D1523992

OVERCOMING OUR EVIL

Moral Traditions Series
James F. Keenan, S.J., Series Editor

American Protestant Ethics and the Legacy of H. Richard Niebuhr
William Werpehowski

Aquinas and Empowerment: Classical Ethics for Ordinary Lives
G. Simon Harak, S.J., Editor

Aquinas, Feminism, and the Common Good
Susanne M. DeCrane

The Banality of Good and Evil: Moral Lessons from the Shoah and Jewish Tradition
David R. Blumenthal

Bridging the Sacred and the Secular: Selected Writings of John Courtney Murray
J. Leon Hooper, S.J., Editor

A Call to Fidelity: On the Moral Theology of Charles E. Curran
James J. Walter, Timothy E. O'Connell, and Thomas A. Shannon, Editors

The Catholic Moral Tradition Today: A Synthesis
Charles E. Curran

Catholic Social Teaching, 1891–Present: A Historical, Theological, and Ethical Analysis
Charles E. Curran

The Christian Case for Virtue Ethics
Joseph J. Kotva, Jr.

The Context of Casuistry
James F. Keenan, S.J., and Thomas A. Shannon, Editors
Foreword by Albert R. Jonsen

The Critical Calling: Reflections on Moral Dilemmas Since Vatican II
Richard A. McCormick, S.J.
Foreword by Lisa Sowle Cahill

Defending Probabilism: The Moral Theology of Juan Caramuel
Julia Fleming

Democracy on Purpose: Justice and the Reality of God
Franklin I. Gamwell

Ethics and Economics of Assisted Reproduction: The Cost of Longing
Maura A. Ryan

The Ethics of Aquinas
Stephen J. Pope, Editor

The Evolution of Altruism and the Ordering of Love
Stephen J. Pope

The Fellowship of Life: Virtue Ethics and Orthodox Christianity
Joseph Woodill

Feminist Ethics and Natural Law: The End of the Anathemas
Cristina L. H. Traina

The Global Face of Public Faith: Politics, Human Rights, and Christian Ethics
David Hollenbach, S.J.

The Ground Beneath the Cross: The Theology of Ignacio Ellacuría
Kevin F. Burke, S.J.

Heroes, Saints, and Ordinary Morality
Andrew Michael Flescher

Introduction to Jewish and Catholic Bioethics: A Comparative Analysis
Aaron L. Mackler

Jewish and Catholic Bioethics: An Ecumenical Dialogue
Edmund D. Pellegrino and Alan I. Faden, Editors

John Paul II and the Legacy of Dignitatis Humanae
Hermínio Rico

Josef Fuchs on Natural Law
Mark Graham

Love, Human and Divine: The Heart of Christian Ethics
Edward Collins Vacek, S.J.

Loyal Dissent: Memoir of a Catholic Theologian
Charles E. Curran

Medicine and the Ethics of Care
Diana Fritz Cates and Paul Lauritzen, Editors

The Moral Theology of Pope John Paul II
Charles E. Curran

The Origins of Moral Theology in the United States: Three Different Approaches
Charles E. Curran

Overcoming Our Evil: Human Nature and Spiritual Exercises in Xunzi and Augustine
Aaron Stalnaker

Prophetic and Public: The Social Witness of U.S. Catholicism
Kristin Heyer

Shaping the Moral Life: An Approach to Moral Theology
Klaus Demmer
James F. Keenan, S.J., Editor

Theological Bioethics: Participation, Justice, and Change
Lisa Sowle Cahill

Theology for a Liberating Church: The New Praxis of Freedom
Alfred T. Hennelly, S.J.

Who Count as Persons? Human Identity and the Ethics of Killing
John F. Kavanaugh, S.J.

OVERCOMING OUR EVIL

Human Nature

and

Spiritual Exercises

in Xunzi

and Augustine

Aaron Stalnaker

Georgetown University Press / Washington, D.C.

As of January 1, 2007, 13-digit ISBNs will replace the current 10-digit system.
Cloth: 978-1-58901-094-9

Georgetown University Press, Washington, D.C.

Library of Congress Cataloging-in-Publication Data

Stalnaker, Aaron.
Overcoming our evil : human nature and spiritual exercises in Xunzi and Augustine / Aaron Stalnaker.
p. cm. — (Moral traditions series)
Includes bibliographical references and index.
ISBN-13: 978-1-58901-094-9 (cloth : alk. paper)
ISBN-10: 1-58901-094-9 (cloth : alk. paper)
1. Good and evil. 2. Augustine, Bishop of Hippo, Saint. 3. Xunzi, 340–245 B.C.
4. Conduct of life. 5. Ethics. I. Title. II. Series.
BJ1401.S82 2006
205—dc22

2005027249

This book is printed on acid-free paper meeting the requirements of the American National Standard for Permanence in Paper for Printed Library Materials.

13 12 11 10 09 08 07 06 9 8 7 6 5 4 3 2
First printing

Printed in the United States of America

Contents

Acknowledgments

I am acutely aware of how much this book has gained from the labor and help of others, and thankful for all that I have learned in the process. Teachers and mentors awakened and refined many of the ideas and passions that animate this study. At Stanford, Lee Yearley first introduced me to the joys and drama of comparative ethics; without his teaching, I would not be who I am today. P. J. Ivanhoe has taught me a great deal about Chinese thought and much else, and has displayed an astonishing willingness to read draft after draft from an old student. Van Harvey provided a model of disciplined engagement with religious thought, and initiated much of my thinking about conceptual diversity. At Brown, Barney Twiss served as my principal adviser and provided trenchant suggestions and criticisms, stimulating intellectual sympathy, and guidance in all things academic. Jock Reeder's vigorous disputations, always with the utmost politeness and care, as well as his searching questions and comments on numerous papers and chapters, were invaluable. I am grateful for Wendell Dietrich's vast erudition, demanding exactitude in expression, and steadfast support. I thank Hal Roth for countless conversations over *nam chau* and iced coffee, for leading me into the world of scholarship on early Chinese texts, and for his patience with my Confucian leanings. And Michael Puett at Harvard has been unfailingly generous in his assistance and counsel, both during graduate school and after.

Many friends and colleagues helped me to think through the issues addressed in this book. I am especially indebted to William Babcock, Eric Hutton, and Bryan Van Norden for their extensive, insightful, and thought-provoking comments on an earlier version of the entire manuscript. Through shared work and delightful intellectual camaraderie, Mark Berkson, Tal Lewis, and Jon Schofer helped develop the ideas in this study in countless ways. Among colleagues at Georgetown I am particularly grateful for exchanges with Fran Cho, Chet Gillis, Tod Linafelt, Beth McKeown, Vince Miller, Jim O'Donnell, Chris Steck, and Diane Yeager. At Indiana, I have enjoyed the benefits of numerous excellent conversations as well as three invigorating colloquia on various aspects of the book; Byron Bangert, Steve Bokenkamp, Gardner Bovington, David Brakke, Rob Campany, David Cockerham, Bob Eno, Sara Friedman, Connie Furey, David Haberman, Bert Harrill, Kevin Jaques, Nancy Levine, Rich Miller, Erin Plunkett, Lisa Sideris, David Smith, Steve Stein, Lynn Struve, Jeff Wasserstrom, Mary Jo Weaver, Steve Weitzman, and Mark Wilson have all been truly helpful in this regard. I appreciate the many fine comments and questions I received from audiences at Davidson College, Georgetown University, Harvard Divinity School, Princeton University, and the University of Michigan, as well as the annual meetings of the American Academy of Religion, the American Philosophical Association, and the Society of Christian Ethics. Others who offered stimulating comments on some or all of the manuscript or related presentations, or in conversation, include Peter Brown, Diana Cates, John Cavadini, David Clairmont, Frank Clooney, Jesse Couenhoven, Mark Csikszentmihalyi, Robert Dodaro, Shari Epstein, Noah Feldman, Andy Flescher, Eric Gregory, Jennifer Herdt, John Kelsay, Jack Kline, Jung Lee, Thomas Martin, Anne Monius, Kevin Madigan, Chuck Mathewes, Jean Porter, Al Raboteau, Frank Reynolds, Ted Slingerland, Jeff Stout, Kirsten Sword, Mark Unno, Jim Wetzel, and Eric Zimmerman, as well as various anonymous reviewers. I have surely failed to profit as fully as I might have from all the suggestions I have received, and I remain responsible for all errors that remain.

The dissertation out of which this book grew was supported by grants from the U.S. Department of Education and the Spencer Foundation. Summer grants and other research support from both Georgetown University and Indiana University greatly assisted the transformation of the dissertation into the subsequent book.

Various bits of chapters 2 through 4 appeared in an earlier form as parts of "Comparative Religious Ethics and the Problem of 'Human Nature,'" in the *Journal of Religious Ethics* (vol. 33, no. 2 [Summer 2005]: 187–224). Significant parts of chapter 7 appeared in an earlier form as "Spiritual Exercises and the Grace of God: Paradoxes of Personal Formation in Augustine," in the *Journal of the Society of Christian Ethics* (vol. 24, no. 2 [Fall/Winter 2004]: 137–70). I thank both of these journals for permission to republish portions of those essays here.

I am grateful to Richard Brown and Jim Keenan for their faith in this project, as well as their thoughtful responses and expert help along the way to the final manuscript. I am also indebted to the thoroughly professional staff at Georgetown University Press for all of their work on this project—not least for the aplomb with which they have handled the issues raised by including Chinese characters in the text.

I owe more than I can say to my family. I thank my parents, Budd Stalnaker and Marcia Stalnaker, for love, friendship, and patience with my many voyages. This book is dedicated to them. I thank my children, Elena and Rowan, for their infectious joy and cheerful disregard for my schedule. And I thank my wife Kirsten for true companionship, courage, and faith that our many gambles were worth the trouble—and they surely have been.

Introduction: To Change One's Life

Does anyone ever really change?[1] Religions tend to answer this question with an emphatic yes. And it does seem that religions can transform people: Some believers become selfless servants of the poor, or even suicide bombers. But how and why might this happen? Similar circumstances push people in quite different ways; "good intentions" alone are not sufficient for real conversion to some demanding new form of life. This book focuses on how ethical and religious commitments are conceived, articulated, and nurtured through methodical practices that guide aspirants through alternative territories of sin and salvation, ignorance and wisdom, or suffering and bliss.

Pierre Hadot has called such transformative practices "spiritual exercises." By this term he means repeated practices that engage thought, imagination, and sensibility, and that have a significant ethical component, yet aim more broadly at a transformation of vision, a metamorphosis of the whole personality. Spiritual exercises in this sense are frequently advocated as potent means to reshape one's own existence.[2]

The emerging interest in practices of personal formation is a natural way to develop what has come to be called virtue ethics. Attending to such practices clarifies not only what human goodness or excellence might be but also how to attain it. Sophisticated theories of spiritual exercises inevitably involve significant reflection on the cultivation of virtuous dispositions, whether conceived in a familiar Aristotelian idiom or not. And religious ethics is uniquely well suited to examine practices designed to help believers internalize particular religious narratives, symbols, and tropes as essential elements of the cultivation of virtue within particular traditions. Furthermore, a focus on spiritual exercises offers one sensible way to address worries that ethical life in a plural, democratic, consumerist context has become diminished, or even incoherent, by directly examining techniques for the cultivation of virtue and reflecting on the "retrieval" of such techniques for contemporary life.

There has been much recent attention to such practices in Greek and Roman antiquity, especially among intellectual historians and to a lesser extent philosophers.[3] The importance of this work for religious ethics is only now becoming apparent.[4] However, the techniques of self-mastery practiced in the Hellenistic schools of philosophy are only one closely related set of traditions of spiritual exercises. The various forms of Hellenistic philosophy share debatable presuppositions about human beings, seeing us as composed of body and soul, with an intrinsic internal conflict between reason and passion (with these contrasts understood differently by different figures, certainly). But these are not the only ways of imagining human existence, and thus living a reflective and humane life. The reason/passion contrast, in particular, can be problematic in the way that it shapes the understanding, content, and ethical goal of spiritual exercises: Attending only to rational restraint easily suggests that desires and emotions are intrinsically antagonistic to wisdom, and obscures the passionate nature of thinking itself.

This study broadens ethical inquiry into spiritual exercises by taking explicitly religious practices such as prayer and ritual more seriously as objects of study, and by examining East Asian as well as classical Western materials. More specifically, this book examines and compares the thought and practice of Augustine of Hippo (354–430 CE), a late antique Christian of immense influence on later Western civilization, and Xun Kuang 荀況 (c. 310–c. 220 BCE), commonly known as Xunzi 荀子 ("Master Xun"), an important early Confucian figure who shaped his tradition in profound if sometimes overlooked ways. Augustine and Xunzi both have sophisticated and insightful accounts of spiritual exercises, and both make such ethical work central to their religious thought and practice.

Attention to their theories of personal formation reveals, however, that their practical proposals are tightly wedded to their distinctive accounts of "human nature" as bad or fallen. (Indeed, they are each the most influential exponents of such a view in their respective traditions.) For both of them, human life calls out for reformation to a higher standard than the satisfaction of our immediate instincts. Their careful attention to our tendencies toward cruelty, deception, self-aggrandizement, lust, and greed gives added depth, as well as believability, to their proposed exercises for personal transformation. Genuine growth in virtue is difficult for us to achieve. It requires sustained effort, wisely directed, with significant outside help.

Despite having no noteworthy cultural or historical connection, Xunzi and Augustine share sufficient similarities and differences to allow nuanced comparative analysis of their positions. Their prescriptions share a general shape: Both have been represented in English as saying that "human nature" is "evil," and so humans need significant reformation to become moral; but such translations mask important differences in anthropology, ethics, metaphysics, and understandings of what counts as the most important history and texts. Interpreting each of them holistically allows nuanced, analogical comparing and contrasting of their ideas around the themes of human nature, personhood, spiritual exercises, and the will.

Such analysis raises the thorny problem of evaluation in a comparative context. Charitable interpretations of sophisticated thinkers always require considered judgments about the sensibleness or rationality of positions attributed to them, given the traditions and contexts in which they worked. At this level, evaluation is inescapable in any study of philosophical or theological materials, even when conceived of as a purely historical exercise. Comparative studies of religious thought raise further questions, however: Not only must later interpreters decide what thinkers were justified in believing in their own contexts, but if the force of their potentially competing universal claims is to be respected, those claims must somehow be evaluated in a contemporary context, comparatively, through imagined conversation or dialogue.

It is a fundamental error, however, to construe this imperative in terms of an antagonism between whole traditions, or even, more modestly, of two unrelated thinkers, one of whom might be rationally "vindicated" in imaginary debate. First, only assiduous and sustained comparative bridge building can produce vocabularies and theories sufficient to position two complex theories within one horizon of interpretation.[5] Even the physical metaphors of space and vision can mislead, however, because the precise relation of different ideas and practices articulated by only two thinkers can vary immensely, as can their relative strength or weakness, from various points of view. More seriously, it must be a matter of interpretation and argument, rather than assumption, that elements of different ethics are in competition or conflict, rather than harmony or some other relation. To reify wholes and see these as antagonists (as in Alasdair MacIntyre's talk of "rival traditions") risks blinding us to the details that make all the difference.[6] It also skews one's interpretive stance so that edification by others, both through and beyond differences, becomes unlikely and suspect, rather than a primary aim of comparative inquiry.

A better goal than the rational vindication of whole traditions (coincidentally always one's own) would be something more like global neighborliness, which seeks to live with others peaceably and learn from them as much as can be learned, and to offer help carefully and respectfully as needed, within imprecise limits set by humility and tact.[7] Such neighborliness may grow into friendship or even something like conversion, but acquaintance must come first. Rivalry is also possible, but hardly to be assumed.

Comparative ethics is valuable, perhaps even desperately needed, in our contemporary context of global interdependence, misunderstanding, and mutual mistrust. Though broad-brush comparisons have their uses, if offered with suitable caution and caveats, disciplined reflection on influential "classic" thinkers is also quite valuable. It can reveal the humanity, and even the sublimity, of unfamiliar traditions and thinkers. It is also able to address fundamental ethical issues at a depth impossible with general summaries. By engaging the details of particular insightful but differing conceptions of a given topic, comparisons of the sort developed here reveal overlooked aspects of particular thinkers and articulate alternative ways of framing important issues. This kind of comparison can carefully relate those alternatives, thereby changing our sense of "the issues" themselves and recasting traditional terms of analysis and debate so that previously seen difficulties on both sides may be reimagined and addressed in new ways.

The present comparison of Augustine and Xunzi refines and broadens our understanding of human nature, spiritual exercises, and moral psychology. I argue that "human nature" is a family of related but conflicting concerns that may or may not be seen as aspects of any one postulated theoretical entity: concerns about our physical, biological existence, about what unites us with other animals (or, conversely, what separates us from them and makes us uniquely "human"), and about the proper or "natural" course of human development. Spiritual exercises can be understood both narrowly as the sorts of primarily intellectual exercises that Hadot examines, or more widely as any practice intended to form us as ethical and religious subjects; taking the latter option allows the development of broader typologies of such exercises, within which familiar phenomena such as study, various forms of meditation and prayer, renunciation (and "asceticism"), ritual, and aesthetic practice can be analyzed and related. Crucial points include the conscious, methodical character of spiritual exercises, their close correlation with theoretical accounts that justify and order them, and their formal and substantive differences correlating with different religious construals of reality, morality, and human anthropology. With regard to the cultivation of virtue, both Augustine and Xunzi develop sophisticated versions of what I call "chastened intellectualism" as a general account of human beings, although their models of human moral psychology differ in significant and interesting ways. The mature Augustine favors a "triune" model of the *mens,* or mind that integrates memory, understanding, and will or love, while Xunzi advocates a model of the *xin* 心, or heart/mind, that relates two distinct but intertwined systems of motivation: conscious assent or dissent, and our spontaneous dispositions to feel and desire in certain ways.

More generally, this comparison suggests (but does not yet establish) the broader hypothesis that religious anthropologies are intrinsically wedded to regimes of person formation, so that both must be studied together for either to be adequately understood. Obviously, any such account of individual formation should not be sundered from religion's role in ordering social life but seen as an essential element of this ordering.

The comparison also highlights important but easily overlooked aspects of each figure individually. I argue that the dusty portrait of Augustine as rigid "doctor of grace" railing against Pelagian freedom needs to be revised: Any account of Augustine's thought must be able to make sense of his unwavering commitment to spiritual exercises as necessary to the Christian life, which he discusses in detail in less frequently read sources such as his sermons. This interpretive lens also highlights tensions in Augustine's thought between different models of human psychology, one familiar to him from his rhetorical education and relatively closer to Neoplatonic accounts, and the genuinely innovative model he develops in *On the Trinity*; the differences between these models play out in his reconceptualization of ancient spiritual exercises. And though past studies have investigated Xunzi's general account of moral development, the present focus on spiritual exercises leads to careful analysis of the actual practices he recommends and the subtle moral psychology on which they rest.

On the basis of detailed interpretations of both Augustine and Xunzi, the present study also argues for a number of particular comparative conclusions, which can only be sketched here in the most telegraphic way. Xunzi's account of patient work at the "artifice" of human goodness seems particularly capable of addressing the everyday struggle to domesticate and train our first-order desires, and thus it better illuminates gradual progress in cultivating virtue; he also articulates a fuller and more positive role for human embodiment in the moral and religious life. Augustine's ethics, conversely, seem better suited to addressing our ongoing, second-order tendencies to rebel against the very idea of this sort of work on ourselves. His focus on pride and the perverse imitation of divinity also provides a better account of what may be called radical evil as a continuing human potential. And regarding the general shape of their regimes of personal formation, Augustine's rigorous focus in his exercises on a hermeneutics of interior movements of the soul stems in significant part from his scripturally grounded conception of what is morally salient. This contrasts sharply with Xunzi's ritually grounded emphasis on the proper performance of duty and virtue, which allows him to rely more heavily on external, communal, performative exercises to effect changes in internal states. Xunzi's "outside-in" approach to spiritual exercises is thus fundamentally different from Augustine's recommendation of perpetual self-scrutiny in community with other imperfect lovers of the divine.

A careful exploration and comparison of the details of these different ethico-religious "vocabularies" of thought and practice allows moderns to reflect on them as candidates for contemporary retrieval, adjustment, and use, and also to reflect more generally on the role of such vocabularies in social and religious life in contemporary, culturally plural societies.

The book's nine chapters address the following themes. Chapter 1 focuses on the role of comparison within the broader field of religious ethics. It develops a version of the pragmatist idea of a "vocabulary" as a way to conceive of multiple ethics, explores some of the strengths and weaknesses of various strategies of comparison, and justifies in more detail the choice of objects and topics compared in the current study, as well as its architecture and approach.

Chapter 2 provides more specific contextualization for the body of the study. It gives brief, orienting accounts of each figure's social and intellectual context, and it then develops limited but sufficient accounts of the "bridge concepts" or themes of comparative analysis upon which the later detailed interpretations of Augustine and Xunzi build: human nature, personhood, spiritual exercises, and the will.

Chapters 3 and 4 outline in turn each thinker's distinctive accounts of human beings, with special attention to Augustine's concept of *natura* and Xunzi's idea of *xing* 性—both traditionally rendered in English as human "nature." Chapter 3 examines Xunzi's contrastive pairing of *xing* 性, the "innate," and *wei* 偽, "artifice," along with his account of the human *xin* 心, "heart/mind," which generally acts on the basis of various spontaneous *qing* 情, "emotions" and "dispositions," and *yu* 欲, "desires" that emerge from them but which can also act more reflectively through *lü* 慮, "deliberation," and *ke* 可, "assent." Chapter 4 weaves together various Augustinian themes, including original sin, human nature and its "fault," and divine imagehood, including the mental activities of remembering, understanding, and willing or loving; these are followed by considerations of body and soul; flesh, spirit, and the two loves; habitual vice and "concupiscence"; and an analysis of the will's debility.

Chapter 5 develops the bridge concept of "human nature" by comparing these two accounts. It explores various moral psychological themes on this basis, most notably desire, emotion, memory, and consent, and it shows how the psychologies and anthropologies developed by Xunzi and Augustine are interwoven with their prescribed regimes of personal formation.

The next chapters turn to Augustine's and Xunzi's positive proposals for ethico-religious education and personal cultivation, offering a sustained treatment of the specific practices they recommend and their accounts of how and why these practices so effectively contribute to human flourishing. Chapter 6 begins by exploring Xunzi's general conception of the *Dao* 道, or "Way," along with his understanding of the process of *xiu shen* 修身, "improving oneself," before giving detailed interpretations of his three core spiritual exercises: *xue* 學, "learning," *li* 禮, "ritual," and *yue* 樂, "music."

Chapter 7 discusses Augustine's metaphors for and theoretical mapping of the life of Christian discipleship, building on his accounts of *exercitationes*, "exercises," and *disciplina*, "teaching" and "discipline." The bulk of the chapter analyzes Augustine's understanding of catechesis and baptism, the classical liberal arts, reading and listening to scripture, literal and symbolic practices of eating (including both fasting and the Eucharist), and different types of prayer.

Chapter 8 compares in more detail their conceptions of personal formation and spiritual exercises. It begins by articulating their distinctive understandings of "subjection" as the necessary form of real human agency, and it charts the differing "spiritual geographies" in which they imagine such agency. It develops and sharpens the various elements of the bridge concept of the "will," analyzing both of their treatments in relation to some themes in contemporary virtue ethics, with special attention to their differing ways of conceiving and addressing conflict within the self. It then examines the underlying logic of Xunzi's "outside-in" and Augustine's "inside-out" approaches to personal formation, and it seeks to show how this contributes to some of the intriguing differences between their sets of spiritual exercises, exploring in depth their differing evaluations of honesty and pretence within religious self-cultivation. This chapter closes by arguing for the merits of what I call "chastened intellectualism" as a general type of moral psychology, reflected differently in both Xunzi and Augustine.

The final chapter examines both the value and sharp limits of abstract or "thin" modern accounts of moral personhood, in relation to "thicker" religious accounts like those considered in this study that are equally universal in their scope and aspirations. It argues that two-level theories of ethics and politics will be needed for the foreseeable future, because most human beings need the resources for personal formation that only religious or quasi-religious traditions provide; however, in current conditions of ineliminable religious diversity, we need as well to cultivate neighborly concern for those who follow other traditions and ideals. It concludes by arguing for a fleshed-out conception of this "global neighborliness" as a governing ideal for cross-traditional interpretation.

NOTES

1. Diane Yeager asked me this question when I first discussed this project with her.

2. The phrase "spiritual exercises" harks back perhaps most directly to Ignatius of Loyola's (1991) foundational text of the same name. It is unfortunately impossible in

this already lengthy study to adequately engage Ignatius's work and its subsequent traditions of interpretation and use. The present book uses the term "spiritual exercises" in dialogue with Hadot and other recent theorists of personal formation, as explained more fully in chapter 2.

3. Important examples include Davidson 1994; Foucault 1985, 1986, 1997; Hadot 1995, 1998, 2002; Harris 2001; Nehamas 1998; Nussbaum 1994; and Sorabji 2000.

4. Excellent recent studies include Antonaccio 1998 and Schofer 2003 and 2005. For an approach to these issues from a modern psychodynamic perspective, see Wallwork 1999.

5. This language of "horizons of interpretation" derives from Gadamer 1989. Note Alasdair MacIntyre's efforts to specify what might be involved in such a process (1988, 349–88).

6. MacIntyre 1988 (e.g., 368) and 1990. But note also MacIntyre's serious and suggestive attempts (1991, 2004a, 2004b) to grapple with Confucianism.

7. Obviously some traditions, such as Nazism, are so vicious that actively opposing them is the only reasonable, ethical response (although carefully studying them is also necessary, to diagnose their success in particular circumstances, and continuing attractiveness for some). I leave to the side questions of how to distinguish truly vicious traditions from those more numerous religious and philosophical traditions worthy of respect and neighborly engagement. "Offering help" to other traditions should certainly include rational criticism of particular points.

Source and Citation Formats

ABBREVIATIONS OF AUGUSTINE'S WORKS

Abbreviated title	*Latin title*	*Translation*
bapt.	*De baptismo*	On Baptism
cat. rud.	*De catechizandis rudibus*	On the Instruction of Beginners
civ. Dei	*De civitate Dei*	City of God
conf.	*Confessiones*	Confessions
c. ep. Pel.	*Contra duas epistulas Pelagianorum*	Against Two Letters of the Pelagians
c. Jul.	*Contra Julianum*	Against Julian
c. Jul. imp.	*Contra Julianum, opus imperfectum*	Against Julian, an Unfinished Work
c. litt. Pet.	*Contra litteras Petiliani*	Against the Letters of Petilianus
c. mend.	*Contra mendacium*	Against Lying
cont.	*De continentia*	On Continence
corrept.	*De correptione et gratia*	On Admonition and Grace
div. qu.	*De diversis quaestionibus octoginta tribus*	On Eighty-Three Varied Questions
doc. Chr.	*De doctrina Christiana*	On Christian Teaching
duab. an.	*De duabus animabus*	On the Two Souls
en. Ps.	*Ennarrationes in Psalmos*	Explanations of the Psalms
ench.	*Enchiridion ad Laurentium de fide spe et caritate*	A Handbook on Faith, Hope, and Love
ep.	*Epistulae*	Letters
ep. Jo.	*In epistulam Joannis ad Parthos tractatus*	Tractates on the First Letter of John
ex. Gal.	*Expositio Epistulae ad Galatas*	Commentary on the Letter to the Galatians
ex. prop. Rm.	*Expositio quarundam propositionum ex epistula Apostoli ad Romanos*	Commentary on Statements in the Letter to the Romans
Gn. adv. Man.	*De Genesi adversus Manicheos*	On Genesis, Against the Manichees

Abbreviated title	*Latin title*	*Translation*
Gn. litt.	*De Genesi ad litteram*	On the Literal Interpretation of Genesis
gr. et lib. arb.	*De gratia et libero arbitrio*	On Grace and Free Will
gr. et pecc. or.	*De gratia Christi et de peccato originali*	On the Grace of Christ and Original Sin
Jo. ev. tr.	*In Johannis evangelium tractatus*	Tractates on the Gospel of John
lib. arb.	*De libero arbitrio voluntatis*	On Free Choice of the Will
mag.	*De magistro*	On the Teacher
mend.	*De mendacio*	On Lying
mor.	*De moribus ecclesiae catholicae et de moribus Manichaeorum*	On the Catholic and Manichean Ways of Life
nat. b.	*De natura boni*	On the Nature of the Good
nat. et grat.	*De natura et gratia*	On Nature and Grace
ord.	*De ordine*	On Order
pat.	*De patientia*	On Patience
pecc. mer.	*De peccatorum meritis et remissione et de baptismo parvulorum*	On the Merits and Forgiveness of Sins and on Infant Baptism
perf. just.	*De perfectione justitiae hominis*	On the Perfection of Human Righteousness
persev.	*De dono perseverantiae*	On the Gift of Perseverance
praed. sanct.	*De praedestinatione sanctorum*	On the Predestination of Saints
qu. Hept.	*Quaestiones in Heptateuchum*	Questions on the Heptateuch
quant.	*De animae quantitate*	On the Greatness of the Soul
reg. 2	*Regula: Ordo monaserii*	The Rule: Monastic Order
retr.	*Retractationes*	Reconsiderations
s.	*Sermones*	Sermons
s. Dom. mon.	*De sermone Domini in monte*	On the Lord's Sermon on the Mount
spir. et litt.	*De spiritu et littera*	On the Spirit and the Letter
Trin.	*De Trinitate*	On the Trinity
vera rel.	*De vera religione*	On True Religion
virg.	*De sancta virginitate*	On Holy Virginity

A NOTE ON CITATIONS

Citations of Xunzi's works are to D. C. Lau's concordance (1996). All citations of this and the other Institute of Chinese Studies concordances will take the form chapter/page/line; so, for example, 19/97/9 would mean chapter 19, page 97, line 9. Lau's concordance is based on the *Sibu Congkan* edition of the *Xunzi*, which itself is a reprint of the *Taizhou* edition from the Song; Lau carefully notes his emendations, which are based on parallel texts and other manuscript traditions. For a discussion of the textual history of the *Xunzi*, see Knoblock 1988–94, vol. 1, 105–28. Unless otherwise noted, citations for Augustine's works refer to Jacques-Paul Migne's commonly accessible *Patrologia Latina*, now widely available via the Internet as a searchable database. Migne is unfortunately based on the Maurist edition of the collected works of Augustine compiled from French sources and published from 1679 to 1700. It thus does not share in the fruits of modern textual scholarship, and merely collects variant readings without attempting to produce true critical editions, as in the ongoing series *Corpus Scriptorum Ecclesiasticorum Latinorum* and *Corpus Christianorum*, which are still not complete. Translations are my own, unless otherwise noted.

CHAPTER ONE

Comparative Ethics

✦

If the term "religious ethics" is to be more than a catchall, a thoughtless expansion of Christian ethics to be as inclusive as possible, then the field of religious ethics needs thoughtful comparison of different "ethics" (in the plural). This comparison can and should go on both within and across religious traditions. Some of the distinctive challenges and possibilities of comparative ethics come into sharpest relief, however, in cross-traditional inquiry.

Indeed, comparison is central, perhaps even essential, to the history of religious studies as a discipline.[1] To talk about religions in the plural generates the problem of what "religions" are, and how they relate to each other. To address these issues, one must compare different religions, which itself requires the differentiation and relation of suitable objects of comparison.[2]

This chapter examines how contemporary ethicists have arrived at a similar point of intellectual departure, with analogous dilemmas and creative possibilities. It addresses four related topics in sequence: why comparison is desirable in religious ethics, how to conceive of multiple ethics, the strengths and weaknesses of various strategies of comparison, and why this study's proposed comparison has been chosen and framed as it has.

COMPARISON IN RELIGIOUS ETHICS

Comparison in ethics shares certain virtues with all other sorts of comparison: First, it can illuminate each of the objects compared in new and sometimes surprising ways, revealing easily overlooked details or themes; second, it provokes, tests, and develops various theoretical generalizations about the compared objects; and third, it can thereby help generate new theories about the substantive domain being considered. In ethics, for example, comparing conceptions of courage found in the early Confucian Mencius and the medieval Christian Thomas Aquinas illuminates both of their treatments, leading to substantive insights into courage and refinement of virtue theory generally.[3]

The potential for theoretical creativity inspired by comparison deserves special comment, because this can occur in various ways, each of which is significant. First, through comparison, the concepts with which analysis is pursued are themselves put to the test and, if need be, revised or discarded. So, for instance, this study attempts to analyze and refine ideas of "human nature" and "spiritual exercises." But these are not just categories for ordering primary material from other sources; they are also topics of inquiry themselves. So to the extent that we can refine such concepts, we also gain greater purchase on the subject matter at hand. Through serious engagement with multiple significant accounts of a topic, comparison can help generate a hypothetical dialogue between various positions, creating a new dialectic that points toward positions that would have been difficult to arrive at without comparison. Explicating how this sort of fruitful juxtaposition can proceed, by exemplifying it as fully as possible, is a central task of this book.

Comparison also holds real potential for theoretical critique. Comparative work can be just as effective as historical and "genealogical" studies in bringing to consciousness the full range of consequences of common contemporary ways of framing ethical issues, and thus calling them into question.[4] Indeed, when comparison crosses traditions from different regions and/or cultural spheres, it promises not only skeptical questioning on the basis of surprising narratives of subtle corruption, or the unmasking of dubious origins, but also the articulation of genuine alternatives. These alternatives may or may not be fully satisfying in themselves, but they at least provide positive possibilities on which to base future constructions.

Comparison has always possessed these general virtues. In the contemporary West, and arguably the entire contemporary world, it takes on an added practical urgency as well. Religious diversity is a significant social fact, and it has shaped the modern West in deep and abiding ways, perhaps most notably by providing an impetus for the creation of secular modes of governance and theories of social and political order, which in turn have reinforced religious diversity by allowing it to proliferate more freely.[5] In the wake of changes in immigration law in the 1960s, the United States has become significantly more religiously complex, and this trend shows no signs of abating; similar if somewhat more limited stories could be told about other Western and non-Western countries.[6] These accelerating social realities mean that thoughtful engagement with neighbors from sometimes vastly different religious backgrounds is becoming a recurrent necessity for larger and larger numbers of people. The challenge of successfully working with people with different religious and ethical orientations is fast becoming an essential component of responsible citizenship in contemporary Western democracies.

Comparative ethics is well positioned to analyze such interreligious negotiations, and also to engage the profound philosophical, theological, and ethical issues such religious plurality poses.[7] Just to mention a few, religious diversity sharpens questions regarding ethical universalism and relativism, how to understand and justly order religiously complex communities, and how to navigate multiple religious and social identities, as well as meta-ethical problems about the nature of moral norms. And sustained comparative attention to specific cases provides a way to base analyses of these broader questions in real data about concrete particulars.

In the past few decades, the most common general theoretical approach to disagreement about "comprehensive visions of the good" has been to develop social contract theories, such as those propounded by John Rawls.[8] But this move can relegate religious life to seeming theoretical irrelevance, as an accidental detail of individuals' private lives. Religious and other critics of liberalism have seized on this as a reason to denounce liberalism as a political theory, and as one more sign that modernity is a supposedly decadent epoch. Even democracy as a mode of governance can be suspected as hostile to religion and to coherent ethical practice.[9]

Partly under the influence of Alasdair MacIntyre's electrifying jeremiad *After Virtue*, both philosophical and religious ethicists have turned to virtue ethics as at least a complement, and sometimes a replacement, for abstract social contract–based accounts of modern societies, as well as the rule-centered moral theories that generally accompanied them in the past. As Jeffrey Stout has argued, however, this somewhat romantic turn to traditions of virtue as a preferable ethical alternative to modernity generates odd dilemmas as people try to square modern democratic commitments with the premodern social presuppositions of, for instance, Aristotle and Aquinas.[10] This dynamic makes it necessary to "retrieve" the ethics of virtue from these past thinkers, saving and amplifying what is still admirable and needed in such classic accounts without importing objectionable premises.[11] Provided that we face the seriousness of the difficulties in such attempted recoveries, I applaud this return to ancient conceptions of virtue, in part because I do not fully share Stout's confidence that the practices of democracy are sufficient in themselves to cultivate virtuous citizens, in the absence of religious or quasi-religious traditions of personal formation.[12]

Grappling with alternative regimes for the cultivation of virtue is a uniquely apt way to address contemporary needs for two things: the cultivation of richly grounded, virtuous human beings; and analysis of the problems and new possibilities created by societies that are culturally and religiously complex and disintegrated. Recovery efforts that stay within the West risk submerging or misconstruing the distance that separates the contemporary Western world, in all its complexity and diversity, from some previous European one. In contrast, a comparative study that addresses multiple sophisticated traditional accounts of personal formation provides a broader and more suitable context for thinking through the contemporary retrieval of past models, theories, and practices of personal formation. In a comparative study, the issues of religious disagreement and social complexity can never be massaged away or misleadingly written off as symptoms of corrupt modernity.[13] To be clear, I am not claiming that "the West" is somehow spiritually bereft or bankrupt, in need of enlightenment from "the East." I am claiming that the multiplicity of traditions now present and interacting in the Western world generates compelling intellectual and indeed moral problems that need to be addressed through disciplined comparative study.

The sort of comparative ethics I propose here provides a way to move beyond the simplistic tradition/modernity dichotomy that often seems presupposed in the analysis of MacIntyre and Hauerwas, while also answering Stout's rejoinder that democratic traditions and practices are themselves sufficient to produce excellent human beings, by addressing the striking power of various religious regimes of spiritual exercises to change and form people into ethical agents.

CONCEPTUAL DIVERSITY, NOT CONCEPTUAL RELATIVISM

At this point, a critic might justifiably ask for a fuller account of these "ethics in the plural" that one is to compare. How are they to be appropriately identified and adequately described and interpreted? This section develops a terminology for discussing different forms of ethics, while avoiding certain widespread philosophical mistakes.

For comparative ethics to have a compelling intellectual rationale, it needs to be able to articulate the possibility of social and conceptual diversity without collapsing into either naive universalism or pernicious relativism. If, for example, eighteenth-century Americans, ancient Chinese, medieval Maya, and contemporary Middle Eastern Muslims all share so much as human beings that their differences of thought and life are not particularly significant, then there is no real point in attending to the differences in ethical conceptions between (let alone within) these groups. But few people who reflect carefully on these matters remain tempted by this possibility for long. The more frequent danger is some form of relativism, which attempts to cordon off distinct cultures or groups and insist that what each believes is "true for them." Versions of this line of thought tend to rely on dubious conceptions of cultures as unified, harmonious, and insulated wholes; have problems accounting for their own pronouncements (i.e., are self-referentially incoherent); and are in effect defensive operations against taking anyone's normative commitments seriously, because all such commitments are not only justified but "true for" those who hold them. (Moral debate becomes hard to fathom under such a model.) Comparative ethics would be pointless and indeed impossible if this sort of relativism were both intelligible and correct.[14]

So what way of framing the issues is most fruitful when trying to articulate social and conceptual diversity, without prematurely throwing up one's hands in despair? I will argue that three contemporary pragmatists and one antiempiricist cousin—specifically Donald Davidson, Richard Rorty, Robert Brandom, and Jeffrey Stout—are most helpful here. This might seem surprising, because Davidson, for one, is renowned for his demolition of "the very idea of a conceptual scheme," which has seemed to many to be exactly the tool to use when examining ethics across cultures.[15] But Davidson and especially the explicitly pragmatist Rorty, Brandom, and Stout provide a better way to address conceptual diversity through their discussion of alternative "vocabularies" for social life. Because these thinkers, especially Davidson, Rorty, and Brandom, are attempting to recast central debates in analytic philosophy of language, epistemology, and even metaphysics, I do not here attempt to give an overview of their projects as wholes but instead focus only on those ideas they develop that are useful for comparative studies of religious thought.[16]

This limited foray into issues of method in religious ethics might seem to be a digression, but in fact it is essential, because it helps clarify what is at stake in cross-traditional comparisons. Though it is true that all thinking is comparative in the sense that it draws distinctions between things that differ in some respects, while being the same or similar in others, there is still a difference worth attending to between comparisons within a tradition, and across traditions. Interpreting different religious ethics as different "vocabularies" for social life, that make both thought and action possible, provides a way to do justice to the interpretive challenges that come up in both sorts of comparisons (within or across traditions). It provides a way to think about the subtle differences that obtain between, for example, Augustine and Calvin on sin and redemption, as well as both the subtle and the massive differences between Augustine on Jesus Christ and Xunzi on the *Dao* 道 or Way.

In sum, the notion of vocabulary I develop here is useful for comparative ethics because (1) it makes human conceptual diversity explicit, undercutting both naive universalism that takes a particular ethical terminology and set of moral "problems" or "questions" for granted, and the common relativism that freezes and hermetically seals vocabularies as if they were never used by real people acting in the world; (2) it provides the conceptual resources necessary for grappling with differences between ethics that share much, as well as those that might appear to share little, and everything in between; and (3) it shows that comparison, even of the sort attempted here, is not intellectually exotic but instead continuous with more typical language use and interpretive practice, even while it makes certain problems of interpretation more explicit. This conception of "vocabulary" is also useful for ethics generally, especially for a study of virtue or spiritual exercises, because of the way it intrinsically links discourse and theory with action and practice.

To summarize, in his famous article on conceptual schemes, Davidson is motivated by the specter of conceptual relativism, which holds that something might be true for one person or group but not for another, differently situated. (Thus God might really exist for Christians but not for strict Theravada Buddhists.) He endeavors to rule out this possibility by demonstrating the unintelligibility of the very idea of a "conceptual scheme"; he targets this idea because relativists often use it to argue that truth is relative to different schemes. Davidson first suggests that the idea of a "scheme" is interchangeable with the idea of a language, so that incommensurability of schemes is equivalent to untranslatability between languages. He then attempts to show that we cannot make sense of complete or even partial untranslatability between human languages, because we cannot even identify a specific confusion or disagreement without an enormous basis of shared background beliefs; this background is required to be sure that we are even talking about the same topic.[17] So, particular difficulties in translation can only emerge when enormous amounts of belief are already shared. Thus, of particular importance, we must interpret strange others charitably, presuming that they are right about most things for it to be even possible to identify topics about which we seem to disagree.[18]

Terry Godlove refers to this line of thought as "content holism," but what he takes this to imply shows the dangers of relying only on Davidson. Godlove thinks Davidson's argument for content holism is important to scholars of religion because it "requires us to reject the notion that religions are alternative conceptual frameworks," and moreover, "it requires us to reject conceptual relativism in any interesting form—say the imputation of divergent epistemes, paradigms, worldviews, forms of life, radical alterity, and so on."[19] This is sloppy. Of course we should reject the absurdly totalizing idea that religions are conceptual frameworks, and not only because we cannot make sense of the idea of neutral content that is organized differently by different schemes. Davidson does help to ward off conceptual relativism. But the idea that refusal of conceptual relativism implies that people from different cultures and religious traditions could never differ significantly in "worldview" or "form of life" is baffling and wrong, given any typical sense of these expressions. The issue here is the tendency to confuse the distinction between conceptual *relativism* and conceptual *diversity*; the latter can be sorted out and analyzed, sometimes only laboriously, but it is certainly quite real. And any assessment of the truth of religious beliefs, or even the responsible identification of certain beliefs and practices as competing with each other, requires heavy interpretive lifting and careful comparative bridge building. (These can and indeed should be construed as Davidsonian points.)

Properly understood, Davidson's theory of radical interpretation can be enlisted to help explicate cross-cultural understanding,[20] but it still tends to obscure certain issues that need to be highlighted in comparative studies of religious thought. Here I discuss two. Davidson is tempted by the idea that human languages, for the most part, share an ontology of simple objects that help provide the "background" before which particular difficulties of translation or understanding can be intelligible.[21] But exactly how much of an ontology particular languages share, from everyday objects to more abstract religious and social matters, is an open question, to be decided by actual inquiry, not transcendental argument. In particular cases, one might be able to identify quite significant differences in ontology, and ethics, and then continue from there with further comparative analysis.[22]

More deeply, the conflation of conceptual scheme with language is a mistake, as others have pointed out.[23] The metaphor of conceptual "schemes" can impute excessive coherence to the ideas of a culture, and it understates the expressive possibilities of any natural language. As P. M. S. Hacker argues, even if we grant "that there is no precise distinction between what is theory and what is pre- or non-theoretical," we can nevertheless distinguish between theories and languages. Languages are in no sense theories, do not fit or predict reality, and can frame many assertions that predict and describe reality in contradictory ways.[24] Put more generally, there are dramatic differences in the degree to which concepts interrelate in a whole language; in a particular milieu with competing schools of thought sharing certain disputed terms; in an identifiable tradition (with its own debates, to be sure); and in the writings of a particular thinker, especially if she or he is a systematic one aiming to produce a coherent theory. Because it can be used for all of these, there is an inevitable looseness to the idea of "conceptual schemes," which helps somewhat to explain the power of the idea in multiple realms and the heat of the debate over its value.

Many of Davidson's critics on this issue wish to resurrect the terminology of conceptual schemes. But I fear that this way of speaking always brings with it hopes for the elusive "given" that lies beyond all such schemes and yet is somehow to be organized by them, which was one of Davidson's rightful targets all along. Comparativists need more precise and less misleading terminology.

A better candidate is the notion, pioneered by Rorty, of alternative "vocabularies" for different social and intellectual practices.[25] Rorty's central idea is that vocabularies are tools for doing things, for helping people to "cope" with reality, and should not be seen as more or less transparent mediums for "representing" reality.[26]

As Brandom notes, thinking about vocabularies as tools implies that vocabularies have purposes, and both he and Rorty vigorously contest the notion that all vocabularies must share the single overriding purpose of "representing reality" as it is in itself—indeed, they think such a purpose is dangerously misconceived. Instead, their antirepresentationalist pragmatism invites what Brandom calls "discursive pluralism." Different vocabularies will aim at different purposes (e.g., social justice, aesthetic fulfillment, or prediction and control), and we have no reason to wish that we might find a super-vocabulary that would be best for all possible purposes. Thus individuals and communities will make use of a variety of vocabularies on this account, and this is a good thing.[27]

More specifically, a vocabulary implies a set of related social practices. Brandom's inferentialist philosophy of language focuses on the practices of inference and reason giving that are essential to linguistic communication. More broadly, human practices in general are discursive, on this model, because they involve interpretation and understanding (of beliefs, intentions, states of affairs, etc.) that can only be conducted with vocabularies, that is, with roughly integrated collections of concepts that stand in complex relations of mutual entailment and interrelation.

The central linguistic practices of inference, commitment, and "licensing" that Brandom charts are normative, and indeed for both Rorty and Brandom norms of *any* sort are only possible for creatures that use languages. Vocabularies and the practices they make possible are shot through with implicit normative "proprieties" concerning everything from when it is appropriate to use certain words to when it is right to take certain actions. These norms can be made explicit through reflection on and articulation of shared social practices, but the implicit norms and practical "know-how" of social actors are primary, at least on Brandom's model.[28] Brandom even defines "vocabularies" as "implicitly normative discursive practices."[29]

This practical context for vocabularies has important implications. New vocabularies make new purposes possible, and thus in some sense create or at least accompany new practices, new forms of life.[30] Rorty and Brandom seem to share a romantic, historicist conception of how such new vocabularies arise: Great geniuses "like Galileo, Yeats, or Hegel" struggle to create a new vocabulary that then "catches on" more widely, changing the way large numbers of people speak, interpret, and act. Charting the rise and fall of vocabularies becomes a mode of intellectual and cultural history.[31]

But Brandom's latest reflections on vocabulary change suggest that such a picture is overdramatized. As he writes, "Every claim and inference we make at once sustains and transforms the tradition in which the conceptual norms that govern that process are implicit." To apply conceptual norms by using concepts is at the same time to transform them, he thinks, because the use of concepts, of words, "consists largely in making novel claims and novel inferences." (He takes it to be an empirically verified claim about language use that the sentences uttered by adults are in large part unprecedented, simply because of the complexity of grammar and the size of our vocabularies.)[32] And this sort of habitual production of novel sentences "leads inexorably to changes, not just in the claims we are disposed to make, but thereby in the concepts themselves. To use a vocabulary is to change it."[33] So human beings, as linguistic creatures, are constantly creative in their use of language, with unpredictable results. Languages in use are languages in flux, albeit slowly, and change is an intrinsic tendency of languages, not merely the result of the intellectual labors of heroic "strong poets" of the past.[34]

One of the vague points in this line of thought is the relation of vocabularies to other vocabularies, and to actual languages such as English or Latin. Rorty speaks of vocabularies as "alternative language games," and he gives a variety of examples, such as "the vocabulary of ancient Athenian politics versus Jefferson's, the moral vocabulary of Saint Paul versus Freud's, the jargon of Newton versus that of Aristotle, the idiom of Blake versus that of Dryden."[35] Thus a vocabulary, on this account, appears to include a normative theory of a given realm (e.g., politics or physics), which is expressed in particular terms, which together reflect the implicit norms (and presumably some explicit ones) governing the use and application of the concepts involved. Thus a vocabulary for Rorty is more like a theory than a language, so that both Blake and Dryden, for instance, can use the English of their respective eras. However, in addition to explicit theoretical commitments, such as claims about reality and standards of judgment or justification, a vocabulary would seem to include characteristic tropes, images, and narratives, adding up to a distinctive style of speaking, interpreting, judging, and acting. So a given language will probably include numerous vocabularies, some of which will rarely come into contact, and others of which might conflict, merge, or alternate as human beings use them to get along in the world.

Although Rorty is prone to speak somewhat antagonistically of "alternative language games" that are incommensurable in the sense of being irreducible to a single master vocabulary,[36] the relations between vocabularies would seem to be almost infinitely various. I develop a brief proposal below for modeling cross-traditional hermeneutics, but for now suffice it to say that problems of translation, interpretation, and judgment are best addressed in particular cases rather than by general accounts or methods that can then be mechanically applied.

Part of what makes vocabulary change possible, on this account, also helps to explain why it might be worthwhile to step back and adopt what Brandom calls the "vocabulary vocabulary" as a way to become more reflective about our own practices and commitments, and more productively inquisitive about other possibilities.[37] Brandom argues that "linguistic norms are special, in that being constrained by them gives us a distinctive kind of freedom." By agreeing to be constrained by the norms of a vocabulary, we give up freedom from constraint, or "negative freedom"; but at the same time, we gain "unparalleled positive freedom" to make new claims, conceive new purposes, and to do things that were previously impossible because inconceivable.[38] We cannot glorify God, for example, without learning a vocabulary of theism.

The recitation of cherished texts serves as one way to begin to learn a vocabulary, but on Brandom's account, as noted above, we most often use vocabularies to produce novel sentences. We thus "spend most of our time on untrodden inferential ground," where commitments implied by novel claims are in some sense "controlled" by the norms implicit in our vocabulary. But the process of speaking, of creating novel utterances and following out their implications, is not at all "determined" by those norms. These norms direct us in a general direction but do not map out a precise path in advance; moreover, they are not guaranteed in advance to be mutually reinforcing and coherent in all their implications.[39]

James Bohman has helpfully described this distinction as the contrast between "enabling" and "limiting" conditions for knowledge. Enabling conditions for knowledge are "variable and alterable," in contrast to limiting conditions, which are "determinate and fixed." The fact that we can, however laboriously, bring any particular part of our own vocabularies to consciousness is critical if interpretation is to have any deep effect on our thoughts or lives. We are not "judgmental dopes," utterly caught up in our culture's roles, norms, and skills, and neither is anyone else.[40]

Just as the eye allows us to see, our normally prereflective command of various vocabularies current within our social setting allows us to act meaningfully and interpret others' actions. Nonskeptical conclusions follow from this understanding. The necessity of using shared vocabularies does not affect the status of any particular belief, skill, or interpretation; this "background" to interpretation is epistemologically neutral. Interpreting in terms of a vocabulary is seen as working within certain flexible constraints, rather than strict limits, and thus leads to fallibilism, not radical contextualism. Bohman calls this general view "weak holism," in contrast to the "strong holism" of the conceptual relativist.

This suggests that learning how to use new vocabularies, and seeing how they relate to ones we already know well, is continuous with normal, intrinsically creative linguistic practice. Even the creation of new vocabularies is not "abnormal," as Rorty once termed the process (in order to praise it), but a response to practical needs to cope with new people and previously unknown texts that speak in unfamiliar ways.

To sum up, vocabularies, languages, and the practices and cultures that go along with them function as enabling conditions. They make social activity possible and undergird any sort of reflective inquiry, whether our own or that of some thinker from the distant past. Though they partially constrain and direct, they do not close us off from each other, and they in no way preclude the very possibility of gaining understanding and knowledge about the world or other people. "Cross-cultural" interpretation is a refinement and continuation of the sort of reflective interpretation to which anyone must resort when it becomes apparent that the person they are trying to understand does not share their assumptions and vocabulary.

The "vocabulary vocabulary" has several virtues. It provides a helpful way to address and analyze conceptual diversity while steering clear of the problems Davidson diagnoses with "conceptual schemes," it highlights the practical context of all language use, and it helps account for my own position as an interpreter in a way that does not presuppose a radical disjunction between theorist and human objects of study.

Nevertheless, certain difficulties remain. First, the vagueness of the scope of "vocabulary" is a minor problem. On the one hand, vocabularies can be seen broadly as a social group's available repertoire of terms and skills that allow the pursuit of various more or less distinctive purposes; on the other, vocabularies can be seen as the creations of particular people or small groups as they pursue and articulate more precise purposes, and practices and modes of life that support these ideals. I thus propose that, where necessary, the more general sense be marked by the term "conceptual repertoire."[41] This captures the sense of multiplicity and openness to varieties of use that seems appropriate for a species as disputatious as our own. It also avoids the imputations of unity, planning, and intentional structure that go with the predecessor notion of "scheme" but are inappropriate for the full panoply of the past ideas in any tradition, whether construed broadly as an entire civilization or more narrowly as a school or a religious group.

I further propose that a "conceptual apparatus" be used when we need to specify the more or less systematic formulation and use of elements of a cultural-linguistic conceptual repertoire by a particular thinker (or small group) in a particular tradition and cultural context. The notion of an apparatus focuses attention on someone's *constructing* a system of thought and practice out of available materials, and it implies both that such a system exists for certain ends and that it is put to use by people with productive results: the ordering of personal and communal life, in a way that is at least potentially sustainable, depending on the extent of its influence. Obviously, a conceptual apparatus is no more inherently unchangeable than a conceptual repertoire or culture, and some do become broadly influential in a larger society (e.g., those of Zhu Xi, Luther, or Calvin). And when we wish to highlight the continuity between these two ends of the spectrum of discursive practice, or when retaining a more general frame of reference, we can simply stick with "vocabulary."

The second difficulty is related, and it concerns the thought that vocabularies are tools with purposes: It seems misleading to think of whole vocabularies as having a single purpose, like a hammer; in my terminology, a conceptual repertoire would have numerous "purposes" that it can articulate and assist. A conceptual apparatus could be usefully thought of as facilitating a single overriding goal, such as the conversion of human beings to God or of ordering the world according to the Way. But even here, one might want to suggest that particular words are more like tools, and that vocabularies consist of numerous tools that together help one to become a particular sort of person or help a group become a certain sort of community (e.g., a guild of plumbers or painters, to follow out the analogy). This, too, seems to be a minor point, however.

A more significant issue concerns the metaphysical and meta-ethical presuppositions, if any, of this view. Rorty and Brandom make occasional crass remarks that mention religious belief and observance, only to link them to fanaticism; and in their more careful moments, they argue that at the very least religiosity should be a strictly private affair.[42] In contrast, Stout's "mild-mannered" pragmatism, including his use of Brandom's inferentialism, highlights the social nature of rational justification and is more conspicuously broad-minded about which beliefs and practices might be rationally justified for conscientious believers, explicitly including religious ones.[43] Though Stout is concerned to argue, successfully to my mind, for the objectivity of moral norms on a purely social basis in a world without an Augustinian God, this does not constitute an argument against theological premises. Nor does the Brandomian inferentialism Stout champions imply that there cannot be divine purposes as well as human ones. It does imply that for human beings to come to understand such purposes, they would need to be articulated in a human vocabulary, or at least a vocabulary that humans could understand well enough to use—but this cannot be controversial for theists, especially for Christians. To borrow Stout's metaphor, the fact that it is possible to play soccer without a referee does not make it impossible to play with a referee.[44] In this book, I rely on the pragmatist notion of a vocabulary simply as a way of articulating human normative practices and recognizing what diversity they possess. None of this "vocabulary vocabulary" should be taken to surreptitiously decide substantive questions in the comparative philosophy of religions.[45] How human purposes and the vocabularies with which they are articulated and pursued relate to any nonhuman or transhuman aims, if there are any, is a question that the notion of "vocabulary" does nothing to settle.

STRUCTURAL CHOICES AND PRODUCTIVE COMPARISONS

Even the most patient and open-minded critic would continue to wonder whether this study can avoid the familiar weaknesses of comparative studies that I have not yet addressed directly, and which the terminology of different vocabularies for ethics does not address by itself. Does not comparison, this critic might ask, rest on unjustified generalizations about whole traditions (e.g., "Hindu ethics" and similar imaginary reifications), and thereby issue in dubious, impressionistic conclusions? And does not the need for quick closure of summary accounts in order to move on to comparison itself mean that all such accounts will be radically inadequate, because they are so decontextualized and simplified that they lose touch with any potential objects of comparison before the inquiry gets off the ground? Other errors of historical interpretation, such as anachronism, are also common. And how could one person possibly develop the scholarly expertise necessary to handle materials from several different cultural and historical complexes? These are important and wise questions, the hard-won fruits of past comparative studies of religion that were often badly flawed. In the process of sketching out what I take to be the intellectually responsible options for comparative ethics, and the trade-offs among them, this section attempts to answer these questions. The responses should be sufficient to win over the curious but skeptical, although perhaps not the hardened despiser of comparative work.

The most basic choice to make when setting up comparisons is between depth and precision of treatment, on the one hand, and generality of scope, on the other.[46] Many of the most objectionable difficulties with past comparisons, whether historical, theological, or philosophical, stem from the quixotic desire to encompass all religions in one study. Whether such efforts attempt to tell a story of universal spirit coming to self-consciousness, or to map the range of psychological archetypes that obtain across all of human history, or to argue for a single "deep structure" of "religious reason" that informs all traditions, the vastness of the ambition involved leads to predictable errors of interpretation, especially overgeneralization and anachronism.[47]

Although there have been some better recent attempts to circumvent the problems of wide scope by using teams of scholars, each bringing specialized expertise, this approach risks other problems, most notably a failure to actually engage in rigorous comparison, rather than merely juxtaposing accounts of various traditions, organized around themes. A heavy burden devolves to the editors of such collected volumes, who must do much of the work to draw out similarities and differences between materials with which they are not deeply familiar.[48] Perhaps the best solution to the group approach is to assemble specialists who are also seriously interested in comparison, who can then work together to develop comparisons jointly, through multiple drafts of interrelated essays or coauthored books. Such projects, obviously, require logistical acumen, personal commitment from all involved, and significant support.[49]

The other possibility is to narrow the scope of a comparative study to focus more precise attention on particular objects to be compared. This path has been followed by the most successful and illuminating recent comparative studies, including Lee Yearley's *Mencius and Aquinas: Theories of Virtue and Conceptions of Courage*, and Karen Carr and Philip Ivanhoe's *The Sense of Antirationalism: The Religious Thought of Zhuangzi and Kierkegaard*.[50] By focusing in depth on only a few figures, in cultures and traditions that an author knows well, it becomes possible to approximate the level of contextualization in capable intellectual history. Most important, tightness of focus, on the basis of real scholarly expertise in the relevant languages, cultures, and traditions, allows a level of precision in both treatment and comparative analysis that is otherwise unattainable. Moreover, generalizations about single thinkers, especially if they have systematic tendencies, are much more defensible, and can be more effectively qualified as necessary, than generalizations about whole religions or traditions.[51] If the figures to be compared are to be taken seriously as thinkers, with theoretical positions and vocabulary that are worthy of careful attention, then the model of comparing two thinkers in depth around a particular theme of interest will be hard to surpass.

The present study aims to continue to develop this mode of comparative ethics. The dangers in this way of proceeding are excessive narrowness and potential limitations of audience, but these dangers are less intellectually serious than those courted by more generalizing approaches. Narrowness, in particular, can be overcome by careful choice among topics and objects to be compared, on the basis of broader debates in religious ethics and knowledge of the relevant traditions, so that tightness of focus in a comparative project is no more objectionable than in a topical study that stays strictly within a single tradition or era or that focuses on a particular figure.[52]

A second general strategic choice is between historical contextualization and creative, emblematic generalization. The virtues of carefully contextualized historical accounts are currently well known and celebrated: insightful interpretations that recreate as closely as possible the initial conditions for a text's reception, and thus perhaps as well authorial intention. Again, if insight into particular "classic" texts or thinkers is desired, this approach will generally be superior.[53]

Against this, David Hall and Roger Ames's collaborative project *Thinking Through Confucius* is based on a method they describe as one of "cross-cultural anachronism," whereby they take a current Anglo-American philosophical problem (the nature and importance of thinking) and look for resources to address it in the *Analects* of Confucius, which does not explicitly entertain such an issue. They argue that only such a course will allow us to recognize what is truly alien and distinctive in Confucius's thought and practice, by uncovering hidden biases and projections inhering in our categories of analysis. Their ultimate goal is to detail certain "fundamental presuppositions" they find underlying conceptions of "thinking" in China and the West.[54] Although Hall and Ames claim at times to be illuminating the *Analects* and even the historical Confucius, several of their interpretive claims are dubious.[55] I think their work is most profitably interpreted, first, as a somewhat exaggerated dialectical response to preceding trends in Western accounts of Confucius, and second, as a creative attempt to articulate a form of "New Confucianism" that draws heavily on American pragmatism.[56] Thus Confucius serves as the emblem and "launch pad" for their own creative philosophizing in a Confucian vein. The main potential virtue of this strategy is the development of novel approaches to familiar material.

I have argued elsewhere that such creative productions on the basis of past sources or exemplars, considered strictly as new theoretical constructions, should be judged on their own intellectual merits, regardless of historical faithfulness to their sources.[57] Nevertheless, though the temptation, even the compulsion, to see oneself as uncovering the essence of Confucian thought for today might be hard to resist, that impulse should not be allowed to obscure the distinctive tasks and responsibilities of the historian. The danger with emblematic generalization, then, is of losing touch with the historical sources that provoked one's efforts in the first place. Depending on the author's abilities, this in turn increases the chance of producing something new but second rate, or not even new.[58]

Robin Lovin and Frank Reynolds have discerned a third fundamental methodological choice between "holistic" interpretations that are sensitive to context and "formalistic" interpretations that attend to the logical structure of ethical beliefs or theories.[59] Their targets are the comparative work of David Little and Sumner Twiss on formal definitions of moral, religious, and legal reasoning; and that of Ron Green on the "deep structure of religious reason" that he discerns in a variety of religious traditions.[60] Lovin and Reynolds's edited volume is noteworthy in that it was the first to borrow an empirical, holistic approach from the history of religions in order to situate the ethics of various thinkers and traditions carefully in their larger cultural and historical contexts; I also adopt such a holistic approach to ensure adequate historical engagement with my sources. Little and Twiss and Green are all concerned, although in different ways, with formal structures of ethical thought; localizing this concern, I look carefully at the vocabulary or conceptual apparatus of each thinker to be compared, the better to attend to the philosophical or theological issues at play in their presentations. In other words, properly constructed comparative studies can have the virtues of both these sorts of studies and can escape the false dilemma of this previously apparent methodological choice.

The current inquiry, then, seeks to transcend past difficulties in comparative studies by carefully focusing attention on the work of two influential thinkers on topics of significant contemporary ethical interest, topics about which both developed sustained reflections. In this way, they can be addressed as theoretical interlocutors and not merely as objects of study awaiting the organizing ministrations of the contemporary interpreter. A tight focus makes it possible for one person to develop the relevant kinds of expertise and to give each party something approaching his or her due as a sophisticated thinker. Careful historical contextualization and depth of treatment ward off the sorts of dubious generalizations that provide more insight into the mind of the comparativist than into different reflective modes of religious life.

BRIDGING RELIGIOUS WORLDS

However it might be structured, any comparative ethical study faces two fundamental challenges: It must bring distant ethical statements into interrelation and conversation, and it must simultaneously preserve their distinctiveness within the interrelation. In the present work, careful analysis of each thinker's distinctive vocabulary meets the second goal; the first goal is pursued by means of "bridge concepts."[61] Bridge concepts are general ideas, such as "virtue" and "human nature," which can be given enough content to be meaningful and guide comparative inquiry yet are still open to greater specification in particular cases. They differ from "thin concepts" only in that they are chosen specifically to facilitate a particular comparison of a delimited number of objects, and so are chosen with those objects in mind. The process of selection and refinement is thus in an important sense inductive, and any broader applicability any given set might possess is essentially hypothetical and subject to further testing and revision in wider inquiries.

Bridge concepts are not, then, hypotheses about transcultural universals that purport to bring a "deep structure" of human religion or ethics to the surface; I am skeptical about all such deep structures or "epistemes" that are supposed somehow to determine or explain thought and practice, whether for humanity as a whole, or merely within a single tradition or era.[62] In contrast, as general topics, bridge concepts may be projected into each thinker or text to be compared as a way to thematize their disparate elements and order their details around these anchoring terms. Bridge concepts often work best if near-equivalent terms for the various aspects of the bridge concept can be found in each set of writings to be compared, but this is not necessary.[63] In this study, the primary bridge concepts—to be discussed in the next chapter—are "human nature" and "spiritual exercises," with secondary attention to ideas of a "person" and the "will."

One might worry that if given too much specific content, bridge concepts could move beyond guiding inquiry to determining it. The projection inherent in this sort of procedure might move beyond what is normally accepted in any historical or philosophical exegesis organized around themes and become boringly self-fulfilling, as unanimity is discovered in the unlikeliest places. More subtly, one might be tempted to find that every thinker in every tradition is deeply concerned with one's own preexisting questions, providing a variety of "answers" to them, rather than proposing questions and answers of their own. In contrast, bridge concepts are designed to elicit theoretical formulations in each object compared (i.e., their "vocabulary"), including questions and basic orientations, but to refrain from reshaping the terms each thinker uses into some fundamentally new form. The analysis of each thinker's vocabulary thus safeguards each side's uniqueness within the comparison. Articulating a vocabulary in this sense focuses attention on the way particular ideas fit into larger visions, and on the metaphorical linkages and logical relations within these larger systems, thereby allowing more nuanced comparisons of seemingly similar ideas across traditions.

This "vocabulary vocabulary" is a productive tool for comparative ethics because it facilitates the construction of what Charles Taylor has called "languages of perspicuous contrast" to distinguish precisely between the elements of different ethics.[64] Bridge concepts can be articulated in the process of comparison in such a way that they highlight both similarities and differences, and even more subtle similarities within differences, and differences within similarities.[65] But bridge concepts are not conceived as junior versions of Esperanto that might come to fully articulate both vocabularies in a new, third idiom; they merely assist in the process of creating comparative relations between distant ethical positions.[66]

Bridge concepts and the comparisons they facilitate serve as important tools for what Rorty calls "edifying philosophy." He writes:

> Since "education" sounds a bit too flat, and *Bildung* a bit too foreign, I shall use "edification" to stand for this project of finding new, better, more interesting, more fruitful ways of speaking. The attempt to edify (ourselves or others) may consist in the hermeneutic activity of making connections between our own culture and some exotic culture or historical period, or between our own discipline and another discipline which seems to pursue incommensurable aims in an incommensurable vocabulary. But it may instead consist in the "poetic" activity of thinking up such new aims, new words, or new disciplines, followed by, so to speak, the inverse of hermeneutics: the attempt to reinterpret our familiar surroundings in the unfamiliar terms of our new inventions. . . . For edifying discourse is *supposed* to be abnormal, to take us out of our old selves by the power of strangeness, to aid us in becoming new beings.[67]

Although I do not wish to go everywhere Rorty wishes to lead us, as far as "more interesting" ways of speaking are concerned, I do second the suggestion that analyzing, critiquing, and thus changing and enriching our own vocabularies, our ways of speaking and acting, is truly edifying. Comparative religious ethics, as argued earlier in this chapter, is a particularly powerful way of bringing preconceptions to consciousness, while simultaneously generating new ethical possibilities, through careful engagement with exotic "others" such as Augustine and Xunzi. By expanding and reordering our own conceptual repertoire, we gain new inspiration for refining or even reconstructing our own conceptual apparatuses. Whether we might become "new beings" in the process is not something that can be judged in advance.

WHY XUNZI AND AUGUSTINE?

Although meta-ethical concerns and curiosity about the potentials of comparative religious ethics certainly played roles in the genesis of this project, the most formative impetus came from attempts to grapple with the specific subject of the cultivation of virtue. How could anyone really become more virtuous over time? Analogous questions were central to widespread debates in ancient China about *xiu shen* 修身, usually translated as "self-cultivation." And as Pierre Hadot has taught us, practical regimens of personal formation, which he calls "spiritual exercises," were equally essential to Greco-Roman "philosophy" as a shared way of life. Engaging sophisticated accounts of such exercises helps to develop virtue ethics in a fruitful new direction, by stressing the intentional cultivation of character through methodical practices. These practices can be described and analyzed in detail, just as particular virtues can, and such close analysis sheds much light on the moral psychology of character development. Whether moderns are able to cultivate virtue is, after all, one of the central issues in critiques of modernity and liberalism. If we wish to understand virtue, and perhaps even become better ourselves, it would be wise to reflect carefully on some of the most sophisticated past accounts of this process.

This leads directly to Augustine and Xunzi. Both develop subtle and insightful accounts of personal formation that include detailed analysis and advocacy of particular practices. They also build their accounts of personal formation on the basis of clear-eyed but distinctive assessments of humanity's propensities to do evil. Their analyses of "human nature" as fallen or bad profoundly shape the practical regimens they each suggest, which are tuned to restrain, ameliorate, or even transform our more questionable impulses.

Although I cannot fully argue the point here, some form of the general view that aspects of human nature are seriously problematic, and thus that people need significant formation to become moral, seems right. But there are many versions of this sort of account, cast in quite different terms. Are human beings selfish rational agents, each seeking to maximize our individual economic benefit regardless of the "costs" to others? Are we delinquent children of God, in sinful rebellion against our creator, seeking our own aggrandizement at the expense of others? Are we social beings whose instincts are foolishly shortsighted and often destructively selfish? Are we servants of our own will to power, or possessors of a death instinct? And what are the implications of such diagnoses for efforts to improve our situation? Grappling with Augustine's and Xunzi's accounts of these matters can help us to reflect both on substantive questions of anthropology and ethical formation, and on various possible vocabularies for such reflection. None of these vocabularies are in any sense necessary for human thought (even certain traditional Western ones that claim such necessity); all of them are candidates for contemporary assessment and use.

The fact that people display tendencies to covetousness, cruelty, revenge, greed, and lust for domination, to name a few of our less splendid propensities, does not rule out the existence of more sociable and compassionate impulses, as both Augustine and Xunzi recognize. Recent efforts to relate "evolutionary psychology" to ethics often carefully attend to these more benign impulses.[68] This study contends that it is inadequate to focus only on "prosocial" human impulses without careful attention to what might be called the "antisocial" side of humans, which as Augustine understood particularly well can twist even the most seemingly sociable motives to destructive ends. For beings like us, the cultivation of virtue requires the restraint and redirection of certain impulses, as well as the cultivation of others.

It is also insufficient to simply take modern contrasts between "altruism" and "egotism" for granted as setting the terms in which "morality" is to be understood. We need to be much more alert to the nuances of different possible vocabularies for understanding ethics, and for understanding "human nature," which is a far from self-evident idea, much less an empirically simple datum to be read off of our genetic code. Significantly different ways of articulating both "human nature" and "ethics" are not only possible but actual, and particular versions of these ideas cannot simply be assumed. Comparative ethics can be particularly helpful in bringing such differences to awareness and in analyzing their philosophical and practical consequences.

At this point, the founding judgment of this study that both Xunzi and Augustine have particularly profound vocabularies for overcoming human evil can only serve as a promissory note, to be cashed in detailed analyses of their prescriptions. But readers should take some comfort in the immense historical significance of both figures in their respective traditions. Augustine is the original "master of suspicion" in the West, at least as profound as his later inheritors Marx, Nietzsche, and Freud.[69] Augustine strove to create a theological-ethical system in order to know and love God better, and his ideas became enormously influential in later Western culture. It is probably safe to say that "the West" would not be "the West" without Augustine. He is also the subject of intense recent interest as a theological and philosophical hero to be restored to his rightful preeminence, so it behooves us to reflect carefully on what is distinctive to his way of framing key issues in ethics.[70]

Xunzi provides a particularly useful object for comparison with Augustine. He shares in a rough way some basic Augustinian presuppositions (that humans have a destructive or bad "nature," and therefore must change to become good) while not sharing others (the preeminence of God, Christ, the Bible, and divine grace). Thus there is reason to hope that fine-grained comparisons can be developed between them, because the similarity in the general morphology of their views is the basis for the bridge concepts used to compare them. Furthermore, Xunzi is an equally sophisticated theorist and thinker, and so he will not be overwhelmed or subtly marginalized in the comparison.[71] Crucially, Xunzi does not articulate his positions as either an acceptance or rejection of central Augustinian doctrines about the will, or God, and so at the level of theoretical detail provides a true alternative rather than another layer of commentary on the Pelagian controversy. And last, Xunzi is an important and influential figure in Chinese intellectual history, although not equivalent in stature to Augustine in the West: Xunzi was eventually eclipsed by his predecessor Mencius in a way that never happened for more than brief periods with Augustine.[72]

NOTES

1. Sharpe 1975.

2. For a recent account of "religion" and related terms that doubles as a brief history of religious studies, see Smith 1998. For an insightful analysis of common modern metaphors for "religion" and their various intellectual consequences, along with a brief comparison with medieval Chinese ways of discussing what could be called "religion-analogues," see Campany 2003.

3. Yearley 1990. Yearley's work is discussed more fully later in this chapter, and in chapter 9.

4. On the issues involved, see Rorty 1984; Herdt 2000, esp. 180; and Lewis et al. 2005. On "genealogy," see, e.g., Nietzsche 1967; Foucault 1977, 1978; and MacIntyre 1990.

5. For a believably modest version of this "secularization" narrative, see Stout 2004, 92–118. For a fuller history of how South and East Asian religions and philosophies have contributed to modern European civilization and its offshoots, see Clarke 1997.

6. For details, see Eck 2001.

7. Bruce Grelle and Sumner Twiss make similar points in the introduction to their coedited volume (1998).

8. Rawls 1971, 1993.

9. I refer here to the work of Alasdair MacIntyre (e.g., 1984, 1988) and Stanley Hauerwas (e.g., 1981), among others.

10. For a fuller narrative of the development I sketch here, along with a distinctive analysis, critique, and alternative proposal, see Stout 2004.

11. Exemplary practitioners of this sort of approach include: Martha Nussbaum (1986) on Aristotle, Alasdair MacIntyre (1984, 1988) on Aristotle and Aquinas, Jean Porter (1990) on Aquinas, Annette Baier (1991) on Hume, and Onora O'Neill (1989) on Kant.

12. Stout 2004, 147–61 (esp. 151–52 on democratic questioning and exchange of reasons), 162–73 (esp. 165 on essay writing as a spiritual exercise), 192–98, 203–24, 278–83, 287–308 (esp. 293 on "social practices directed toward excellence" and the "discursive practices of ethical deliberation and political debate").

13. Indeed, the sort of unified, harmonious, clearly bounded community MacIntyre (1988, 370–88) sketches as part of his analysis of "languages-in-use" seems to be at best a rare accident of history, when compared with the much more frequent cases of changing, conflicted, interconnected communities that contemporary historical research reveals. For a trenchant critique of the conception of culture embodied in MacIntyre's account, see Tanner 1997. Tanner argues that cultures cannot be precisely individuated, tend to be subject to internal conflicts, and have been in a more or less continuous process of change as our many interrelated histories have rolled forward. For similar arguments, see Moody-Adams 1997. For a powerful feminist critique of the traditionalism MacIntyre has espoused, see Okin 1989, 41–73.

14. Much of the best contemporary work on relativism grows out of twentieth-century Anglo-American philosophical debates about the rationality of alien cultural practices, which have often revolved around the objective truth of beliefs apparently presupposed by such practices. Important publications in this line include Evans-Pritchard 1937; Winch 1958, 1970 [1964]; MacIntyre 1970a [1967], 1970b [1964]; Wilson 1970; Hollis and Lukes 1982; Krausz 1989; and Simon 1990. For an excellent book-length study of moral relativism informed by early Chinese thought, see Wong 1984. On the relation of culture(s) to ethics, see Fleischacker 1994 and Moody-Adams 1997.

15. Davidson 1984, 183–98.

16. The best introduction to this line of thought for a religious studies audience is Stout 2002. See also the broad but clear and relatively concise introduction in Brandom 2000a, 1–44. Brandom 1994 gives the fullest version of this general approach. I am indebted to Jeff Stout, John Reeder, and John Kelsay for probing questions and helpful discussions regarding the relation of these lines of thought to comparative ethics.

17. To be more precise, Davidson (1984, 191–92, 195–97) is ruling out zones of untranslatability between languages, e.g., over religious matters, but leaving space for particular difficulties of translation, of specific words such as "grace" or *qi* 氣.

18. For a fuller and more precise analysis of Davidson's arguments and the subsequent debate about conceptual schemes, see Stalnaker 2001, 19–38.

19. Godlove 2002, 12. Note also his important earlier work, Godlove 1989.

20. See, e.g., the more congenial statements about the complexities of "coming to understand one another" in Godlove 2002, 15–16.

21. Davidson (1984) writes at one point: "A language may contain simple predicates whose extensions are matched by no simple predicates, or even by any predicates at all, in some other language. What enables us to make this point in particular cases is an ontology common to the two languages, with concepts that individuate the same objects. We can be clear about breakdowns in translation when they are local enough, for a background of generally successful translation provides what is needed to make the failures intelligible" (192). But compare this from his closing comments: "It would be equally wrong to announce the glorious news that all mankind—all speakers of language, at least—share a common scheme and ontology" (198).

22. For a general critique of Davidson on this issue, see Kraut 1986, esp. 406, 409, 415. A. C. Graham has reflected extensively on this issue in relation to the Chinese case. For a concise, late summary, see Graham 1989, 389–428. For more detailed statements, see Graham 1990b, 1990c, and 1991.

23. See, e.g., Hacker 1996 and Case 1997.

24. Hacker 1996, 297.

25. See Rorty 1979, esp. chaps. 7 and 8, and Rorty 1989, esp. chaps. 1–3. Robert Brandom (2000) has written an excellent analysis of this theme in Rorty's thought. See also Rorty's (2000) appreciative response in the same volume.

26. Brandom 2000b, 159; Rorty 1989, 13–15; Rorty 1979, 368. Similarly, according to Rorty, it would be a mistake to think of languages as a barrier between people or cultures; instead, they should be seen as the main tools people use to deal with each other.

27. Brandom 2000b, 168ff.

28. For fuller discussion see Stout 2002, 35–41.

29. Brandom 2000b, 167. See also the briefer definition of "vocabularies" as "linguistic practices" on 178.

30. Rorty 1989, 12–13. Foucault is perhaps the most notable recent theorist of the social productivity of discourses, and of the complex interplay between the development of discourses and practices. See particularly Foucault 1977 and 1978.

31. Rorty 1989, 12–22; Brandom 2000b, 168–81.

32. Brandom 2000b, 175.

33. All quotations in this paragraph are from Brandom 2000b, 177.

34. In other words tradition, understood in a certain way, is the right category for the analysis of vocabulary change over time. Brandom puts these points in terms of traditions of language use in Brandom 2000b, 177. For broader discussion, see Shils 1981; cf. MacIntyre 1988.

35. Rorty 1989, 5.

36. See, e.g., Rorty 1979, 388, and 1989, 11–13. He is of course not alone in this habit; MacIntyre's theory of conflicting traditions develops such an account in much

greater detail. See, e.g., MacIntyre 1988, esp. 164–82, 349–403, and MacIntyre 1990.

37. Brandom 2000b, 177.

38. Brandom 2000b, 178.

39. Brandom 2000b, 176.

40. Bohman 1991, 119–21.

41. Rorty at one point (1989, 22) suggests that we think of our "intuitions" as "the habitual use of a certain repertoire of terms," but he does not develop this remark. Rob Campany (2003, 317–19) has recently proposed that we think of religions "as repertoires of resources" for human social life. He is building on the empirical and theoretical work of Ann Swidler (2001) on cultures as repertoires.

42. See e.g., Brandom: "We can all too easily imagine our scientific institutions falling into the hands of theological fanatics who can describe in excruciating detail just how the revolutionary change from present day science to their loopy theories represents decisive progress along the essential dimension of pleasingness to God" (2000b, 171). On the inappropriateness of religious discourse in public political deliberation, see Rorty 1994.

43. Stout 1988, 13–33 and passim; Stout 2004, 92–117, 163–79 (note esp. 317 n. 8.), 199–202, 256–69. Note as well the similarity of this account to the "cultural-linguistic" approach to religion developed in Lindbeck 1984 for ecumenical reasons, and with theological intent.

44. Stout 2004, 183–286, esp. 270–78. The image of God as the referee of a game is at best very limited. To speak more theologically, to talk of God as judge does not rule out discussing God as creator, sustainer, father, mother, etc.

45. For a serious and commendable effort to grapple with these questions, see McKim 2001.

46. For capable recent surveys of the methodological terrain in comparative religious ethics, each with fuller bibliography, see Twiss 1998b and Lewis 1998.

47. Although I would vigorously contest Hegel's account of the history of Chinese thought, for example, I do not question his considerable significance for modern Western thought. Here I simply want to address the adequacy of certain sorts of comparisons as comparisons. For a thoughtful development of certain Hegelian themes for the purposes of comparative ethics, see Lewis 2005. The other references are to the work of Carl Jung and his admirers, such as Joseph Campbell, and to Ronald Green. Green's work (1978, 1988), while flawed by his efforts to find a basically Kantian structure of practical reasoning in numerous different traditions, is nonetheless illuminating in several ways, partly through the very effort to find the "deep structure of religious rationality" in places where it is not obviously present.

48. Noteworthy examples of group efforts include Lovin and Reynolds 1985; Reynolds and Tracy 1990, 1992, 1994; and Cabezón 1998.

49. The most ambitious and admirably self-conscious recent effort along these lines is the Comparative Religious Ideas Project, which culminated in three volumes edited by Robert Cummings Neville (2001a, 2001b, 2001c). For a fine coauthored volume, see Carr and Ivanhoe 2000. Another collaborative effort at comparison is the

Journal of Religious Ethics 33, no. 2 (Summer 2005), a focus issue titled "Anthropos and Ethics," which includes essays by Berkson, Lewis, Schofer, and Stalnaker, and a jointly authored introduction.

50. For comparative theological works that exemplify the virtues of this general approach, see Clooney 1993, 2001.

51. Jonathan Z. Smith (1990, 117–18) rightly criticizes this sort of "holism," by which he means the assumption of homogeneity of whole "religions" in such a way that, for example, different Christianities in antiquity can be presumed to share more with each other than with contemporaneous Judaisms or other varieties of antique religions, when in fact this assumption is false. Needless to say, this assumption of homogeneity is very different than the sort of holism in interpretation that the present study advocates.

52. Narrowness can have more subtle consequences, of course: One might simply be unaware of particularly profound treatments of a given topic in traditions that are beyond one's competency, or even outside one's awareness, and so choose poorly when constructing a study of that topic. But those who work within only one historical complex or tradition are even more prone to this intellectual vice than comparativists.

53. Awareness of later commentaries, interpretations, and reworkings is obviously also very helpful. Thus, for example, we can gain greater insight into Augustine's thought, and our own modern reactions to it, by having at least some awareness of how he has been read and used by Aquinas, Erasmus, Luther, Calvin, Kant, Kierkegaard, and many others.

54. Hall and Ames (1987, 11–25) contend, for example, that the "deep presuppositions" supposedly "dominating" "Anglo-European" and Chinese thought can be summarized in dichotomies between "transcendence" and "immanence," "conceptual disjunction" and "conceptual polarity," and "history" and "tradition," with the first of each pair describing the orientation of Western culture and the second that of Chinese culture. Such historical shorthand is equally unfair to the complex traditions of both China and Europe. For a more developed argument against these sorts of essentialist claims, see Puett 2002. Although I disagree with them on some basic issues of methodology, Hall and Ames's work is rich with specific insights and intriguing suggestions, and a full assessment of it is far beyond the scope of this chapter.

55. For example, consider their account of *yi* 義, normally translated as "righteousness" or "justice," as something more like "disclosure of personal significance" (Hall and Ames 1987, 83–84, 89–110).

56. In particular, Hall and Ames rightly seek to counter Herbert Fingarette's (1972) treatment of Confucianism as lacking a sense of interiority or individuality. On their desire to make Confucian thought a viable participant in contemporary philosophical conversation, see Hall and Ames 1987, 6, 313–36.

57. Stalnaker 2005. Please see this article for fuller discussion and necessary qualifications.

58. There are deep and difficult issues here, particularly with regard to personal engagement with and appropriation of classical sources, that I cannot pursue in this venue. The best work on these issues is still Gadamer 1989.

59. Lovin and Reynolds 1985, 1–35.

60. Little and Twiss 1978; Green 1978, 1988.

61. I owe this way of framing things originally to John Reeder. And although arrived at independently, my "bridge concepts" and Neville's "vague categories" of comparison seem to function in similar ways in the process of inquiry (Neville 2001a, 9–16). Perhaps the main difference is one of scope: Neville's Comparative Religious Ideas Project aims to bring six different traditions (conceived and articulated in various ways by various authors) into mutual imagined dialogue, and to flesh out their vague categories in the process into a metavocabulary capable of accurately relating all six traditions' claims about the topic marked out by the category. I am less hopeful than Neville and his fellows that this degree of scope will yield rich insights, when compared with more carefully specified and delimited comparisons, but this is only partly a matter of judgment, partly a hunch, and partly a result of my own limitations as an investigator.

62. For different versions of this sort of "deep structure" view, see Green 1978 and 1988, and Foucault 1971. Foucault, at least in this work, is the more straightforward determinist; Green recognizes the possibility of deviation from his "deep structure of religious reason," as for example in early China, but still argues that such occurrences are rare and have predictable negative consequences.

63. Sometimes a thinker might have several words that cover the territory of a particular English word, sometimes none at all. The deeper issue is to take care to map a thinker's use of a particular concept or concepts, even if he or she does not have a word that translates easily into English as the bridge concept in question. To assume that someone cannot have a concept for something unless they possess a word for it has been called the "lexical fallacy." On this, see Van Norden 2003b.

64. Taylor 1985b.

65. For discussion, see Yearley 1990, 4–6, 170–75.

66. To be more precise, the present study attempts to represent the ethical thought and practice of Xunzi and Augustine in the English language, obviously not the native tongue of either thinker, by means of bridge concepts that are themselves articulated in English. These bridge concepts are designed to guide inquiry into the "vocabularies" of each thinker, originally framed in late antique Latin and classical Chinese. The transliteration, translation, paraphrase, and exegesis involved in this process of representation are essential to the interpretation of both thinkers, and to the comparison of them. The English-language interpretations offered here are not exhaustive but are oriented to and shaped by the comparative purposes of this study.

67. Rorty 1979, 360.

68. See, e.g., Thomas 1989; de Waal 1996; Sober and Wilson 1998; Katz 2000.

69. The phrase "master of suspicion" comes from Ricoeur 1970, 32.

70. Probably the most prominent such Augustinian is the theologian John Milbank. But note also younger scholars such as Charles Mathewes (2001).

71. This issue haunts Yearley's book on Mencius and Aquinas (1990), because of the centrality of virtue *theory* to both Aquinas's thought and Yearley's comparative project.

72. For a fuller accounting of Xunzi's historical influence, see Knoblock 1988–94, vol. 1, 36–49.

CHAPTER TWO

Contexts for Interpretation

✦

I argued in chapter 1 that if one's goal is to engage culturally distant thinkers precisely as thinkers, as theorists who have developed religious conceptions worthy of careful study, then the best comparative strategy is to interpret them with sensitivity, alert to the various contexts and traditions in which they moved and worked. This is not particularly controversial, but neither is it obvious what this implies. Proper contextualization of interpretations does not require a lengthy account of "the context" that would duplicate or mimic specialist histories; it is rather a matter of perceptive interpretation of particular points in each thinker, leading to insight into broader themes in their visions of life. Thus to charge that a historical account has been "decontextualized" must be a reasonable critique of specific aspects of the account in question, not some sort of blanket complaint about the amount of generalized discussion of the historical background presumed by the account.

Moreover, readers often generate conflicting interpretations of profound and broad-ranging thinkers such as Augustine and Xunzi. Choices of organization and emphasis must be made in any study; evidence and counterevidence must be weighed. In important respects, the investigator constitutes the objects of her study by choosing the approach and themes that guide it, as well as the evidence to be given greatest prominence. It behooves all interpreters to remember that even the most articulate objects of study do not determine some proper form that interpretations of their words must take; Augustine and Xunzi tell many stories, not just one, and it is up to us as readers to be clear about how we approach them and why.

Accordingly, in this chapter, I first offer very brief introductions to the life and historical context of Xunzi and Augustine, designed only to orient readers who may be unfamiliar with either. I then discuss in more detail the "bridge concepts" to be used as organizing themes in this study: human nature, personhood, spiritual exercises, and the will.

XUNZI AND AUGUSTINE

Obviously Xunzi lived in a profoundly different culture from the modern United States, used a language unrelated to English, and was responding to a distinctive (and in certain ways quite alien) intellectual scene. With Augustine, we may be misled by the thought that he is Western, and hence "ours." Peter Brown rightly insists that "the Christianity of the . . . Middle Ages—to say nothing of the Christianity of our own times—is separated from the Christianity of the Roman world by a chasm almost as vast as that which still appears to separate us from the moral horizons of a Mediterranean Islamic country."[1] We must be alert to the distance between contemporary ideas that descend from Augustine and his own conceptions expressed in similar or even apparently identical terms, as well as to a cultural world almost as foreign as ancient China. In many ways, the problems generated by historical and cultural distance are quite parallel, and similar skills are necessary to navigate both. I thus provide brief introductions to the life, context, and thought of each of our subjects.[2]

Xunzi was born in the state of Zhao around 310 BCE, during the Warring States period of Chinese history, and he probably lived just past the unification of China by Qin Shihuang in 221 BCE. This era was marked by continuing strife between several states seeking to conquer the others and succeed the clearly moribund Zhou Dynasty. In this environment, violence and social disruption were common, and ongoing debates over the proper ordering of self and society took on a new intensity as a "hundred schools of thought" contended for influence with rulers seeking the proper Way of human existence.

Xunzi seems to have been precocious: He left home at fifteen to go to perhaps the preeminent center of learning of his day, the Jixia "Academy" in the capital of the state of Qi, where scholars of every philosophical and religious persuasion debated each other and enjoyed the king's largesse. In such an environment, Xunzi was exposed to all the major intellectual currents of his day, and he distinguished himself sufficiently among the attending thinkers that he was honored three times as head libationer at the official ancestral sacrifices. He also traveled fairly widely. In between extended stays at Jixia in Qi, he spent a number of years at the court of the southern state of Chu after King Min of Qi overreached militarily and was hunted down and killed. He also visited Qin, the eventual victor in the internecine conflicts, where he was confronted with a powerful and ruthless state that impressed but saddened him.

Near the end of his life, Xunzi was appointed magistrate of Lanling in Chu, a post of uncertain but probably not enormous gravity, where he continued to teach his students and in all likelihood worked to put his literary legacy in order. A perhaps apocryphal story describes a very old Xunzi, having lived to see the unification of China by Qin with the help of his own turncoat student Li Si, declining an honorary post in the new regime offered by his renegade pupil. In any case, Xunzi died shortly thereafter, having failed to convince any of the kingly pretenders to adopt his Way. The future official "triumph" of Confucianism could not have been foreseen.[3]

Xunzi borrowed ideas from numerous sources to rearticulate the tradition of the Zhou Dynasty passed on by Confucius and his followers; he self-consciously described himself as one of this group of *Ru* 需, generally termed "Confucians." In particular, he took issue with his Confucian predecessor Mencius over the character of human *xing* 性, or "nature." Where Mencius suggests that human *xing* is good, Xunzi argues instead that it is bad, and that any human goodness is a matter of "artifice." The innate desires that make up our *xing* often aim at real goods, Xunzi thinks, but tend to be destructively shortsighted and selfish. They disrupt our lives, gnawing at us if unsatisfied, growing without limit if we do manage briefly to fulfill them, turning families and communities against themselves in a chaotic struggle for scarce goods. Reforming these desires is the task of a demanding program of traditional Confucian ethico-religious cultivation, centering on ritual practice, musical performance, and textual study, which Xunzi likens to straightening crooked wood in a steam press or hammering blunt metal on an anvil. If this is pursued over many years, he thinks, a complete transformation of human dispositions and desires is possible, so that even a "person in the street" can become a sage.

Xunzi's influence was most profound in shaping the Confucianism that followed him, which was officially declared orthodoxy in the Han Dynasty. His students transmitted several of the versions of key classical texts that survive today, and his general turn back to the importance of textual study was decisive in shaping later Confucianism. Nevertheless, his direct influence seems to have waned as the Han Dynasty continued, and the first extant commentary on his works dates from the Tang Dynasty, written by one Yang Liang in 818 CE. Xunzi was further eclipsed by the ascent of Zhu Xi's Mencian-inflected "Neo-Confucianism" in the Song Dynasty, which relegated Xunzi's position on human nature to the status of heterodoxy until the twentieth century. Nevertheless, since the eighteenth century, interest in Xunzi has been growing, inspired mostly by the sophistication of his thought and the development of indigenous traditions of modern historical-critical scholarship in China and Japan, and augmented since the 1920s by a slow but steady stream of Western studies.[4]

Although we know a relatively large amount about Xunzi's life when compared with other early Chinese thinkers, and can even speculate about the chronology of some of his writings, scholars know vastly more about Augustine's life, context, and works, many of which can be dated quite precisely. Augustine was born on November 13, 354 CE, in Thagaste, a town in Roman North Africa. His parents had limited means, and they barely managed to provide him with a classical literary education, at a time when mastery of the shared literary and rhetorical culture of the Roman Empire was one of few avenues for social and economic advancement. In 370, he gained sufficient support to go to Carthage to continue his studies, and while there took a mistress, with whom he had a son.

In Carthage, Augustine was inspired to seek wisdom by reading a now-lost work of Cicero, and after rejecting the Christian scriptures as stylistically uncouth, he became a Manichean "hearer." He became a teacher of rhetoric, first in Thagaste, then in Carthage, and finally in Rome. His fame as a rhetorician grew, and in 384 he moved to Milan, seat of the Western imperial court, where he continued to teach rhetoric, gave occasional panegyrics for famous men at court, and drifted into a circle of intellectually refined Neoplatonic Christians centered around Ambrose, bishop of Milan. His mother followed him to Milan, and arranged a marriage to a very young heiress; Augustine's longtime concubine was forced to return to Africa, although their son remained with him. Augustine admired Ambrose's sermons, first for their stylistic refinement, and later for their content; after an initial serious study of Paul's letters, Augustine converted to Christianity, which was also for him a conversion to sexual abstinence. He called off his socially advantageous marriage, resigned his post in Milan, and retired to the countryside in philosophical retreat with some like-minded friends. That spring, on Easter in 387, Augustine was baptized by Ambrose in Milan, and shortly thereafter his mother died, after they shared a vision of God.

After a delay in Rome, Augustine returned to Africa in 388 and founded a small monastic community dedicated to the shared practice of spiritual exercises; during this time, his son also died, quite young. On a visit to Hippo in 391, Augustine was compelled by the local populace to be ordained as a priest. He again organized a monastic community, undertook an intensive reading of Christian scripture, and eventually succeeded Valerius as bishop of Hippo in approximately 396. As bishop, Augustine had immense responsibilities. He preached numerous sermons each week, was the chief minister in the celebration of the Eucharist and the giving of baptism, and was in charge of his congregation, his clergy, the ecclesiastical property, and the administration of the church and its alms distribution. As Roman authority weakened (Rome itself was sacked in 410), he also took on increasing local authority, judging legal cases such as familial disputes over wills. He publicly debated opponents, whether Manichees, Donatists, or others, and as a Catholic in a heavily Donatist area of North Africa, he was the leader of a minority religious population in a time of violent clashes between factions.

Augustine traveled frequently, attending church councils and preaching at distant churches. Despite all this, he kept up a voluminous correspondence and wrote more than one hundred books, many but not all polemical, in a variety of genres. He lived a long and trying life, exercising considerable influence and power, and died on August 28, 430. While he lay on his deathbed, the Vandals—who in a single year had swept across North Africa, destroying much of the Roman Christian civilization he had labored to rejuvenate—laid siege to Hippo, the last Roman town standing in North Africa. Hippo fell and was partly burned a year later, but Augustine's library survived.[5]

Augustine teaches that humans live in a "fallen" and "penal" state, possessing a damaged *natura* that bears only a shadowy resemblance to our "nature" as originally created by God. For Augustine, this *natura* does not stand for uncultivated impulses, but is our essential being, locating us in the divinely ordered hierarchy of existence. On this account, people are afflicted with "ignorance" and "difficulty," and more broadly with "concupiscence," a syndrome of covetous and ill-directed desire. With hearts darkened and chilled, we no longer have the power to love the good and act rightly. As the mature Augustine argues against his Pelagian enemies, only divine grace can heal the wound of original sin, and during this earthly life such healing can only be partial. And yet, for Augustine, we should also seek the aid provided within the church by *exercitationes*, "exercises," and *disciplina*, "teaching," "training," and "discipline." By "crucifying the [fallen] inner man" and "refashioning" the divine image within our minds, we can "make progress day by day" in righteousness. As the love of God is poured into our hearts, our desire for God will be kindled and our minds illuminated.

Augustine's influence on the West has been profound and multifaceted. He is one of few authors to have been read constantly from his death until the present day, having been carefully studied by such diverse thinkers as Boethius, Bede, Anselm, Aquinas, Erasmus, Luther, Calvin, Descartes, Pascal, Rousseau, Kant, Kierkegaard, and Heidegger.

The distance between these two thinkers and ourselves should be clear. Nevertheless, relying on advances in understanding made possible by modern historical and linguistic scholarship, we are now, paradoxically, in a relatively better position than those in intervening eras to try to engage Augustine and Xunzi on their own and their contemporaries' terms.

What such study reveals, however, is not always particularly congenial to modern sensibilities, or, more important, to considered ethical and political judgments worthy of our committed allegiance. Some of these thinkers' views present serious barriers to our appreciation of their ideas and thus need to be addressed before going further. The most glaring obstacle is presented by the hierarchical, stratified, and thoroughly patriarchal social orders Augustine and Xunzi both took for granted and, to varying extents, lauded as good.

Although powerful arguments justifying certain sorts of hierarchy may be extracted from Xunzi and Augustine (e.g., concerning appropriate teacher–student relationships), their assumptions about sex and class hierarchy should be exposed and rejected.[6] How should one approach this issue? First, it is essential to face the problems head on, with appropriate criticism, rather than attempting to ignore real issues through, for instance, quietly importing gender-neutral language into translations or explications of ancient texts that presuppose male dominance.[7]

Moreover, one may use universalistic aspects of their thought (according to Augustine, men and women's minds are both created in the image of God, in identical positions relative to God and salvation; according to Xunzi, all "people in the street" have the potential to become sages) to argue against unjustifiably particularistic aspects, oriented to sex and class. One may also excuse both thinkers for not foreseeing many centuries of political and economic development that make possible more egalitarian societies, which would have been unimaginable in the fundamentally agrarian economies of ancient China and Roman North Africa. A final, more difficult step is to articulate "Augustinian" and "Xunzian" views in more contemporary idioms, at least when moving beyond description to retrieval, so that the burden of imaginative reconstruction does not rest wholly on the reader. At the same time, it is important to remember that one reason both Xunzi and Augustine deserve attention today is that they are suspicious of easy narratives of social progress and pleasant proclamations of humanity's goodwill and sociability. I hope this study allows them to interrogate the present as much as it allows the present to interrogate them.

BRIDGE CONCEPTS

One of the ironies of comparative ethics is the sharp disjunction between the process of research and representations of the results of that research.

The actual process of comparative study is one of moving back and forth between religious worlds, trying not to become disoriented and confused. While doing this, one slowly refines both the categories of analysis (what I call bridge concepts), and one's initial hunches about the salient similarities and differences between the objects compared. Thus what I am about to say about the four bridge concepts used in this study will give every appearance of determining the structure of inquiry into Augustine and Xunzi, but in fact emerged out of the comparison, as I attempted to place them in imaginary dialogue with each other. This is important, because the analysis and refinement of concepts such as "human nature" is one of the important intellectual results of this sort of comparison.

As noted above, bridge concepts are general ideas that guide and thematize comparative inquiry, while leaving space for greater specification in particular cases. My primary bridge concepts in this work are "human nature" and "spiritual exercises," each of which can be linked to a range of ideas and specific terms of art in both Xunzi and Augustine. In the course of further comparison, I also deploy ideas of "person" and "will." In this section, I specify what I mean by these terms and give preliminary defenses of their aptness and utility in a study of this sort.

These bridge concepts were chosen from among many possibilities. The overarching goals were substantive and were derived from my sense that virtue ethicists need to attend more carefully to religious models and practices of training, personal formation, and even transformation. Thus, in setting up this comparison, I needed a way to represent both the "raw" and the "cooked" state of human beings, as well as the proper methods and techniques for the cooking, religiously speaking. The question in this case could be framed more precisely as follows: What are human beings like before, during, and after the processes of ethico-religious change advocated by Augustine and Xunzi, why do they think such changes are necessary, and how practically are they accomplished? Numerous rubrics—including "self-cultivation," "technologies of the self," "subjection," "asceticism," and "spiritual exercises"—have all been used to examine such processes of personal cultivation, formation, or development.

Pierre Hadot is perhaps the most illuminating of several recent writers on these topics. As I discuss more fully below, his focus on particular practices of cultivation, and not only general theories of moral reformation over time, opens up a new angle of vision on Xunzi, as well as both the Roman philosophy that entranced the young Augustine and the mature Augustine's own ethics of lifelong Christian discipleship. Michel Foucault, at least in his last published works, also provides helpful guidance for analyzing the components of personal formation across traditions or cultures.

Hadot at times seems to undercut the importance of theory for the practice of spiritual exercises, and at one point he even suggests breezily that moderns can still practice ancient exercises while simply jettisoning the ancient views of nature and universal reason that justified them.[8] But from another angle, his historical analyses can be read as showing the practical import and power of ethical theory and even metaphysics: His emphasis on how worldviews are passed on via traditions of quite specific practices that sustain and invigorate those same conceptions of life is relevant to many religious thinkers. Furthermore, his methods of textual interpretation prompt interpreters to attend much more carefully to the practical context and consequences of what might seem to be purely "theological" works. An Augustinian example would be *On the Trinity*, which is in fact centrally concerned with human spiritual "reformation" to the image of God and is a rich resource for Augustine's understanding of spiritual exercises.

Turning now to Foucault, both Hadot and Maria Antonaccio, among others, criticize Foucault for giving his account of ancient spiritual exercises an excessively "aesthetic" cast that focuses on the cultivation of a particular "style" of existence while submerging the universalistic philosophical underpinnings of ancient spiritual exercises, as well as the universalistic moral claims that were essential to them.[9] Though this judgment is generally apt, especially with regard to Foucault's interest in the potential relation of ancient spiritual exercises to contemporary modes of self-cultivation, it ironically overlooks some significant and original Foucaultian contributions to religious ethics. Arnold Davidson has compellingly articulated what is at stake in Foucault's general account of "ethics" in volume 2 of *The History of Sexuality*.[10]

Perhaps most significant is Foucault's innovative mapping of ethics, in self-conscious reaction against a rule-centered conception of morality, as involving four main aspects: first, the "ethical substance," or an account of moral personhood, that part of the self properly subject to moral evaluation; second, the "mode of subjection," meaning the way in which one conceives of one's relation to moral obligations; third, the "ethical work," or practices of self-formation by which one transforms oneself into an ethical subject (what I, following Hadot, call "spiritual exercises," and what Foucault elsewhere describes as "technologies of the self"); and fourth, the ethical *telos* or ideal at which one aims.[11] Though this admittedly does suggest a remarkably subjectivist account of ethics, Foucault is in this context only attempting to analyze the ethics of self-formation, leaving other aspects to the side. And Davidson rightly argues that with regard to the history of ancient ethics, Foucault's errors of interpretation do not undercut the fruitfulness of his analytical *conceptualization* of the ethics of personal formation, which need not be tied to a relativistic aestheticization of existence.

Indeed, Foucault's schema can illuminate the ethics of thinkers committed to universalistic conceptions of ethics, including both Xunzi and Augustine.[12] Though I do not adopt his conceptions wholesale, they inform my choice and construal of bridge concepts. "Human nature" is a particularly common way of interpreting our "ethical substance," in Foucault's terminology (i.e., the parts of ourselves for which we are morally responsible, and thus also the parts that we attempt to change if needed). Thus "human nature" deserves close scrutiny and analysis, particularly in this case given past readings of Xunzi, and to a lesser extent Augustine. But what is "natural" to us may not cover all the elements of our being that these figures believe we can and should change or develop—so some broader conception of human beings will be needed as well. For this I use the English "person," among various possibilities, for reasons discussed below. As a bridge concept, however, "person" points as well to Foucault's "ethical telos," the ideal person or state that is the object of self-formative striving.

I interpret Foucault's "mode of subjection" as referring to the cognitive and imaginative resources made available by a particular ethical vocabulary, the usually traditional stories, images, metaphors, and symbols that constitute some particular conception of existence. More narrowly, Foucault's concern with subjection, evident even before his last works on the care of the self in antiquity, suggests the fruitfulness as well of particular attention to the role of various authorities, conceived in distinctive ways, to the spiritual exercises advocated by Augustine and Xunzi. And last, Foucault's conception of the "ethical work" we do on ourselves maps directly onto Hadot's conception of spiritual exercises.

So "human nature," "person," and "spiritual exercises" have each been chosen as a way to focus attention on particular points within the larger problematic of studying ethical formation or cultivation. I add a fourth bridge concept, "the will," in order to focus more specifically on various aspects of moral psychology that are central to Western conceptions of ethics.

I chose these particular bridge concepts because they seemed fairest to both Xunzi and Augustine, offering thematic guides for sympathetic yet critical investigations that could reveal detailed contours of their strengths without hiding their weaknesses. In general, this meant choosing topics that could elicit significant formulations from both thinkers, but at least in some cases risked highlighting differential levels of treatment of particular issues (e.g., regarding the "will").

As with other sorts of concepts, bridge concepts can vary in character. Most simply, they can be univocal and strictly delimited. More frequently, however, bridge concepts multiply under comparative scrutiny to cover a cluster of related ideas that can be specified more precisely, but that may or may not cohere in any systematic way; in cases of this sort, comparison serves as a prod to conceptual analysis, and it uncovers the complexity and tension in frequently used terms such as "human nature" and "the will."[13] Such clusters, incidentally, will often but not always seem to share a "family resemblance" in the sense explored by Wittgenstein, once we free ourselves from their intuitive simplicity and obviousness; their precise constituents, and mutual logical coherence, are a matter of complex but contingent historical processes. Bridge concepts may also take the form of a focal meaning with specifiable features, accompanied by various secondary meanings that share some but not all of these characteristics.[14] In the present study, "spiritual exercises" is closest to this model. Other forms are of course possible, but they will be left to the side for present purposes.

Human Nature

Richard Rorty suggested in 1989 that historicist thinkers have taught us that "socialization, and thus historical circumstance, goes all the way down." There is nothing, he thinks, "beneath" socialization or "prior" to history that makes or defines us as human. More specifically, there is no such thing as a "human nature" that might help us know who we really are, or how best to live.[15]

For better or worse, Rorty's ironist philosophical therapy is not carrying the day. The idea of human nature seems to be making a vigorous comeback, in both popular and scholarly publishing, propelled by increasing excitement about the "new sciences of human nature," such as cognitive neuroscience, behavioral genetics, and evolutionary psychology.[16] But not everyone is excited, and there seem to be good historical reasons to be worried.

I would suggest that at least some of both the anxiety and excitement stems from intermingling very different senses of what "human nature" might mean, and that it would be helpful to get clear on these differences. On the basis of reflecting on classical Chinese and Christian conceptions of human beings, it now seems to me that talk about "human nature" is a way of addressing at least four distinct sorts of issues. First, it points to human beings' physicality and animality, our most basic, inevitable needs to breathe, drink, eat, and sleep; our needs for care and feeding when young, old, or disabled; and with our less clear-cut but still hard-to-resist desires and aversions (e.g., for food, companionship, attention, sex, status, activity, learning, and expression; and against pain, hunger, humiliation, and death). Second, "human nature" is also a way of discussing what is common to all or most people, underneath or alongside our many individual and group differences. Sometimes it carries a third meaning, in tension with the first:

It marks out what is distinctively "human" about human beings, what does or should separate us from other animals; this is true of Augustine's account of *natura* but not of Xunzi's understanding of *xing*. These three senses are often related to a fourth issue, which is the idea of a natural course of human development, which is often seen as good and desirable, or sometimes lamentable and dangerous. For all these senses or uses—especially the first, third, and fourth—the conjunction of "nature," however conceived, with normative accounts of personal development is quite common. Thus "human nature" is hardly one thing at all but a family of related concerns that may or may not be seen as aspects of any one postulated theoretical entity.[17]

As noted in the first section of this chapter, in their own ways Augustine and Xunzi each regard the fallenness or badness of "human nature" as the paramount problem in human life. It thwarts our sometimes confused aspirations to ethical existence, and it is a crucial part of any explanation for the cruelty and suffering endemic to human societies. Articulating a manifold bridge concept of human nature allows us to tease out the complexities of their views, going beyond a blinkered focus only on the words previously translated into English as "human nature" in each figure. In this way, we can more precisely locate different aspects of their accounts in relation to their larger visions, and to each other.

A critic, perhaps a friend of Rorty, might ask why anyone today should take such a retrograde idea seriously, no matter how it is sliced up. A comparison of multiple versions of such an idea would be particularly pointless—at best a repetition of autopsies. There is no "metaphysical biology" or "essence" shaping human beings, this popular line of thinking goes, and to pretend otherwise is to smuggle dubious presuppositions into the inquiry, perhaps for reactionary political ends. There are two different sorts of criticism in this reply: an antimetaphysical factual objection, and a political worry.

Regarding the first objection—although, in the Western tradition, there certainly have been some highly metaphysical conceptions of human nature as essentially determining each person's status in the cosmos and their proper course of development and form of life—these aspects are not essential to the conception as just laid out. A thin conception of human nature such as the bridge concept I use here aims as much as possible to bracket questions of metaphysics and cosmology, concentrating on our shared organismic life as animals, and what this implies about our developing and living as distinctively human beings. In his most recent book, *Dependent Rational Animals*, Alasdair MacIntyre develops an argument to the effect that humans are a type of animal sharing important resemblances to and commonality with other intelligent animals.

Most notably, these resemblances include intentionality directed toward the satisfaction of certain basic needs and desires, vulnerability to disability and death throughout our life span, and especially in our case weakness and neediness in childhood and old age, leading to significant and at times inescapable dependence on other people.[18] Evaluations of these facts about our animality may vary, but in this study I consider two subtle statements that at least some of these biologically based, mammalian, and more specifically primate needs and desires are seriously problematic. If all such views are wrong (including Freud's and Nietzsche's), and all our natural promptings are benevolent and constructive, then our repeated, spectacularly foul behavior toward each other, in this and every other century, remains a great mystery.[19] One of the points of this study is to examine the different ways Augustine and Xunzi conceive of such an aspect of our being and to grapple with the significant differences in their conceptions. That elements of Augustine's conception of human nature may in the end be objectionable does not rule out all uses of the idea; instead, it ought to spur us to disentangle the various strands of his account and to search for other formulations as well.

The political objection might appear to have more bite. In the not so distant past, conceptions of distinctive natures shaping different "races" were used to justify the most heinous abominations: mass killing of different ethnic groups and systematic racial slavery.[20] In our own time, some natural law theorists argue for the unnaturalness and hence wrongness of homosexual sex acts and thus of any relationships of which they might form a part.[21] And yet here again I will argue that a suitable version of the idea of human nature does not imply ultravicious or even conservative consequences; on the contrary, versions of this line of thought have been deployed for liberatory ends. Martha Nussbaum's and Amartya Sen's "capabilities approach" to development economics and politics is a prime example.[22] Nussbaum argues on neo-Aristotelian premises that there are nine basic capabilities that are distinctive to humanity and therefore ought to be safeguarded by any regime and systematically supported by any developmental scheme. Her approach is thoroughly feminist in its commitment to the dignity and potential of girls and women, and friendly to homosexuality. Though her conception of human nature is again "thicker" than the one I deploy here to facilitate comparison, it does serve as a counterexample to the objection.

A third possible exception needs to be considered as well. Even if my analysis of the complexity of "human nature" as a topic is granted, one could still question whether there is anything common to human beings, including aspects of our physical existence, that is sufficiently robust and significant that it can provide anything like a "baseline" for personal formation. Even if we abstract from differences of upbringing and experience, this critic could say, individual temperaments and talents are too various to allow illuminating ethical generalizations about spiritual exercises, which must be tailored to particular individuals, as differential treatment by "masters" of various "disciples" suggests. This is a fundamental and important objection, but its force can only be evaluated with regard to particular conceptions of human nature, as they are interpreted within larger programs of personal cultivation. (In other words, it is not a direct objection to the bridge concept itself but to theories that such a concept might be used to study.) To forecast later arguments, Augustine is somewhat more vulnerable to this sort of criticism because of his account of the universal pervasiveness of extremely serious sin, while Xunzi's view can accommodate a relatively greater variation in natural moral "talent." However, both Xunzi and Augustine should be read as intelligently arguing against this sort of objection, which can itself be read as a competing account of "human nature" as either (1) very limited in import and scope, or (2) being defined almost entirely in terms of each individual's "natural course of development," to the exclusion of the other elements of my fourfold sketch, with this natural course understood as extremely various across different individuals.

Spiritual Exercises

A common theme in the study of Chinese philosophy and religion is "self-cultivation," the theory and practice of becoming a flourishing, ethical human being. A classic distinction separates "discovery" and "development" models of this process.[23] A development model, as found paradigmatically in Xunzi's predecessor Mencius, sees self-cultivation as a process of nurturing one's nature, on an analogy to plants, through which it will grow slowly but steadily into fully formed moral personhood; Mencius describes this process as the cultivation of four "beginnings" or "sprouts" of virtue, which when developed become humaneness, righteousness, ritual propriety, and wisdom.[24] A discovery model, by contrast, as found in the Neo-Confucian Wang Yangming and certain Chan Buddhists, sees self "cultivation" as a profound and sudden transformation of vision and orientation, resulting from a breakthrough to a previously obscured layer of the self, one's true underlying nature, which is complete and perfect in its moral and cosmic awareness.[25] This schema has been supplemented by Jonathan Schofer, who suggests that Xunzi represents a third way, a "reformation" model, wherein human nature is seen as inadequate on its own and must be reshaped like raw material into a better, finished form: full ethical personhood.[26]

Although this tripartite model of types of self-cultivation has proven useful within the study of Chinese religions, it will not be particularly helpful in the current comparative study. Augustine and Xunzi are both, in their own ways, examples of a reformation model, so some finer theoretical tool is necessary to bring out the details of each of their views.

Many examinations of this sort in patristic sources construct an object of study in terms of "asceticism," a highly controverted term.[27] However, despite recent attempts to rehabilitate *askesis* as a way of talking about practices of personal formation, "asceticism" often still suggests a focus on the renunciation or suppression of physical desires like hunger and sexual appetite. Such practices are important to Augustine, but they are not as determinative as they might seem to casual contemporary readers of his *Confessions*, and if focused on exclusively could skew the interpretation of Augustine's overall understanding of personal formation. "Monasticism," another common category in Christian studies, similarly implies too much about the scope and social location of such formative practices.

Hadot has investigated phenomena in the ancient Greco-Roman world that were similar to those classed as "self-cultivation" in the study of China, and "asceticism" and "monasticism" in the study of early Christianity. My second bridge concept, "spiritual exercises," is a premodern coinage that Hadot has recently revived. He argues that all the Hellenistic schools of philosophy were centered around a variety of partially shared "spiritual exercises." By this term, he means certain methodical practices that engage thought, imagination, and sensibility; that have a significant ethical component; and that ultimately aim at a broader transformation of vision, a metamorphosis of the whole personality. Drawing on lists of such practices by Philo of Alexandria, Hadot divides them into four rough types: (1) disciplines of attention, particularly to one's own thoughts and feelings, or to what is occurring at the present moment; (2) meditations, often on maxims of one's tradition, or on trying to see and respond to the world as they suggest, but also frequently on death and suffering; (3) other intellectual exercises, such as reading, writing, listening, philosophical dialogue, and exegesis of authoritative texts, designed to expand and reshape one's awareness and "inner discourse" of interpretation; and (4) active exercises of various sorts, intended to create habits. On Hadot's view, ancient philosophy was primarily therapeutics, concerned especially with rationally regulating the passions. It was a way of life that was also training for death, for the separation of the soul from the body with its desires. Philosophical theories, Hadot claims, served these deeper practices of personal transformation and were not the primary end of ancient philosophy. In his view, the goal of philosophical speech and writing was almost always to pull the hearer onto or further along the path of spiritual progress.[28]

Hadot's work on Marcus Aurelius's *Meditations* shows the strengths of his way of proceeding. Cautioning against the sort of "psychohistory" that on the basis of his *Meditations* has wrongly judged Marcus to have been pessimistic, despairing, or even an opium addict, Hadot insists on situating the received text in the context of ancient philosophy generally, and of Stoicism in particular, as a way of life and a tradition of spiritual exercises. Hadot argues that ancient authors were not expressing their own personal creativity and idiosyncratic views, which might justify such psychological analyses of their works. Rather, they were strictly constrained by rules of rhetoric concerning literary genre, structure of exposition, style, and figures of thought, and by rules concerning the subject matter and themes that must be addressed. According to Hadot,

> In the case of Marcus Aurelius, we have seen that the spiritual exercises that he wrote down were prescribed by the Stoic tradition, and in particular by the form of Stoicism defined by Epictetus. Canvas, themes, arguments, and images were provided for him in advance. For Marcus, the essential thing was not to invent or to compose, but to influence himself and produce an effect upon himself.[29]

Marcus was following Epictetus's counsel to write daily to vivify the dogmas and principles of Stoicism within one's mind. Apparently "pessimistic" musings on the vanity of human activities, the certainty of death, and the alarming "brute facts" about food or sex are actually traditional figures that Marcus reenacted by writing them down, repeatedly, in various vivid forms, to impress the truths of Stoicism more firmly on his mind in the course of his duties as emperor.[30] Marcus's writing was thus itself a spiritual exercise, an attempt to master his "inner discourse" about things and events, in accord with Stoic doctrine. This doctrine was both theoretical and practical: It described the world and human life in order to rationally justify a certain form of philosophical life.[31]

Although a full discussion of Marcus's exercises is beyond the scope of this chapter, a few remarks are in order. First, these disciplines or exercises aim to internalize certain theoretical positions about the cosmos and human beings, ones that are seen as true and rationally justified. Marcus tries to reshape himself according to Stoic doctrines that the only real good is moral good, that is, virtue, the purity of intention, which is within our power as free, reason-possessing human beings. Similarly, the only real evil is moral evil. Everything that does not depend upon our inner freedom is subject to Destiny, necessarily determined by the will of universal Nature and Reason, and morally indifferent (although not valueless). As exercises, these ideas are mobilized in the practices of developing and assenting only to "adequate" or rigorously objective descriptions of events, stripped of any personal interest, and of stamping out judgments that include typical self-interested hopes and fears; of limiting our passive desires to the pious hope that everything will happen according to Destiny, the will of the All, and rejecting selfish desires for fame, wealth, and even life; and of restricting our active impulses to those spontaneously and purely seeking the common good of humanity as "one body" of rational beings.[32] Theoretical structures are thus integral to the orientation and emotional tonality of a distinctive way of life; practicing the appropriate spiritual exercises internalizes these ideas and cultivates related habits of judgment, feeling, and action.

Second, the form of the relevant spiritual exercises is closely correlated with, and arguably even derived from, a theoretical account of the activities of the human soul or psyche, and of the human person more generally.[33] The present study examines how analogous practices are structured both within and outside the ancient Roman context, without some of its largely shared presuppositions about the structure of the human person and psyche. One could expect that such practices would correlate with whatever account of personhood is offered by the thinker in question; for the cases of Xunzi and Augustine, whether this is true, and if so, exactly how, remains to be seen.

More generally, Hadot rightly insists on attention to literary genre and rhetorical style for the proper interpretation of ancient texts, and he highlights the importance of the social context, literary traditions, and practices behind a text that may motivate it and shape its form and content, and are essential to what it recommends. Though neither Augustine's nor Xunzi's writings provide examples as extreme and obvious (in hindsight) as Marcus Aurelius's *Meditations*, Hadot's interpretive emphases do illuminate several of their texts; and some of the specific traditions he discusses, such as Stoicism and Neoplatonism, shed light on Augustine's works.[34] Conversely, Xunzi's social and literary context is quite different from Augustine's Roman North Africa, and so the precise content of ancient Greco-Roman spiritual exercises is less relevant in his case than Hadot's methods of interpreting texts. Hadot argues that discovering authorial intention is still the primary interpretive goal, and that contextual analysis of the sort discussed above is the best way to reach this goal. These views are especially compelling in a case like the present one, where the texts in question are religious and philosophical ones that promote a certain set of ideas and a certain form of life, community, and polity.

Finally, the idea of spiritual exercises also hits the right note for both Xunzi and Augustine, encompassing yet transcending common references to "self-cultivation" and pointing to the crucial importance placed by both men on teachers and companions on the path of ethico-religious development. It is important for us not to read into ancient Roman and Chinese authors a modern sense of individuality and distinctive selfhood, where the depth of one's interiority may be cast in terms of one's distance from the "crowd" or "herd," and one's depth of purpose tied to a degree of distance from sociality.[35] Augustine and especially Xunzi had strongly communal orientations, which is visible in numerous ways, including their accounts of spiritual exercises, most of which involve other people. Both recognize the importance of individual, solitary work at spiritual cultivation, but this is not the norm for either of them, and it is but one aspect of much larger programs for developing flourishing personhood.

As with "human nature," I have deployed the idea of "spiritual exercises" not only because it seems to illuminate important issues in the texts of both Xunzi and Augustine but also because both of them in fact used analogous concepts and practiced analogous exercises. For Xunzi, "spiritual exercises" correspond in a narrow sense to his idea of *xiu shen* 修身, usually translated as "self-cultivation" but meaning more precisely something like "improving oneself." More broadly, his conceptions of *li* 禮, ritual, and *yue* 樂, music, can also be profitably interpreted as being in significant ways spiritual exercises, aimed at personal and social transformation. For Augustine, his discussions of *exercitationes animi*, "exercises of the soul," and *disciplina*, "teaching" or "training," are sometimes overlooked but provide a distinctive avenue of entrance to his better-known theological teachings about grace and the will. More broadly, two contexts that might be seen primarily as concerning ritual, Augustine's monastic societies and his church congregations, can also be analyzed as settings for spiritual exercises. And as remarked above, Augustine as a young man became a passionate student of philosophy, and thus he came into personal contact with some form of the traditions Hadot has investigated; their influence is perhaps most noticeable in his early works, written before his entrance into the priesthood in 391.

To sum up, then, "spiritual exercises" as a bridge concept guides us to examine particular practices of personal formation in their full imaginative and theoretical context, which includes but goes well beyond explicit theories about proper ethico-religious development. We can hypothesize that these exercises will correlate quite precisely with the conceptions of human beings, and especially human psychology, that each figure develops. We can also test some of Hadot's other interpretive generalizations—such as his fourfold schema for types of exercises, his focus on training for death, and his picture of spiritual exercises as bringing the passions into congruence with the demands of universal reason—against a wider array of evidence.[36]

Self or Person?

In this section, I begin by introducing the influential recent line of philosophical thought about personhood pioneered by Harry Frankfurt and continued by Charles Taylor. This analysis accomplishes two tasks: It supplies context and precedent for the somewhat abstract account I develop of "person" as a bridge concept. It also provides a basis for later assessment of the strengths and weaknesses of this sort of highly general and abstract modern account, when compared with the "thicker" accounts proffered by Augustine and Xunzi, which are no less universal in aspiration.[37] In the rest of this subsection, I examine the strengths and weaknesses for comparative inquiry of several general terms for human beings used by Frankfurt and Taylor: self, subject, agent, and person. I argue that this analysis requires only a bridge concept, not a full-fledged theory of personhood, and that "person" is the best candidate for such a concept, because it distorts Augustine's and Xunzi's thought least, is most capacious, and fits well with the themes of this study.

Frankfurt, in his much-read essay "Freedom of the Will and the Concept of a Person," presents a fairly minimal contemporary account of what we mean when we use the word "person."[38] He begins by distinguishing between "first-order" and "second-order" desires. First-order desires are simply desires to do or not do something. Second-order desires are those a person has for some first-order desire to move him or her effectively to action (or to refrain from acting, according to the case). For example, on some hot July day, I might want to go swimming, which would be a first-order desire. I might also want my desire to go swimming to become stronger and more regular, so that I would get into shape and enjoy the benefits of good health; this would be a second-order desire. First-order desires are common to all animals, Frankfurt thinks, whereas second-order desires are unique to humans and are the products of reflective self-evaluation of one's existent first-order desires. He defines "will" simply as the first-order desire that is or will be effective in moving one to act. When someone has a second-order desire for some first-order desire to become effective (i.e., to become his will), he or she has a "second-order volition"; Frankfurt thinks having second-order volitions is essential to being a person, in contrast to being merely a member of the human species. Humans without second-order volitions he terms "wantons," because such creatures would simply not care about their wills; and regardless of how rational and deliberative they might be in the pursuit of satisfying their first-order desires, they still would fail to evaluate them and thus would follow them blindly. True persons not only seek to fulfill their desires but also care reflectively about what sort of desiring person they are and might become.[39]

Taylor deploys Frankfurt's ideas about first- and second-order desires, but he goes beyond Frankfurt's focus on desire, arguing in more detail for the importance of evaluation as constitutive of fully human *selfhood*, a change in terminology to which I shall return. Taylor suggests that the "reflective self-evaluation" Frankfurt discerns as intrinsic to second-order volition comes in two varieties, which Taylor calls "weak" and "strong" evaluation. Weak evaluation concerns outcomes only and typically reduces to matters of ungrounded personal preference. In weak evaluations, it is sufficient that something be desired to judge it good, and some other desire might be set aside only because it is contingently incompatible with the one chosen. For example, I feel like both going for a swim and eating lunch; I decide to go swimming because the pool is only open now and I will be able to eat lunch later, but not vice versa. Strong evaluation, by contrast, concerns the "qualitative worth" of different desires, motivations, and actions. It typically rests on evaluative distinctions that are not contingent, and it deploys vocabularies of qualitative contrast such as good and bad, noble and base, deep and shallow. Refraining from some cowardly evasion of duty rests on qualitative distinctions between courageous and cowardly behavior that would not change depending on scheduling or some other contingent factor.[40]

These two kinds of evaluation are related, Taylor thinks, to two different kinds of self. Someone who evaluates only weakly Taylor calls a "simple weigher of alternatives," in contrast to a "strong evaluator." A simple weigher would be capable of evaluating alternative courses of action and acting on something other than the impress of immediate desire; he or she would thus possess reflection, evaluation, and will, but not "depth." Such a person could give no further reason beyond greater attractiveness (or circumstantial conflicts between desires) for choosing one thing over another. A strong evaluator, however, can articulate the superiority of some courses of action over others in terms of the qualities those actions possess. Such qualities are built on contrasts between "different possible modes of being of the agent." In fact, Taylor holds that there could be no true "simple weighers of alternatives," and that "the capacity for strong evaluation in particular is essential to our notion of the human subject."[41] Taylor writes:

> To characterize one desire or inclination as worthier, or nobler, or more integrated, etc. than others is to speak of it in terms of the kind of quality of life that it expresses and sustains. I eschew the cowardly act above because I want to be a courageous and honorable human being. . . . [For

> the strong evaluator,] motivations or desires do not only count in virtue of the attraction of the consummations but also in virtue of the kind of life and kind of subject that these desires properly belong to.[42]

Strong evaluations are the vehicle by which people become the kind of subjects they intend to become. They are the means by which one seeks and perhaps attains a definite ethical and religious shape.

Taylor goes on to argue that we are not completely free to choose the criteria for our strong evaluations, and that these criteria define our identity as persons and agents. They provide the "horizon of evaluation" within which we may live. Our strong evaluations, according to Taylor, are "articulations" of our deepest, generally inchoate sense of what is decisively important, higher, more worthy, and the like. Through repeated attempts to articulate our deepest motivations and ideals, we become partially responsible for our character as subjects.

Owen Flanagan has criticized Taylor's view as excessively intellectualist and moralistic, and inferior to a position more akin to Frankfurt's, from which Flanagan thinks Taylor has departed. Flanagan argues that Taylor's notion of strong evaluation hinges not so much on qualitative distinctions as on qualitative *moral* distinctions, conceived as such. This seems to me to be a plain misreading of Taylor's original position, where strong evaluation is definitionally linked to qualitative distinctions per se and the possibility of nonethical evaluative distinctions is explicitly recognized.[43] Taylor can perfectly well accept Flanagan's point that people need not see themselves primarily in ethical terms, nor make only or primarily moral evaluative distinctions, in order to be recognizably human agents. Flanagan's second point, that Taylor overemphasizes the role of reflection and articulateness in human agency, providing an excessively linguistic and intellectualist view, has more bite. Nevertheless, Taylor can parry the objection, as he does in *Sources of the Self*, by accepting that strong evaluations can be unspoken assumptions absorbed in one's upbringing and yet function as guides to action, even if the actor cannot articulate the reasons for such action.[44] In any case, Flanagan is happier with Frankfurt's more minimalist approach; but as I argue below, even this is more than is needed in the present study, so I shall leave Flanagan's own position to the side.

Taylor's use of the term "horizon" of evaluation signifies his debt to Hans-Georg Gadamer, as does his use of "articulation" as a way of theorizing the importance of interpretation in human life (even if one wanted, like Flanagan, to press on Taylor the possibility of inarticulate, unreflective action based on inchoate interpretations of social realities). Like Gadamer, Taylor recognizes that such horizons of self-interpretation and -evaluation are passed on to each of us through the traditions within which we are raised and live.[45] But this attention to tradition ought to lead quickly to the recognition that there are many different traditions capable of providing terms and ideals sufficient for strong evaluation. Alternative vocabularies for making these qualitative distinctions are crucial, however reflectively they are held and used, and produce distinctively different sorts of "subjectivity."

Before two such alternatives can be addressed in later chapters, however, basic theoretical choices must be made regarding the terms in which this study is to be cast. Where Frankfurt restricts himself to the notion of a "person," Taylor also uses the words "self," "agent," and "subject" to make his points. These four bridge concept candidates, although certainly similar, are not identical. Even when a stipulative definition is at issue, it is useful to interrogate typical usages to see which is closest to what is needed.

To assess these possibilities, one should note the implied contrast terms in each case, and what aspects of human existence are thereby highlighted. The increasingly ubiquitous "self"[46] is typically contrasted with "other," perhaps the vaguest and most equivocal term in all contemporary philosophical writing. This self–other combination carries echoes of a Hegelian dialectic of self-consciousness, and the term "self" at least denotes conscious inner awareness or understanding of one's existence. Even if I were to define the term to leave this heritage behind, it would still encourage a uniquely modern individualism wherein a human being is conceived as making a fundamental distinction between her- or himself on the one hand, and everything and everyone else on the other. Though this term certainly can be helpful as a way of discussing different modes of internal awareness and self-understanding, I will not use it as a primary bridge concept because some of its associations are misleading when trying to explicate the thought of both Augustine and Xunzi.

"Subject" carries many of the same associations with German Idealism and its offshoots, and in this aspect is often contrasted with "object," again focusing attention on consciousness and inner awareness, but also on perception of external realities. At least this term, unlike "self," has the advantageous implication that other human beings are recognized as other subjects, leading to discussions of ideas like "intersubjectivity." An older usage of the term relates a "subject" to a "sovereign," a lord or ruler who looks over and commands the subject, and to whom he or she owes loyalty and even devotion; in this aspect, the word conjures up feudal social hierarchy. (Alternatively, one may be "subject" in this sense to some greater power simply by virtue of one's weakness, and feel toward it nothing but resentment, fear, and perhaps awe.) Issues of authority are important to distinguishing Augustine's and Xunzi's proposals, so I will attend to their differing accounts of "subjection." But it would be counterproductive to try to build some general account of subjection into my theoretical tools before beginning, rather than describing the relevant differences as they are manifest in each thinker's conceptual apparatus. Nor is the issue so central to the comparison that it should be made preeminent through terminological choice.

"Agent," like "subject," has desirable features but is not in the end the best overarching choice. It describes the human being as an actor, moving through a world of other agents and inert things upon which they may act. "Agent" comes from a tradition of discourse stretching back to Kant, which has become a subfield within contemporary analytic philosophy, the philosophy of action. It is also part of the classical liberal tradition of political philosophy, which is alien in significant ways to both Augustine and Xunzi.[47] Recent philosophical approaches centered on agency often view the capacity to choose rationally among alternatives as the most essential and definitive human characteristic—a stance that also conflicts with both our subjects. Though exactly how people act or fail to act is an important part of this study, it is not its sole focus, and in particular I am less concerned with an assessment of what acts might be good or bad than with what kind of person it would be best to be, and how Xunzi and Augustine answered that question and its natural follow-up, how to become such a person.

With "person," the entities to which it is to be contrasted are on the one hand animals, the not fully human and thus not, properly speaking, persons. On the other hand, there are superhuman contrasts like spirits, angels, Heaven and Earth, and gods or God, which might be analogized as "personal" but are not (or are at least no longer) persons in the usual sense. These contrasts, moreover, are relations of some sort of implied hierarchy on a continuum containing many members, which suits both Xunzi and Augustine, although each would specify the hierarchy differently. "Person," moreover, is not essentially a matter of inward self-awareness or conscious self-conception, although it doesn't exclude these. And in contrast to "self" and "subject," it essentially includes the notion that we are physically existing animal beings, although without specifying exactly how persons are to be understood or analyzed into parts or aspects. All these elements are useful for present purposes.

As discussed above, the theoretical impetus behind the use of bridge concepts is the desire to bring culturally distant religious figures into an imagined dialogue, to relate their distinctive bodies of thought and associated practices by describing them around certain shared themes. The paradigmatic danger of such a move is to obscure or confuse differences. Thus, when choosing bridge concepts, we should strive to take nothing for granted that may be at issue between the two, and in general to be as spare as possible. In cross-traditional interpretation, we need to open ourselves to other conceptions and formulations of personhood more than we need to test them by familiar standards. Ergo, this study needs a bridge concept, not a full-blown theory of personhood; a minimal, "thin" concept rather than a thicker, more complex one articulated in familiar categories like volition. In comparative ethical studies, one should take as little as possible for granted, the better to learn more.

In this case, all I need is a contrastive term to recognize the goal of spiritual exercises: developed, flourishing personhood, in contrast to raw animality. "Person" fits the bill. It also can be used in a more inclusive sense to recognize simple membership in our species, with our typical characteristics, that is, human nature, and so is congruent with the first part of the study. (Furthermore, when this contrast needs to be explicitly drawn, as it is when explicating Xunzi, I can distinguish merely being a member of the human species from being a fully cultivated person.)[48] Corresponding to Augustine's Latin term *persona*, and to Xunzi's classical Chinese *ren* 人, "person" does not import alien notions into either man's ideas or overemphasize particular aspects of human existence such as choice, agency, or inner reflexivity.

This concept of personhood takes little for granted about how exactly to understand "human nature," what the constituent elements of a person are (i.e., what sort of general account of the human person ought to be given), why spiritual exercises are necessary, what they are, what their ultimate *telos* might be, or how they produce their effects. In other words, this bridge concept is compatible with the desired comparative questions, without smuggling in answers ahead of time or focusing on extraneous or misleading issues. Only after describing the relevant parts of Xunzi's and Augustine's views, each forming a distinctive vocabulary of personhood, will it be profitable to return to Frankfurt's and Taylor's theories for comparison.

The Will

The idea of the "will" presents more serious difficulties than the previously discussed bridge concepts. To begin with, the word derives from Augustine's Latin term *voluntas* (still visible in the French *volonté* and English "voluntary"), which has no exact equivalent in Xunzi's philosophy or in early Chinese thought generally. *Voluntas* is absolutely central to Augustine's theological system, but the term in Xunzi often translated "will," *zhi* 志, though certainly worthy of sustained attention, is relatively less important overall to his views, occurring a total of ninety-four times in the extant corpus of his works. Just as the crucial role of spiritual exercises in Xunzi's ethical theory has prompted me to investigate analogous disciplines advocated by

Augustine, Augustine's preoccupation with the human will has led me to focus on the place of *zhi* 志 in Xunzi's system, along with other terms he uses that cover related philosophical and psychological territory. But even here, we should resist premature identification of the Augustinian *voluntas* with the modern English "will."

In this section, I review the conclusions of an essay by Charles Kahn on the "discovery of the will" in ancient Greek and Roman philosophy, which capably analyzes some of the tangled threads making up our modern ideas about the will, with attention to Augustine and his predecessors and successors.[49] Suitably emended, Kahn's list of aspects of different ideas of the will may serve as a guide to inquiry into Xunzi's account, and for comparison of his ideas with Augustine's complex concept of *voluntas*.[50]

As Kahn points out, it is far from clear what exactly our conception of the will is, or if there is only one such idea. Current discussion of "the will" is sometimes a way of talking about making decisions, rationally or otherwise; sometimes about the strength of motivation or commitment; sometimes about moral responsibility for actions; sometimes about our intentions when acting; and sometimes about freedom and determinism as global metaphysical issues. Kahn discerns four different modern perspectives on the will, "each of which might lead to a different account of the history of this concept" if it were used as the basis for such a narrative.[51] The first he calls the "theological concept of the will," which begins with Augustine and culminates in Aquinas and the medieval "voluntarists," where the human will is seen as modeled on and responding to the prior will of God, which for this family of theories is the primary referent for the term. The second is the post-Cartesian idea of the will as volition, an inner mental event that causes or accompanies any outer movement of the physical body, and which is wedded to a dualism of mental and physical entities. The third is the Kantian notion of will as self-legislation, wherein we become aware of our existence as noumenal, nonempirical beings, and which is the root of stronger theories of the will such as Schopenhauer's and Nietzsche's. The fourth is more of a theme, the problem of free will and determinism, which cuts across the previous three, and "in fact precedes them all, since it can be clearly traced back to Aristotle and Epicurus."[52]

Kahn's concern is to produce a more complex, philosophically oriented history of the notion of the will than the one provided in Albrecht Dihle's pathbreaking and influential account of the concept, which Kahn finds to be uniquely interested in the theological strand and its problematic of human response to divine will.[53] He thus systematically compares Aristotle's and Aquinas's theoretical accounts of human action and the psyche, finding a unified concept in Aquinas (*voluntas*) that draws together four largely unrelated elements of Aristotle's thought. He then turns to the historical developments intervening between these two men, and he discerns four major landmarks between them: first, the Stoic theory of action centered on the notion of *sunkatathesis* or "assent" standing guard between any "impression" (*phantasia*) and an "impulse" to action (*horme*); second, the translation of Greek philosophy into Latin, where disparate notions about action became expressed through *voluntas* and cognates like *voluntarium*, and the metaphor of freedom from constraint becomes habitually related to *voluntas* through the new Latin technical term *libertas*; third, the convergence of these trends in the later Stoicism of Epictetus and Seneca, writing in Greek and Latin, respectively, who expand the notion of assent into a broader conception of moral character and personal commitment, which is to affect and shape all our daily experiences of thought, feeling, and action through the thorough practical application of reason (what Hadot would call spiritual exercises); and fourth, Augustine's doctrine of the will, whereby on Kahn's account "Neoplatonic and Christian levels of spirituality are added to the Stoic and Roman conceptions of *voluntas* we have traced so far."[54] Kahn's thesis is that Augustine's and Aquinas's theories of the will certainly presuppose commitment to Christian traditions as an indispensable condition, but that the other Greek and Roman trends he documents are preconditions as well; in sum, their accounts of the will "have proved to be two of the most powerful and durable examples of eclecticism in Western intellectual history."[55]

As apt as this judgment may be, my goal here is not historical narrative but comparative ethical analysis. Furthermore, I reject Kahn's contentions that Augustine lacks a "systematic theory of human action" and especially that his concept of will is not part of a "theoretical model for the psyche," upon which Kahn bases his turn to Aquinas.[56] Augustine's views on these issues are outlined in chapters 4, 5, and 7.

Nevertheless, Kahn is right to distinguish different and even competing strands in modern statements about "the will." As a bridge concept, "will" is a list of areas of related inquiry: I examine Xunzi's and Augustine's accounts of human action; theories of what a person and "mind" are that undergird these accounts; assessments of human capacities for choice and decisive commitment; and any characteristic limitations, flaws, or dangers that afflict human decision and action. Precisely what terms each thinker uses, and how they are related, if at all, are central questions. For Augustine, obviously, *voluntas*, *libertas*, and *arbitrium* (meaning "choice" or "decision") are crucial. For Xunzi, I focus on *zhi* 志, roughly "intent"; *ke* 可, "assent"; and his various words for feeling and desiring, especially *qing* 情 and *yu* 欲. Furthermore, Kahn's discussion of the theological strand of thinking about the will, drawing on Dihle's insightful work, where human willing is seen as modeled on and responding to divine willing, is useful for contrasting Augustine's and Xunzi's understanding of human ethico-religious life.

NOTES

1. Brown 1988, xvii.

2. Citations of Xunzi's works are to D. C. Lau's concordance (1996). All citations of this and the other Institute of Chinese Studies concordances will take the form chapter/page/line, so for example 19/97/9 would mean chapter 19, page 97, line 9. Lau's concordance is based on the *Sibu Congkan* edition of the *Xunzi*, which itself is a reprint of the *Taizhou* edition from the Song; Lau carefully notes his emendations, which are based on parallel texts and other manuscript traditions. For a discussion of the textual history of the *Xunzi*, see Knoblock 1988–94, vol. 1, 105–28. I have departed from Lau's text only three times, for reasons discussed in the notes. Unless otherwise noted, citations for Augustine's works refer to Jacques-Paul Migne's commonly accessible *Patrologia Latina*, now widely available via the Internet as a searchable database. Migne is unfortunately based on the Maurist edition of the collected works of Augustine compiled from French sources and published from 1679 to 1700. It thus does not share in the fruits of modern textual scholarship, and merely collects variant readings without attempting to produce true critical editions, as in the ongoing series *Corpus Scriptorum Ecclesiasticorum Latinorum* and *Corpus Christianorum*, which are still not complete.

3. On Xunzi's life and influence, see Knoblock 1982–83, and 1988–94, vol. 1, 3–49.

4. For fuller discussion and bibliography, see Knoblock 1988–94, vol. 1, 105–20.

5. The classic biography of Augustine is Brown 1967, which was supplemented with a lengthy new epilogue in 2000. For a good, short sketch more detailed than the one offered here, see Markus 1999. For recent revisionist accounts, see Wills 1999 and O'Donnell 2005.

6. To summarize roughly, Augustine lived in a society based economically on tenant farmers and slaves, and he saw slavery as a condition justly imposed on sinners, i.e., all of humanity. He also thought that hierarchical relations of dominance were intrinsic to human society, and that family relationships (e.g., husband–wife, parent–child, and master–slave) were defined by the giving and obeying of orders; ideally such relationships are governed by genuine concern for the welfare of the subordinate parties, rather than lust for domination (*civ. Dei* 19.15, 14). Xunzi takes for granted a system of tenant farming that supported government administration primarily via tax revenues, and a patrilineal social and kinship system where women's life possibilities centered on maintenance of male lines of descent. In his writings, Xunzi barely mentions women, remarking only occasionally on such things as women's role of nurturing (or perhaps feeding) children while men instruct them (19/97/9), and on the dangers of women's sexual attractiveness to (male) practitioners of Confucian disciplines (20/100/2).

7. For an outstanding example of this sort of critique applied to contemporary thinkers, see Okin 1989.

8. Hadot 1995, 211; see also 212, 273. For insightful discussion, see Antonaccio 1998, 75–78.

9. Hadot 1995, 206–13, Antonaccio 1998, 78–79. Against Hadot and Antonaccio, Nehamas 1998 tries to make this cultivation of a Nietzschean and Foucauldian "aesthetics of existence" essential to his conception of spiritual exercises, so that the true practitioner of such exercises both aims at and succeeds in shaping his or her life into something unprecedented and new.

10. Davidson 1994.

11. Foucault 1985, 25–33; see also Davidson 1994, 118ff.

12. For a much broader attempt to bring Augustine and Foucault into conversation, see Schuld 2003.

13. I thus use "concept cluster" differently than Rosemont 1988 and Berkson 2005. Rosemont and Berkson mean by this something more like what I call "conceptual apparatus," whereas I intend to focus on an apparently single idea like "human nature" that when tracked into multiple accounts in different languages can be analyzed into various constituent ideas of no necessary mutual relationship.

14. A famous example would be Aristotle's account in *Nicomachean Ethics* 1156a6–1157b5 of the three kinds of friendship: complete friendship or friendships of virtue (the focal meaning), friendships of utility, and friendships of pleasure (the secondary meanings).

15. Rorty 1989, xiii.

16. The phrase comes from Pinker 2002.

17. Probably the most important recent book on human nature is Midgley 1995. Also valuable is MacIntyre 1999.

18. MacIntyre 1999, esp. 1–79.

19. And if, as some hopeful socialists and Marxists might contend, exploitive or otherwise unjust social arrangements cause our apparent viciousness, the question is merely pushed back another level. What is it about human impulses and/or sociality that often leads to such destructively organized communities?

20. My point here concerns using ideas about nature to support abominations like genocide; I am not trying to suggest that such horrors no longer occur, however they are "justified."

21. Obviously the moral status of homosexual sexual activity is controversial in contemporary U.S. society. I leave to the side any justification for my views on these questions; seriously examining these issues would stray too far from present purposes.

22. Nussbaum 1993, 1995, 1997.

23. For a fuller exploration of the general theme of self-cultivation in Confucianism, as well as of these and other models of the process, see Ivanhoe 2000a.

24. *Mencius* 2A6.

25. Ivanhoe 2002, 96ff.

26. Schofer 2000 [1993].

27. On the study of "asceticism" in early Christianity, see Clark 1999, 14–42. On asceticism more generally, see Wimbush and Valantasis 1995. On asceticism in Augustine, see Lawless 2000.

28. Hadot 1995, esp. 49–70, 81–125. Evaluation of Hadot's specific historical claims about ancient philosophy is beyond the scope of this study.

29. Hadot 1998, 243–44.

30. Hadot 1998, 243–306, 49–50, 102–5.

31. Hadot 1998, 35–53.

32. Hadot 1998, 35–231.

33. Hadot 1998, 40–53, 73–100.

34. Hadot 1993.

35. As with any generalization, there are likely to be exceptions, especially in this case with regard to eremitic traditions, of which both Augustine and Xunzi were aware. (Interestingly, Augustine admires and takes them quite seriously, as for instance in his *Confessions*, but Xunzi mocks them as ineffective; see *Xunzi* 21/105/14–16; cf. 24/6/8–10 on "reclusive scholars.") My point is to be alert to the possibility of deceptive projections of contemporary presuppositions.

36. For further discussion of the suitability of this category for analyzing Xunzi, see chapter 6, esp. n. 15.

37. Note also the outstanding essay collection building on a classic lecture by Marcel Mauss: Carrithers, Collins, and Lukes 1985.

38. Frankfurt 1988.

39. Frankfurt 1988, 12–19.

40. Taylor 1985c, 15–21.

41. Taylor 1985c, 21–27, 25, 28.

42. Taylor 1985c, 25.

43. Flanagan 1990, passim, 37–41. For counterevidence, see esp. Taylor 1985c, 24 n. 7; Flanagan 1990, 42, quotes another recognition of this by Taylor (1985a, 239).

44. Taylor 1989, 77–78, 91–92. Flanagan 1990, 53, cites these passages and discusses the issue.

45. His concern with these issues shows in works like Taylor 1991 and esp. 1989.

46. For a review of some recent literature on this idea, see Lauritzen 1994. Some recent collections of essays on the subject are Rouner 1992; Ames, Dissanayake, and Kasulis 1994, 1996; and Allen 1997.

47. This is currently a hotly debated topic. See, e.g., the perceptive essays by Dawson, Jackson, Meilaender, Santurri, and White (all 1997) in *The Journal for Peace and Justice Studies* 8, no. 2 (1997), which focus on Augustine and modern liberalism. Note also Gregory n.d.

48. "Humanity" often plays a similar evaluative role, pointing to an achieved level of ethical cultivation. In the end, "person" seemed to have the connotations closest to

what I was looking for, whereas "human" was closer to a straightforward attribution of membership in the species *homo sapiens*.

49. Kahn 1988.

50. The best survey of the growth of ideas of "will" in the West is Sorabji 2000, 303–40, although I depart from him in one crucial way in my reading of Augustine's psychology (see chapter 5, n. 14). His notes also serve as a more extensive guide to bibliography on this issue than I can provide here. Sorabji's analysis is closely tied to a range of related developments in the ancient Mediterranean and medieval Europe. Thus his analysis of the gradual clustering of the components of "will" into one idea is too closely related to Augustine (whom he sees as the pivotal figure in this development) to be the best choice for a bridge concept in the current study.

51. Kahn 1988, 235.

52. Kahn 1988, 235–36.

53. Dihle 1982. For Kahn's comments, see Kahn 1988, 236–38.

54. Kahn 1988, 238–56.

55. Kahn 1988, 259.

56. Kahn 1988, 238.

CHAPTER THREE

Ugly Impulses and a Muddy Heart

✦

A few commentators have noted in passing the similarity between Xunzi's apparent teaching that "human nature is evil" and Augustine's notions of original sin. H. H. Dubs inaugurated this line of thought in a 1956 article, in which he argued tendentiously that "like Augustine, [Xunzi] saw that the only safe foundation for authoritarianism is the belief that human nature is fundamentally evil, for then man cannot trust his own reasoning."[1] More recently A. C. Graham and P. J. Ivanhoe have both rejected this judgment of similarity to Augustine and have argued that a more accurate translation of Xunzi's slogan *ren zhi xing e* 人之性惡 would be "human nature is bad."[2] This more recent line of argument is more insightful, but to grapple with the full complexities of the comparison requires sustained attention to both Xunzi *and* Augustine, combined with deeper reflection about just what "human nature" might mean to these thinkers, and to us.

To advance beyond previous interpretations, it is crucial to see both the analogies and disanalogies between contemporary notions of human "nature" and Xunzi's understanding of several key ideas—*xing* 性, what is "innate"; *qing* 情, usually "disposition" but sometimes "emotion"; and *yu* 欲, "desires"—as well as his completely separate account of what makes human beings distinctive among animals. Only if these issues are carefully sorted out can we avoid illegitimate inferences about Xunzi's anthropology. I offer my account in the first section of this chapter. It is equally vital to properly recognize Xunzi's sharp contrast between *xing*, the "innate," and *wei* 僞, the purposefully created "artifice" that makes us truly human. Giving this deep distinction its proper weight necessitates reading Xunzi's understanding of human nature in relation to his views of the *xin* 心, "heart/mind," and his broader account of personal formation, which I analyze in the second section.

XUNZI ON HUMAN NATURE

The word in classical Chinese usually translated as human "nature" is *xing* 性. *Xing* became a problem for the followers of Confucius in the fourth century BCE, when other groups challenged the value and justification of their ethical and political prescriptions. In this case Yang Zhu, a shadowy figure who left no surviving writings, was the posthumous figurehead for a critical tendency that advocated "keeping one's nature intact, protecting one's genuineness, and not letting the body be tied by other things."[3] On the basis of later writings of a generally similar tenor, A. C. Graham has reconstructed these doctrines. One's *xing*, for a Yangist, is above all the natural tendency of a human being to live a full term of life, unless thwarted by outside influences such as disease, violence, or anxiety. More broadly speaking, "The *xing* of a thing . . . is its proper course of development" over the course of its whole life span.[4] For Yangists, it is crucial to use things to nourish one's own *xing*, and not the other way around, which would be to sacrifice oneself foolishly, even for the sake of something as apparently grand as the rulership of a large territory. "Protecting the genuine" means rejecting ceremony and rituals, and not allowing one's spontaneous impulses to be deformed by custom or training.[5]

Together, these ideas were a direct attack on Confucian ritual practice and political commitment.[6] If, as most took for granted, one's *xing* is endowed by Heaven, the same Heaven that mandated the ritual order of the Confucian-venerated Zhou Dynasty, then one should not damage or deform it. But Yangism contended that Confucian ritual practices themselves, along with their attempts to exercise political power, were harmful and dangerous.

The most prominent surviving response to this challenge is that of Mencius (or Mengzi), a fourth-century BCE Confucian. As Graham has shown, the debate over *xing* flourished in the fourth century, especially because the Yangist position seemed to counsel egoism and undercut any sort of governmental involvement. Graham contends that Mencius's conception is formally similar to the more complex notions of *xing* current in his time, wherein the *xing* of a living thing is "the way in which it develops and declines from birth to death when uninjured and adequately nourished, for example its condition in full health and its term of life."[7] Mencius himself sees human *xing* as the spontaneous sociable inclinations, distinctive to humans, which are initially small and fragile but tend to grow naturally when properly nurtured, developing into full-fledged moral inclinations.

Mencius's primary metaphors for human psychology and moral development are agricultural, expressed in terms of the growth of barley or trees (e.g., 6A7, 6A8). His technical term for our incipient moral dispositions is *duan* 端, "sprouts." For Mencius, our *xing* consists primarily in four such sprouts, which all people have from birth (6A7), and which have an inherent developmental trajectory toward becoming the full moral virtues of benevolence, righteousness, ritual propriety, and wisdom (2A6). They begin as weak emotional promptings that are revealed in certain situations by our spontaneous moral reactions, which depending on our degree of cultivation may or may not result in action. If nurtured properly, these sprouts will follow what we might call their genetic pathways and "fill out" into virtues. Failure to arrive at virtuous, flourishing personhood can for Mencius be the result of failure to nourish these sprouts (through deprivation), or outright damage to or destruction of them through consciously thwarting their motivational promptings (6A8).

Xunzi, in the third century, reformulates this conception of *xing* and completely rejects the metaphors and moral psychology that attend it.[8] Though for Mencius our *xing* is what ties us to the great sages of the past (6A7), for Xunzi "human *xing* is definitely that of the petty person" (15/4/14). Xunzi redefines *xing* as follows: "That which is so from birth is called *xing*. What the *xing's* harmonious operation generates, the vital essence effortlessly and spontaneously uniting arousal and response, this is [also] called *xing*" (107/22/22–23).[9] Thus what because of its teleological and biological aspects could reasonably be translated as "human nature" for Mencius has become for Xunzi merely what is "innate," done without effort or thought.

So far, this definition does not seem to carry any evaluative judgment, positive or negative. But Xunzi makes his substantive views clear at the beginning of his chapter on *xing*:

> Human *xing* is bad; our goodness is artifice. Now, human *xing* is such that from birth it has a love of profit. Following this will produce wrangling and strife, and courtesy and deference will perish. From birth there is envy and hatred in it; following these will produce violence and crime, and loyalty and trust will perish. From birth it has the desires of the ears and eyes, and a love of sounds and colors. Following these will produce wantonness and chaos, and ritual, obligations, proper form, and good order will all perish. (23/113/3–5)

Xunzi tends to pair *xing* 性 contrastively with *wei* 偽, "artifice" or "artificial," as in his repeated motto that "Human *xing* is bad; our goodness is *wei*." For Xunzi, *xing* does not exhaust our human capabilities; in particular, it leaves out the human heart/mind (*xin* 心) and its capacities to respond to the world and direct action while remaining empty, unified, and tranquil. (These issues are discussed more fully in the next section.)

By a love of *li* 利, "profit" or "benefit," Xunzi is pointing to a basic selfishness and acquisitiveness he finds to be characteristic of the human heart/mind (23/114/12). He argues that even brothers, if they had valuable goods to apportion between themselves, would fight and rob each other, if they acted spontaneously, on the basis of their innate impulses alone. In contrast to this, Xunzi suggests that even fellow countrymen will treat each other with deference in a similar situation if they have undertaken the Confucian program of ritual reformation (23/114/16–18).

Xunzi repeatedly notes that this innate selfishness is characteristic of the uncultivated "petty person," and he laments the ugliness of common human inclinations to envy and hatred (23/116/25–26). Nevertheless, he occasionally notes more positive emotional tendencies, such as the general propensity of animals with conscious awareness (*zhi* 知) to cherish other members of their own species, even beyond death. (Xunzi remarks on this in the midst of a discussion of mourning rituals, and he argues that this instinct is most pronounced among people because we have the most acute conscious awareness [19/96/10–13].)

Xunzi's interest in the problem of fascination via the various modes of sensation is a consequence of his theory of natural spontaneous reactions to environmental cues, which he thinks form a large subset of all human actions. He writes, "All people have that which unites them: when hungry they desire to eat, when cold they desire warmth, when exhausted they desire rest, they love benefit and hate harm. This is what people have from birth, what is so without waiting, what [sage king] Yu and [tyrant] Jie had in common" (4/15/7–8; see also 23/114/2–6). Humans display a large set of typical responses to certain events and situations; active responsiveness seems to be built into Xunzi's notion of humanity's instincts.

Furthermore, each sense tends spontaneously to distinguish qualities of its proper objects, some of which seem to be emotionally and motivationally loaded, such as the eye distinguishing "beauty and ugliness," and the nose "fragrant and rotten" (4/15/8–10).[10] As Xunzi notes cryptically above, part of what is innate is the "vital essence effortlessly and spontaneously joining arousal and response," wherein a human organism responds naturally and spontaneously, without working at it or thinking, as when a person becomes hungry and desires food.[11] He seems to think that our inherent tendency to prefer fragrant smells, pleasant sounds, and arresting sights is the engine of a potentially unending spiral of desire, punctuated by envy and anger when such desires are frustrated.[12]

To sort out these issues more fully, I need to lay out Xunzi's understanding of two other technical terms that he frequently uses in combination with *xing*: *yu* 欲, rendered well in English as "desire"; and *qing* 情, often translated as "passions" or "emotions" but sometimes as "the essential," "circumstances," "natural responses," or several other hotly debated possibilities.[13] I begin with the more complicated case of *qing*.

First, it is clear that Xunzi uses *qing* in a variety of senses. He uses it in the broad sense of "circumstances" or "general facts" when he entertains the hypothetical objection that "the past and the present have different *qing*; therefore they require different Ways to order chaotic elements" (5/18/24; see also 3/11/18). He uses the word in the sense of "fundamental quality" or "definitional core" when he says "regulating inner and outer, higher and lower, is the *qing* of social obligations (*yi* 義)" (16/79/7; see also 17/82/18, 20/100/15, 22/108/15). He even uses it in the sense of what is "genuine" or "authentic" when he suggests that the "real educated man," *zhen shi* 真士, does not resent his lord for failing to notice his good qualities, nor does he accept rewards when superiors fail to notice his shortcomings; "he does not adorn his strengths or weaknesses, but uses [his] *qing* to recommend himself" (3/11/22–23).

Most important, Xunzi also uses the term in a technical sense with regard to human beings. Helpfully, he defines the relation of *xing* 性, *qing* 情, and *yu* 欲. He writes:

> The *xing* consists of the Heavenly tendencies (*jiu* 就); the *qing* are the substance of the *xing*; desires are the responses of the *qing*. What the *qing* cannot avoid is seeking after an object of desire when one thinks the object may be attained; [but] judging that something is permissible and finding a path to it, these must emerge from the understanding (*zhi* 知). (22/111/14–15)[14]

Xunzi ties *xing*, *qing*, and *yu* tightly together, as three analytically separable aspects of the same system of human responsiveness to stimuli. For Xunzi, "Heaven" stands for spontaneous and effortless natural processes of generation and completion, both in the cosmos and human life, which are generally constant and inevitable.[15] Thus *xing* is what all humans regularly receive at birth: It is our innate endowment, which predictably tends in certain directions; we might even call it the collection of our "instincts."[16] Xunzi then uses the broadly suggestive term *qing* to give content to this idea of a uniform endowment; *qing* are what we all share (3/11/15; see also 23/115/23). Xunzi identifies *qing* itself as the spontaneously responsive aspect of human beings, and the desires *yu* 欲 as the responses of *qing* to a person's environment. Xunzi then goes on to underline the impulsive force of desires as the actively motivational aspect of a person's *qing*, while integrating this with an emphasis on the centrality of intellectual recognition and judgment to the overall process of human action. All of this is treated in greater detail below in my discussion of Xunzi's account of the *xin* 心, or "heart/mind."

Another equally crucial definitional passage has been partly quoted above. Immediately subsequent to his definition of *xing*, Xunzi writes: "The liking and disliking, delight and anger, sorrow and joy of the innate endowment are called *qing*" (107/22/22–23). For Xunzi *qing*, the "substance of the innate endowment," at least appears to be a set of paired positive and negative emotions. These *qing*, he thinks, become aroused by stimuli, generating more specific desires and aversions in any particular situation. Moreover, he occasionally uses *qing* as a way of counting particular feelings, as when he says that "from birth humans have the sprouts of these two *qing* [i.e., sorrow and happiness]" (19/49/19).

It should seem odd that Xunzi might represent a set of evaluatively charged emotions as the "substance" of our innate endowment, which are aroused to form desires and aversions, rather than themselves being the reactions of some more basic stuff, perhaps *xing* understood substantively. Emotions seem more like reactions to events than the "substance" of our psyches that can generate more specific object-centered movements such as desires. The way out of this bind is to take Xunzi's use of *qing*, at least in its psychological sense, as ambiguous between "emotions" that occur at specific times for specific reasons, such as sorrow and joy, and more enduring "dispositions" to respond to the world in various ways.[17] Indeed, the use of *qing* as "disposition" is generally more common in Xunzi, although the very term *qing* underlines the centrality of emotional reactivity to his conception of disposition or habit.

To sum up, then, Xunzi uses *xing* and *qing* as nearly interchangeable technical terms for the collection of our spontaneously occurring innate instincts. If he wants to stress its givenness, unconsciousness, or general character, he discusses it as *xing*, as for example when he speaks of *xing* as "the root, beginning, material, and raw wood," to be contrasted with artifice, which is "the refined form and pattern, the development and flourishing" (19/95/1). If instead he wants to stress its active, responsive character in relation to things and events in the larger environment, or to talk about more specific manifestations of general tendencies, he will usually talk about human *qing*. Given these nuances of emphasis, his use of *xing* is usually best translated as "instincts" or what is "innate," and his use of *qing* as "disposition" or occasionally "emotion," either singular or plural, depending on the context.

This may still seem somewhat vague. I do not mean that *qing* are dispositions only to have certain feelings. For Xunzi, our *qing* are best thought of as tendencies to feel, desire, and act in certain ways. To describe them as an observer, one would need to specify what sorts of objects and situations engaged a person's delight, what sorts anger, and so on. As a whole, such dispositions make up a person's character. As a corollary, one would expect that interpretive judgment would be crucial to the ways in which our *qing* are manifested as desires and actions; as we shall see below, Xunzi does indeed hold such a view.

Compare the following statements about our common human disposition with the passage quoted above about humanity's innate endowment:

> The human disposition is such that it desires to have grass- and grain-fed animals for food, desires to have patterned, embroidered clothing, desires to have carriages and horses for travel, and moreover desires the wealth of surplus money and accumulated stores. To have things be thus and not know insufficiency over the whole course of one's life, this is the disposition of human beings. (4/16/5–6; cf. 4/16/18)
>
> [The sage king] Yao asked [the sage king] Shun: "What is the human disposition like?" Shun answered: "The human disposition is exceedingly ugly—why would you ask about it? When a man has wife and son together, his filial treatment of his parents declines; when he satisfies his fondest desires, his trustworthiness with his friends withers; when his rank and pay swell his loyalty to his lord slackens. Oh humanity's disposition! Humanity's disposition! Exceedingly ugly—why would you ask about it? Only the worthy make this become untrue. (23/116/25–23/117/1)

Xunzi's assessment of human *qing* is remarkably consonant with his assessment of our *xing*. Humans have a disposition tending toward strongly selfish desires and actions. When these desires are partially satisfied, moral conduct tends to wither as one's circle of concern contracts. But even this satisfaction will only be partial, because Xunzi thinks everyone's disposition is such that we all desire "to be as eminent as the Son of Heaven, to be so rich that one possesses the whole world, to be as widely acclaimed as the sage kings, and to rule over all people but be ruled by no one" (11/53/12–13). For Xunzi, each of us yearns to be an emperor, giving every order but taking none.

The motive power and proliferating expansiveness of desire are hallmarks of Xunzi's view. At the beginning of his chapter on ritual, he lays out the origin and twofold justification of ritual, all on the basis of human desire. He writes:

> How did ritual arise? I say people have desires from the moment of birth. If they desire something but cannot attain it, then it is impossible for them not to seek after it. If in this search for satisfaction people have no measure to apportion things within boundaries, then it will be impossible for them not to come into conflict. This conflict in turn produces social chaos, and chaos leads to destitution. The Ancient Kings abhorred such chaos, so they established ritual and social obligations in order to apportion things, to nurture the desires of men, and to provide sufficiently what people seek. They made it so that desires should not be destitute of things [that satisfy them] and goods would not be exhausted by desires, so that the two of them, desires and goods, support each other and mature. This is the origin of ritual. (19/90/3–5)[18]

For Xunzi, human desire restlessly seeks satisfaction, and only the Confucian ritual order can provide a way for people to live in harmony with each other and the natural environment, moderating and ordering everyone's pursuit of satisfaction, for the greater good as well as individual flourishing. Xunzi here presents, in capsule form, what might be called his negative and positive justifications for Confucian ritual.[19] The negative argument proceeds from untutored human desires, to a widespread, heedless search for their satisfaction, to social conflict and societal collapse, leading to an abhorrent state of widespread poverty and suffering. Ritual breaks this chain of consequences by channeling the search for satisfaction within wise boundaries. The positive justification for ritual sees this restraint as an ordered transformation, both of human beings and their environment, considered as both natural and economic. By reforming desires and the quest for satisfaction, a higher flourishing is possible, wherein all receive what they need (food, clothing, shelter, adequate rest), and some at least receive more, and more beautiful, things than would ever be possible without social order and cooperation. "Desires and goods support each other and mature" under the guidance of ritual and social obligations, the apparent constraints that actually free up greater powers and lead to more and finer enjoyment.

This illuminates Xunzi's basic assumption that desires are not in any sense wicked. They aim at real human goods, whether basic and essential, or luxurious; it is primarily the consequences of everyone blindly following their innate desires that are disastrous. Xunzi makes no apologies for arguing that Confucianism is not only the best Way to avoid these consequences but also the most satisfying possible Way (22/111/16–18). He has no patience with opponents who argue that good government requires the elimination or even reduction of human desires; we do, however, need to reform and redirect our desires. Indeed, he argues that having desires is intrinsic to being alive—the only people who truly lack desire are dead (22/111/4–6). He explains:

> Desires do not wait for the possibility of satisfying them, but those who seek [something] follow that to which they assent (*ke* 可). That desires do not wait for the possibility of satisfying them is received from Heaven; that when seeking [something] we follow what we assent to is received from the heart/mind. When a single desire received from Heaven is controlled by the many aims received from our heart/mind, it is certainly difficult to categorize it as being received from Heaven. (22/111/6–8)[20]

Desires gain their force spontaneously, but as I discuss more fully in the next section, actual human action is frequently a complex process involving conscious assent to particular aims. In such cases, we can no longer call a particular desire merely "innate," because it has been overridden and reshaped by our assent to particular plans of action or standards of judgment. Some of our desires, such as hunger, are surely spontaneous and innate throughout life, but even "the stupid" reflect on and assent to particular courses of action (10/42/13), though their judgments are presumably only framed with the "petty" evaluative categories of benefit and harm (4/15/14–16). For Xunzi our conscious aims, and the practices we engage in to reform our emotions and desires (or alternatively to follow them wherever they lead), are the crucial determinants of virtue and vice, success and failure, good government and destructive anarchy.

Having laid out in some detail Xunzi's views of what is innate, *xing* 性, our disposition and emotions, *qing* 情, and our desires, *yu* 欲, we are in a better position to take stock of Xunzi's claim that "human *xing* is bad" and how his general picture relates to the bridge concept of "human nature."

As pointed out above, the general context for Xunzi's pronouncement is his controversy with Mencius over moral psychology and personal development. Where Mencius saw four "sprouts" of virtue in nearly all human beings, even the vicious or untutored, Xunzi strongly rejects this suggestion. For him, our innate endowment contains nothing moral; everything higher in human life is produced out of and to a certain extent in spite of our instinctive feelings and desires. Where Mencius favors agricultural metaphors of spontaneous growth and maturation, Xunzi turns to tougher craft metaphors, such as a blacksmith sharpening metal or a carpenter straightening crooked timber on a steam press (23/113/9–14).

By saying that humanity's innate endowment is bad, Xunzi is really making two claims: first, and most strongly, about the consequences of following our *xing*; and second, about the character of *xing* itself. As T. C. Kline has argued, Xunzi repeatedly argues for the terrible *consequences* of thoughtlessly following our innate emotions and desires; to do so is to invite competition, conflict, destructive disorder, and extreme poverty, as outlined above.[21]

Although our *xing* does seem to have some positive and more or less neutral elements—such as the basic concern for other members of the same species that all animals share, and sense capacities that make life possible—Xunzi also seems to be making a slightly stronger claim about the general drift of our innate endowment as an active force. We are like warped wood, in contrast to straight, like dull metal instead of a sharp sword. As Xunzi recounts his version of Chinese history,

> In antiquity sages viewed human *xing* as bad, and saw that it became prejudiced and wicked, not upright; rebellious and chaotic, not orderly. Therefore they established the superior position of lords to watch over it, clarified ritual and norms of justice (*liyi* 禮義) in order to transform it, raised up models and standards in order to govern it, made punishments heavy in order to curb it. They caused the whole world to display good governance, and unite with the good. This is the government of the sage kings and the transforming influence of ritual and just norms. Now suppose we got rid of the superior position of lords, lacked the transforming influence of ritual and just norms, got rid of governance through models and standards, lacked the curbs of punishments. Let us rely on this scenario and examine how the people of the world would treat each other: if it were thus then the strong would harm the weak and rob them, the many would tyrannize the few and extort from them, in an instant the whole world would fall to rebellion and chaos, destroying each other. Using this to examine it, it is clear that human *xing* is bad, and our goodness is artifice. (23/115/3–8)

Although Xunzi shies away from the Mencian emphasis on *xing* as having a genetic developmental trajectory, in favor of an alternate emphasis on what is thoughtless, spontaneous, and innate, in this passage we get a glimmer at least of a general tendency to our *xing*. What is at first a set of selfish, biologically based needs, drives, and capacities, will if free of the influence of education, good government, and the threat of punishment become "wicked" and "rebellious," actively recalcitrant to the aims of social harmony and peace. Thus not only are the consequences of following such an innate endowment bad, but the endowment itself is deeply problematic. Nevertheless, our *xing* is neither thoroughly bad, in the sense that every element of it is contemptuous, nor truly "evil," in the sense that we would take any innate delight in destructive or cruel actions for their own sake. Although Xunzi thought many engaged in such crimes in his day, he saw these as derivative of a larger struggle for political dominance and personal aggrandizement that came from rulers with undisciplined dispositions and desires.

How might this account of Xunzi's ideas about *xing* 性, *qing* 情, and *yu* 欲 be related to the resonant English phrase "human nature"? Recall that for the purposes of this study I specified the meaning of "human nature" in four ways. First, I suggested the term points to human beings' physicality and animality (i.e., what connects us to other animals and living things); our most basic, inevitable needs, such as breathing and eating; and to our common but more variable desires and aversions, whether for attractive goods like companionship and pleasure or against evils like humiliation and death. Second, it is also a way of discussing what is common to all or most people, underneath or alongside our many differences. Sometimes, in tension with the first sense, there is a third meaning of that which is distinctively "human" about human beings, what separates us from other animals. And fourth, the term sometimes points to a natural or spontaneous course of development over the life span.

It should be clear that Xunzi's account so far fits the first and second aspects much better than the third; it also at least implicitly addresses the fourth, precisely by rejecting its value and centrality. For Xunzi, our innate endowment, *xing* 性, is made up of a responsive set of dispositions, *qing* 情, which generate any number of more specific desires depending on events and circumstances. He asserts certain widespread responsive tendencies related to hunger, thirst, and fatigue, paired positive and negative emotions, and desires for personal benefit and power. And as for the connection between human *xing* and animals, he makes it explicit, arguing that without the transforming influence of ritual, our *xing* leads us to be "like wild beasts" (26/123/13). Thus our merely natural pattern of development leads to a moral wilderness where people are vicious and suffering, and communities are riven by destructive conflicts. He also asserts that human *xing* and *qing* are common to all people (23/115/23, 3/11/15), in contrast to social customs, *su* 俗, which diverge depending on group affiliation and different teaching (1/1/8).

Turning to Xunzi's account of what makes human beings distinct from other animals, however, reveals interesting nuances in his views. He gives two accounts of humanity's distinctiveness. The first runs as follows:

> What makes human beings truly human? I say it is because they make distinctions. . . . Now the Sheng Sheng ape resembles a human being in form; it too is a featherless biped. But the noble man sips Sheng Sheng soup and eats Sheng Sheng meat. Therefore, what makes human beings human is not that they are featherless bipeds; it is because they make

> distinctions. Even though there are parents and offspring among animals, they lack the proper affectionate relationship between father and son, and though there are males and females, they lack the proper separation between the sexes. Therefore among human ways of life none lack distinctions. Of distinctions, none is more important than those concerning social hierarchy, and of the ways to distinguish social hierarchy, none is more important than ritual. Of rituals, none is more important than those of the sage kings. (5/18/13–18)[22]

Just as the senses can distinguish differing objects, the human heart/mind may draw distinctions of its own, on the basis of any standard that can be articulated and understood.[23] For Xunzi, our instincts and disposition, as well as our physical form, are largely similar to that of a great ape; our ability to make distinctions and live accordingly is what separates us from other animals. In particular, the sages' ritually prescribed, hierarchical social distinctions, *fen* 分, are the key to our dominance as a species, which Xunzi graphically illustrates through the meat-eating habits of the noble man.

Xunzi pursues this line of thought even further in another passage, where he places humankind in relation to all things in the cosmos. He writes:

> Water and fire have *qi* 氣, but are without life. Grasses and trees are alive but lack awareness. Birds and beasts have awareness but lack norms of justice (*yi* 義). People possess *qi*, life, and moreover norms of justice, and thus they are the most honored beings under Heaven. In strength we are inferior to the ox, in walking inferior to the horse, yet we use these animals—how can this be? I say it is because people can form communities, while animals cannot. How can people form communities? I say it is through hierarchical divisions. How can hierarchical divisions be enacted? I say by means of justice. Thus if people use just norms to divide themselves then they will be harmonious; if harmonious, they will be unified, if unified they will have greater strength, with greater strength they will be powerful, when powerful they will triumph over things, and thus may gain palaces and houses to live in. Thus when people properly follow the sequence of the seasons, employ the myriad things, and universally benefit the world, there is no other reason for this but that they have obtained these hierarchical divisions and norms of justice. (9/39/9–13)

In Xunzi's worldview, active but still inanimate things possess *qi* 氣, which for him appears to mean the "vital energy" that animates the rhythmic, cyclical flux of the cosmos; by implication, inanimate things like rocks would apparently not possess *qi*. Some more complex and active entities, such as plants, possess life. Beyond this, animals have awareness (*zhi* 知), and thus they can respond actively to their environments, although as Xunzi says elsewhere, humans have the most acute awareness or understanding of any animal (19/96/10–13). What in this passage sets us apart as a species, however, is not just hierarchical social divisions, *fen* 分, but *yi* 義, a resonant Confucian term often translated as "justice" or "righteousness," which for Xunzi clearly implies a large set of mutual obligations tied to interrelated social roles and their attendant relationships. We can draw complex webs of distinctions between ourselves, Xunzi thinks, precisely in order to constitute subtle and humane relationships. We can thereby form cohesive and powerful communities and can obtain much more than could be gotten through our feeble capacities for strength and speed. It should be noted that this distinctive human feature is hardly innate, in the sense of being part of our *xing*; *yi* is something we need to "obtain," and which Xunzi cautions us not to let go of for an instant (9/39/16).[24]

Thus for Xunzi, what is truly distinctive about human beings is our learned, consciously sought ability to live in complex, interrelated communities, living within complex social roles that are bound by mutual expectations, tied by affections and shared understandings of these differentiated roles. Our physical form and typical desires and drives are not particularly unusual among animals, although one might speculate that for Xunzi, humanity's tendency to move beyond satiation of a set of basic desires to an endless spiral of lack, frustration, and greater desires is unique, a consequence of our ability to draw many more distinctions than other animals, and to live in large part according to socially constituted distinctions. Xunzi comes close to this sort of linkage, claiming that desires stem from judgments of lack (23/114/18–20),[25] noting the heart/mind's tendency to reshape desires according to conscious aims (22/111/6–8), and insisting that our understanding of the proper Way is crucial to human flourishing, in order to rule out misguided evaluation (23/103/15–23). To fully explore these questions, however, we will need to move beyond an outline of Xunzi's view of "human nature" to his larger anthropology and consider other aspects of his account of personhood.

XUNZI'S CONCEPTION OF A PERSON

The word *ren* 人, or "person," is by far the most commonly occurring substantive noun in the Xunzian corpus, with *tian* 天, "Heaven," a distant second.[26] Though I leave to the side platitudes about the "this-worldliness" of Confucianism as a tradition, it is clear that Xunzi was very concerned about human beings and human problems, both individual and social. The outlines of his conception should be clear from the preceding section: Human beings are complex and actively reflective beings, possessing a spontaneously responsive innate endowment, *xing*, and disposition, *qing*, along with a heart/mind that makes distinctions, articulates and argues about them in language, and guides the whole person as he or she follows such distinctions in conjunction with the rest of the community.

In this section, I address aspects of Xunzi's view of the human person not adequately covered above, starting with two famous discussions of the various constituent parts of a human being and moving on to a sustained examination of his account of the human heart/mind, or *xin* 心. One of these passages has been partially quoted above, but it needs to be read in full:

> The various names for what pertains to people [are as follows]: That which is so from birth is called *xing* "innate." What the *xing*'s harmonious operation generates, the vital essence effortlessly and spontaneously uniting arousal and response, this is [also] called innate. The liking and disliking, delight and anger, sorrow and joy of the innate endowment are called "dispositions." The dispositions being a certain way and the heart/mind choosing on their behalf is called "deliberation." The heart/mind deliberating and the abilities putting it into action is called "artifice." What is completed only after deliberation accumulates and the abilities practice it in this way is [also] called "artifice." . . . That by which a person knows is called "awareness" [or "understanding"] (*zhi* 知). The awareness having something with which it accords is called "knowledge." That by which people are capable of doing things are called "abilities." The abilities having something which they match is called "being able." . . . These are the various names for what pertains to people; these are the perfect names of the later kings. (107/22/22–108/22/2)

For Xunzi, our dispositions motivate us to deliberate about possible courses of action that might satisfy our inclinations. When a person's abilities carry this process into action, so that what would be "too little" or "too much" is brought to the proper ritual mean, such actions fulfill Xunzi's short-term definition of *wei* 偽, "artifice" (19/94/8ff). This deliberation is also central to the longer-term process of personal reformation that Xunzi advocates. For him, when deliberation "accumulates" over time, and when the abilities become practiced at carrying it out, the more profound "artifice" of noble character is achieved. (These matters are discussed in more detail in chapter 6.) One should note, however, that Xunzi suggests elsewhere that this ability to *lü* 慮, "deliberate," in a full and proper sense, comes only with considerable progress down the Confucian Way, subsequent to sufficient understanding and practice of ritual (19/92/16–19). As I explore below, it is a ticklish interpretive problem to tease out the relations in Xunzi's thought between the limited but real powers of an undeveloped heart/mind, the greater capacities of a noble man, and the perfected heart/mind of the sage.

This passage, when combined with others supporting such a conclusion, also shows that Xunzi possesses a strong sense of the objective reality of the world, and of the Way as its normative order, because he defines knowledge and true capability for action (as opposed to the mere logical possibility of doing something) in terms of *he* 合, "matching" or "tallying" with external situations and authoritative models for action.[27]

The next passage about the constituent elements of persons has occasionally been used to argue that Xunzi's understanding of human nature is confused. He writes:

> When Heaven's responsibilities are already fulfilled, Heaven's accomplishments already complete, the physical form is whole and the spirit has been born, like and dislike, delight and anger, sorrow and joy are stored there; these are called the "heavenly dispositions" (*tian qing* 天情). Ears and eyes, nose and mouth, the physical form and [its] abilities, each has that with which it [properly] meets and cannot interchange abilities with the others; these are called the "heavenly officials" [and also "senses"] (*guan* 官). The heart/mind dwells in the central cavity in order to govern the five officials; it is called the "heavenly lord." To use what is not of one's kind as resources, in order to nurture one's own kind, this is called "heavenly nurturance" (*yang* 養).[28] Those who accord with their own kind are called "fortunate," those who oppose their own kind are called "unfortunate;" this is called the "heavenly policy." To darken one's heavenly lord, throw one's heavenly officials into chaos, cast aside one's heavenly nurturance, thwart the heavenly policy, turn one's back on the heavenly dispositions, and thereby lose Heaven's accomplishments, this is called "the greatest calamity." [In contrast,] the sage purifies his heavenly ruler, rectifies his heavenly officials, prepares his heavenly nurturance, accords with the heavenly policy, and nurtures his heavenly dispositions, in order to make Heaven's accomplishments complete. (17/80/9–13)

Xunzi uses extended bureaucratic metaphors to illuminate the relation of *tian* 天, "Heaven," and human beings, and to argue for a particular vision of the interior psychological "government" of persons. The key to understanding this passage is recognizing that for Xunzi, the cosmic order is a ritual order, and the human ritual order is continuous with, although not identical to, the cosmic order.[29] However, this is not to say that for Xunzi *tian* and people have the same Way to follow or roles to play in the cosmos; they most certainly do not. For Xunzi, the traditional Zhou deity *tian* occupies the apex of the cosmic hierarchy, the most honored position. On his account, its duties or "official responsibilities," *zhi* 職, are the mostly constant movements of the various celestial bodies, and in addition those natural processes of generation and development that "develop without [people] acting purposefully, and are attained without seeking [the results]" (17/80/1). These heavenly powers Xunzi calls *shen* 神, "spiritual" or "numinous," meaning that they are mysteriously productive without human effort or visible activity, producing "Heaven's accomplishments," such as the changing but orderly sequence of the seasons (17/80/5–7). Heaven for Xunzi is like the sage ruler, who takes no apparent action yet governs and orders the entire realm. In this aspect of the metaphor, however, it is human beings who must act as the faithful ministers, implementing policies and following their own Way, which is to actively order the cosmos. "Heaven has its seasons, Earth its resources, and humanity its ordering government; this is called 'being able to form a triad' [with Heaven and Earth]" (17/80/2–3). The cosmic order is a ritual order in that each element has its proper role and place in the hierarchy, with its due honors and deserts, and its own tasks; Xunzi cautions that we must not "compete with Heaven over responsibilities," but accept our own role and Way (17/80/2).

This passage also illuminates Xunzi's moral psychology.[30] In a way characteristic of late Warring States theoretical discourses, he likens the interior elements of persons to a bureaucratic government while simultaneously linking this imaginative description to his larger vision of the cosmic order. On his account, certain elements of human beings and human life are decreed and provided by Heaven, according to spontaneous, mysterious processes. Most noticeably, Heaven provides our *qing* 情, dispositions, as well as our sense organs and body as a whole, all as part of our innate endowment. This includes our *xin* 心, "heart/mind," which should play the role of ruler within the psychophysical system of the human person, directing and ordering our actions and, over the long term, the reformation of our emotions and desires, which lead to action.[31] Xunzi even speaks about "heavenly nurturance" and the "heavenly policy," which reflect humanity's crucial but delimited role as steward and overseer (i.e., performing the governmental function of high ministers) of "all under Heaven," the traditional locution for the entire world.

Some have seen in Xunzi's implied injunction to "nurture the heavenly emotions" a conflict with his doctrine about "human nature." Understood properly in terms of the Chinese terms he uses, the apparent conflict evaporates. The word *yang* 養, translated by "nurture," "rear," or "nurse," typically refers to the proper treatment of domesticated animals, which need to be fed, cared for, and above all trained into useful work; and as Anthony Yu has pointed out, it is also a word for "treating" an illness.[32] By extension, it is used of children, and in Xunzi's time it had even taken on the sense of "cultivate" and was applied by others with alternative views to such entities as the human *xing* 性, the *shen* 神, or "spirit," or sometimes just "life" or the physical form. Xunzi is clearly using it here in the older sense. In parallel to his statements about the animality of our *xing* and *qing*, he means that we must care for and look after the development of our *qing* so that it reaches its proper transformed state. That our *qing* is "heavenly" means merely that it is given to us as is by Heaven's spontaneous productive processes when we are conceived and then born. It does not mean that it is somehow orderly "by nature," in contrast to Xunzi's many other statements about our *xing* and *qing*. As he points out right before the passage quoted above, to order the products of Heaven is humanity's role and task, and human *qing* is no exception to this.

Further support for this reading comes from Xunzi's contention that what is innate in us is not and cannot be discarded but still needs to be transformed. He writes:

> Innate endowment (*xing* 性) is the root and beginning, the raw material and rough timber. Artifice (*wei* 偽) is the form and order, the development and flourishing. If there were no innate endowment, there would be nothing for artifice to improve; if there were no artifice, then the innate endowment could not make itself splendid. Only after innate endowment and artifice have been merged is the reputation of the sage perfected, and the achievement of uniting the world thereby fulfilled. Thus it is said: Heaven and Earth join and the myriad things are generated, *yin* and *yang* meet and changes and transformations arise, innate endowment and artifice merge and all under Heaven is well-ordered. Heaven is able to generate things, but cannot distinguish things; Earth is able to support people, but cannot order them; the world's myriad things, the category of living people, [all] await the sage and only afterward are they divided. (19/95/1–4)

Our *xing* may be bad, but it is still sufficiently pliable to serve as the raw material that artifice remolds into educated men, noble men, and sages. Our dispositions and desires are reformed but not exchanged; they are ordered and ornamented, not demolished and replaced. Further, this process of transformation and ordering is precisely our proper role in the cosmos, as followers of the human Way. For Xunzi, we reform ourselves and order the larger natural world, for the greater good of human beings and the entire range of the myriad things.

This ordering is to be accomplished, according to Xunzi, by means of the human *xin* 心, "heart/mind," the conception of which is absolutely central to his vision, and essential to its overall coherence.[33] He describes this organ as follows:

> The heart/mind is the lord of the body, and the ruler of the numinous clarity. It issues commands but receives none. By itself it prohibits or allows, seizes or grasps, moves or stops. Thus, the mouth can be forced to be silent or to speak, the body can be forced to crouch down or stretch out, but the heart/mind cannot be forced to change its ideas. If it judges something right, it will accept it; if it judges something wrong, it will reject it. (21/104/10–12)

On this rather stark formulation the heart/mind rules, and the rest of the body obeys. We are not at the mercy of our immediate desires unless we consent to them. This is because "no person does not follow that to which they assent (*ke* 可) and reject that from which they dissent" (22/111/20). Although we are prompted by our desires and aversions, our heart/mind at least has the potential to command us to refrain from following these promptings or to go beyond them. Though we can become capable of acting against these spontaneous attractions and repulsions, we initially see no reason to do so, and we will only restrict our pursuit of apparent goods if our mind commits to some larger plan of action, like the Confucian Way. As Xunzi puts it, everyone approves of certain things, and this is what separates the stupid from the wise: The wise assent to the Way, whereas the rest of us "see only profit" and reflect only to the extent that we might more effectively satisfy our immediate desires (10/42/13, 4/15/14–16). In Harry Frankfurt's terminology, Xunzi thinks uncultivated people are "wantons" with no larger plan of life than getting as much of what they desire as possible.

As Bryan Van Norden has perceptively argued, this notion of *ke* 可, "approval" or, better, "assent," is the second pillar of Xunzi's understanding of human action, and an important departure from Mencius.[34] The word *ke* is richly multivalent, including the notions of *possibility* (sometimes contrasted with actual ability to do something),[35] as well as what is worthy of social, aesthetic, and/or moral *approval*. It can also be used verbally to express a judgment of either possibility or approval or, as I would argue, the stronger idea of assent, which rules out a merely notional approval in favor of a real, motivating recognition of action-compelling factors in a situation. Xunzi uses the word to express both possibility and assent in turn, as in the passage from the "Rectifying Names" chapter quoted in the previous section where he begins by stating that "desires do not wait for the possibility of satisfying them, but those who seek [something] follow that to which they assent" (22/111/6). This double meaning helps him to express the force of this sort of judgment: *suo ke* 所可, "what we assent to" is expressed identically to "what [we think] is possible."

Xunzi is not arguing that there is some desiring faculty of the heart/mind, distinct from some approving and directing faculty. He is saying that we normally do whatever we desire but that sometimes the heart/mind assents to some other course of action, dissenting from what we immediately desire. After the passage quoted above about desires and the aims of the heart/mind, he continues as follows:

> Life is definitely what people desire most, and death what they hate most. Nevertheless, some people follow life [in this way] yet end up dead; it is not that these people do not desire to live and instead desire to die, but rather that they dissent from the means by which they could live, and assent to the means by which they will die. Thus when desires are excessive yet one's actions do not reach so far, it is the heart/mind stopping them. If that to which the heart assents hits the target of Pattern (*li* 理), then although one has many desires, how could this harm the social order (*zhi* 治)? If one's desires do not reach a certain point yet one's action moves beyond it, this is the heart/mind making it happen. If that to which the heart assents misses the target of Pattern, then although one has few desires, how could one stop before plunging into chaos? Thus order and chaos lie in what the heart assents to, not in what the disposition desires. (22/111/8–11)[36]

Xunzi thinks that assent simply trumps desire when the two come into conflict; this shows that his conception of *ke* 可 is particularly strong, more than mere approval of a possible course of action as fine or good. (That this could make sense hinges in part on the sense of *ke* as covering what the actor can conceive of doing in a given situation; some actions are simply impossible to contemplate doing.) In consequence, for Xunzi our judgments are ultimately more ethically significant than our desires, because our desires can and will be reshaped as our understanding changes, and can be resisted or surpassed in any given instance.

This picture appears to generate certain conundrums that parallel western debates about "weakness of will." For Xunzi, given his understanding of the character of our instincts and uncultivated dispositions, if we could not override our desires for some higher goal, we would be doomed to a chaotic, brutish existence. But if even the "stupid" and uncultivated can assent to a better plan that overrides immediate desires, Xunzi appears to flirt with an unrealistic understanding, wherein one can simply decide to be good and thereby become a sage in a single great leap. More deeply, does he not notice the fact that people can be torn between different impulses, and even different standards for judgment, and so fail on particular occasions to live up to what they think in tranquillity to be their highest aspirations? I treat these issues at greatest depth in chapters 5 and 6, but suffice it to say here that Xunzi does recognize these issues, and that he thinks it takes great effort and extended practice to learn to assent reliably and steadily to the Way above all. For Xunzi, our ability to assent to courses of action is of very little use to undeveloped people, because they will only assent to those courses of action that serve their dispositions (22/107/23–24), or more specifically those that will "benefit" them most by satisfying their actual desires (4/15/14–16).

To put this another way, Xunzi is not drawing a distinction between moral and nonmoral motivating factors when he separates assent from desire. For him, assent can be based on any judgment or (mis)understanding, expressed in any set of evaluative categories; this is why he is so alarmed by the "obscuration" of human understanding by partial or slanted views (23/102–7, passim). As he notes in the above quotation, these judgments can correctly target the "Great Pattern" underlying the incipient order in both natural and human realms, or they can miss it partially or completely.[37] If "assent" were only moral, this would not be possible.

As Van Norden and others have pointed out, Xunzi is articulating theoretically a very common human experience of self-restraint for larger purposes or ideals, however conceived. A toddler's father, enraged by one more pointless tantrum from his son, raises his hand to strike his misbehaving offspring. Just before he delivers the blow, however, he catches himself, pulls back, breathes deeply, and counts to ten. On a Xunzian account, the father's heart/mind has dissented from his misguided and potentially very destructive desire and has instead assented to a conscious if brief regimen of self-calming. On some evening years later, this child's mother desires, weakly, to help him with his schoolwork, even though she is also exhausted and would probably fall asleep without concentrated effort to the contrary; her conscious assent to the possibility of sharing time with and tutoring him is again the crucial factor in determining what action she takes, both to rouse herself and to attend to him and his needs, beyond her insufficient desire to do so. These judgments, in the thick of life, depend on the whole web of ideas one holds about the world and other people, articulated in whatever categories one has learned to use; in these cases, conceptions of human development and expectations about family roles and responsibilities would be central.

Xunzi likens the process of practical judgment to using a balance or scale to compare weights, and he sees the crucial question as being what one uses as the standard for weighing various factors. For him, of course, the sage uses the accumulated tradition of the Confucian Way as his "scale" for the myriad factors relevant to practical judgment and thus assents only to what is consonant with this Way (22/111/24–22/112/2, 21/103/16–18). But this is only possible if one has already come to understand the Way, and thus Xunzi thinks how one can understand the Way is the crucial question to be examined (21/103/15–23). This becomes all the more pressing because, presumably because of our innate endowment and disposition, "if one's heart/mind does not understand the Way then it will not assent to the Way, but rather to what is against it" (21/103/18–19). We must learn about the Way before we can possibly assent to it; as long as we are ignorant of it, we shall misguide ourselves, to the extent that we guide ourselves at all.[38]

In answering the question of how the heart/mind can come to understand the Way, Xunzi articulates what he takes to be its three most significant potential abilities.[39] He writes:

> Thus the crucial points of ordering are to be found in understanding the Way. What does a person use to understand the Way? I say it is the heart/mind. What does the heart/mind use to understand? I say it is emptiness, unity, and tranquillity. The heart/mind never stops storing, yet it has/there is (*you* 有) what is called emptiness. The heart/mind never lacks duality, yet it has what is called unity. The heart/mind never stops moving, yet it has what is called tranquillity. People from birth have awareness [and understanding] (*zhi* 知). Having awareness, there is memory.[40] Memory is storing up, yet the heart/mind has what is called emptiness. Not allowing what has previously been stored to interfere with what will be received is called emptiness. From birth the heart/mind has awareness. Having awareness, it perceives difference. [Perception of] difference is awareness of two aspects of things at the same time, . . . [which] is duality, yet [the heart/mind] has what is called unity. Not allowing this one to interfere with that one is called unity. When the heart/mind is asleep it dreams. When it is at ease, it moves on its own. When one employs it, it plans. Thus the heart/mind never stops moving, yet it has what is called tranquillity. Not allowing dreams and irritations to disorder awareness is called tranquillity. (21/103/25–21/104/4)

Xunzi sees the heart/mind as having three important potential abilities. "Emptiness," *xu* 虛, is being constantly receptive to new impressions and thoughts, and being able to keep memories and preconceptions from interfering with this process of exploration and discovery; in contemporary parlance, it might be rendered as "openness." "Unity," *yi* 壹, denotes an ability to focus on and pursue one aim without interference from other thoughts, perceptions, or desires; it also points to the capacity to balance diverse perceptions and ideas in harmonious combination, without allowing some to obscure others. "Tranquillity," *jing* 靜, refers to the capacity of the heart/mind to remain calm and alert in the midst of its many natural movements of perception and thought, and even dreams; a tranquil heart/mind can avoid being swept away by any particular movement, yet without requiring inactivity or relying on withdrawal from thought, feeling, stimulation, or even irritation (21/105/14–21/106/1).

In this account of emptiness, unity, and tranquillity, Xunzi moves carefully between two extremes. On the one hand, he cannot give an account of the human heart/mind as completely powerless and incompetent. The ability to assent to courses of action other than those suggested by immediate impulses would only exacerbate the problems of a bad innate endowment and disposition, unless we could somehow distance ourselves not only from our spontaneous desires but also from the calculus of pleasure and pain, benefit and harm that accompanies them from the beginning. Thus Xunzi implies that even from childhood, in parallel to people's *zhi* 知, awareness/understanding, and *zhi* 誌, memory, our heart/minds are receptive to new impressions, are to some degree capable of focused attention and complex thought, and perhaps even have some capacity to resist the confusion and irritation of life and reflect.[41]

On the other hand, Xunzi cannot attribute so much to the heart/mind that the problem of desire and its reformation is falsely mitigated. If it were as easy as simply deciding to be sociable, after sizing up the facts and then assenting to a better Way, then the violent and chaotic era in Chinese history in which Xunzi lived would not have been called the "Warring States." Xunzi does not see the heart/mind as already possessing a (temporarily obscured) power of perfect insight on the order of the Ming Dynasty Confucian Wang Yangming's *liang zhi* 良知, "innate understanding."[42] The heart/mind has the *potential* to lead each person to attain sagehood, but few will be able to complete the journey (23/116/6–15). The rudimentary capacities of the untutored heart/mind to be empty, unified, and tranquil are only enough to allow one to begin to discern and follow the Way, if one is lucky enough to find a good teacher; they are hardly sufficient to teleport one to its conclusion, sagehood.

Thus it is also a mistake to see these as simple, commonsense "cognitive capacities," fully present in all people.[43] Xunzi sees them as growing and strengthening over time, if properly developed. What start out as minimal abilities can grow into full-fledged intellectual virtues. Following the previous quotation, he writes:

> One who has not yet attained the Way but is seeking it should be told of emptiness, unity, and tranquillity, and should make them his model. If you intend to seek the Way, become empty and you can enter into it. If you intend to serve the Way, attain unity and you can exhaust it. If you intend to ponder the Way, attain tranquillity and you can discern its details. One who understands the Way with discernment and puts it into practice embodies the Way. Emptiness, unity, and tranquillity are called the Great Pure Understanding. (21/104/4–7)[44]

Xunzi here commends emptiness, unity, and tranquillity to those "who seek the Way but have not yet attained the Way," that is, to aspirants already on the Xunzian religious path rather than to absolute beginners or potential converts. This suggests that these terms primarily refer to the full virtues that make up the "great pure understanding" of the sage. For Xunzi, it appears that most of us will fail to use the beginnings of these three abilities without some external notification of their existence and extended instruction in their cultivation. Elsewhere, he calls this process of emotional and intellectual development "purifying one's Heavenly ruler" (17/80/13); I examine this process more closely in chapter 6.

Xunzi likens the heart/mind to a pan of water with particles of dirt in it. When "placed upright and not moved," that is, developed and used properly, the mud will settle at the bottom and the "clear and bright" water in the top of the pan will reflect external reality perfectly. But if the water is stirred up by even "a slight wind," it will become turbid, barely reflective at all, and inadequate to judge even the grossest outlines of things and events (21/105/5–7). "Thus," he continues,

> If [the heart/mind] is guided with good order, nurtured with clarity, and no thing can tilt it, then it will be sufficient to settle questions of right and wrong and resolve suspicions and doubts. But if a little thing pulls it, then externally one's correctness will be altered and inwardly one's heart/mind will be tilted, and then it will be insufficient to decide even coarse patterns. (21/105/7–8)

For Xunzi, the beginner's heart/mind is highly liable to disruption and confusion. Attractive things and possibilities "pull" (*yin* 引) and "tilt" (*qing* 傾) it, upsetting its balance and clouding its perceptions. Our innate endowment and disposition respond too quickly with inappropriate or destructive desires; we lose our inner equilibrium and openness to other perceptions, and we judge poorly. But if properly "nurtured" and "guided," the heart/mind can develop its emptiness, unity, and tranquillity, becoming able to make better, more subtle and accurate judgments, and turning the ability to assent to planned courses of action a real asset, rather than a means of acceleration toward the struggle of all against all for the satisfaction of proliferating desires. At the climax of this process of developing the heart/mind, Xunzi reports that the sage attains a comprehensive understanding of the human Way, completely free of confusion, partiality, and obscuration (21/104/7–10; 21/106/18–20).

Xunzi, in sum, charts human personhood as follows. We move from conception to birth by means of spontaneous processes, as these are properly carried out by Heaven. We thus have an innate endowment, the "raw material" and "rough timber" of personhood, which is made up of sensory capacities and a responsive disposition. This disposition consists of paired positive and negative dispositions, and it generates numerous desires as the sense organs discern objects and the heart/mind becomes aware of various possibilities. The heart/mind, however, can learn to affect these spontaneous processes in ways unavailable to other animals that share similar sensory constitution, physical appearance, and responsive, desiring modes of action. It can examine and plan, consider possible actions and consequences, relate disparate perceptions and ideas into complex wholes, and even learn to overrule the spontaneous search for the satisfaction of desire by assenting to particular aims or goals. It can learn to remain empty, unified, and tranquil in the midst of these processes, even if at first these nascent abilities are very limited and weak, easily swayed by desires and aversions.

By means of these three developing abilities, the heart/mind can gain knowledge of the world and perhaps the Way. This knowledge accumulates and comes more and more to affect the judgments one makes, and the actions to which one assents; if one is lucky enough to gain an understanding of proper Confucian ritual, this will provide the best possible standard for practical judgment in a variety of circumstances. If sufficiently developed by these ritual practices (19/92/16–19), the heart/mind can deliberate effectively about alternative possibilities, weighing them with the *Dao* as if on a scale to assess the numerous factors affecting any significant decision. Together, Xunzi calls these short- and long-term processes of self-control "artifice," to separate them clearly from the patterns of action to which we gravitate without thought or effort, and which are destructive and ugly. For Xunzi, the possibility of artifice, itself relying on the developing powers of the heart/mind, makes Confucian ritual reformation possible, and it opens a window of possibility for true human flourishing, both individual and communal.

NOTES

1. Dubs 1956, 218. I owe this reference to T. C. Kline.

2. Graham 1989, 248; Ivanhoe 2000b [1994], 29.

3. *Huainanzi* 13/123/21 (Lau 1992, 123); the translation is from Graham 1989, 54.

4. Graham 1990a, 10.

5. Graham 1989, 53–64, esp. 56–58.

6. Like most scholars, I regard both ritual practice and political commitment to their vision of good government to be essential to the early Ru ("Confucians") as a social group. For an alternative view, wherein the Ru's commitment to ritualized education and life are seen as having undercut political action, and justified political failure and withdrawal, see Eno 1990.

7. Graham 1990a, 27–28.

8. Recent archeological discoveries show that this account is oversimplified; in particular, newly recovered texts that were roughly contemporaneous with Mencius, and thus earlier than Xunzi, advocated something like Xunzi's position on *xing*. For fuller discussion, see Goldin 2000.

9. I thank Hal Roth, P. J. Ivanhoe, and Eric Hutton for suggestions on how to render this line.

10. It is possible that Xunzi is merely saying that the operation of the senses is part of our innate endowment as humans, and not that perceptions tend to carry evaluative force as well. However, I think one of the points of the larger context is to show the linkage between sense perceptions and desire, which Xunzi goes on to discuss throughout the remainder of the paragraph. In particular, we should note 4/15/17–21, where being moved to follow the Way is compared to eating new and initially strange food, which upon reflection and experience smells and tastes good, is healthy for our body, and is therefore obviously preferable. The larger point concerns the importance of cultivating "good taste" in the whole of life; our untutored responses to a degraded or impoverished environment are insufficient in themselves to lead us to goodness; indeed, our initial response to the finest delicacies and highest culture is likely to be surprise and confusion, rather than immediate, visceral delight. For fuller discussion, see chapters 6 and 8 below, and also Hutton 2001, 94–102. For a survey and analysis of early Chinese views of the senses, see Geaney 2002.

11. For a fuller discussion of the psychophysical terminology of "vital essence," along with an investigation of the sources of such ideas, see Stalnaker 2003.

12. Xunzi says at various points that all people desire to live as richly as a king, and to enjoy the utmost sensual satisfactions (4/16/5–6, 4/16/18, 11/51/24–11/52/1), although in another passage just discussed above (4/15/17–21), he notes that people will assume that what they are aware of constitutes the field of possibility for satisfying their desires, even if it does not include the "fine things" he mentions in the earlier set of passages. The implication seems to be that our desires tend to expand and seek the limits of their possible fulfillment in any setting, and that this is a potentially very serious problem for individual and communal life.

13. Graham (1990a, 59–61) argued that *qing* in early China never means passions, even in the *Xunzi*, but rather "the facts," "genuine," or "what is genuinely X" about some object X, i.e., what defines it as X. Hansen 1995 attacks Graham, proposing "inputs from reality" as a single, unified meaning in the early period, but is ultimately unconvincing. Puett 2004 argues for the manifest diversity of usage of *qing* in early texts, which use and redefine the term for various purposes. See Stalnaker 2001, 69–71, and Hutton 2001, 145–59, for fuller discussion.

14. On *jiu* 就 as "tendency" or "tend toward," see, e.g., Xunzi 1/2/4–5. I thank P. J. Ivanhoe for comments on this passage.

15. *Xunzi*, chap. 17; on Heaven's constancy, see 17/79/16 and 17/81/1. For longer discussions of Xunzi's account of *tian* 天, "Heaven," see Machle 1993; and Goldin 1999, esp. chap. 2. Machle has argued that other commentators have overstated Xunzi's emphasis on the constancy and regularity of *tian*, because, e.g., mysterious plagues, stellar events, and weather disruptions are also produced by *tian*. His point is well taken, but Xunzi nevertheless does seem to see constancy as the primary feature of the Way of *tian*.

16. I thank Hal Roth for prompting this identification of *xing* with "instincts," even if it was not exactly what he originally proposed.

17. On these points see Hutton 2001, 145–49.

18. I have provided what might be called a "gentler" interpretation of this passage, as being primarily about the apportionment of goods. The word *fen* 分 can certainly mean "apportion" in this sense, and is commonly used in precisely this way in early texts. But in Xunzi, it often refers to hierarchical social divisions, as Eric Hutton has argued. If taken in this sense, the passage advocates instituting such divisions as the primary policy to curb the disorder generated by competing desires. On *fen* in the *Xunzi*, see Hutton 1996.

19. For fuller discussion of Xunzi's "positive" and "negative" justifications of Confucianism as a socially instantiated tradition, see chapter 6, n. 36, on 10/45/6–10/46/4.

20. There is a lacuna in this passage. For a brief survey of previous suggestions, see Xunzi 1988a, 427–28. For the most compelling suggestion to date, which makes good sense of the sentence, and fits the overall pattern of parallel constructions in the passage, and which I have adopted, see Lau 1996, 111 n. 4. For an alternative view, see Knoblock 1988–94, vol. 3, 22.5a, 343–34 n. 97. I have also benefited from Eric Hutton's (2001, 151–52) analysis of this passage.

21. Kline 1998, 109.

22. Translation adapted from Ivanhoe 1991, 313. My understanding of this passage has been helped by conversations with P. J. Ivanhoe.

23. On the heart/mind's ability to draw distinctions, which Xunzi does not explicitly mark as either innate or acquired, but which surely relies on learning, and is thus largely a matter of teaching, learning, and artifice, see, in addition, 22/108/16–22/109/3, 22/110/7–9, 22/110/14–15, 23/117/16–8. For fuller discussion, see Stalnaker 2004, 53–68.

24. This passage is at the center of an ongoing controversy about the proper interpretation of the *Xunzi*. Donald Munro (1996) has argued that *yi* in this passage refers to an innate moral sense, which vitiates any contrast Xunzi might want to draw between himself and Mencius. David Nivison (1996) reads it as an unfilled capacity to regard something as a duty. I think Eric Hutton (1996) has successfully argued against both of these interpretations, and I follow his reading: *Yi* is distinctive to human beings, but it is far more than a bare capacity, because it can minutely organize all of human society, and cannot be anything innate, because it must be "obtained," and can be abandoned (for another case where Xunzi clearly says we must *de* 得, "obtain," *yi*, see 23/113/10). Furthermore, it is something that is "used," like an external tool, to implement social divisions. For Hutton's interpretation of *yi* itself in the Xunzi as closer to "social roles" than some vague sense of "righteousness," see Hutton 1996. Hutton now has some doubts about the grammar of the clause about *yi* in the passage quoted above, but I am still convinced by his larger point, and regard this passage as evidence for it.

25. T. C. Kline (1998, 110–11) makes this point nicely.

26. Xunzi uses *ren* 1260 times, and *tian* 598 times. He uses the character *zi* 子, by itself meaning "son," 746 times, but this is artificially inflated due to frequent discussion of the noble man or *junzi* 君子. All the other words used so frequently are basic grammatical particles that crop up in a variety of sentences. Usage figures are from Lau 1996, 783.

27. On Xunzi's penchant for epistemological objectivity, based in his account of the *dali* 大理, "Great Pattern," which underlies all reality, natural and social, and is the ultimate justification for the rightness of the Confucian Way, see Stalnaker 2004. For an account of Xunzi's general "epistemological optimism," see Kline 1998, 166–72.

28. "Nurturance" is Eno's rendering (1990, 199). See also Machle 1993, 100. For a slightly different reading of the word *yang* 養, to account for early references to "*yang*-ing"—i.e., treating, an illness—see Yu 1997, 74.

29. On these points, I have gained from Machle 1993, especially 147–78.

30. I thank Hal Roth for helpful comments on the significance of this aspect of the passage.

31. The *xin* is literally the organ of the heart, but includes all the "affective," "cognitive," and "connative" functions that in English are divided between the "heart" and the "mind." Despite the best efforts of analytic philosophers, to educated English speakers "mind" still often connotes a mysterious, nonphysical substance or entity. Xunzi and other ancient Chinese had no similar traditions of thought about the *xin*, which they saw as thoroughly integrated into the energetic psycho–spiritual–physical system of the human body. Depending on context, I will render *xin* as "mind" or as "heart/mind," but readers should attend to the Chinese idea behind these somewhat misleading locutions.

32. Yu 1997, 74 n. 74.

33. Goldin 1999 recognizes the crucial role of the mind in Xunzi's larger account of human life.

34. Van Norden 1992. David Wong (1996), taking up a challenge Van Norden considers in his essay, argues that the distinction between approval and desire cannot be sustained. His argument is roughly as follows. The distinction can be given either a strong or a weak interpretation. In the strong one, approval can override desire absolutely; in the weak one, approval can override immediate desires in favor of longer-term desires. The strong interpretation would require either independently existing Platonic moral qualities, which the mind can perceive, or a faculty of mind akin to Kantian pure practical reason, either of which could do the work of overriding desire; however, Xunzi believes in neither of these things, so the strong interpretation cannot be correct. The weak interpretation, however, collapses into Mencius's position that desire is the only human motivator, making the problem of how people could possibly become virtuous acute for Xunzi. T. C. Kline (1998, 113–20) argues convincingly against Wong that these strong and weak interpretations do not exhaust the field of possibility. Instead, he suggests that reading Xunzi as a theorist of ethical virtue solves the problem neatly, by connecting desire to understanding and evaluation in terms of ethical ideals and moral categories of evaluation, beyond calculation of benefit and harm or desire and satisfaction. According to Kline, the entire process of motivation via approval is not part of the natural processes of desire, but of deliberative activity, or as I render it, "artifice."

35. This distinction appears in the discussion in chapter 23 of the universal possibility of the "person in the street" to become a sage, even if in actual life most are unable to carry this out. See 23/116/6–23, esp. line 20.

36. As Van Norden 1992 points out, this is a direct attack on the ideas in *Mencius* 6A10.

37. See, e.g., 21/102/5 and 9/39/5–6. For further discussion, see Stalnaker 2004.

38. In Ivanhoe's (1994, 173) memorable phrase, we are born "in a state of complete moral blindness."

39. The subsequent and related passages from the *Xunzi* have been the subject of intense scholarly interest. I have responded to previous scholarship in Stalnaker 2003. The most careful and precise treatment of these issues, cast in terms of an analysis of Xunzi's epistemology, is Hutton 2001, 102–31. Hutton and I agree that *xu*, *yi*, and *jing* are best understand as virtues or excellences that are achieved after long and demanding practice of Confucian disciplines. Hutton may disagree with my contention that Xunzi presupposes some minimal initial beginnings of these virtues if Confucian learning is to get off the ground for the complete beginner; we also interpret *yi* and *jing* slightly differently.

40. Xunzi uses *zhi* 知 in two senses: Minimally, it means only awareness. But maximally, it means not only awareness of something but understanding of it, as for instance the Way, where the "crucial points of ordering" society are to be found not just in being aware that the Way exists, but in truly understanding it. I also follow the common emendation of *zhi* 志, "intention," to *zhi* 誌, "memory," as a common graphic variant, because it makes better sense of the reference to "storing" and the subsequent

explanation of "emptiness." For a defense of the less frequent alternative reading, see Hutton 2001, 114–15.

41. In particular, it would be very odd if Xunzi did not think children were receptive to new impressions. As I have argued elsewhere (2003, 91), there are hints in Xunzi of a sequential ordering of these three excellences of the heart/mind, so if pressed I would argue most strongly for early protoversions of *xu*, emptiness or receptiveness, and to some lesser degree *yi*, unity, as explanations of how Confucian practice can begin at all. *Jing*, or tranquillity, however, seems like something that might only be attainable, even in a minimal way, only subsequent to some degree of training.

42. On Wang Yangming's views and their distance from classical Confucians, especially Mencius, see Ivanhoe 2002.

43. Cf. Nivison 1991.

44. Translation adapted from Knoblock 1988–94, vol. 3, 21.5d. Knoblock follows the punctuation of Kubo Ai and other Japanese scholars; Yang Liang confesses his own confusion over the interpretation of this difficult passage. See Knoblock 1988–94, vol. 3, 330 n. 41. The point I make about this passage would not be affected by the details of various renderings, because the overall drift is clear: to truly pursue the Way one must develop one's emptiness, unity, and tranquillity until they become the "Great Pure Understanding" of the sage.

CHAPTER FOUR

Broken Images of the Divine

✦

Rather than providing a supposedly static summary, much of the best contemporary work on Augustine carefully traces the development of his thought, often correlating it to events in his life.[1] One great virtue of this approach is that it maps the changes in his views over time, illuminating every contour and ridge of his evolving conceptions, and thereby aids a more precise grappling with his ideas. Another virtue is suitability to Augustine's thought itself, which "proceeds by way of ceaseless inquiry"[2] and is preserved in a vast collection of writings, almost all of which were provoked by particular circumstantial needs or controversies, and most of which can be dated quite precisely, thus presenting an almost irresistible field for historical investigation and narration, wherein the dynamism of Augustine's intellectual production can be represented afresh.

Nevertheless, I do not follow such an approach here, for reasons both of substance and of compositional necessity. The necessity is obvious: To give a full account of the development of Augustine's anthropological ideas would dreadfully prolong the present study and would overwhelm the comparison with Xunzi. Furthermore, others have done this work, and done it well.[3] I proceed instead by giving my own relatively brief analysis of Augustine's mature views of the human person, which I take to be developed most compellingly in *On the Trinity*, although present in numerous other texts as well. The bridge concepts of human nature and personhood outlined in chapter 2 provide the organizing architecture. I thus present Augustine's developed anthropological thought as a generally unified systematic edifice that at least aims at comprehensiveness and coherence, even if it sometimes falls short. I would contend that this interpretive strategy is justified by Augustine's own understanding of truth as unified in and indeed identical to the one God, eternal and unchanging (*Conf.* 10.23.33, 13.29.44). Augustine recognized that his own human attempts to articulate an account of divine truth varied somewhat, but he did not think this undercut the unity and stability of the truth he sought (*Retr*., prologue). In other words, despite his splendidly profligate creativity, Augustine himself aimed at systematic unity of thought, and so it is not inherently distorting to attempt to reconstruct his ideas in this way. However, at times it will still be useful to discuss changes and tensions in his views, and I will not hesitate to do so when it will clarify his ideas or the comparison with Xunzi's. To suggest that such a unified account is necessarily "static," already dead, is perilously close to an anachronistic misrepresentation of some of Augustine's own deepest intellectual commitments. It also bespeaks a veiled distaste for his final positions on God and humanity, without directly engaging them.

In this chapter, I explore those ideas of Augustine that can be grouped under the bridge concepts of "human nature" and "person." I examine his accounts of *natura* and its role in his metaphysics, salvation history, and anthropology, and the integrally related idea that humans are created in the image of God, with minds that remember, understand, and will. I then fill out the background to these themes by discussing his concept of *persona*, his ideas about the human mixture of body and soul, the question of the orientation of the soul and its loves, and his views on "concupiscence" and "habit," concluding with a synthetic treatment of his conception of the will and its debility.

AUGUSTINE ON HUMAN NATURE

Augustine uses the word *natura* and its cognates, derived from the deponent verb *nascor*, "to be born," about 5,000 times in his works, and he specifically discusses the *natura* of humans more than 800 times.[4] Appearances are in this case not especially deceiving, for *natura* overlaps closely with its English derivative "nature." Augustine sometimes uses the word to refer to Nature in general, the orderly, created cosmos (e.g., *Trin*. 3.7), but more often he means by it the particular nature of a certain sort of thing, that is, its constitution and mode of being and activity, its essential characteristics that define it as a unified class (*Trin*. 6.4, 7.7).

The immediate context for Augustine's frequent use of these terms is his youthful affiliation with and later renunciation of Manicheism. Manicheism was a variant form of late antique Christianity, with a supplementary revelation from Mani, a third-century Babylonian. Mani taught a baroque cosmology marked by a radical dualism of light and darkness, good and evil, which were originally separate but became intermingled due to an invasion of the realm of light by the forces of darkness. This produced the present state of the universe, where particles of light are held prisoner by the darkness and seek to free themselves to rejoin the realm of light; human beings are microcosms of this larger pattern, and accordingly our religious task is to release the immaterial light within us from the evil darkness of our bodies, through a complex system of asceticism, including dietary and sexual controls.[5]

Central to the Manichean system of thought and practice was the idea of two dueling natures, one good and one evil. With the vivid cosmological backdrop, Manicheans present these contrasting natures as two antagonistic substances, opposed to each other in their very being. On this view, existence is sundered between rival creative principles, and human beings' sense of internal conflict is explicable as the conflict between the trapped particle of light, who we truly are, and the entrapping body of darkness, chaining us to the cycle of procreation, birth, and death, enslaved to the forces of evil via carnal desires.

Although this radical diagnosis of our predicament spoke to Augustine as a young man, he became disillusioned with it and turned against it decisively.[6] In early works such as *On True Religion* and *On the Nature of the Good*, he laid out his theological-metaphysical response, the basic outlines of which he never altered. For Augustine, the universe is centered on the one true God: "The Supreme Good beyond all others is God. It is thereby unchangeable good, truly eternal, truly immortal. All other good things derive their origin from him but are not part of him" (*nat. b.* 1).[7] Out of nothing God creates all lesser things, which are therefore mutable (*nat. b.* 1). All such things are arranged in a hierarchy of being and goodness, where degrees of nearness to God reflect greater amounts of both being and goodness, which in this account are identical (*nat. b.* 1, 5). "For all existence as such is good" (*vera rel.* 11.21),[8] says Augustine, and is derived from and sustained by God, the supreme existent (*nat. b.* 1; *civ. Dei* 12.26).

This hierarchy of existence and goodness is correlated precisely to the idea of *natura*, so that different natures mark out different types of beings on the scale of existences (*civ. Dei* 12.2). In fact, Augustine seems to view the ideas of *substantia* ("substance"), *essentia* ("essence" or "being"), and *natura* ("nature") as interchangeable concepts for the constitution and form of a class of things (*vera rel.* 7.13; see also *lib. arb.* 3.13). This "order of nature" below the immutable God Augustine specifies as follows, in ascending order: inanimate objects, living things, living things with an impulse to reproduction, sentient beings (i.e., animals in contrast to plants), intelligent beings (i.e., humans instead of other animals), and immortal beings (angels over humans) (*civ. Dei* 11.16).

Contra the Manichees, there is no evil substance whatsoever. Augustine writes: "Every nature is good. If we ask whence comes evil, we should first ask what evil is. It is nothing but the corruption of natural measure, form, or order. What is called an evil nature is a corrupted nature. . . . But even when it has been corrupted, insofar as it is a nature it is good, insofar as it is corrupted it is evil" (*nat. b.* 3–4).[9] All existing beings are formed with divinely ordained *modus* ("measure," with the senses of both quantity and limit, or "manner" of being), *species* ("form" or "appearance"), and *ordo* ("order" or "rank"). These characteristics define the essence of each type of being, and by virtue of their being created by God, are intrinsically good and beautiful. Evil is not a countersubstance for Augustine, at war with a set of good substances, but the corruption or perversion of an always intrinsically good nature. Evil has no existence of its own but is always parasitic on and disruptive of the good. In Augustine's famous formulation, the field of evil is completely exhausted by sin and its penalty, that is, by love that disorders God's ordering of nature, the hierarchy of being, and God's justly imposed penalty for such wrong loving (*vera rel.* 23, 38–39, 44; *civ. Dei* 12.2–3). Now of course, because all existing things are good, they are all worthy of praise and indeed love, but only in proportion to their place in the hierarchy of being: God is supreme existence and goodness, and thus deserves supreme love (*Trin.* 9.13). To give one's greatest love to created things is one of Augustine's models for sin, or "carnality," in his lexicon.

From the very beginning, then, there is a double movement in Augustine's understanding of specifically human nature: Its true and basic state, its "original" or "pristine" condition as created by God, is "perfect," that is, with its loves correctly ordered to the cosmic scale of existence; but insofar as it is mutable, it is nevertheless subject to corruption, and our universal lived experience of our *natura* is of its corrupted condition, not its original purity (*ver. rel.* 46.88).

Originale peccatum

To fill out this sketch of Augustine's abstract understanding of human *natura*, we need to turn to his account of what is often called "salvation history," or God's working out of the divine purpose in time. According to Augustine, there are four central episodes in this narrative, three of which have already occurred: the Creation; the Fall; the life, death, and resurrection of Christ; and the last judgment.

His accounts of the Creation and the Fall are obviously dependent on Augustine's reading, and rereading, of Genesis, but they are also fruits of his long search to "know God and the soul" above all (*sol.* 1.2.7). His views are thus not simply *derived* from scriptural exegesis but also correlate with his reflections on his own experience, and his intellectual quest to understand the human condition.[10]

In *City of God*, Augustine proposes various allegorical readings of the description of paradise in Genesis, and he suggests that there may be other valuable interpretations along these lines besides his own. He cautions, however, that "there is no prohibition against such exegesis, provided that we also believe in the truth of the story as a faithful record of historical fact" (*civ. Dei* 13.21; cf. 15.27, 16.2).[11] Thus Augustine saw the Genesis account as not only symbolizing and prefiguring important truths about the church and the life of the blessed but also as, in some sense, a completely accurate account of the creation of the first human beings, if allowance is made for perhaps overly concrete modes of expression for God's action as immutable, immaterial creator (*civ. Dei* 12.24, 13.24).

Augustine discusses the Creation and Fall of both humans and angels in some detail, but helpfully provides the following summary, oriented to the effects on human *natura*:

> God created man aright, for God is the author of natures, though certainly not of their defects. But man was willingly perverted and justly condemned, and so begot perverted and condemned offspring. For we were all in that one man, seeing that we all *were* that one man who fell into sin through the woman who was made from him before the first sin. We did not yet possess forms individually created and assigned to us for us to live in them as individuals; but there already existed the seminal nature from which we were to be begotten. And of course, when this was vitiated through sin, and bound with death's fetters in its just condemnation, man could not be born of man in any other condition. Hence from the misuse of free choice there started a chain of disasters: humanity is led from that original perversion, a kind of corruption at the root, right up to the disaster of the second death, which has no end. Only those who are set free through God's grace escape from this calamitous sequence. (*civ. Dei* 13.14)[12]

This compressed version of the narrative may serve as a guide to the various elements of Augustine's vision of divine creation and original sin.

"God created man aright, for God is the author of natures, though certainly not of their defects." Without doubt, human *natura* was for Augustine completely good and orderly as originally created. God fashioned the bodies of Adam and Eve out of dust, and then He directly implanted their souls (*civ. Dei* 12.8, 12.24). Human nature includes both elements, soul and body (*ep.* 137.2.8, *civ. Dei* 13.24, *Trin.* 15.11).

God's plan was to create humans "as a kind of mean between angels and beasts," partaking of both the physical and intelligible realms, and owing obedience to their creator. This obedience, if actual, was to be rewarded with immortal life, and fellowship with the good angels; if they disobeyed, they were to live like beasts, destined to die (*civ. Dei* 12.22). God benevolently arranged the initial conditions of human life as favorably as possible: All of Adam and Eve's physical needs were abundantly provided for, they were "not distressed by any agitations of the mind, nor pained by any disorders of the body,"[13] with their loves ordered and the supreme object of their delight (i.e., God) always present. Furthermore, God's command of obedience regarding the fruit of one tree was simple, memorable, and easy to obey, as well as being a sensible reminder that God is Lord, and free service to Him is in every creature's best interests (*civ. Dei* 14.10, 15).

"But man was willingly perverted." Despite all this, inexplicably, Adam and Eve rebelled. Augustine provides detailed analyses of the first, angelic fall, and multiple assays of the elements of the Fall of the first human beings.[14] In *City of God*, he returns to this theme several times in books 12 to 14, working over the ground repeatedly in his quest to answer one of his perennial questions, "*Unde malum?*"—"From whence comes evil?"

The outer story is simple enough. Satan and the other evil angels preferred their own glory to the service of God, and they fell away from Him (*civ. Dei* 11.11, 13; 12.1, 6; 14.11). In Eden, where Adam and Eve enjoyed a perfectly suitable and harmonious existence, Satan used a serpent as his mouthpiece. He first attacked Eve, the "inferior" and more "gullible" of the two, supposing that Adam could not be entrapped directly but "only if he yielded to another's mistake." Eve was deceived, and she believed the serpent's suggestion to eat from the forbidden tree, not realizing this was a sin. Adam, however, "was not seduced" (1 *Tim.* 2.14) but "refused to be separated from his only companion, even if it involved sharing her sin" (*civ. Dei* 14.11).[15] Though he may have been mistaken about the consequences of this decision, being unacquainted with God's strictness (14.11), Adam nevertheless consciously and freely chose to put a lesser good, human companionship, above a greater, obedient love for the divine (see also *conf.* 2.8.16–2.9.17).

Augustine assures us, however, that this outward manifestation of evil could not have occurred without a previous, hidden evil will. He writes:

> It was in secret that the first human beings began to be evil; and the result was that they slipped into open disobedience. For they would not have arrived at the evil act if an evil will had not preceded it. Now could anything but pride have been the start of the evil will? . . . For it is a perverse kind of exaltation to abandon the basis on which the mind should be firmly fixed [i.e., God], and to become, as it were, based on oneself, and so remain. . . . This desertion is voluntary, for if the will had remained

> unshaken in its love of the higher changeless Good, which shed on it light to see and kindled in it fire to love, it would not have been diverted from this love to follow its own pleasure; and the will would not have been so darkened and chilled in consequence as to let the woman believe that the serpent had spoken the truth and the man to put his wife's will above God's commandment. (14.13)[16]

The primal drama is interior, for Augustine, and the primeval sin is pride, improper self-love and self-satisfaction, "a longing for perverse exaltation" (14.13). As William Babcock argues, pride is not so much the cause of the first evil will as its content, the essence of "defection" away from God to oneself.[17] Turning away from God, the source of all illuminated understanding and any fire of love that we possess, simply *is* to be "darkened and chilled" so that self-deception and disordered loving become possible.

As many commentators have noted, however, these moves only deepen the mystery of original sin. In Eden, human beings' every need was splendidly met, and they loved God above all, with emotions and desires perfectly suited to God's objective order of value in creation (14.10); how could such creatures possibly choose to turn away from God, the source of their felicity? As Babcock has noted, by describing Adam's fall as both conscious and voluntary disobedience to God's command, Augustine makes the human case structurally parallel to the even more difficult case of the fallen angels, who are at the summit of created reality, closest to God in being, rational and already immortal, but whose company is somehow split: All the angels share the same perfectly favorable "initial conditions" and character, but only a portion choose to remain in them, while others fall away (12.1).[18]

In book 12 of *City of God*, Augustine analyzes the angelic fall in much the same terms as the human Fall. After remarking on the fineness of angels' and all other creatures' natures, as given to them by God, and insisting that evil contravenes and perverts these natures, Augustine identifies the turn of some of the angels to themselves from God with the fault of pride (*civ. Dei* 12.1–6). He writes that this "was the first defect, the first impoverishment, the first fault of that [angelic] nature," which was capable of attaining blessedness by enjoying the supremely existent God, but turned away to a lower state of being, and thus became miserable.[19] He goes on: "If in turn one seeks the efficient cause of this evil will, one finds nothing." The first evil will simply has no cause, he thinks (12.6).

What does this mean? In *City of God* 12.6, Augustine pursues a remarkable thought experiment about two men, of precisely similar mental and physical disposition, who both "see the beauty of the same woman's body, and the sight stirs one of them to enjoy her unlawfully, while the other continues unmoved in his decision of chastity."[20] As explanatory factors, he rules out in turn the beauty of the woman, differences in mind or body, and unequal temptation from malignant spirits, all of which were equal in or equally present to both. Nothing remains but each man's individual will (*proprius voluntas*) as possible cause. He then considers the very possibility of defection from God, adamantly rejecting the (Manichean) idea that this would stem from human nature, and he settles instead on the fact that our natural being is created from nothing (12.6). Despite the ambiguity of *civ. Dei* 12.6 and a few similar passages, it is clear that Augustine thinks creation ex nihilo explains the possibility, but not necessity, of defection from God (*civ. Dei* 12.8).[21] This is a metaphysical point about degrees of being; for Augustine, the highest being is the immutable God, but everything lower, existing in time, is subject to change and thus may defect from God.

Augustine's final words on this problem are appropriately mysterious:

> Therefore no one should try to find an efficient cause for an evil will. It is not a matter of effecting [something], but of defecting; the evil will itself is not effective but defective. For to defect from him who is the Supreme Existence, to something of less reality, this is to begin to have an evil will. To wish to discover the causes of such defection—deficient, not efficient causes—is like wanting to see darkness or hear silence. Yet we are familiar with darkness and silence, and we can only be aware of them by means of eyes and ears, but this is not by perception but by absence of perception. No one therefore must try to get to know from me what I know that I do not know, unless perhaps in order to learn not to know what must be known to be impossible to know![22]

"Deficient causation," a mysterious nothingness like silence and darkness, is the imperceptible and unknowable beginning of human defection from God. This seems to be Augustine's final pseudo-explanation for the origins of evil, both human and angelic.

Evaluations of this account vary.[23] It is easy for critical analysis of these questions to sprawl, so I will make my case as briefly as possible and move on. As stated above, I think Augustine's view is that creation ex nihilo leads only to the possibility of sinning, *posse peccare*, not the necessity of it, or even the near inevitability of sin, as John Rist would have it.[24] Refraining from sin was very much a "live" option for Adam and Eve, and this was God's intention for them. But this original *posse peccare* is freedom in the modern sense: Adam and Eve were for some time able to, that is, had the power and capacity to choose truly different possibilities in an unconstrained way; as intellectual natures they had, in other words, "freedom of choice" (*liberum arbitrium*) sufficient to follow or desert God (*civ. Dei* 22.1). (It should be noted that this sort of "freedom" is not at all what Augustine himself means by *libertas*, which is the unconstrained power to do what is right, that is, the will of God.)

Saying this, however, does not resolve the difficulties seen by James Wetzel and especially William Babcock. Whether the initial turn away from God is described as self-deception about the order of goods (thus Eve, according to Augustine, although this clashes with his account of Adam's full understanding that he chose to sin) or left as a perverse surd (the apparently correct interpretation of Adam's case), a chasm yawns between the prelapsarian state of Adam and Eve and their first sinful acts. Wetzel, by focusing on the intelligibility of reasons for action, is left with a contradiction between Augustine's account of Adam's (inadequate) reason for sin, which is that he did not want to lose the companionship or marital solidarity of Eve, and Augustine's objectivity about knowledge and values, about which Adam "was not deceived." Babcock puts the point more generally, showing that Adam and Eve could not have had any motivation, given the order of their loves, to fall away from God.[25]

A distinction needs to be made between the unintelligibility of a particular agent's action, and the failure of a general account or explanation of that action, which is a second-order problem. Even if Adam thought that he had a good or at least sufficient reason for joining with Eve in her sampling of the forbidden fruit, Augustine's general account of their unfallen condition does make such a judgment "utterly inexplicable."[26] Given their integrated characters, they should have been using their freedom to explore paradise and enjoy any of the innumerable other goods of creation, doing anything to avoid displeasing Him whom they loved above all else.

To say in response, however anachronistically, that true freedom just is the possibility to do anything whatsoever, however contrary to one's strongest loves and most compelling reasons (but only if those loves and reasons are good, as we shall see below), is only to push the problem back a step. If *posse peccare* is an accurate description of the freedom Augustine usually describes as *liberum arbitrium*, freedom of choice, it is baffling why God would create beings with this as a fundamental, indeed natural, characteristic (*c. Jul. imp.* 5.60); human nature would then be intrinsically vitiated, and Augustine would have compromised the goodness of God's creative action.[27]

Perhaps the most charitable reading is that Augustine sees the Fall as a highly unlikely, indeed nearly incomprehensible event, which nevertheless certainly occurred (from biblical, social, and personal evidence), and which therefore must be grappled with intellectually: Precisely because of its senselessness, Adam's action deserved the severest punishment (this near impossibility would be the inversion of Rist's contention of near inevitability). It is clear, at least, that Augustine thinks God's goodness is uncompromised by the prelapsarian possibility of human sinning (whose actuality is foreknown and accepted by God), and that God's sovereignty and goodness are only reemphasized by His inscrutable decision to allow the Fall to occur (*civ. Dei* 12.28, 22.1), so that he could bring goodness out of that and subsequent evils, to demonstrate conclusively that his providential design could not be thwarted, but only made more complex and beautiful (14.11, 22.1; 11.21–22).[28]

Regardless of modern distaste, for Augustine the human Fall is absolutely central to a proper understanding of human beings and human *natura*. To return to our summary quotation from *City of God* 13.14: "But there already existed the seminal nature from which we were to be begotten. And of course, when this was vitiated through sin, and bound with death's fetters in its just condemnation, man could not be born of man in any other condition." Adam and Eve's defection from God was, paradigmatically, a sin, and so warranted punishment. Indeed, according to Augustine, because of the ease of fulfilling God's requirement and avoiding sin, the Fall was immensely wicked and warranted a particularly severe judgment (*civ. Dei* 14.15). Augustine writes:

> In fact, because of the magnitude of that offense, the condemnation changed human nature for the worse; so that what first happened as a matter of punishment in the case of the first human beings, continued in their posterity as something natural and congenital. . . . But human nature in him [Adam] was vitiated and altered, so that he experienced the rebellion and disobedience of concupiscence in his body, and was bound by the necessity of dying; and he produced offspring in the same condition to which his fault and its punishment had reduced him, that is, liable to sin and death. (both *civ. Dei* 13.3)[29]

Adam's *natura* was *mutata*, "changed," and, more precisely, *vitiata*, "vitiated" or "marred," so that all his offspring would be *obnoxius*, a richly suggestive word meaning "liable," "subject," "obedient," "exposed," "obliged," and even "addicted," to sinning and death. According to Augustine, the just punishment for rebellion and disobedience is rebellion redoubled, so that man is "handed over to himself" but rendered internally at odds, disobedient to himself. Man's *caro*, "flesh," and even his *animus*, "mind" or "soul," do not submit to his *voluntas*, "will," so that both soul and flesh are frequently troubled (14.15; see also *nat. et grat.* 28). This trouble includes our emotional life: "Man was distracted and tossed about by violent and conflicting emotions, a very different being from what he was in paradise before his sin" (*civ. Dei* 14.12). Augustine also makes it clear that without the Fall human beings would never have suffered either physical death or the processes of decay that lead to it; death is not natural but a punishment for sin (14.12, 13.15; also 12.22; 13.3, 9, 13). Thus the internal conflict for which Augustine's vision of humanity is noted is for him a primary symptom of fallenness, and it is properly speaking a divine punishment for original sin, which through human action generates more sinning.

We should also note that for Augustine *natura* crosses the divide between metaphysical immateriality and material creation, so that it may at least in part be properly described as *natura seminalis*, the "seminal nature" or "seed" by which humanity is propagated (*civ. Dei* 13.14). Thus not only is human *natura* vitiated in the abstract but the *semen* "seed" also carries a *vitium*, a "fault," "defect," "failing," or "blemish" (*civ. Dei* 22.24, *c. Jul. imp.* 2.216). Using the metaphor of cultivated olive trees that can nevertheless only produce wild olive trees as offspring, Augustine suggests that in the wake of Adam's defection, the procreative seed of all human beings is marred, so that all human offspring, including those of baptized parents, are prone to sinning and moving inexorably toward death (e.g., *gr. et pecc. or.* 2.40.45–46). As Elizabeth Clark has argued, Augustine develops the theme of vitiated seeds not only in *City of God* but also in several later works, with the most detail in the *Unfinished Work Against Julian*. This sort of biotheological doctrine provided the Pelagian Julian of Eclanum with enormous ammunition to charge Augustine with resurgent Manicheism in his understanding of sin and redemption.[30]

Indeed, for Augustine, sex is deeply implicated in human fallenness, in several distinct ways. As noted, sexual reproduction in the wake of the Fall passes on a vitiated nature, ensuring that without grace all human beings will sin with necessity (*nat. et grat.* 11). Thus "carnal generation" itself is not only "frail" but also "condemned" (*pecc. mer.* 2.15). Augustine also finds in the unruliness of sexual desire, especially male sexual desire as he understands it, a paradigm for our destructive internal conflicts, our disobedience to ourselves. Moving unpredictably and embarrassingly on their own, failing to be aroused when called, Augustine sees the disobedient behavior of human sexual organs as a suitably symbolic punishment for human rejection of God's just dominion (*civ. Dei* 14.16, 19, 23).

Imago Dei

Augustine's serious indictment of our vitiated nature, and of humanity's original and continuing sinfulness, is very well known, perhaps in part because of the long-standing popularity of Augustine's *Confessions*, which contains some of his more vivid and personalized statements on this theme.

Yet even in the *Confessions*, there are signs that this is not all Augustine has to say on the matter of human nature. In the very first paragraph of the work, he announces what is arguably its central theme: "You stir us to take pleasure in praising you, because you have made us for yourself, and our heart is restless until it rests in you" (*conf.* 1.1.1).[31] Later he writes: "In seeking for you I followed not the mind's intelligence, by which you willed that I should surpass the beasts, but fleshly sensation. But you were more inward than my most inward part and higher than the highest within me" (3.6.11; see also *Trin.* 8.11).[32] For Augustine, God is the absolute basis of our existence, including our self-awareness. God illuminates our mind from within as our inner teacher and standard of judgment (*mag.* 11.38ff., *conf.* 10.65, *civ. Dei* 14.13) and kindles our love for Him, by the Holy Spirit pouring the love of God into our hearts (e.g., *spir. et litt.* 32.56, from Rom. 5.5).

Augustine articulates these themes most forcefully in his treatment of the doctrine that human beings are made in the image of God, "the image in which we were created in terms of our nature" (*spir. et litt.* 27.47; see also *civ. Dei* 11.26, *Trin.* 12.4).[33] This deepest aspect of our *natura* is never lost, despite the Fall, and remains within us, to be reenergized by grace and renewed and purified through Christian discipleship, as I discuss more fully in chapter 7 (*spir. et. litt.* 28.48–49). More specifically, for Augustine, the human mind in its activity is the image of the triune God, Father, Son, and Holy Spirit (*Trin.* 7.12, 12.4, 12.12).

Augustine's account of the traditional motif of divine imagehood takes shape against the background of his theory of the human soul, especially as this is developed in *On the Trinity*. Using Pauline language, he makes a basic distinction between the "inner man" and "outer man." He writes:

> Now then, let us see where we are to locate what you might call the border between the outer and the inner man. Anything in our consciousness (*animus*) that we have in common with animals is rightly said to be still part of the outer man. It is not just the body alone that is to be reckoned as the outer man, but the body with its own kind of life attached, which quickens the body's structure and all the senses it is equipped with in order to sense things outside. And when the images of things sensed that are fixed in the memory are looked over again in recollection, it is still something belonging to the outer man that is being done. In all these things the only way that we differ from animals is that we are upright, not horizontal, in posture. This is a reminder to us from him who made us that in our better part, that is our consciousness, we should not be like the beasts we differ from in our upright posture. Not indeed that we

> should throw ourselves onto what is most sublime in bodies; for to seek repose for the will even in such noble bodies is to fell the consciousness into a prone position. But just as our body is raised up by nature to what is highest in bodies, that is, to the heavens, so our consciousness being a spiritual substance should be raised up toward what is highest in spiritual things—not of course by the elevation of pride but by the dutiful piety of justice. (*Trin*. 12.1)[34]

The inner/outer distinction thus does not simply reproduce the distinction between body and soul. Instead, it tracks the boundary between what is animal in us and what is distinctively human, marked out by our lofty *ratio* or "reason" (12.2). The soul, then, includes a higher, distinctively human element, which Augustine calls the *mens* or "mind," which is what he means by the "inner man" (12.2–4). The "outer man," by contrast, includes both the body and those lower elements of the soul that deal directly with bodies: sensation, and the mental functions that concern sensation, which are shared by all animals, such as memory of sense impressions and impulses to seek advantageous things and shun harmful ones (12.2). This schema is always both descriptive and normative, as his symbolic analysis of our upright posture and heavenly spiritual orientation suggests; what is "higher" is better, more worthy of love and respect, and is our proper end as rational beings (11.6, 10).

And although he is not always precise about his terminology, Augustine generally conveys this distinction between the animal and human sides of our soul via two different words for soul: the masculine *animus*, which accents our rational, human capacities; and the feminine *anima*, which connotes more the vivifying force of the soul within the body. In fact, he once defines these terms as the higher and lower halves of the soul, with *animus* equivalent to the inner man or *mens* and *anima* equivalent to that animal-like portion of the outer man dealing with sensation, spontaneous reactions, and the unguided operation of the memory in connection with basic biological drives (15.1). He also uses *anima* with adjectival modifiers, especially *rationalis* and *irrationalis*, to designate these higher and lower parts of the soul (e.g., *civ. Dei* 19.13).[35] In terms of his habitual use of the words, however, both often seem to include both the inner man or mind, and also the psychic parts of the outer man. His use of *cor*, "heart," although perhaps even vaguer, seems to cover the same full range of the psyche as *animus* and *anima*, but with the accent falling on the will and the emotions, topics to be discussed more fully below.[36]

For Augustine, being the image of something implies likeness to it but not vice versa, because being an image implies further that the image is created with reference to an original, to which it naturally tends in its activity (7.12, 8.5). All created things have some distant likeness to spiritual things, and thus in a limited way to God, showing *vestigia*, "traces," of their distinctive eternal forms (12.5). Only humans, however, created as images of the triune God, have a direct likeness to deity. Augustine's search for the image of God in humanity leads him in the end to the mind and its various functions.

There are a number of ways to parse the structure of *On the Trinity*; but in its overarching trajectory, it is inarguably a quest to understand the difficult theological doctrine of a triune God (*Trin*. 2.1, 9.1). Thus Augustine's investigations of the divine image in humanity in the second half of the work are pursued with constant reference to the problematic of how fallen yet graced humans may come to understand the Christian God, who is one yet a trinity. The text simultaneously advocates, directs, and symbolizes the human ascent to God, by leading the understanding from earthly things to heavenly, tracing trinitarian structures in various levels of created reality to illuminate the trinitarian structure of uncreated reality, God. At the same time, because trinitarian structures are most visible in the human mind, Augustine in the process of this ascent gives a detailed account of the mind's structure and functioning.

At the most rudimentary level, there is a trinity of sensation discernible in the activity of the "outer man," in the combination of perceivable external objects, the senses being formed or impressed by the likenesses of these objects, and the *intentio animi*, the "application"[37] of the soul (*animus*), which holds the senses on the object (11.2ff.). Related to this is an analogous but more inward trinity of recollection, which consists of (1) "memory retaining the appearance that the soul drank in through bodily sense"; (2) an *intus visio*, "internal sight," when the *acies animi*, "soul's eye" or "conscious attention," is formed by what memory retains; and (3) "the same will" (*voluntas*) that directed the senses to objects now directs the *acies animi* to memory in a conscious act of recollection, producing in thought something like sight (12.6). Note how memory and will are crucial to even the lowest levels of human psychic functioning, for Augustine. In his account, the mind is the ruling part of the soul and has a remarkable influence on and control over the body (6.10, 10.7, 12.2, 15.11; 10.9, 11.7).

For Augustine, the *mens* itself is undoubtedly one unified entity, a single nature, but it can be analyzed into two aspects or functions: *sapientia* or "wisdom," and *scientia* or "knowledge" (12.1–4). *Sapientia* concerns the activities of the mind with respect to the intelligible world of eternal forms; *scientia* covers the mind's understanding and management of temporal and bodily affairs, and includes reflective action in the world (12. 3–4, 22–25).

Both aspects of the *mens* involve the use of Augustine's famous psychological trinity of *memoria*, "memory," *intelligentia*, "understanding," and *voluntas*, "will." He summarizes their interrelation as follows:

> These three, then, memory, understanding, and will, are not three lives but one life, not three minds but one mind. So it follows of course that they are not three substances but one substance. When memory is called life, and mind, and substance, it is called so with reference to itself; but when it is called memory it is called so with reference to another. I can say the same about understanding and will; both understanding and will are so called with reference to another. But each of them is life and mind and being with reference to itself. For this reason these three are one in that they are one life, one mind, one being. . . . But they are three in that they have reference to each other. And if they were not equal, not only each to the others but also each to them all together, they would not of course contain each other. In fact though they are not only each contained by each, they are all contained by each as well. (10.18)[38]

Memory, understanding, and will are thus not three separate minds, or even truly different parts or regions within the mind, like faculties, but rather are functions or activities of the single human mind, which is a whole, of one substance and *natura*. Trinitarian theological imperatives should be clear as well in the description of these three as equal and mutually coinhering, yet analytically separable as interrelated activities of mind. Let us examine each of these activities in turn.

As mentioned above, the metaphor of "internal sight" inside memory conceived as a kind of "storehouse" of impressions with "fields and vast palaces," a "huge cavern with its mysterious, secret, and indescribable nooks and crannies," opens up interior "space" within the soul (*conf.* 10.8.12–13; *Trin.* 9.10–11, 11.13–14). Within this space, the soul's "eye" or attention can move purposefully among memories, recollecting past events and imagining almost infinite possibilities by recombining elements or qualities of past experiences (*Trin.* 11.13, 17). But one's inner attention may also be seized, whether by the exceptionally "lively" powers of the senses themselves (12.20) or the compelling power of certain recollected sense impressions, which can provoke the strongest desire and fear and can even lead to delusory experiences of the false presence of alluring or terrifying objects (*Trin.* 11.7, *conf.* 10.8.12). Memory also includes skills "acquired through the liberal arts" (*conf.* 10.9.16), as well as the unchanging principles of mathematics

(10.12.19), and past *affectiones*, "emotions," of the soul (10.14.21). Memory is crucial to the sense of time for Augustine, where the vanishing present moment passes continuously into memory, flashing between expectation and recollection (11.17.36–18.37).

Memoria thus has two main aspects, as a repository for all experiences, ideas, emotions, and thoughts, and as the field for recollection, imagination, and thought itself (10.14.22). Thinking, *cogitatio*, consists in gathering together and ordering the dispersed contents of memory (10.9.18); these gathered and ordered thoughts can themselves be committed to memory "through the disciplines the *animus* is trained in" for later recall (*Trin*. 12.23). Augustine thus has a complex picture of an "inner world" within each of us, wherein we can roam over and examine our past acts, feelings, and thoughts, and consider the state and history of our souls. Indeed, at one point in the *Confessions*, he is moved to say of the "great power" of memory, which is "an awe-inspiring mystery," that "this is the soul (*animus*), and this I myself am" (*conf*. 10.17.26). Much can and has been said in comment on the influence of the *Confessions* as a stylized and highly theological project of remembering; its appearance is at the very least a significant event in the history of what may be justly called "the introspective conscience of the West."[39] For Augustine, in some sense we are our memories, and the project of gaining self-knowledge essentially includes self-examination via recollection of one's past, although Augustinian personal formation cannot be reduced to such recollection.[40]

Intelligentia, or "understanding," is arguably the activity most proper to *mens*, reflecting its high rank in the order of being (see *Trin*. 10.7, 10.11). I say this because it is the aspect of the mind concerned with the contemplation of eternal truths, and thus of God (12.22–25). Both wisdom (*sapientia*), "the intellectual cognizance of eternal things," and knowledge (*scientia*), "the rational cognizance of temporal things" (12.25), rely on the eternal form of truth. Augustine writes:

> Thus it is that we make judgments about these things [human character and works of art] according to that form of truth, and we perceive that by insight of the rational mind. . . . Thus it is that in the eternal truth according to which all temporal things were made we observe with the eye of the mind the form according to which we are and according to which we do anything with true and right reason, either in ourselves or in bodies. (9.11–12; see also 12.2)[41]

In other words, judgment in any temporal or physical matter relies on the eternal truths descried by the *sapientia* of the mind, the most basic of which is the *forma* of truth itself. Here, in a crucial move that underpins his theocentric anthropology, Augustine suggests that such awareness of eternity is possible because the human *mens* is "subjoined," *subjungeretur*, from below to the divine store of "non-bodily and everlasting ideas," *rationes incorporales et sempiternas*, which are permanent and unchanging (12.2). More precisely, by means of "the rational substance of our minds," we "cling from underneath to the intelligible and unchanging truth" (12.3). These eternal ideas are the proper subject of *sapientia*, and the means by which *scientia* may be attained; they are as it were a light within and above the darkness of the soul, and the voice of truth whispering in the mind's ear (*conf.* 7.10.16, *Trin.* 7.4–5; *conf.* 11.10).

The judgments of temporal matters that make up the substance of *scientia* are not merely "intellectual," in contemporary parlance, but are always evaluative and motivating:

> And by this form we conceive true knowledge (*notitia*) of things, which we have with us as a kind of word that we beget by uttering inwardly, and that does not depart from us when it is born. . . . And so there is nothing that we do with our bodies in deeds or words to express approval or disapproval of the behavior of men, which we have not anticipated with a word uttered inside ourselves. Nobody voluntarily does anything that he has not previously uttered as a word in his heart. This word is conceived in love of either the creature or the creator, that is of changeable nature or unchangeable truth; which means either in covetousness or in charity. (*Trin.* 9.12-13)[42]

As I discuss in more detail below in the discussion of will, Augustine holds a sophisticated view of the emotions as cognitive, depending on interpretive judgments, whether rational or misguided; or one might say that he views ideas and thoughts as inherently passionate and moving. As he says here, just as we have "internal sight" by which to scan our memory, we utter an "internal word" of judgment whenever we interpret some person or object in the world, rooted either in eternal truth and the love of God, or covetous desire for changeable things. This word is the beginning of action, its prerequisite, and it ought to be based on the unchanging forms or ideas of God, the "form[s] by which [we] love," take pleasure in objects, or decide to put something right if it is flawed, if our minds are properly ordered (9.11).[43]

The third primary mental activity, for Augustine, is *voluntas*, usually translated as "will." Augustine uses *voluntas* in a number of senses over the course of his many writings, and he never dedicates a treatise to a unified treatment of it.[44] A full accounting of the development of his views is beyond the scope of this chapter, and of this work as a whole.[45] Nevertheless, I think a powerful and largely consistent understanding of the will is discernible in Augustine's middle and late works, and that is what I sketch here.

In general, Augustine sees *voluntas* as the sum or collection of a person's loves, which aim at delighting in some end or ends (*civ. Dei* 14.7, *Trin.* 9.2).[46] He writes, in a crucial passage from *City of God*:

> And so a rightly directed will is good love and a perverted will is evil love. Therefore a love that strains after the possession of the loved object is desire; and the love that possesses and enjoys that object is joy. The love that shuns what opposes it is fear, while the love that feels that opposition when it happens is grief. Consequently, these feelings are evil, if the love is evil, and good if the love is good. (*civ. Dei* 14.7)[47]

Will *is* love, and not only that; the four classical emotions (desire, joy, fear, and grief, according to the Stoics, and Augustine) are forms of love, and thus will.[48] *Voluntas* is always intentionally directed toward some object, which it aims to possess and delight in, and it may derivatively be said to avoid some opposing object. *Voluntas* also may be said to oversee the selection or choice of different ends to be sought or shunned, according to its internal hierarchy of loves. Let us take each of these aspects in turn: will as emotion, will as intention, and will as the foundation of choice.

Augustine uses several different Latin terms for our English "emotion" (rather as English, derivatively, includes words such as "feeling," "passion," "affection," and "sentiment," each with different bloodlines and shadings). He sometimes speaks of *motus animi*, "motions of the soul"; sometimes of *affectus* or *affectio*, both meaning "feeling," "inclination," or "affection"; and sometimes even of *passio* or *perturbatio*, "passion" or "perturbation," when highlighting the soul's passivity.[49] In a passage from *City of God* slightly earlier than the one quoted above, he also considers the four emotions of desire, fear, joy, and grief:

> The important factor is the quality of a man's will (*voluntas*). If the will is perverse, it will have perverse emotions [or: movements] (*motus*); if the will is upright, they will be not only blameless, but praiseworthy. Certainly the will is involved in all of them; in fact they are all nothing other than wills (*voluntates*). For what is desire or joy but a will in agreement with what we wish for? And what is fear or grief but a will in disagreement with what we reject? . . . And in general, as a man's will is attracted or repelled in accordance with the varied character of different things which are pursued or shunned, so it changes and turns into feelings (*affectus*) of various kinds. (*civ. Dei* 14.6)[50]

The "movements of the soul" that are emotions, for Augustine, are *voluntates*, "wills" in the plural. This suggests that *voluntas* can have both a general and a specific sense: either a particular love, or the overall set or collection, however ordered or chaotic, of such loves (see *conf.* 8.8.19–8.12.30); the general use seems to be more prevalent. In what seems to be Augustine's only definition of the term "*voluntas*," in the relatively early anti-Manichean work *On the Two Souls*, he writes: "And so it is defined in this manner: *voluntas* is a motion of the soul, under no compulsion, toward either not losing or acquiring something" (*duab. an.* 10.14; also 12.16). Although much later Julian uses this definition insistently to hammer against Augustine's account of original sin, Augustine never renounces the definition itself, either in debate with Julian or in the *Reconsiderations*.[51] This suggests that he was content with the idea of *voluntas* as *animi motus*, and thus "emotion," throughout his adult life.

On this account, then, for Augustine *voluntas* is a blanket term for the emotional or appetitive forces in the soul that move a person to act.[52] *Voluntas* is the internal, felt component of our movements to pursue or shun desirable or fearful objects.

As reflected in the preceding quotation, the moral quality of one's *voluntas* is of paramount importance for Augustine, and this is discernible in terms of its end, that at which it aims. Augustine makes a distinction between "proper" or immediate ends and "final" ends that motivate more specific *voluntates*. He writes:

> For example, if someone wishes to see a scar in order to prove that here has been a wound; or if he wishes to see the window in order to see the passersby through the window; all such wills (*voluntates*) as these have their own proper ends which are referred to the end of that will by which we wish to live the happy life, . . . [which] will be all-sufficient to the lover in itself. . . . Now all wills are straight, and all the ones linked with them too, if the one to which they are all referred is good; but if that is bent then they are all bent. And thus a sequence of straight wills is a ladder for those who would climb to happiness, to be negotiated by definite steps; but a skein of bent and twisted wills is a rope to bind anyone who acts so, and have him cast into outer darkness. (*Trin.* 11.10)[53]

For Augustine, the final end of all human beings' wills is "the happy (or blessed) life," the *beata vita*; but the routes we think will take us there vary. The crucial dividing point, in his view, is whether we "refer" all of our subsidiary willing to the love of God or to the love of created reality, as diverging paths to happiness (*Trin.* 9.13). Certainly, however, in any given case one's *voluntas*, both general and specific, is intentional, aiming at some proximate, penultimate, and ultimate ends; and depending on the character of the higher-order ends, it is either a ladder to beatitude or an entangling rope by which we are caught and tied in carnality.

In the modern West, "will" has often seemed to denote a faculty of decision or choice, and the tendency of Augustine's Platonizing Latin to hypostatize abstractions into entities sometimes makes it seem as if he also views *voluntas* as this sort of executive power within the soul (e.g., *Trin.* 11.9, *conf.* 8.9.21ff.). For Augustine, willing as mental activity is executive in the sense that it is the motivating appetite and judgment of the *mens* leading to action, which may be distinguished as a result of an analysis of that action. But when he discusses the subject in detail, he generally separates out the subsidiary aspect of *voluntas* known as *liberum arbitrium*, "freedom of choice" or "free decision," as a way of focusing the issue.[54]

In debate with Pelagians, Augustine arrives at the position that true *libertas*—that is, freedom in the sense of the ability to love God fully, and hence will the good with complete righteousness—perished as a result of the Fall. Nevertheless, "freedom of choice" continues unaffected, in the sense that we choose without external constraint (as, e.g., by an evil Manichean god) to follow whatever we desire, that is, our *voluntas* (e.g., *c. ep. Pel.* 1.2.5). He writes: "In fact, all people sin by free choice, but in particular all those who sin with a delight in and with a love for the sin and who choose to do what pleases them. . . . They are free from righteousness only by the choice of the will, but they do not become free from sin except by the grace of the savior" (*c. ep. Pel.* 1.2.5).[55] Choice freely serves the will, but in our fallen state it is completely compromised in the sense that it cannot by itself effect a morally significant reversal of personal orientation to God; only God's grace can effect such a change (*spir. et litt.* 33.57ff.). *Liberum arbitrium* only confirms unregenerate humans in sinfulness, as will be discussed more fully in the following section. Similarly, in *On the Spirit and the Letter* Augustine remarks that "agreement" or "consent" *consentio* (as well as "disagreement" *dissentio*), whether to God's effective call or to some temptation, "belongs to the will"; as the discussion preceding this statement makes clear, this is a particular case of the use of *liberum arbitrium* (*spir. et litt.* 34.60).[56]

We are now in a better position to take stock of Augustine's final position on humans having been created in the "image" of God. Strictly speaking, we need to be "refashioned to the image of God" (*Trin.* 7.5); imaging God is a process, consisting of certain activities of the mind, not a state of being (7.12). Those activities are remembering, understanding, and willing/loving—not, however, when used for knowledge of temporal things but when activated as elements of wisdom, the contemplation of eternal truths (12.4). The mind's contemplation of itself provides a sort of proto-image, superior to the trinity discernible in the operations of *scientia*, which even with regard to the temporal data of Christian faith are "adventitious" to the operations of the mind itself (14.4–5, 11). The final and real image of the

Trinity can be seen in the mind remembering, understanding, and loving God, whereby it attains true wisdom (14.15). For temporal beings like us, according to Augustine, this love is a lifelong quest. He writes:

> Let us copy the example of this divine image, the Son, and not draw away from God. For we too are the image of God. . . . We are image because we are illuminated with light; that one [i.e., the Son, Christ] is so because it is the light that illuminates, and therefore it provides a model for us without having a model itself. . . . But we by pressing on imitate him who abides motionless; we follow him who stands still, and by walking in him we move toward him, because for us he became a road or a way in time by his humility, while being for us an eternal abode by his divinity. (7.5)[57]

For Augustine, being created in the image of God is not so much a fact as a task: the imitation of Christ, a difficult project that nonetheless leads to beatitude and the highest delight. (Chapter 7 addresses this process in more detail.)

This account of the soul and especially the mind as divine image also provides Augustine with theoretical support for a symbolic reading of the Fall in psychological terms. He explicitly offers an allegorical reading of the Genesis account of Eden, with Adam serving as the higher portion of the mind and Eve as the lower "assistant" portion of the mind that administers temporal realities, as they succumb to the temptation to delight in the forbidden fruit of love of bodies (*Trin.* 12.13). According to Augustine, "What happens is that the soul, loving its own power, slides away from the whole which is common to all into the part which is its own private property" (12.14). This greed is "the root of all evils," and it leads to anxious striving for possession of parts of creation, via use of one's own body, delighting in bodily shapes and movements. The soul thus "wraps itself in their images" and defiles itself by "fornicating" with created reality, taking subsidiary material ends as ultimate through worldly curiosity, searching for sensory experience, conceit and self-aggrandizement, or carnal pleasure (12.15). Because it is "in the things that it thinks about with love," the mind itself sticks with "the glue of love" to bodily images of things, and so it arrives by force of habit to be unable to imagine anything else (10.11; cf. 12.15). The mind cannot then recognize itself as immaterial and loses sight of eternal things, turning away from divine illumination (12.13). Little by little, the soul "in its private avarice is loaded with error and in its private prodigality is emptied of strength" (12.15). "For just as a snake does not walk with open strides but wriggles along by the tiny little movements of its scales, so the careless glide little by little along the slippery path of failure, and beginning from a distorted appetite for being like God they end up by becoming like beasts" (12.16).[58]

Apart from divine intervention, Augustine suggests, we each reenact the Fall in our own lives, puffing ourselves up in prideful imitation of God, only to fall into a disgraceful bestial existence unworthy of our station in the scale of being (see also 10.7).[59]

Summary

For Augustine, the concept of *natura* links together the inner and outer worlds, the unchanging and unseen with the apparent flux of our existence. He writes:

> Why then is the mind commanded to know itself? I believe it means that it should think about itself and live according to its nature, that is it should want to be placed according to its nature, under him it should be subject to and over all that it should be in control of; under him it should be ruled by, over all that it ought to rule. In fact many of the things it does show that it has twisted its desires the wrong way round as though it had forgotten itself. (*Trin*. 10.7)[60]

The scale of *naturae* is ordained by God, and it is thus not only the actual structure of reality, for Augustine, but also its proper structure, which can be momentarily and locally disrupted but not thwarted in its overall design. Both the scale and all the *naturae* that make it up are inherently good as created, and thus we ought to want (*appetere*) to take our proper place in the hierarchy and treat other elements of creation as they deserve to be treated, according to their true natures. But in the wake of the Fall, this hope has become vain, if our desires (*cupiditates*) are unaided by grace.

For Augustine, the events in Eden involving Adam, Eve, and the serpent were actual historical occurrences, with momentous and unmistakable consequences. They also, as recorded in the text of Genesis, symbolize important truths about the Catholic Church and the life of the blessed (in the description of paradise itself), and perhaps above all about human psychology and our inevitable tendency, in the wake of the Fall, to defect willingly from God in our own lives. He summarizes this aspect of his teachings in his exegesis of Paul in 1 Corinthians 15:21–22, where he writes:

> The Apostle puts this in more striking terms in the same letter: "It was by a man that death came; and by a man came the resurrection of the dead. For just as all die in Adam, thus will all be brought to life in Christ." Now undoubtedly this will be in a spiritual body that will exist in relation to a life-giving spirit. But it does not mean that all who die in Adam will be members of Christ, for the great majority of them will be punished with

> the second death, which is for ever. What the Apostle means by using "all" in both parts of the statement is that no one dies in his animal body except in Adam; and in the same way no one is brought to life in a spiritual body except in Christ. (*civ. Dei* 13.23)[61]

All human beings are derived from Adam, and in him our shared *natura* was vitiated and corrupted when he chose to turn away from God. All human beings pass on this vitiated nature to their offspring, even if they receive the grace of baptism. However, even though fallen, we never cease to be in the image of God. Nevertheless, we are now radically susceptible to further corruption, so that even the highest aspect of the soul, the *mens* or mind, is liable to turn away from eternal truth and become fascinated and enslaved by temporal and bodily reality. That remnant who will be regenerated by grace, although in this life only partially, will receive it only in and through Christ. Thus at least some will be "refashioned to the image of God," with the love of God poured into their hearts by the Holy Spirit, so that they may progressively advance in righteousness and be purified in will.

How does this account of the different aspects of human *natura* correlate with the bridge concept of human nature used in this study? As outlined in chapter 2, I have for present purposes specified the meaning of "human nature" in four ways. First, the term concerns human beings' physicality and animality (i.e., what connects us to other animals and living things), including our most basic, inevitable needs, and our common but more variable desires and aversions. Second, it is also a way of discussing what is common to all or most people. Sometimes, in tension with the first sense, it carries a third meaning of what is distinctively "human" about human beings, what separates them from other animals. Fourth, it concerns a spontaneous or "natural" course of human development.

Xunzi's treatment of *xing* 性 did not cover all of this terrain with equivalent depth of interest but was weighted strongly toward the first and second areas, leaving the fourth submerged and the third purposefully rejected (i.e., our *xing* is not what makes us distinctively human). Augustine's discussion of *natura*, however, is skewed differently, but it is perhaps remarkable in that it includes elements of each aspect while also extending beyond them. For Augustine, human *natura* is what we essentially are as a species of living thing: It is our "substance," our distinctive "being." This is primarily a metaphysically loaded version of the second aspect of human nature, that is, what is common to human beings, with some overlap with the third, what is distinctively human about them. It should be noted, however, that this "distinctiveness" means only that we, like every other type of existing thing, have a unique and definitive *natura* that places us in the divinely ordered scale of being. What that nature includes is not only what is *distinctively* human, that is, the rational mind, which other animals lack (*Trin.* 10.11, 12.1–2). Our *natura* also contains many elements shared with other animals, who have memory, habits, sensation, desires, and fears (*Trin.* 12.2, *conf.* 10.17.26); indeed, Augustine says that our vitiated nature makes us become similar to animals in our carnal existence, although no amount of sinfulness can make someone cease to be a human being (*gr. et pecc. or.* 2.40.46).[62] Though our nature as originally created by God prepared us perfectly to delight in our role in the divinely ordered hierarchy of being, our vitiated postlapsarian nature has led to an indefinitely extended repetition of the Fall in each person's life. Instead of spontaneously and naturally tending toward God in love and obedience, we are beset by concupiscence. Thus our spontaneous "natural" development as creatures will be, at least without sufficient divine grace, a slide into sinful, disintegrated oblivion. As for the first area of "human nature," our inevitable needs and vulnerability, Augustine certainly includes these as elements of our nature as bodies and souls or, in other words, as persons. I fill in more of the details of his account in the next section, on Augustine's conception of a person.

AUGUSTINIAN PERSONHOOD

As with *natura*, Augustine's word *persona* is the root of the English "person." "*Persona*" is rooted in the theater, with its primary meaning being a mask, often of clay or bark, worn by an actor to cover the head; it seems to be derived from the verb *persono*, "to sound through." Derivatively, it may mean a role, part, or character in a play. Cicero, however, also uses it to mean an individual or personality.[63] Augustine uses the word in two important senses, for the three "persons" of the divine Trinity, a usage bequeathed to him from previous Latin Christian tradition (*Trin.* 7.7), and as a shorthand notation for what human beings are; but these two senses are not simply or straightforwardly related.[64]

As Augustine applies it to human beings, *persona* seems to pick out individual human beings, in contrast to *homo*, which can refer either to an individual man or to the species of humankind (*Trin.* 12.18, 15.11; cf. 7.11). Above all, *persona* conveys the fact that a human being consists of both *anima*, soul, and *corpus*, body (*Trin.* 15.11). As Rist has argued, Augustine uses various terms for the nature of this combination, including *contemperatio*, a "proper" or "suitable mixture" (*quant.* 30.59); *mixtura*, a "mixing" or "blending" (*ep.* 137.3.11); *permixtio*, "mixture" (*Gn. litt.* 3.16.25); and a *conjunctum*, "conjunction" of the two parts (*civ. Dei* 13.24).[65] A mixing or blending seems to be the dominant metaphor, although with the caveat that each element retains its distinctive character, in contrast to the blending of material fluids into a composite (*ep*. 137.3.11). Augustine writes: "For just as soul is united to body in a single person so as to constitute man, in the same way is God united to man in a single person so as to constitute Christ. Thus in that person there is a blending of soul and body; in this person there is a blending of God and man" (*ep*. 137.3.11). It seems that Augustine's growing theological confidence in his understanding of Christ as a mysterious unity of God and man in one person made the everyday *coapto*, "joining together," by God of soul and body in persons intellectually palatable, if no less miraculous and astounding to merely human intellects (*civ. Dei* 22.24).[66] Augustine, then, sees the soul and body as highly suited to each other, as superior and inferior partners, conjoined most intimately and thoroughly (*quant*. 13.22, *civ. Dei* 13.24).

The relationship between soul and body within persons has altered with the damage to human nature due to the Fall, and it will change again at the final resurrection of the dead. Human souls and bodies were originally smoothly integrated in prelapsarian Adam and Eve, but our bodies are now prone to "disobedience" to the "commands" of the soul. The redeemed may look forward in hope to a full reintegration around a holy will, with an indestructible "spiritual body" free from disease, death, and shameful urges (*civ. Dei* 13.22–24; see also 12.24).

In his mature writings, Augustine does consistently hold that God created humans with sexed bodies, and that sex is in no sense a defect of human nature, contrary to the many in the ancient world who held that females were defective males. In the resurrection, all defects of our nature will be removed, but in our revivified spiritual bodies sex will remain, although there will be no need for marriage, intercourse, or childbirth in Heaven (*civ. Dei* 22.17). Furthermore, Augustine is quite clear that fundamentally speaking, male and female human beings are in an identical position: Both are made in the image of God insofar as both equally possess a mind that by means of *sapientia* images the triune God, a mind that in itself has no sex. He uses Genesis 1:27 to reread in a symbolic manner Paul's notorious statement in 1 Corinthians 11:7 that though man is the image and glory of God, woman is merely the glory of man, and so ought to be veiled; without such a reading the Pauline passage would be *inanis*, "pointless," Augustine thinks. Augustine contends that the apostle was symbolically referencing Augustine's own schema of *sapientia*, the masculine, directive part of the mind, and *scientia*, the lower feminine assistant, which ought to be "covered" or restrained to maximize the priority of contemplation (*Trin*. 12.10–12). Nevertheless, as this reading suggests, Augustine is hardly a feminist. He accepts male dominance in this life as a given, part of the hierarchical structures of fallen society that are divinely sanctioned insofar as they sustain earthly peace, and are partially redeemed insofar as they are motivated by loving concern for those ruled (e.g., women, slaves, children) instead of lust for domination (*civ. Dei* 19.14–15).

We can begin to untangle Augustine's concerns about the value of fallen human appetites by examining his related distinction between *caro*, "flesh," and *spiritus*, "spirit." On the basis of his reading of scripture, Augustine uses these terms, especially "the flesh," with purposeful double meanings (civ. *Dei* 14.2). In one sense, *caro* simply is another way to refer to the bodily dimension of human existence, precisely as fallen. Thus Augustine can write:

> The so-called pains of the flesh are really pains of the soul, experienced in the flesh and from the flesh. The flesh can surely feel no desire or pain by itself, apart from the soul. . . . Bodily pain is really nothing but a distress of the soul arising from the body, and a kind of disagreement with what happens to the body, in the same way as mental pain, which is called grief, is a disagreement with what has happened to us against our will. (14.15)[67]

Because of the fallen body's corruption, such experiences are now numerous and harrowing, instead of unknown, as in Eden (14.10–11, 15). But to see the flesh in this literal sense as the cause of our frequent sinning, due to its influence on the soul, is to err badly in assessing human nature (14.3).

For Augustine, "flesh" and "spirit" refer most properly to alternative modes of living, that is, to alternative orientations of the soul and its loves (14.1–2).[68] He writes:

> And so we are weighed down by the corruptible body; and yet we know that the cause of our being weighed down is not the true nature and substance of our body but its corruption; and therefore we do not wish to be stripped of it, but to be clothed with the immortality of the body. . . . For the corruption of the body, which weighs down the soul, is not the cause of the first sin, but its punishment. And it was not the corruptible flesh that made the soul sinful; it was the sinful soul that made the flesh corruptible. (14.3)[69]

The soul's voluntary self-corruption has led to the corruption of the body as a punishment; yet even understood thus, the locus of corruption is still the proud soul and not the frail, disobedient flesh. In his context, Augustine is remarkably positive about the value of the human body, far in spirit from the stridently antimarriage Jerome and from the Manichees, who saw the body as intrinsically evil; yet he still had considerable reservations about the desires of the body as fallen, significantly more than his late antagonist

Julian, for instance.[70] In the passage quoted above, Augustine consciously and explicitly contrasts his version of Christian teaching with the views of Virgil and Plato, who see the soul and body as opposed, and the body as the source of the emotions or passions, themselves regarded as the origin of sin and moral failure (14.3). Though Augustine allows that "the corruption of the flesh results in some incitements to wrongdoing and in actual vicious longings," the root problem is always the pride that has infected the entire human soul, including the mind, causing us "to live according to self, that is according to man [rather than God]" (14.3).[71]

These contrasting orientations of the soul, whether to God or to the self and the flesh, form the basis of the heavenly and earthly cities (*civ. Dei* 14.28, 15.1–2). He reflects this basic divide in his terminology about love and appetite, grouping all such yearnings under two headings, often called the "two loves": *caritas*, the holy but still burningly passionate love of God, and thus of God's creation and providential governance; and *cupiditas*, the inordinate desire for things of this world in themselves and for the private enjoyment of the lover, rather than with reference to God as their creator and ultimate end (*Gn. litt.* 11.15.20, *div. qu.* 35–36, *Trin.* 9.13, *gr. et pecc. or.* 1.20.21, *pat.* 20, *en. Ps.* 31.2.5, *s.* 90.6).[72] As discussed above in the context of the will, all "love"—that is, the more general terms *amor* and *dilectio*, as well as *caritas* and *cupiditas* (see *civ. De*i 14.7)—is a "striving" or "desiring," *appetendus*, a "movement," *motus*, toward something that is sought (*div. qu.* 35.1). According to Augustine, our hearts are perpetually unquiet, roaming and searching, and our desires can only be lastingly satisfied by God (*conf.* 1.1.1; cf. *civ. Dei* 14.25).

Given this picture, for Augustine we are never resting quietly (unless we are in the presence of God, beatified); we are constantly following some love or loves, and thus we are ascending or descending the scale of being and value at any given moment. Augustine writes, of the "interior words" that constitute the ongoing life of our minds:

> [Each word] is conceived in love (*amor*) of either the creature or the creator, that is of changeable nature or unchangeable truth; which means either in covetousness (*cupiditas*) or in charity (*caritas*). Not that the creature is not to be loved, but if that love is related to the creator it will no longer be covetousness but charity. It is only covetousness when the creature is loved on its own account. In this case it does not help you in your use of it, but corrupts you in your enjoyment of it. Now a creature can either be on a par with us or lower than us; the lower creature should be used to bring us to God, the creature on a par should be enjoyed, but in God. Just as you ought to enjoy yourself not in yourself but in him who

> made you, so too with the one whom you love as yourself. Let us then enjoy both ourselves and our brothers in the Lord, and from that level let us not dare to lower ourselves down even to our own, and so slacken off in a downward direction. (*Trin*. 9.13)[73]

The two loves are never static; we are always in motion, integrating ourselves in Christ or dispersing ourselves throughout temporal and bodily reality. Though I can do no more here than allude to the Augustinian distinction between *uti*, "to use," and *frui*, "to enjoy," suffice it to say that "using" things and people is highly idiomatic in Latin in a way that cannot be reproduced directly in English. Augustine uses the distinction itself primarily to mark the difference between properly loving people and things "in God," in the sense that they are properly understood and valued as dependent creations of God, and improperly loving them "in themselves," that is, apart from God and for one's own selfish delight in them. This latter love, *cupiditas* or "covetousness," is always decisively shaped by pride, Augustine thinks.

In the fallen and indeed "penal" state of our earthly existence, our loves never achieve complete purity; even the saints are plagued by the enduring presence within of *cupiditas* (*gr. et pecc. or.* 2.40.44; also *spir. et litt*. 36.65; *perf. just*. 11.28, 21.44). For Augustine, in general this is because of our inveterate *concupiscentia*, "concupiscence"; and more specifically, it is due to the intransigent power of *consuetudo*, "habit."

Concupiscence is present as a theme even in Augustine's early works. But especially with the advent of the Pelagian controversy, he begins to use it systematically as a way to summarize and specify the *vitium*, "fault," in our inherited *natura*, that is, the enduring damage caused by the Fall (*gr. et pecc. or.* 2.39.44).[74] Briefly, concupiscence is our tendency to feel covetous desire, even against our conscious rejection of such desire. Augustine, following 1 John 2:16, sees this tendency as having three main forms: "the concupiscence of the flesh and the concupiscence of the eyes and the ambition of the world," or sexual and other bodily lusts; misplaced curiosity[75] and the desire for sensory gratification; and above all, pride and the lust for dominance and acclaim (*gr. et pecc. or.* 1.20.21; *conf.* 10.30.41, 10.35.54; *vera. rel*. 38.69–71).[76] As the fault in our nature, such greedy concupiscence is present from birth, Augustine thinks (*civ. Dei* 13.13). It is evident even in infants, who petulantly strike their caregivers in misplaced anger and are overwhelmed with jealousy and bitterness when even their own siblings receive necessary sustenance from their mother, when there is plenty to go around (*conf*. 1.7.11). Furthermore, concupiscence seems to be magnified in human community: Our innate solidarity with other humans, stemming from the unity of our origin in Adam (*civ. Dei* 12.22, 14.1), easily becomes perverted into *inimica amicitia*, an "unfriendly friendliness" that scrambles our moral reservations and draws us more deeply into sin as we engage in acts we would never do alone, as in Augustine's famously pointless shared theft of pears (*conf.* 2.9.17; see also 9.2.2).

According to Augustine, the force of our concupiscence is so great that we all sin, necessarily (*nat. et grat.* 49.57–50.58, *perf. just.* 12.28, 13.31). Our fallen situation is even graver, however, given the power of habit. Writing of his current state of mind, as already converted to Christianity, baptized, and made priest and recently bishop, Augustine addresses God late in the *Confessions*:

> And sometimes you cause me to enter into an extraordinary depth of feeling marked by a strange sweetness. If it were brought to perfection in me, it would be an experience quite beyond anything in this life. But I fall back into my usual ways under my miserable burdens. I am reabsorbed by my habitual practices. I am held in their grip. I weep profusely, but still I am held. Such is the strength of the burden of habit. Here I have the power to be, but do not wish it. There I wish to be, but lack the power. On both grounds I am in misery. (*conf.* 10.40.65)[77]

For Augustine the new bishop, communion with God is fleeting but real, while habit steadily weighs on his soul like a heavy burden, making life not just a foreign sojourn but also a long trial.

The situation is even worse for the unredeemed. Without grace, habit dooms us to a spiral of ever greater depravity. Augustine writes of his spiritual state before conversion:

> The enemy had a grip on my will and so made a chain for me to hold me a prisoner. The consequence of a perverse will is desire (*libido*). By servitude to desire, habit is formed, and habit to which there is no resistance becomes necessity. By these links as it were, connected one to another, . . . a harsh bondage held me under restraint. (*conf.* 8.5.10)[78]

According to Augustine, the pleasure of satisfying our concupiscent desires has an intoxicating effect: By consenting to the pleasures they afford, we become slaves to our desires for temporal enjoyment. Our freedom to choose becomes attenuated, and eventually ceases, and even as the pleasure fades with repetition, we are chained to sin in such a way that stopping and turning back to God is impossible for us.[79] In this way, concupiscence infects us even more profoundly, thoroughly binding our will to the transitory things of this world, scattering our attention away from God, as we live a reactive, bestial existence, enslaved to passions beyond our control.[80]

Our wills, then, according to Augustine, are fundamentally damaged: They start out debilitated, and under our own machinations *secundum carnem*, "following the flesh," only become weaker and confirmed in vice. We do not ourselves possess the strength necessary to rise up to heavenly things but are dragged back to Earth by the weight of our earthly loves.

Given this analysis, Augustine's frequently discussed conception of the "divided will" is actually a step forward, a sign of significant spiritual progress. This is the condition wherein God by grace has awakened us to our sinful state and has begun illuminating our minds' understanding and kindling love for God in our hearts, but we have not yet received grace sufficient for conversion. In the continuation of the previously quoted passage, Augustine writes:

> The new will, which was beginning to be within me a will to serve you freely and to enjoy you, God, the only sure source of delight, was not yet strong enough to conquer my older will which had the strength of old habit. So my two wills, one old, the other new, one carnal, the other spiritual, were in conflict with one another, and their discord scattered my soul. (*conf.* 8.5.10)[81]

The beginning of active love for God in the soul generates a conflict of loves, with the varieties of *cupiditas* now opposed by the purity of *caritas*. This is not so much the "monstrous split" between willing and not willing the good that it might appear to be to someone straining to make a commitment to God and Christianity. It is rather an "illness of the soul which, when it is lifted up by the truth, does not unreservedly rise to it but is weighed down by habit. So there are two wills. Neither of them is complete, and what is present in the one is lacking to the other" (8.9.21).[82] Augustine rejects any multiplicity of substances, natures, or minds in human persons, but he does recognize a plurality of wills or loves within the overall will, the cumulative sum of these loves, in the sense discussed in more detail in the previous section (8.10.24). Such diverse wills are not *tota*, "complete" or "whole," and so fail to move the person to action or decision (8.9.21).

Much more can and has been written about conversion in Augustine.[83] Here, however, I need to deal with a possible criticism of my account of his views of understanding and willing. I have presented him as saying both that emotions are forms of love, and thus of will, and that emotions (and loves) are cognitive, integrated with evaluative judgments made by the mind's active understanding. A critic might argue, however, that such an account is false to a crucial element of Augustine's self-presentation in the *Confessions*, where he claims in book 7 to have come to an intellectual understanding of the truth but was only able to convert to it in the form of Christianity, with his *tota voluntas*, after further suffering and direct divine admonition, in book 8. On such a reading, Augustine wants to safeguard the possibility of intellectual judgment and will diverging; this would be the whole point of positing the will as a separate faculty or aspect of the mind.[84]

I argue that this common picture is misguided and misunderstands the ways in which Augustine thinks people can be divided against themselves. It also misreads the *Confessions*. In book 7, he does report an awesome initial vision of God, provoked by his reading of "Platonic books" (*conf*. 7.10.16). Here his weak internal sight is shocked by the strong radiance of the divine, revealed as truth, love, and eternity themselves, and above all as Being itself. "All doubt left me," he writes, concerning the supreme value and basic immaterial, unchangeable nature of God (7.10.16, 7.17.23). But this vision does not last, and he "was quickly torn away from [God] by my weight," the weight of carnal habit, and "with a groan I crashed into inferior things," left with only a loving memory of and desire for God (7.17.23).

Although thus far Augustine's report might be compatible with the objection, he goes on to explain his failure to remain with God not just in terms of habit but also because of a lack of sufficient understanding: "To possess my God, the humble Jesus, I was not yet humble enough. I did not know what his weakness was meant to teach" (7.18.24). At this point, Augustine thought of Christ as merely a wise man, and "had not begun to guess the mystery of the Word made flesh" (7.19.25). He wished to return his attention to God's immaterial nature, "but from the disappointment I suffered I perceived that the darknesses of my soul would not allow me to contemplate these sublimities" (7.20.26). He was "puffed up" with this new but limited knowledge of God, acting as if he were a wise man, but had learned nothing of *caritas* or humility from the Platonists. Reflecting on this later, he supposes that this sequence of incremental increases in wisdom was divinely directed, lest he suppose "that the same [Christian] ideas could be gained from those [Platonic] books by someone who had read only them" (7.20.26).[85] In sum, Augustine had been given insight into God's general nature (not material, not changeable, supreme in being) and recognized God as the supremely lovable entity in the universe; but because he was ignorant of Christ's true significance, he was also ignorant of how humans can come to blessedness, and thus he also did not know that his own pride was the final and most fearsome adversary to his redemption (7.21.27).

Augustine in retrospect saw that his carnal habit weighed him down, and pulled him back from God, but this tore him away from God only because pride still infected his soul. In terms of judgment, his mind had not yet turned away from the selfish enjoyment of worldly things and back to God; his standard was still the flesh, even if he had awakened to both the value and attractiveness of God as the supreme end and path to human beatitude. Augustine was simply not fully convinced—he still wanted continence in the abstract, but not quite yet (8.7.17). As he narrates the approach to the moment of his conversion, with multiple warring wills and the inability to will one thing fully and completely, complete with the figure of Lady Continence beckoning to him, he remarks: "I blushed with embarrassment because I was still listening to the mutterings of those vanities [his old loves, i.e., his carnal habits] and racked by hesitations I remained undecided." This was a "debate in my heart," a "struggle of myself against myself." His mind was still uttering inner words that were carnal in orientation, and Lady Continence bids him to stop his (internal) ear to them (8.11.27). Finally, his inner discourse is decisively interrupted by God—admonishing him, via the double mediation of a child's voice and Paul's Letter to the Romans, to "make no provision for the flesh in its lusts" but instead to "put on the Lord Jesus Christ" (8.12.29; Rom. 13:13–14). At last, "all the shadows of *dubitatio* [both 'hesitation' and 'doubt'] were dispelled" (8.12.29).[86]

Obviously, much could and has been said about the various literary and theological aspects of Augustine's account of his conversion in the *Confessions*. With respect to the issue at hand, however, during this narration Augustine never departs from the view presented above that evaluative judgments are part of all human willing, and thus all human love and emotion. Augustine needs grace to overcome his carnal habits and his pride, which form an interlocking system of judgment and impulse that has led him away from God and that perpetually threatens to turn him away from God again, should he consent to the concupiscence that remains in him even after his conversion and baptism. Only after the final healing of the resurrection will this struggle completely cease.

There is thus a basic asymmetry in the power of the human will, according to Augustine, which is only exacerbated by the effects of the Fall.[87] Human persons are always capable of willing evil, of loving mutable things, under our own power; yet by ourselves we are incapable of fully willing the good, and loving God effectively. Indeed, the cause of our evil actions is always the human will, and the cause of good actions is God's grace filling us with sufficient love (*civ. Dei* 12.9, *spir. et litt*. 7.11). We have received every good thing in us from God, Augustine reasons, following Paul, and so there is no reason for boasting of our merits, which warrant only condemnation. The lasting damage of the Fall remains with us in the form of concupiscence even in the regenerate, as well as the tendency of all flesh to sickness, decrepitude, and eventual death. Carnal habits remain an obstacle to the purity and steadfastness of our love. But with divine support, we may yet progress day by day in righteousness, and finally be free of sin and death. Some of the techniques for this "crucifixion of the inner man" (*Trin.* 4.6) will be examined in chapter 7.

NOTES

1. See, e.g., Brown 1967, Chadwick 1986, Rist 1994, TeSelle 1970, and Wetzel 1992.

2. Thus TeSelle 1970, 20.

3. Rist 1994 is a case in point.

4. Van Fleteren 1999.

5. On Manicheism generally, see Lieu 1992. For Augustine's comments on Manichean practices, with a systematic contrast to Catholic Christian practices, see *mor.* For an illuminating recent study of Manichean practice, see BeDuhn 2000.

6. He was, however, charged near the end of his life by Julian of Eclanum with having failed to break sufficiently with Manichean doctrines, particularly regarding, sex, sin, and the body. On this, see especially Brown 1967, Clark 1986, and Fredriksen 1988.

7. As translated in Burleigh 1953, 326.

8. As translated in Burleigh 1953, 236.

9. Translation adapted from Burleigh 1953, 327.

10. Rist 1994, 8, 13, 20–21.

11. As translated in Bettenson 1984, 535.

12. Translation adapted from Bettenson 1984, 523.

13. As translated in Bettenson 1984, 567.

14. The best secondary accounts of these Augustinian falls, simultaneously accurate, sympathetic, and critical, are Babcock 1991b, 87–113, and Babcock 1992.

15. As translated in Bettenson 1984, 570.

16. As translated in Bettenson 1984, 571–72.

17. Babcock 1991b, 111 n. 16. His target here is Brown 1978.

18. Babcock 1991b, 103.

19. As translated in Bettenson 1984, 477.

20. As translated in Bettenson 1984, 478.

21. See also *civ. Dei* 14.13, *c. Jul. imp.* 5.35–39. On this point, see also Babcock 1991b, 111 n. 16.

22. Translation adapted from Bettenson 1984, 479–80.

23. Charles Mathewes (1999, esp. 208, 210–11) finds the undamaged will's inexplicable defection to be the sine qua non of freedom of choice, in the modern sense of an unconstrained capacity to pursue genuinely divergent ends, and a successful theological bulwark against divine responsibility for evil. He also suggests that the first sin is unintelligible qua voluntary sin, but that it can be described as a perverse affirmation of a lesser good above a greater one. Robert F. Brown (1978; cf. Babcock 1991b, 111 n. 16) contends that "an absolute origin of evil, arising from the free will of a creature, must be incomprehensible," but then suggests that Augustine only inconsistently recognized this,

and provided various inadequate causal explanations despite his better judgment. John Rist (1994, 104–8) suggests that creation not only comes from but tends to nothingness, and nothingness is thus created beings' "localization of weakness;" the fall then is "almost inevitable," yet still senseless, and Adam's reasons for choosing sin are "utterly incomprehensible."This is, however, purposeful on Augustine's part: he refuses to give a full but false explanation for what is truly inexplicable. Babcock (1991b, 101–5) suggests that because of the discontinuity between the character, emotions, and context of the Edenic agents and their first sinful acts, the turn away from God is "utterly inexplicable," and that the notion of deficient causation is too thin to be distinguished from pure chance (perhaps the ultimate case of bad luck); humans and the rebel angels are not finally recognizable as moral agents. James Wetzel (1992, 213) concurs with Babcock, but puts the point in terms of the unintelligibility of Adam and Eve's reasons for sinning, i.e., their misrepresentations of lesser as greater goods, given their favorable initial conditions of sufficient knowledge of and love for the Good; again their moral agency is fatally compromised.

24. Rist 1994, 104–8, esp. 106–7. See the previous note for discussion.

25. See note 23 above for citations.

26. Babcock 1991b, 101–5.

27. Interestingly, Augustine once seems to suggest that it was a (misguided) desire for freedom that motivated Adam to disobey God's command (*civ. Dei* 14.15; cf. 13.13). In the full context of that chapter, however, this seems to be a description of Adam's pride in turning away from God, more than an explanation for the defection.

28. On the "aesthetic theme" in Augustine, see Hick 1977.

29. Translation adapted from Bettenson 1984, 512–13.

30. Clark 1986.

31. Translation adapted from Chadwick 1991, 3.

32. Translation adapted from Chadwick 1991, 43.

33. As translated in Teske 1997, 180.

34. Translation adapted from Hill 1991, 322.

35. O'Daly (1987, 7–8) provides an acute analysis of Augustine's various uses of *anima* and *animus*.

36. In *Trin.* 10.9 Augustine distinguishes between the physical organ of the heart, and the frequent, perhaps even "improper" figurative use of the term in Biblical texts as a synonym for *animus*, a rhetorical move in which he frequently engages as well.

37. *Intentio* literally means a stretching or tension, and figuratively suggests exertion, effort, and attention, as well as purpose or intention.

38. As translated in Hill 1991, 298–99.

39. A classic source for this is Stendahl 1976; see also Taylor 1989, 127–42. The beginning of sophisticated contemporary analyses of the *Confessions* is Courcelle 1950. For a concise but fuller review of the most important scholarship, see O'Donnell 1992, vol. 1, xx–xxxii.

40. Wetzel 1992, 160, 168, 215, and in general chapters 4 and 5. Note however, that this is not an omnipresent and unambiguous theme in Augustine's other writings. In *Trin.* 9.1, for example, he interprets Paul in Phillipians 3:13–15 as counseling that

"perfection in this life . . . is nothing but forgetting what lies behind and stretching out to what lies ahead intently. The safest intent, after all, until we finally get where we are intent on getting and where we are stretching out to, is that of the seeker" (as translated in Hill 1991, 270). See also *en. Ps.* 83.1.3–4 for further discussion and scriptural citations.

41. As translated in Hill 1991, 277.

42. As translated in Hill 1991, 277–78.

43. As translated in Hill 1991, 277. The Latin is: "Statim amor ille, quo in eum ferebar, offensus, et quasi repercussus, atque ab indigno homine ablatus, in ea forma permanet, ex qua eum talem credens amaveram." Obviously the English rendition reorders the Latin, but the idea of a form by which someone is loved when they are believed to resemble it is explicitly present.

44. Djuth 1999 is particularly illuminating on this point.

45. For more comprehensive assays of his ideas on the will, see Rist 1994 and Wetzel 1992.

46. Rist 1994, 140.

47. Translation adapted from Bettenson 1984, 557.

48. In what follows, I owe a great deal to Wetzel's analysis in 1992, 99ff.

49. *Motus animi* (or *animi motus*), e.g., *doc. Chr.* 2.2, 2.3, *civ. Dei* 8.17, *en. Ps.* 4.6, 9.8; *affectus*, e.g., *conf.* 2.9.17, 8.7.17, 10.14.21; *affectio*, e.g., *lib. arb.* 3.9.26, *Gn. litt.* 11.34.46, *civ. Dei* 12.6; *passio* and *perturbatio*, e.g., *civ. Dei* 14.8-9.

50. Translation changed in several ways from Bettenson 1984, 555–56. See Wetzel 1992, 101, for discussion. See the section on "consent" in chapter 5 below for fuller analysis of *consensio/consentire* in this passage.

51. See *c. Jul. imp.* 5.40–43, 5.51. In *retr.* 14.3, Augustine notes that his point in this passage was to distinguish cases where someone willed from cases where they did not will, and that strictly speaking this occurred only in Eden. After the Fall, carnal habit binds us in such a way that the lack of compulsion in the definition must be qualified, if not renounced (for Augustine, there is never an evil substance compelling sinful action, as the Manichees attest). These matters are discussed in more detail in the next section of this chapter.

52. For a discussion of love as essentially appetitive, and a correlation of these appetites with the various natures of those entities in the order of being that feel them, see *civ. Dei* 11.28.

53. Translation adapted from Hill 1991, 312.

54. Over his lifetime, Augustine's ideas and terminology in this area were even more fluid than in some other areas of his thought. Particularly misleading is the idiosyncrasy of his treatment in the now widely read but early *De libero arbitrio*, which was completed in two stages, before and after a significant change in his thinking about human willing. Again see Wetzel 1992 and Rist 1994 for more precise historical accounts of the changes in his views and use of terms.

55. As translated in Teske 1998, 118.

56. For further reflection on "consent" in Augustine, see the relevant section of chapter 5.

57. As translated in Hill 1991, 223.

58. As translated in Hill 1991, 331.

59. Augustine also, in *Trin*. 12.17, offers a second allegory of the Genesis account of the Fall in terms of particular sinful acts, analyzed in terms of the different parts of the soul. The account is problematic and somewhat ambiguous, but I think it should be understood, in an apparent but superficial paradox, as discussing our experience as already fallen, carnal beings. Augustine here talks, rather platonically, as if sensual appetite seduces *scientia* by suggesting to it opportunities for selfish sensual enjoyment (like the serpent addressing Eve). If the mind consents at a merely notional level, but *sapientia* restrains it from actively sinning, this is "as if the woman alone ate the forbidden food," a truly mysterious possibility. But if full consent is given, this is as if both shared the food, and the mind at its highest levels ("that application of the mind which has the supreme power to move the limbs to action or restrain them from action" [translation adapted from Hill 1991, 332]) plunges into and enslaves itself to temporal reality. It is especially odd for Augustine to speak as if sensation itself, and not carnal concupiscence, is evil; this seems to me to be contrary to his considered positions on concupiscence and the appetites of the body, to be discussed more fully in the following section. As I read Augustine, pride is a disorder of the whole soul, centered in the mind, and this is why some sensations are even interpreted as opportunities for selfish enjoyment contravening the divine order of creation; the problem is in the mind itself, not in our sensations. For further discussion, see the section on "consent" in chapter five.

60. As translated in Hill 1991, 292.

61. Translation adapted from Bettenson 1984, 539–40.

62. Augustine makes the point in the same place, however, that of course animals are not subject to condemnation, because they cannot share in beatitude, and so are also exempt from misery in the condition proper to them. For humans to live like beasts, however, is disgraceful.

63. Lewis 1995, 607; Katz 1999.

64. Cf. Katz 1999, who asserts that the theological sense is fundamental. Augustine seems to recognize the incongruity between the two uses in *Trin*. 15.11.

65. See Rist 1994, 99.

66. Rist 1994, 100. On *coapto* as the manner in which God both joins human nature to Himself in Christ, and joins body to soul in people, see *ep*. 137.3.12.

67. As translated in Bettenson 1984, 576.

68. On the sense of Augustine's phrases *secundum carnem* and *secundum spiritum* in *City of God*, see Carney 1991, esp. 35 n. 5.

69. As translated in Bettenson 1984, 550–51.

70. On this, see Brown 1988. See also Miles 1979.

71. First translation Bettenson 1984, 551. On pride as the root sin responsible for the conflict between flesh and spirit, see Burns 1991, 82, and Rist 1994, 96–97.

72. For insightful discussion of this, see Babcock 1991a, 39–66, esp. 58–59.

73. As translated in Hill 1991, 278.

74. A helpful introduction to these issues and some of the secondary literature is Burnell 1999.

75. Curiosity in this pejorative sense may be contrasted with the "appetite for finding out," the "sort of love that the studious have" that is highly praiseworthy, because it is directed to the understanding of God (*Trin.* 9.18, 10.1).

76. As translated in Teske 1997, 414.

77. As translated in Chadwick 1991, 218.

78. Translation adapted from Chadwick 1991, 140.

79. For a comprehensive survey of this theme, see Prendiville 1972. See also Rist 1994, 175ff., who errs only by glossing the important distinction between the "fault" *vitium* in our actual nature as fallen, and the literary trope of "second nature" that Augustine occasionally borrows from classical authors as a way of talking about the force of habit, especially for sin.

80. This state of flourishing concupiscence, however, can for Augustine have a role in the economy of salvation: It undercuts pride by exposing our frailty and sinfulness in an unmistakeable way, so that we see no other choice but to call on Christ for aid (*corrept.* 9.24). On this, see Burns 1991, 83.

81. Translation adapted from Chadwick 1991, 140.

82. Translation adapted from Chadwick 1991, 148.

83. Wetzel 1992 is a searching analysis of Augustine's changing views of conversion.

84. This objection is a modified form of the one Wetzel (1992, 2ff.) considers in his introductory chapter. Thinking about his discussion of these matters has provoked much of my interpretation of Augustine, which is quite similar to his. Nevertheless, I do not resolve all the difficulties in exactly the way he does, nor do I read books 7 and 8 of the *Confessions* just as he does. Briefly, I reject the idea that Augustine receives a complete "intellectual" vision of God in 7.10.16; he receives only a partial one, as much as he can absorb, and besides freedom from the force of habit he does still need "more and better knowledge of God," contra Wetzel 1992, 2 (although it is sometimes difficult, given Wetzel's style, to tell exactly when he is giving his own views and when he is offering a hypothetical alternative). In general, my interpretation is close to Carney 1991, which reads the mature Augustine as propounding a "double-matrix ethic" of truth *and* love.

85. As translated in Chadwick 1991, 127, 128 (adapted), 128, 130, 130.

86. As translated in Chadwick 1991, 152, 153.

87. Babcock 1991b, 105–7.

CHAPTER FIVE

Comparing Human "Natures"

✦

REVISITING BRIDGE CONCEPTS

Bridge concepts aim to provoke accounts of widely separated figures in terms of a common set of topics that highlight particular points of similarity and difference. By creating more precise points of contact, the comparativist can provide the basis for an imaginary dialogue between the two positions thus articulated and thereby pursue more substantive investigations of the general topic the bridge concept specifies. Thus a bridge concept like "human nature" can serve to generate what might be called a *problématique* for inquiry. The process works as follows: Comparison provokes conceptual analysis of what at first seemed to be a straightforward idea such as "human nature," which in turn provokes deeper interpretive investigations on each side, which lead to articulated positions that can be seen, at least partially, to speak to each other in various ways. Sorting out the issues thus raised spurs further ethical analysis of the subtopics in question.

Most crucially in the present case, Augustine's and Xunzi's accounts of human nature are not theoretically isolated but are themselves enmeshed in larger projects of person formation. At the most general level, at least, both thinkers charge "human nature" with grave flaws and deficits, as well as important potentials. Both the deficits and the potentials, however, describe possible arcs of development, whether ascending toward the angels or sage kings, or descending into corruption and pettiness. This chapter begins to chart this motive aspect of accounts of human nature as justifications and guides for self-cultivation more explicitly, in preparation for the subsequent chapters on their proposed spiritual exercises.

To make headway with this comparison, then, we must first attend closely to the various aspects of "human nature" as a bridge concept and thereby delve beyond the surface similarities in the views of Augustine and Xunzi to begin to grapple with the distinctive strengths and weaknesses of each figure's ethical vocabulary. Despite the facile identification of Augustine's and Xunzi's positions by Dubs in the middle of the twentieth century, the evidence adduced in chapters 3 and 4 suggests that the differences between their two accounts are quite significant.

For Augustine, the bridge concept of "human nature" correlates fairly well with his own term *natura*. According to him, human *natura* is our essential being, placing us high in the divinely ordained hierarchy of being, superior to inanimate things, plants, and animals but inferior to angels and God. This *natura* is shared by all human beings, and it is distinctive to us as a species in comparison with other types of things, each of which has its own *natura*. *Natura* includes every salient aspect of human beings, including what is distinctive to us, our rational minds, as well as what is shared with other animals: memory, habits, sensation, desires and fears, and the bodily existence that makes these things possible. In the wake of the primordial Fall, we have been justly punished with a vitiated version of our original nature, and our existence as persons, as mixtures of body, *corpus*, and soul, *anima* and *animus* (including mind, *mens*), is marked by profound deficits: a tendency toward covetous desire for earthly goods, including food, sex, companionship, praise, wealth, and power; and susceptibility to destructive habits that cement these desires into our memories in such a way that we become enslaved to a bestial and corrupt existence.

Although for Augustine our embodied existence has become a locus for the punishment of original sin, and for the repetition of sin, our mind still carries the indelible imprint of its creator. Our minds are made in the image of God, and no amount of sinning can destroy this. Our deepest desire remains fixed on God, and so we can never truly rest without full divine presence. Given this deep yearning for the divine, to the extent that we become entangled in carnal delight (i.e., the love of created things in themselves rather than as creations of God), we are inwardly at war with ourselves. For Augustine, however, this internal struggle does not map cleanly onto different psychological faculties, such as reason and emotion, or warring substances, such as light and darkness, or even aspects of human personhood like body and soul. On his account, we are composites of different substances joined in a "mixture" or "marriage" that should be loving and marked by obedience of lower to higher but is instead marked by disobedience and chaotic impulses of rebellion against just order. Perhaps surprisingly, Augustine characterizes this tendency to rebellion in terms of a structurally unified mind that speaks internal "words" involving the integrated activity of memory, understanding, and will or love. However, in spite of its formal unity, the mind has been infected at the highest levels with a pride that divides it from God and, in a cascade of deviations, divides the mind against itself and the body from the soul.

For Xunzi, by contrast, the standard identification of *xing* 性 with "human nature" is incorrect, given my analysis of the idea as a multifaceted bridge concept. To get at Xunzi's views of human nature in a contemporary sense, one must attend not only to *xing*, "innate endowment" or "instincts," but also to *qing* 情, "disposition" and "emotion," as well as to Xunzi's separate discussions of what is unique about human beings and what is common to humans and other animals, as well as his larger accounts of psychology and moral development. Indeed, when considered in this larger context, it is clear that *xing* does not even exhaust what is common to human beings but instead focuses on what we do spontaneously and effortlessly, without thought, in contrast to all that is *wei* 偽, "artificial" or constructed in human life.

According to Xunzi, human beings have an innate endowment, the "raw material" of personhood, which is made up of sensory capacities and a responsive disposition. He construes this disposition as made up of certain positive and negative emotional tendencies, or rather he appears to conceive of emotions primarily as dispositions to feel and act in certain ways. These *qing* generate more specific desires as the sense organs discern objects and the heart/mind becomes aware of various possibilities. Our innate emotions and desires, however, are "bad" for two reasons. First, they produce awful consequences if followed without external or internal restraint. And second, they tend generally toward destructive, shortsighted selfishness (although they do include some sociable instincts as well). If dependably satisfied, they are liable to proliferate well beyond our basic needs. Except for our ability to form and follow distinctions, which seems also to underlie our metastasizing desires, human beings are no different from other animals, such as apes, who share similar appearance, sensory constitution, and responsive, desiring modes of action. According to Xunzi, our spontaneous impulses include our shared desires for food, sex, shelter, rest when tired, companionship with similar creatures, and social dominance.

The human heart/mind, however, can affect these spontaneous, instinctual processes in ways unavailable to other animals. It can examine and plan, consider possible actions and consequences, relate disparate perceptions and ideas into complex wholes, and above all learn new skills and information. All these activities can interpenetrate with our spontaneous desires in any given situation, especially through the heart/mind's ability to overrule spontaneous desires by assenting to particular aims or goals. Over time, the heart/mind can learn to remain empty, unified, and tranquil in the midst of this active deliberation, even if at first these nascent abilities are limited and weak, and easily swayed by desires and aversions. Learning, whether correct or misguided, tends to accumulate and affect the judgments one makes and the actions one is moved to take. For Xunzi, the Confucian Way is the comprehensive object of learning, the pursuit of which will nurture these capacities into full flower.

Thus Xunzi takes *qing* and *xing*, terms that had been used before him in relatively strong ways to mark the "fundamental nature" or "essence" of a thing and its genetic trajectory of birth, growth, decline, and death, and redefines them in minimalist ways. Our *xing*, for Xunzi, is what is innate, thoughtless, and instinctive, what requires no work or delay to become so; in contrast, *wei* 偽, or "artifice," is necessary to develop the heart/mind and become truly human, to become persons in any strong sense. Our *qing* consists of evaluatively loaded dispositions to feel and act in certain ways, which in turn generate specific desires in response to particular situations. As a matter of logic, Xunzi seems to be assuming that certain potential capacities must exist in the heart/mind for it to be capable of learning complex theories about human life and the cosmos, restraining and reshaping emotion and desire, and commanding socially prescribed actions. Yet he does not ascribe these to our *xing* but to the heart/mind and to "artifice," his marker for that which takes conscious effort over time to achieve.

Xunzi and Augustine, then, differ both in the architecture and the substance of their moral anthropologies. Augustine unifies all human beings in the concept of *natura*, which he then specifies in terms of body, soul, "inner" and "outer man," and mind, each of which he analyzes in itself and in its relations to the other elements of human personhood. For Xunzi, what "makes us human" is our capacity to make distinctions, by means of the heart/mind; our innate endowment, dispositions, and desires are no different from other primates' and deserve no special respect. To become genuinely humane persons, Xunzi thinks, we must develop and rely on the educated heart/mind, and this process of development will eventually transform us from our animalistic beginnings.

The various aspects of "human nature" can have rather different theoretical valences. For both Augustine and Xunzi, accounts of our instinctive desires and aversions provide grounds for pointed criticism of some of our drives, and thereby partly define the problems and objectives for their regimes of personal formation. The powers that should be brought to bear on these drives, however, are for Xunzi at least emphatically not instinctive or spontaneous. For both thinkers, attention to human desires pushes us beyond a consideration of "human nature" alone, toward a broader account of moral psychology and even moral anthropology. Much of the rest of this chapter comparatively develops various themes in this area, examining topics such as desire, emotion, habit, and will, in preparation for the subsequent analysis of their proposed spiritual exercises.

Both thinkers' assessments of what is common to all human beings, as well as what is distinctive to us as a species, help develop the substance of their moral anthropologies. These accounts of commonality and distinction also serve to place human beings in a broader religious cosmos. Contrary to readings of Augustine and Xunzi as pessimistic, both these thinkers give humans rather lofty stations in the broader ecology of existence. Strikingly, both place us in what could be called penultimate positions: inferior and subject to the greatest beings (angels and God, for Augustine) or powers (Heaven and Earth, for Xunzi), but superior to everything else in the universe. Their distinctive cosmologies help provide the tenor or color of their pictures of personal formation. (These themes are developed in greater detail in chapters 6 and 7.) For Augustine, we must take care to do all we can to ascend toward divinity, reversing the fall "downward," using lower beings only insofar as they contribute to this process, and cultivating grateful obedience, humble dependence on Christ, and active, joyful service. By such means we may eventually return to our true home and true rest, in effect leaving our current station and ascending to a more stable and blessed angelic position (*corrept.* 10.27). For Xunzi, we are to actively administrate the existence of all living things, especially ourselves, like good and capable ministers serving their lord. Xunzi explicitly warns us not to try to ascend in the cosmic hierarchy but to come to dwell happily and well in our current, inevitable station, which can be made splendid and beautiful, or wretched and chaotic, depending on the character of shared human activity. Eternal beatitude beckons Augustine; Xunzi dreams of the beautiful order of the Way prevailing completely under Heaven. Both figures are concerned to inspire their audiences toward dramatically better possibilities that can and will be achieved, if their proposals are followed.[1]

Last, both thinkers chart courses of "natural" development in order to warn us away from predictable doom; both decry the social chaos, war, and human degradation that uncorrected human action is prone to foment, and Augustine points as well to damnation as the final, just result of these evils for the individual souls that pursue them. This fourth aspect of the bridge concept serves to articulate more fully the dangerous consequences of human sinfulness, to use Augustinian language. At the micro level of individual formation, however, this developmental dimension serves to condition each figure's account of spiritual exercises by articulating various dangers and weaknesses that must be avoided or corrected over time if a person is to become virtuous.

Let us turn now to develop some of the deeper issues implied by both thinkers' moral anthropologies, through more precise comparisons of particular issues.

COMPARATIVE MORAL PSYCHOLOGY: THEMES FOR FURTHER DEVELOPMENT

The mind (i.e., *mens* for Augustine, *xin* 心 for Xunzi) is for both our subjects the unified center of thought and feeling. Both use imagery of rulership to describe the mind's role within the person, although for Augustine this metaphor is double-edged: The human mind is in the midst of a chain of command, subject to God, its rightful lord. Trying to command oneself apart from God is one of Augustine's paradigms for sin. Thus for Augustine obedience to God is essential to the mind's proper functioning, whereas for Xunzi there is no such requirement, although we can only learn to feel and think wisely through inculcation into the practices of the Confucian Way. (Their differing senses of appropriate "subjection" or dependence are examined more carefully in chapter 8.) For Xunzi, the mind is always capable of ruling the body, although its abilities to analyze, reflect, and judge need significant development to have any positive effect on our existence. We might say that for Augustine the fallen mind is fundamentally weakened, out of joint with reality, its view of the truth congenitally but not totally obscured, and it needs surgery and a convalescent period to come to understand and love the truth. For Xunzi, by contrast, the mind's capacities are at risk because of the general direction and tenor of our innate impulses, but it carries undamaged potential and suffers no fundamental epistemological deficits other than complete ignorance. For Xunzi, truly dangerous obscuration of the heart/mind is the result of miseducation, misplaced conviction, and the often natural development of vicious customs or habits.

The unity of the different aspects of the mind is a striking feature of both their accounts, although how exactly they analyze the various powers and activities of the mind varies. (I pursue this theme most fully in chapter 8 by developing an account of the two figures' distinctive versions of "chastened intellectualism" in moral anthropology; I lay some of the groundwork for that account here.) For Xunzi, the mind can be—and must develop its capacities to be—empty, unified, and tranquil, and it can make and observe numerous distinctions with increasing precision. By this he means that we are and remain open to new experience, and yet can store memories of past ideas and observations without disrupting our ongoing openness; we can learn to relate our ideas, impressions, and memories together into a whole without losing sight of particular ones, and "unify" or focus our attention on particular objects, thoughts, and goals; we can learn to remain unperturbed and alert in the process of living, acting, and thinking; and we can make subtle distinctions and judgments between phenomena, especially concerning human social life, and act on those judgments. For his part, Augustine analyzes the mind as a single immaterial substance that remembers, understands, and loves, and he explicates this by means of the metaphor of the mind as a person within oneself, with an "inner ear," "inner eye," and "inner mouth" that hear, see, and speak inner words that precede normal language and action. Our interior perception can gradually become strong enough to contemplate and love eternal truths; but in the unregenerate state, such "divine light" appears so strong that it is painful to us, and we would turn away from it without help to withstand the shock.

To fill out these general pictures, and to articulate specific points of agreement and disagreement between Augustine and Xunzi, I turn now to a sequence of anthropological and psychological themes that have been broached in chapters 3 and 4 but that need to be developed further in tandem. These themes are (1) desire, (2) the complex relations of emotions and dispositions as a first assay of the topic of "the will," (3) the powers and debilities of memory and habit, and (4) the idea of assent or consent as a second approach to willing.

Desire

Both Xunzi and Augustine conceive of desire as a fundamental aspect of human motivation, and thus they see desire as in large part defining the field of what is problematic in human life—why do we desire wrongly, and how might we come fully to desire what is good? Thus for both thinkers, the human tendency to desire merely apparent rather than real goods is a deep-seated ethical difficulty.[2]

Despite their relatively similar lists of what our typical desires include, however, profound differences appear in the two thinkers' general analyses of desire. Augustine links his psychology of desire at its deepest levels to the metaphysical hierarchy ordained by God, and to humanity's defection from this just and beautiful order. For Augustine, desire always has a "vertical" dimension—up toward God or down away from Him—which corresponds to a fundamental formal difference between expansive desires (*caritas*) to share in universally present, unchanging goods like God, and constrictive, covetous desires (*cupiditas, libido*) to hold and possess earthly goods in a private manner for one's own enjoyment. Almost all our damaged "natural" desires fall into this category for Augustine, although our deepest natural desire is still for rest in God.

For Xunzi, in contrast, there is no categorical contrast between types or forms of desire. Human desires aim at real goods, in the sense that the objects desired are not intrinsically evil; but these goods may or may not be properly ordered within the highest good, which for Xunzi consists of following the human Way. For Xunzi, then, impulses to action can be consonant with the Way or disruptive of it, but the fundamental structure of desire (judgment of lack, felt yearning, and frustration or satisfaction) remains the same regardless of the object of desire. Though Xunzi does distinguish between good and bad desires, he does not conceive of this distinction in terms of an absolute contrast between opposing orientations to good and evil. Tempting alternatives to the Way are skewed and incomplete, according to Xunzi, and will therefore lead us astray, but they are not thereby fundamentally opposed to the goodness of the Way.

The first thing to note here is the centrality of metaphysics to each figure's account. For Augustine, not only is God the ultimate object of desire; God's perfection essentially includes eternal constancy. In contrast, created things, although intrinsically good and testifying through their measure, form, and order to the goodness of their maker, are subject to change, including decay and destruction. This seems to be a necessary condition of Augustine's judgment that created things can never make us happy and thus cannot serve as fit objects for our strongest desire. When we misdirect our longing this way, we will be stalked by anxiety, born from the threat of loss; this anxiety will inevitably give way to despair as the people and things we love covetously (i.e., with *cupiditas*) fail or desert us (e.g., *en. Ps.* 83.3, *conf.* 4.4.9ff.).

God, by contrast, will never fail us. God gives us *caritas*, the passion for what is divine, which we yearn to participate in and serve. Although *caritas* can issue in fear of and sorrow over evils, it will never take the form of anxiety. Sorrow is still compatible with appropriate religious hope, but anxiety is incompatible with human happiness, which must in its final fullness be peacefully and surely at rest in God.[3] To sum up, according to Augustine, human desire tends to deify its objects in the hopes that they might fulfill our longings for beatitude; but this passionate projection makes idols out of things and people, and it tempts us to sin to defend the unstable illusions of happiness to which we cling.

It is illuminating to compare this account with Xunzi's view of the relation of the Confucian Way to the various goods we desire. For Xunzi, in contrast to Augustine,[4] the human Way is a way *only* within and through the world, which orders and maximizes its beauty and productivity. This can be achieved by giving beautiful form and proper order (*wenli* 文理) to human social life, especially by means of Confucian ritual in Xunzi's broad sense of the term. This makes sense as a model for human life because Xunzi thinks there is no hope of eternal beatitude in Augustine's sense; he does not even entertain the possibility of such a state. Instead of sharing Augustine's Neoplatonic metaphysics, Xunzi sees the cosmos as governed by temporal patterns of cyclical change, such as day and night, the cycles of the moon, the seasons, and the motions of the stars and planets.

Such changes are not absolutely invariant and stable (e.g., eclipses and droughts occur), but they are generally regular and recurring. The Way utilizes and relies on these patterns to achieve its glorious effects. (These themes are all developed in greater detail in chapter 6.) So though people and things pass away, we know that others will take their place, and that others will take our place eventually as family lineages and religious traditions continue across human generations. Eternal rest is not a possibility in such a view, and so the satisfaction and subsequent renewal of desire can never be stripped of their rhythmic, cyclical character. There can be no higher happiness than enacting the Way fully over time, for Xunzi; for him, the highest good is an ongoing performance, not a final end.

Xunzi thinks we all possess impatient instinctive desires for food, beautiful things, and sex, among other things, and one of the chief tasks of Confucian self-cultivation is to reshape these desires over time. This requires restraint, on the one hand, but also a development of a stronger taste for the beauties of the Way, on the other. When these new desires are awakened and strengthened by Confucian training and experience, the beauty and justice of the proper means for securing satisfaction will heighten our pleasures.

For Xunzi, then, sensory pleasure is an unalloyed good, and he thinks one of the prime features of his Confucian Way is that it provides so much satisfaction for so many, not only the wealthy and powerful but also the poor and defenseless (although he thinks these groups' pleasures will be, and should be, decidedly unequal). For Augustine, in contrast, the pleasure that comes with the satisfaction of desire is almost always a trap, an entanglement in carnality that binds us to earthly goods and pulls us "down," away from God. The only safe delights are the joys to be found in the service and worship of God; but while these are at times profound and intense, in this life they apparently cannot completely overwhelm the competing pull of carnal delights, even in fully committed and practicing Christians. Thus Augustine is extremely interested in the regulation of "natural" desires like hunger and sexual libido, and he wants as much as possible to minimize them; whereas for Xunzi, such desires need to be shaped and ordered so that they may be satisfied in beautiful, religiously meaningful, and socially constructive ways. Xunzi thinks trying to eliminate or even minimize such desires is foolish, because he judges such a project to be impossible (22/111/4–6); we need to redirect such desires, not try to extinguish them.

Augustine might query Xunzi about anxiety and fear—how could any sage be free of such things? No matter how thoroughly the Way prevailed at a given moment, as for example in the heyday of the revered Zhou Dynasty, the social instantiation of the Way could eventually decay and lapse, as Xunzi agrees it had lapsed during his own time. Of course, such things can happen, Xunzi could reply, but the only solution is to reinvigorate the Way itself; if you have wandered off the path and become lost, you must simply return to the correct path. Such vicissitudes are horrible, and we should strive to avoid them, but one's faith must be in the Way itself and its proven potency. More specifically, Xunzi could distinguish between, on the one hand, the debilitating anxiety and fear felt by "petty" people who are ignorant of the Way and know all too well the dangers they face from others who might hurt or steal from them; and on the other, the wise but not complacent vigilance of the sage who knows the limits of his own life and powers, and the endlessly recurring difficulties engendered by the unfortunate character of untutored human instincts. Of course, a wise follower of the Way may suffer greatly as he struggles to establish the Way in a corrupt age; but such suffering is more akin to Augustinian sorrow over evil than to the anxiety and despair provoked by covetous love for people and things. A Xunzian "noble man" will remain assured that he is on the right path, even if it becomes clear that he must die an early or painful death.[5]

So we can say that Augustine and Xunzi disagree about something quite important: Does the fact that we, like all people and things, are subject to change lead to dissatisfactions and anxieties so fundamental that nothing deserving the name of happiness can be found in human life as we know it, which at best is only a foretaste of an ultimate, indestructible happiness?[6] Xunzi and Augustine agree that what might be called normal anxiety and fear drive us to religious solutions to our problematic ways of living; they disagree about the extent to which such fears and anxieties can be ameliorated here on Earth. For Xunzi, we are inevitably vulnerable to misrule and social chaos, but we can protect ourselves and each other from many varieties of bad luck through careful planning and foresight. However, this vulnerability, precisely because it is inevitable, can and must be accommodated within a flourishing human life by means of such things as both wise government and the Confucian death rituals (to be analyzed in the next chapter). Augustine agrees that we remain vulnerable in this life; but ironically, because of his religious hope for a revolutionary end to this vulnerability, his account of our predicament becomes all the more radical in its assessment of our misdirected and idolatrous desires.

Emotions, Dispositions, and the Will

Xunzi and Augustine both stress the critical importance to the religious and moral life of having correct emotions. Normatively, both reject as inadequate merely correct beliefs without the right feelings and desires. Descriptively, the question is more complex. Xunzi seems to think most aspiring Confucians will have beliefs that come closer to the truth than do their desires, although both will approach greater adequacy together over time. On my reading, Augustine ties beliefs and desires quite closely together, in complex ways, given his views of the unity of the *mens*; like Xunzi, however, he thinks beliefs and desires grow together toward the truth, if they do so at all.[7]

Strikingly, Augustine and Xunzi share numerous important ideas about emotions. Both provide accounts of the emotions that stress their cognitive character, and specifically the importance of interpretation to the generation of feelings. Furthermore, both Xunzi and Augustine link emotion and desire together as analytically separable aspects of a single system of human motivation and action, although exactly how they parse the parts of this system varies.

For Augustine, the four classical emotions (desire, joy, fear, and grief) are forms of love, and thus will. These emotions are "movements of the soul" and even *voluntates* or "wills," which are each intrinsically integrated with the other aspects of the internal "word" that constitutes them, that is, with memory and thought. Thus the emotions themselves, for Augustine, could be considered desires, because they are the intentional "movements" of the soul toward or away from various objects. The entire account centers on the quality and direction of our loves. These movements must be called cognitive, in contemporary terms, because they exist in the form of "internal words" that are by nature discursive, describing and responding to situations and objects in linguistic terms.

For his part, Xunzi understands emotions primarily as dispositions to feel, desire, and act in certain ways, depending on circumstances. Desires gain their force spontaneously, but human action is always a complex process involving interpretations of circumstances based on whatever theories an actor holds true, and sometimes even on conscious assent to particular goals. Xunzi makes it clear that there is an element of interpretation even in cases of apparently spontaneous desires and feelings, because the heart/mind must first identify an object as something in particular (e.g., a bear rather than a bush), and apparently also make a judgment about the relation of the object to oneself (e.g., we are in the woods, not a zoo, and that bear is 10 yards away from me), in order to feel fear and desire to run (22/111/14–15). Such cognitive content is also obviously present in cases of conscious assent to discursively articulated goals.

As discussed in chapter 3, it is odd that Xunzi uses only one word, *qing* 情, for both emotion and disposition; indeed, the idea of emotion is relatively submerged even here, because the accent most often seems to fall on steady patterns of responsiveness. This terminology leads Xunzi to interpret human emotional life largely in terms of how it affects the long-term process of personal reformation: as I argue in chapter 6, Xunzi focuses not on desire per se as the object that spiritual exercises are supposed to change, but on *qing*, our relatively stable but still plastic dispositions to feel and act. He seems, then—despite his clear separation of habitual, relatively stable disposition from particular response at a given moment—to have left what we think of as emotions (particular feelings in response to particular situations) in a theoretical netherworld, doubling the position of specific, object-directed desires that are "the responses of the *qing*" (22/111/14–15). Perhaps we should think of Xunzian emotions as more generalized responses to situations (I fear that the bear will hurt me), and of desires as more specific (I want to run away from the bear and seek cover over there).

In his works, Augustine makes explicit the connection—or rather identity—between emotion, love, and *voluntas*, which shows that proper emotions and desires are essential to righteousness, from his point of view. This identification also shows that his account of love must be the central element of any contemporary account of his views of "the will." However, his use of two interchangeable groups of terms (*voluntas* and the various terms for love, e.g., *amor*, *caritas*, and *cupiditas*) for *both* dispositions *and* particular emotions/desires has far-reaching effects in his account of spiritual exercises and his caution regarding the very idea of virtue. (I develop these ideas further in chapters 7 and 8.)

Xunzi more clearly distinguishes disposition and desire, while remaining somewhat murky on emotions. This allows him to articulate clearly how over time spiritual exercises transform our dispositions, which in turn lead us to spontaneously desire different things. In other words, Xunzi's terminology makes it easier for him to develop a sort of virtue theory and to give a nuanced account of how religious practices both respond to what we already feel and desire but also slowly change us in what are ultimately very dramatic ways, so that we come to desire and pursue different, higher goods.

Augustine is not being sloppy, however. He has what he judges to be the most serious reasons for his worries about previous understandings of virtue as an ethical concept, which lead him to articulate human progress in righteousness not in terms of correct knowledge alone, or increasingly secure dispositions to act well, but rather in terms of a physics of increasingly ordered and powerful love that depends on God, not self. (I discuss Augustine's attempt to respond to the ambiguities of the pursuit of virtue more fully in chapters 7 and 8.) To begin to see why he thinks such a theoretical maneuver is necessary, we must examine his account of memory and his strikingly negative assessment of habit.

Memory, Habit, Sin

Augustine makes considerably more of memory than does Xunzi. For Augustine, the vast inner expanses of our memories are in some sense ourselves, and they provide the field for reflection and much of our personal reformation. Memory holds not just old thoughts and sense impressions, according to Augustine, but also skills and (most important) habits, which continue to weigh us down even after baptism. Xunzi, in contrast, sees memory as a relatively unproblematic aspect of the mind, worthy of mention but no serious analysis; he appears to conceive of memory as a storehouse or library that can be consulted when we wish to recall particular bits of information (21/104/1), although he does not develop this image. According to Xunzi, while we can become *bi* 蔽, "obsessed" (literally "obscured"), by partially true doctrines or particular goals, hopes, or fears, this seems to be a problem of understanding and attentiveness as much as a failure of "emptiness" or the openness to new impressions in memory. Once obsession is resolved, for Xunzi, it is apparently gone; but for Augustine, the momentum of past sins continues to trouble us even after we have repudiated them and tried for years to eradicate their aftereffects.

This sketch is perhaps unfair to Xunzi. His account of obsession hinges on the idea that people become partly aware of the truth, become unduly attached to what they have learned and experienced, and thereby become blinded to the complexity of reality. We love what we have learned from our own experience, and we become resentful of anyone who might question whether we fully understand things (21/102/5–10). Xunzi is here underlining the difficulty of truly coming to understand and grasp the Way, which cannot be articulated in simple formulas or an invariable ranking of various criteria for judgment.[8] Life is complicated, and it is not easy to become wise. Not surprisingly, for Xunzi, we are prone to overestimate our own moral attainment and understanding, and we resist those who could be our teachers. There are at least hints here of an account of self-justification and defensiveness as a deep moral problem, making us prone to failure when we do not systematically engage in study of what is in fact the right Way; if we pursue some merely partial and thus wrong way intensively, we will be all too certain that we are becoming wiser and better, even as we wander further away from the right path. Intellectual patterns are habit forming, and we should take the utmost care to pursue the right patterns, those that continue to open us up to correction from reality in all its complexity.

From an Augustinian point of view, however, this account of moral failure is still too shallow: It rests on a simplistic and truncated account of memory, and it underestimates the scope of the negative effects of habit in our present fallen condition. Most strikingly, Augustine would question whether we are the sovereign masters of a flawless but essentially passive memory. For him, we cannot always easily recall whatever we might wish to recall; but even more alarmingly, we cannot forget what we might wish to forget: illicit pleasures and the taste for sin they have groomed. Our memory "whispers" to us against our better judgment, tempting us with possibilities we would prefer to reject: Augustine as bishop famously confesses that in dreams he still gives in to such temptations (*conf.* 8.11.27, 10.30.41). Even the most righteous have much to regret, according to him, because of the stringent inwardness of his ethic of desire—even to lust is a sin, whether or not one succeeds in satisfying such a lust outwardly.[9] So for Augustine, past sins present an ongoing problem, one that can be attenuated but not completely resolved until death.

The primary engine of this ongoing difficulty is of course habit, as discussed in chapter 4. According to Augustine, when lusts are satisfied in action, they bring a deceptive pleasure that chains us to particular sins, so that even after the pleasure diminishes, as it will with repetition, we can no longer avoid the illicit act in question. As John G. Prendiville has shown in his exhaustive survey of Augustine's views of habit, Augustine relentlessly focuses on the power of habit formation for evil.[10] Sinful habits become chains so strong that only God can break them, but what virtuous habits we develop are fragile, liable at any moment to slippage and collapse without incessant divine support. Our virtues are gifts from God, and "perseverance to the end" is a further gift, which all believers need to secure the continuation of such virtues (*conf.* 10.32.48, *civ. Dei* 19.27, *corrept.* 9.24, *persev.* 17.42, 45–46).

This theorization of habit allows Augustine to delve deeply into various aspects of our resistance to moral goodness, in ways that Xunzi never even approaches. But it comes at a high price. Augustine has portrayed habit—the most obvious tool for conceiving of virtue as a disposition to think, feel, and act rightly—as a paradigmatic aspect of human sinfulness. Nor is this a theoretical tic that might be corrected without repercussions. Augustine conceives of habit this way because of his account of lust (in the broad sense of all covetous desire) and what he sees as the unique power of pleasure to mold us toward vice.

Xunzi, for his part, seems to think it likely that if whole groups of people fail to follow the Way but instead seek directly to satisfy their instinctive desires, they will generate and follow "chaotic customs." This is "the petty redoubling the petty," with each person's heart/mind operating as thoughtlessly as his or her stomach, to disastrous social and moral effect (4/15/14–17). Xunzi, like Augustine, sees the possibility of habitual vice deepening our bad instincts into real depravity; but in contrast to Augustine, he does not appear to think that there is an asymmetry of habit formation in favor of vice, even though this might seem to follow from his account of our spontaneous desires. As I show in the next chapter, Xunzi focuses with remarkable consistency on the power of habit formation for good, as in his account of the "accumulation" of goodness through repetitive Confucian practice. He recognizes the possibility of "deviant" and "chaotic" customs, but he is not unduly troubled by them or the vices they generate. Such things can generally be restrained and even reformed by good government, he thinks, except when people's habits have been truly hardened over many years. Human motivation is more pliable, for Xunzi, for good and for ill.

So Augustine and Xunzi again differ about quite significant issues. Though both agree that many of our spontaneous, innate desires misdirect us, Augustine thinks such desires are uniquely habit forming and thus powerful and dangerous. Xunzi disagrees, thinking that our desires can follow numerous different channels, and that habituation can occur in many directions, to quite various moral results. For Augustine, in our fallen state we are innately prone to vice, and we find it particularly difficult to escape its clutches even with sustained effort and divine aid; whereas for Xunzi, we are merely susceptible to vice, given the general tenor of our instincts. It is certainly hard and painful to retrain ourselves and our tastes, according to Xunzi, but it can be done.

As we shall see in the following three chapters, Xunzi thinks that dependable self-mastery is difficult to achieve but eventually attainable, and he may even believe in the possibility of perfect, sagely virtue. Augustine, however, thinks self-mastery is a mirage, a subtle trap set by pride. Sin's continuing vigor, reaching out of our past via memory to seduce our present and destroy our future, is an ongoing source of dismay and anxiety for Augustine. The only solution, he thinks, is to trust in God's mercy (*conf.* 10.32.48).

The Will Once More: Assent, Consent, and Dissent

Both Augustine and Xunzi attend carefully to our conscious assent and dissent from particular courses of action. Such decisive responses to the world seem to be essential to the idea of having a will, and to pursuing purposes or ideals, as distinct from mere satisfaction. Xunzi isolates *ke* 可, "assent," as a characteristic and important activity of the heart/mind, and in the course of his treatment it becomes clear that he views this as one of the crucial human powers making human reformation possible. Augustine does not build such an operation into his mature structural account of the mind in *On the Trinity*, but very early he develops an account of sinful willing in terms of suggestion, delight, and consent that he struggles to integrate with his later account of the unified *mens*. This section of the chapter explores the similarities and differences between Augustine's and Xunzi's views of consent and attempts to identify the relative strengths and weaknesses in their positions.

Xunzi's account is simpler, and so I treat it here first. As noted in chapter 3, Xunzi thinks all people, even the uncultivated, will do what they *ke*, "accept" or "assent to," even when their existing desires point in another direction. Assent seems to be a natural human power for Xunzi, not something that might fail on occasion because of the strength of our desires; when desire and assent conflict, assent just trumps desires, according to Xunzi, and we suffer deprivation willingly (22/111/6, 20). On the face of it, such a position seems blind to common human experiences of "weakness of will" and internal conflict and indecision. But Xunzi is aware of such problems. He clearly believes that many people simply assent to seeking what they desire, and that all people start out this way. Only experienced difficulties can prompt us to question ourselves and our desires, and only the conscious articulation of our difficulties can open the logical possibility of overriding our desires. Because our desires do not cease to clamor for attention, on Xunzi's view, we only dissent from following them if we are convinced that they will lead us into relatively greater trouble and suffering—or in other words, we dissent from them when we believe they are dangerous. This does make sense; even the vicious can usually control themselves when they think their life or some other important interest is at stake. Such a judgment of personal danger provides some foothold, Xunzi thinks, for people to judge actions to be wrong, at least in the most limited, prudential sense. How Xunzi thinks such a limited sense of morality may grow into full-fledged commitment to the Confucian Way is the subject of chapter 6.

But even this sketch raises important questions. In essence, Xunzi has moved some of the problems to a new location. When, on his view, are we really convinced by the rightness of various principles or ideals? Might we be uncertain or confused, and how should we remedy this? Could we forget our convictions by not attending to them, and default to acting on spontaneous desires? One might also ask, with Augustine, if desires could tempt us to betray even our settled convictions. Xunzi is not very articulate here, but he at least implies that these are real problems simply by virtue of his insistence on personal reformation: We need to reform our *qing* in order to reshape our desires, because we cannot depend on assenting repeatedly to what we do not desire. More specifically, he seems to think that disordered desires "pull" and "tilt" our perceptions so that we become grossly insensitive to important countervailing considerations, and so we blithely assent to actions that a clear-eyed observer would quickly reject (21/105/5–8). The need to transform our dispositions, and thereby our whole experience as perceiving, desiring beings, at least saves Xunzi from the charge of blindness to the difficulty of our predicament. But it does reveal him to be a sort of intellectualist in his account of morality and personal formation, in the sense that right understanding is the key to successfully transforming our feelings and desires. Assent, for Xunzi, is a matter of correctly recognizing and interpreting the morally compelling features of a situation, so that we correctly grasp what is at stake and thereby know what we *must* do; in Xunzi's vocabulary, *suo ke* 所可 means both "what we assent to" and "what [we think] is possible." Xunzi's challenge, then, is to account for our motivation to begin to learn, and to continue learning, about the Way, and to explain how such learning relates to the transformation of our dispositions and to the development of our heart/mind's abilities. For Augustine, of course, this is no problem at all: God calls whom He will, initiating and sustaining redemption in every member of the elect.

Augustine's analysis of consent is more complicated and occurs on multiple fronts. He develops his analysis of sinful willing in terms of suggestion, delight, and consent (*suggestio*, *delectatio*, *consensio*) as part of his exegesis of the story of Adam and Eve, beginning as early as 389 in his first commentary on Genesis (*Gn. adv. Man.* 2.14.20–21).[11] On this account, all sin begins with a suggestion, whether through sensation or memory, of some illicit possibility; this is akin to the serpent's whispering to Eve in the garden. Augustine gives the example of seeing delicious food during a fast. Next, we spontaneously delight in the prospect of the suggestion, for example, relishing the thought of eating the food before us. This is akin to Eve in fact being seduced by the serpent, so that she delights in what he proposes, and in her allegorical role as stand-in for carnal appetite, she actually eats the forbidden fruit. Last and most crucially, for sin to be "complete," we must consciously consent to the illicit prospect before us. In the example, this would be a conscious decision to break our fast wrongly and eat the food before us; the Genesis parallel is Adam choosing, even though "not seduced" as was Eve, to join her in eating the forbidden fruit. Such consent is itself sinful, even if our bad intentions are never realized in action (*s. Dom. mon.* 1.12.34).

This picture is fundamentally an account of temptation, but it captures broader issues in Augustine's vision of human motivation and action. Most notably, it highlights the spontaneity and centrality of delight in the operations of the will: Our *voluntas* is the collection of our loves, and our loves are movements of yearning toward various objects that delight us. Delight and yearning are two alternate descriptions of the same experience. As Augustine says, "A love that strains after the possession of the loved object is desire; and the love that possesses and enjoys that object is joy" (*civ. Dei* 14.7). Various possibilities attract us according to the character and orientation of our loves, and we long to "possess and enjoy" what delights us.

Let us try to coordinate this schema of suggestion, delight, and consent with the account given in chapter 4 of Augustine's psychology, especially as articulated most fully in *On the Trinity*. "Suggestion" correlates fairly easily with the discussion of sensation and memory in the "outer man" in book 11, both of which provide objects for our awareness, although even here Augustine wants to insist on the centrality of our *voluntas* in both picking out and remaining attentive to various possible objects of attention (*Trin.* 11.1–16, 15). The trouble begins with the differentiation of delight and consent. It appears that to capture the motive force of love, and thus *voluntas*, we must assimilate *delectatio* or "delight" to Augustine's various words for love and desire (*amor*, *diligo*, *caritas*, *cupiditas*, *libido*, *desiderium*, etc.). Given the account of the psyche developed in *On the Trinity*, such strong feelings take the form of "internal words" that we speak to ourselves as if reporting on our environment: This ongoing flow of words is the discursive structure of consciousness, according to Augustine. But how then are we to differentiate words spoken to articulate recognition of some delightful object from words spoken in judgment of that delight?

The problem is sharpened by the crucial passage from *City of God* that identifies emotion with *voluntas*. Augustine writes:

> Certainly the will is involved in all [emotions]; in fact they are all nothing other than wills (*voluntates*). For what is desire or joy but a will in agreement (*in . . . consensionem*) with what we wish for? And what is fear or grief but a will in disagreement with what we reject? . . . And in general, as a man's will is attracted or repelled in accordance with the varied character of different things that are pursued or shunned, so it changes and turns into feelings (*affectus*) of various kinds. (*civ. Dei* 14.6)[12]

The Latin generally translated as "consent" is *consensio* (verb form: *consentio*, *consentire*), here rendered quite properly as "agreement," the word's principal meaning. Augustine is saying, in other words, that emotions just are *voluntates* or "wills" consenting to or dissenting from particular objects, that is, "in agreement" or "disagreement" with them. So it appears that *delight itself* is a form of spontaneously given consent or agreement, for Augustine, which muddies the waters as fully as possible.

What are we to make of this? At the very least, it appears that Augustine wants and needs to be able to separate out the spontaneous and involuntary *consensio* that constitutes our emotions from the purposefully chosen *consensio* that constitutes a judgment about what delights or repulses us. But his various ways of talking about *voluntas* and the mind do not make this easy.

One reasonable place to look for a resolution would be Augustine's treatment of the allegory of Adam, Eve, and the serpent in *On the Trinity* 12.17, where he interprets it in terms of different *intentiones*, "intentions" or "applications," of the triune human mind. The superior application, symbolized by Adam, is *sapientia*, "wisdom," and concerns the contemplation of eternal, spiritual realities. The inferior application, symbolized by Eve, concerns material reality, and is called *scientia*, "knowledge," presumably in allusion to the knowledge of good and evil provided by the tree in Eden. The allegory plays out similarly to the earlier texts, with sensation offering a tempting suggestion, and Eve consenting, but this time as *scientia*, rather than as *appetitus carnalis*, "carnal appetite." This apparent reallocation of psychic territory would have one very important benefit: Our concupiscent delight in sinful possibilities would not be localized in an "appetite" that could be seen as outside ourselves, given that Augustine wants to insist that in the deepest sense we are our souls, and more specifically our minds, above all. So it would be our mind feeling delight and yearning, our own *voluntates* that were engaged by both licit and illicit possibilities. Augustine goes on to attribute to *sapientia* a superior role in judgment, as "that *intentio* of the mind that has the supreme power to move the limbs to action or restrain them from action."[13] When the mind consents at its highest levels, this is full, conscious consent.

Unfortunately, this proposed reading will not work. First of all, the distinction between *scientia* and *sapientia* tracks the distinctions between what is material and temporal, on the one hand, from what is spiritual and eternal, on the other. So any sort of consent to good or bad possibilities must be occurring in our *scientia*. Moreover, in this same passage (*Trin.* 12.17), Augustine clearly differentiates *appetitus* "appetite" from "the reasoning of knowledge," because the business of our *scientia* or "knowledge" is to attend to and reason about sensible, material things. He speaks of the "carnal" or "sensual" "movements of the soul," common to humans and animals, which are *intenditur*, "stretched out," toward material realities in such a way that they quite easily become "cut off" from our *sapientia* or wisdom. So Augustine in this passage is distinguishing between what we might call notional and real consent (both consciously chosen), not between spontaneous and considered consent. He also argues that our appetites or "movements of the soul" (recall that this is one of his characteristic ways of speaking about emotions) are "close to" but distinct from the *intentiones* of our mind, particular our *scientia* or knowledge.

On the one hand, this way of parsing things allows Augustine to argue, as he does repeatedly, that merely feeling tempted by some delight is not in itself sinful, as long as we do not consent to pursuing it (e.g., *cont*. 8.20); such a situation is lamentable, part of our fallen condition, but is in itself only dangerous, not damning. But on the other hand, it also creates serious tensions with his considered account of desires and emotions as discussed in *City of God*. How are we to make sense of "movements of the soul" that move us to action that are somehow outside our minds? How could emotions and desires be inarticulate and yet still move us toward rather specific sorts of illicit pleasures? Our *voluntas* seems simultaneously to be one essential aspect of our unified minds, and yet also to include spontaneous movements that are in some sense outside our minds.

In some places, Augustine writes as if our "internal mouth" speaks only the words or thoughts to which we consent, and that tempting "suggestions" are somehow not verbalized internally, despite being within our hearts (*cont*. 1.2–2.3). But even the metaphors he uses, for example of "suggestion," work against this unfortunate quarantine maneuver. And in one of his most famous and penetrating accounts of the divided will, book 8 of the *Confessions*, the old, sensual temptations are described as *voluntates*, or "wills," that are quite specifically articulate "whispers" from out of the depths of our memories (*conf*. 8.11.26). These can only be construed as "words" spoken by our minds, in his fully developed psychological terminology. The issue may be put sharply this way: Who is talking internally when we "hear," that is, feel, such tempting suggestions? For Augustine, it must be us, not some alien substance in the form of our own bodies. The locus of sin is in our fallen minds, not just our souls, and certainly not in our bodies.

To revise Augustine slightly in the service of what I take to be the strongest version of his account of human psychology, our minds operate by means of an ongoing internal discourse. In contrast to some recent accounts, I suggest that for Augustine when we feel tempted we ourselves are affected, at the "highest" level of our soul, that of our *mens* or mind.[14] This means that our inner discourse is not entirely under our own control. Our minds speak words we wish they did not, and so if we are to pursue righteousness and the service due to God, we inevitably end up talking to ourselves, at least internally; our own minds are thus the deepest battlegrounds of "Christian combat." As Augustine insists, we cannot master our own inner discourse without divine aid. What grace provides is a stronger delight in divine things, strong enough to overpower our previous loves decisively, even if not completely. Without sufficient delight, we are unable to consent, even if we might in some ineffective sense wish to (mere wishes would be an alternative construal of weak delight).

Delight and consent, then, are two different sorts of "internal words." The distinction between them tracks the distinction Frankfurt and Taylor draw between first-order and second-order desires, as long as we understand second-order "desires" to be products of some more or less articulate evaluation, as Taylor's account suggests.[15] Furthermore, Augustine is at pains to emphasize that people cannot effectively consent to anything without sufficient delight in the prospect. Without sufficient delight, "consent" is ineffective yearning, a second-order desire that registers as a form of suffering because it cannot be fulfilled.

Indeed, what is striking about Augustine's account is that our choices to assent or dissent from particular things are only logically superior to our desires; in actual experience, choice freely serves our *voluntas*, in the sense of the sum of our actual loves. As sinners with divided loves, we may have second-order wishes not to follow certain desires that now seem wretched, but we cannot simply choose not to follow them. In fact, we may be powerless to do anything other than consent to them, even with some awareness of how horrible they are; this is precisely the force of Augustine's account of sinful habit.

Obviously, this could not be more divergent from Xunzi's account of consent, at least on the surface. We frequently fail, according to Augustine, to do what we would wish or choose, although this raises at least a logical need for something like partial consent to effective sinful desires (i.e., those we carry out in action).[16] A patient, charitable Augustinian would want to query Xunzi about the exact scope of his confidence about consent. What sort of grounds would one need to dissent effectively from strong desires, whether for food, fame, or whatever? Xunzi's account seems to trade on the linguistic ambiguity of *ke* 可, ranging from "possible" to "permissible" to "approved" or "assented to." Suppose for now that any sane person will avoid what they take to be suicidal or impossible, but does that mean that anyone can be convinced to go against their own strong desires?[17] Xunzi does seem to want to say yes, but with some very significant caveats: Most will not see any point in dissenting from their existing desires, and even when we do become dissatisfied with a primarily instinctive existence, we need very significant outside aid to have any hope of reorienting ourselves to higher goods; without such a strong reorientation, the power of assent will not win us much, because we will not know what to assent to.

Xunzi's moral psychological point is that assent is a different sort of motivating factor than mere desire, although the two relate intimately. He is not concerned with heroic feats of moral strength so much as the actual experience of self-control. The sort of case Xunzi would want to point to is not the case of struggling against an addiction but of controlling oneself in day-to-day activities of the sort referenced in chapter 3 (e.g., fighting off sleep to help a child with homework, or restraining oneself from lashing out in anger). In his view, it is just a misunderstanding to say that people who can control themselves in this way have some deep desire to avoid lashing out in anger. Xunzi is not particularly interested in cases where people are overpowered by their passions. Because at that point nothing can be done against the flood, one should avoid reaching such a state in the first place. And indeed, the places where Xunzi thinks human beings will be most desperate are often either amenable to political correction (making sure famines and wars do not occur), or can be properly mediated and even "saved," if I can say such a thing, by means of ritual (e.g., responding to the death of intimates). All of this implies that he thinks most people are for the most part not as far gone in viciousness as an Augustinian account suggests. The two men differ, then, about the actual quality of our inclinations, as well as our capacity to resist them if we are genuinely convinced we must, whether by force of circumstance or personal conviction.

From Xunzi's point of view, Augustinian consent seems like a meaningless psychological epiphenomenon, merely the conscious recognition that our strongest desire is indeed moving us to action. Perhaps Xunzi could accept this sort of picture as an account of how the "petty person" deliberates and acts most of the time, because they merely consent to what they think will be beneficial, which is also their strongest desire. But he would insist that such a picture cannot do justice to the crucial case of the religious student who must struggle to overcome disordered inclinations on the basis of a conscious commitment to something higher than immediate satisfaction, that is, staying on the Way.

Xunzi would have to give ground, I think, regarding the possibility of something like addiction: habitual vice that cannot be overcome even when it is no longer wished for or even accepted. But I suspect that he would resist any move to universalize this phenomenon as indicative of the deep character of human existence. He lived in desperate, dangerous times, and he seems to have thought that the urge to survive, and if possible, thrive, would be sufficient to scare significant numbers of people into real openness to his

Confucian Way, even if some others would inevitably succumb to their own, or someone else's, avarice and lust for power. Whether anyone would ever hear of finer possibilities was the responsibility of Xunzi and others like him.

We should expect that Xunzi and Augustine differ, then, on the role of assent or consent in the process of personal reformation. Crucial points of contrast might be expected at the start, concerning how one begins a new religious way of life, for example, through a dramatic conversion experience; in the middle, as beginners and more advanced practitioners struggle along the path of advancement (specifically, how does consent relate to the character and perhaps overcoming of internal division?); and at the end, when consent and desire are finally reunited in something like perfect virtue, if such an end ever comes.

"HUMAN NATURE" IN THE CONTEXT OF FORMATIVE PRACTICES

Augustine is deeply impressed by human resistance to moral reformation. He views this resistance as overwhelming, in effect, because no human being can become good through any combination of personal effort and merely worldly assistance; our lusts for pleasure, acclaim, and power are simply too pervasive and deep to be overcome without shattering experiences and a humble, grateful reliance on the God who pulls us back mercifully from the brink. If we fail to make a decisive break with our penultimate yearnings (not for God but for this world), they will remain hidden and effectively subvert whatever projects for goodness we attempt to pursue. Only by openly facing our paradoxical situation, as beings so close and yet so far from God, can we hope to escape it, having at last clearly understood what we need and where to get help.

Xunzi, by contrast, is deeply impressed by both the human need and potential for reformation. Our instincts cannot lead us to goodness; following them blindly is a trap into which too many fall. Luckily, though, there is a trustworthy tradition of reformation available that marks out the path we need to follow to become good: Confucianism. Until we understand the danger we are in, we are unlikely to seek help; but after we do start to understand, we may come across a suitable teacher who can show us this proper Way. As we pursue the Way, we will gradually come to understand both it and ourselves better, and in the process be transformed, intellectually, emotionally, and morally. Reinventing the Way by oneself is not even logically possible. Nor is hearing the Way simply a matter of hearing some directions that we are then able to practice without difficulty; it is a long, demanding process. Xunzi clearly recognizes that many will not become convinced by the majesty of the Confucian Way from outside, and some are so far gone in vice that they will need to be coerced into sociability or even executed. But the majority would welcome a Confucian society, he is convinced, even if their initial evaluations were based on petty and self-interested calculation.

These differing senses of the possibilities for human reformation deeply shape both Augustine's and Xunzi's conceptions of human nature. However the various elements of "human nature" are conceived, such ideas are theoretical projections based on experience conditioned by tradition, and so serve to explain and justify that experience and further shape the relevant tradition(s) of reflection and practice. Without Xunzi's and Augustine's distinctive experiences of the difficulty of becoming good, it is hard to see what motive they would have had for developing their fully realized accounts of human nature. Thus "human nature" is an exceptionally ironic idea: Versions of it must be articulated in culturally conditioned vocabularies of reflection, but it aims to articulate human existence in a raw or undeveloped form, precisely to provide an account of continuing resistance to enculturation. Nothing else is possible for us, however, as linguistically, culturally, and historically conditioned beings, so we should not worry that there is something illicit in such an attempt to get behind, underneath, or before culture.

Nevertheless, all such attempts are linguistically articulated, and as my analysis above has shown, respond to a variety of different but related questions about human beings. There seems to be no easy and obvious way to decide which possible combination and framing of these questions is best, so interpretive, humanistic studies of "human nature" as a culturally deployed concept cannot simply be superseded by empirical inquiries into genetics, brain function, and the like. It is unlikely that inquiries into human nature can be conducted in abstraction from concerns about what humans can and should become (or avoid). Explicitly examining the intellectual linkages between conceptions of "human nature" and normative ideals of human formation and flourishing can serve to clarify various possible ways of proceeding, along with their strengths and weaknesses.

One rather obvious point does need to be made. In contrast to Augustine, who believes he has certain, divinely revealed knowledge of such matters, Xunzi does not speculate about the origins of the world or the human species. Xunzi confines his account of normative history to human culture, as developed by a succession of ancient sage-kings and carried into his own day as the Confucian tradition. By implication, on his account, there has been no change for the worse or the better in human nature or the structure of persons, only an improvement in techniques for reforming them. Death, disease, hunger, and sexual desire are central and inevitable aspects of human existence, and they have always been so. For Augustine, as I have shown, this is not the case. Death, illness, and spontaneously arising "fleshly" desire are all punishments for humanity's original disobedience. Not to belabor the point, but Xunzi's views are much closer to a tenable view informed by modern evolutionary biology, even if they propound an idealized conception of ancient Chinese kings; Augustine, in contrast, seems wedded at a deep level to an erroneous account of human origins, which colors his perception of our instinctive desires, as well as his sense of our relative alienation from the rest of our ecosystem.

The rather more interesting question, however, is which of them provides a more insightful account of the character of observable human impulses, and of moral anthropology more generally. But deciding such questions without resolving their underlying religious and philosophical disagreements about sacred history and the structure of the cosmos will be nearly impossible, at least without begging crucial questions.[18] In lieu of such a quixotic attempt at global theological judgment, we can focus instead on particular areas of human experience that each thinker's vocabulary highlights, as a way to at least generate hypotheses about greater depth and insight. At this point in the study, such hypotheses can serve to generate questions that look forward to the forthcoming accounts of each thinker's regimes of spiritual exercises.

Augustine's accounts of memory and habit provide a particularly powerful way to conceive of inner depth and complexity within human beings. This accent is only heightened by his striking account of the mind as structurally unified and yet internally divided when looked at over time: Our inner discourse produces a stream of sometimes diametrically opposed "inner words" of love and knowledge. Both of these theoretical moves help him to question and "problematize" the very idea of moral progress. And yet as I argue in chapter 7, Augustine is clearly committed to the possibility, indeed necessity, of "making progress in righteousness." So the strength of his anthropological and psychological vocabulary for talking about hidden, inward rebellion against justice generates questions as well. What is the theoretical point of his deep suspicion of human motives? More specifically, how does this suspicion relate to his critique of pagan virtue, and his conceptualization of Christian redemption and increasing righteousness? Comparatively, what sort of account of internal moral conflict during the process of personal reformation does Xunzi provide? Is it shallow and inappropriately truncated? Or if not, might it instead be seen as reasonable and humane rather than inappropriately fixated on certain recurrent instinctive desires?

As pointed out earlier in this chapter, Augustine conceives of our desires as always possessing what might be called a "vertical" dimension in relation to God. This relation decisively shapes the character and orientation of all our loving, and it effectively sorts our loves into two types, which he conceives as diametrically opposed. This schema provides him with powerful ways of discussing and analyzing what might be called radical evil, to borrow Kant's terminology.[19] Radical evil would be evil that is deep, willful, and potentially devastating in effect, given sufficient opportunity. What is perhaps striking about Augustine's vision, in comparison with Xunzi's, is Augustine's conviction that truly radical evil lurks within every one of us in the form of rebellious lusts that have infected our minds like a disease. In relatively short order, absolutely anyone—even professing Christians—can go from being a seemingly good citizen to being truly maleficent, given the collapse of love for the divine in the wake of consent to sin. For Augustine, the radicality of the disease demands the most stringent cure and careful ongoing therapy, as we shall see.

Xunzi, by contrast, seems to accent the relative shallowness of the disease. In fact, he eschews all language of disease or impurity, and instead he focuses on craft metaphors, giving examples of patient artisans slowly making something beautiful and useful out of difficult-to-work-with materials. Steady commitment will lead to gradual improvement, on this view, with at least the hope of eventual perfection. One basic question this contrast raises is whether Xunzi is missing something. He certainly seems aware of radical evil, at least in the form of tyranny and predatory crime, but he seems to view this as a contingent matter of bad tendencies allowed to grow under the pressure of violent, chaotic circumstances, without any countervailing forces. Radical evil is extreme and unusual, for Xunzi, not pervasively present in the form of latent possibilities. He seems much more concerned about what might be called day-to-day evil, where people allow their appetites to guide them without consideration of any larger factors, or they evaluate plans merely in terms of a calculation of individual or familial benefit. But it is still an open question whether Xunzi is belittling difficulties that he ought to take much more seriously, as Augustine would surely argue. From another angle, however, this contrast should make us question whether Augustine can finally give a convincing account of something recognizable as human goodness, especially when compared with Xunzi. Or in other words, is Augustine's suspicion of human motives too thoroughgoing and categorical, in the end?

Given his analysis of human instincts as bad but not truly perverse, Xunzi's focus on assent and dissent makes sense. We need to wake up and examine ourselves, on Xunzi's account. For him, moral failure is a matter of inattention and lack of seriousness, and above all a lack of sustained effort, which takes the form of assenting to Confucian disciplines. (Moral failure can also be due to misrule that makes real teachers scarce.) But it remains somewhat mysterious that Xunzi does not assimilate assent to his gradualist paradigm of latent potential and cultivated power, which governs his views of the excellences of the mind, for example (emptiness, unity, and tranquillity). It would seem that he could assimilate assent to this model without endangering at least the possibility of moral development, but he does not. Why? Furthermore, how is this related to the question of how someone begins on the Confucian Way, and the perhaps even more vexing question of how one moves from merely calculating what is beneficial to truly pursuing what is just and good for its own sake?

Let us turn now to examine Augustine's and Xunzi's constructive proposals for personal reformation in more detail.

NOTES

1. It is tempting to interpret Xunzi and Augustine as respectively representing highly intellectual versions of what J. Z. Smith has called "locative" and "utopian" religions, although this mapping sits easier with Augustine than Xunzi. However, because my comparative target is "spiritual exercises" rather than "religion" per se, I will leave these issues to the side. On these terms, see Smith 1978, xi–xv, 67–207; and 1990, 116–43. Note also Yearley 1990, 42ff.

2. For Xunzi, this focus on desire needs to be qualified by equal attention to his account of assent, which on his account apparently trumps desire when the two conflict. These issues are examined in more detail below in the section on "consent."

3. I thank Richard Miller and William Babcock for assistance on these points.

4. I have no wish to contribute to the long-standing error of reading Augustine as "otherworldly," when he is so clearly concerned with the character of human life in this world, as well as committed at the deepest level to the fundamental goodness of created, temporal reality. Nevertheless, for Augustine the proper understanding and "use" of created reality can only be achieved in relation to the eternal, which is humanity's ultimate ground and proper destiny. All of this is very different from Xunzi's conception of the human Way.

5. A modern-day Xunzian might press back on this exact point, charging that Augustine's reading of concupiscent desire as an ever-present, genuinely dangerous lure even among the most serious and committed Christians leads to deep anxiety, especially when combined with a clear-eyed awareness of the doctrine of predestination. Some who appear, even to themselves, to be loving Christians may fall away when God, in His inscrutable judgment, withdraws the grace that lifted them heavenward (*persev*. 9.21). Augustine does not seem to be as aware as he might be of the potentially destabilizing anxiety such ideas can produce, but he would likely attribute such difficulties to our justly deserved penal state after the Fall. The objection would only serve to underline his general point about human happiness in this life.

6. Nussbaum 1986 is an important study in this area. In the broader philosophical literature, such issues tend to be analyzed in terms of "moral luck."

7. The strongest counterevidence to my reading of Augustine's psychology is not the *Confessions* (as argued in chapter 4) but his occasional remarks in *On Christian Teaching* about the need for certain sorts of rhetoric (the "grand style," borrowing from Cicero) to move people when they know something to be true but will not follow it (*doc. Chr.* 4.4.6, 4.12.28, 4.13.29, but cf. 1.9.9; see also *pecc. mer.* 2.19.33). I find this to be in flat contradiction to the subtle picture developed in *On the Trinity*, and speculate that it is a holdover from classical traditions of rhetoric that rested on a view of the soul where reason is opposed by and seeks to rule the passions, which had gradually come to seem not weaker than reason but stronger. Strikingly, these passages were written in the late 420s, near the end of Augustine's life, so this reflects a real tension in his thinking, not a transition between different positions that can be arranged in a temporal sequence.

8. On these points, see Hutton 2001, 74–137, which argues in detail that for Xunzi the Way cannot be codified.

9. The complications Augustine's notion of consent introduces into this picture are addressed in the next section of this chapter.

10. Prendiville 1972.

11. For insightful discussion, see TeSelle 1994. (I owe this reference to Jesse Couenhoven.) In this essay, TeSelle provides further references to Augustine's exegeses of the Edenic drama in terms of willing in notes 1 and 2, p. 355, although several of these do not directly corroborate the threefold analysis that is at issue here. The clearly supportive texts that work out the idea in detail are both very early: *Gn. adv. Man.* 2.14.20–21 (written in 389), and *s. Dom. mon.* 1.12.33–36 (393). Augustine also alludes to the schema in *en. Ps.* 48.1.6, 83.1.7, and 103.4.6, which are surely later, although hard to date precisely. The most interesting testimony for present purposes is the problematic account in *Trin.* 12.17 (written perhaps between 415 and 420), discussed above in chapter 4, n. 59, and again below in the current section of this chapter. TeSelle's other citations are *Gn. adv. Man.* 2.18.28, *cat. rud.* 18.30, *civ. Dei* 14.11, and *c. Jul.* 6.22.68. Note also s. 352.8, preached between 396 and 400. Delight and consent are referenced together in *conf.* 10.30.41, and several other places, especially in *en. Ps.*

12. This translation has been changed in several ways from Bettenson 1984, 555–56.

13. Translation adapted from Hill 1991, 332.

14. The alternative possible line of interpretation here is that taken by Sorabji 2000, 372–84, 400–17; and Knuuttila 2004, 152–72, who attend closely to Augustine's understanding of "consent" and see at least some of the conflicts involved. They read Augustine as advocating a literal separation of "carnal" and "spiritual" wills (*conf.* 8), with the former being an aspect of a lower, "emotional" part of the soul, and only the latter being part of the *mens*, which is thereby rendered more purely rational, and more purely good. This recalls Platonic models of a tripartite soul, analogous to Augustine's very early conception in *quant.*, written in 388 before his ordination, and at least foreshadows Thomistic faculty psychology, which may be part of the hermeneutical attraction. Oddly, however, as Knuuttila recognizes (2004, 161), such a reading requires that

Augustine think good, divinely inspired emotions inhere in the mind, while all other emotions rest in the postulated lower, affective part, which seems capricious. This stratification of consciousness also softens the radicality of Augustine's understanding of both sin and inner conflict, by assimilating these to more familiar contests between reason and passion conceived as different layers of the soul. (On this issue, see my discussion in chapter 8 of different ways of modeling a "divided self.") They thus lose the distinctiveness of Augustine's account of the human mind as deformed but still *triune* image of God proffered in *On the Trinity*, in favor of a more *psychologically* Platonizing reading. There is certainly some evidence for the other interpretation, such as *Trin.* 12.17, discussed above; *Trin.* 12.1–2 on animals and the outer man (depending on how one reads the issue of "animal appetites" in human beings—on my account, because we have the sort of minds we do such "appetites" can only be experienced as desire, via the activity of the mind); one remark in *civ. Dei* 14.19, in the midst of an analysis of Platonic psychology, that implies a separation between *affectiones* and *voluntas*, contradicting 14.6; and Augustine's discussion (in debate with Julian of Eclanum at the end of his life) of sexual lust as bypassing our *voluntas*. Nevertheless, I think the costs of such a resolution are too high. After all, Augustine instructs us to crucify the "inner man," not the "outer" one, if we would follow Christ (*Trin.* 4.6).

15. On these issues, see Couenhoven 2004, chap. 3, sec. 6. I have profited greatly from thinking through Couenhoven's reading of Augustine in terms of modern debates about free will and determinism, especially with regard to his analysis of Augustine on consent.

16. Our *arbitrium*, or choice, would seem to serve this need in Augustine's account of human action, at least in cases where we succumb to desires we (partly) wish to resist.

17. We should note that on an Augustinian account sin is indeed strong enough to drive us all the way from spiritual to physical suicide.

18. The problems with such attempts are manifold: First, incompatible basic premises cannot be judged by appeal to neutral facts or standards. Second, even in cases where it seems we can appeal to relatively neutral grounds (e.g., modern confidence in evolutionary theory as an explanation for human origins), judgments about possible responses of either side are difficult and often question begging. For instance, a contemporary Augustinian might very well be able to assimilate evolutionary theory and to restrict his or her exegesis of the Genesis account of Adam and Eve to the realm of moral psychology. MacIntyre's contrast between "progress" and mere "epicycles" only shows the depth of the difficulty, since one person's progress is another's pathetic failure. Important recent works on such questions include MacIntyre 1988, Stout 1988, Fleishacker 1994, and Moody-Adams 1997.

19. Kant 1960, 15 and passim.

CHAPTER SIX

Artifice Is the Way

✦

In this chapter, I outline Xunzi's understanding of human ethical and religious development. The first section sets the stage by considering Xunzi's general conception of the Confucian Way. Here I explore and analyze his various evocative metaphors for personal formation, and the theories into which they are interwoven. The second section begins by relating the bridge concept of spiritual exercises to the early Chinese problematic of *xiu shen* 修身, usually translated as "self-cultivation." The bulk of this section, and of the chapter as a whole, examines Xunzi's general account of the exercises he advocates most strongly: study, ritual practice, and musical performance and appreciation. The third section pulls back to sketch Xunzi's account of what might be called a ladder of ethical development and excellence, which includes four broad stages: the petty person, the educated man, the noble man, and the sage.

FOLLOWING THE WAY

Although many religious thinkers, including Augustine, make use of the idea of religion as a "way" of life, in early China the word *Dao* 道, aptly translated in its most basic sense as "path" or "way," was uniquely important. What the real or best *Dao* might be was the ultimate topic of political, ethical, religious, and cosmological debate, and the idea was widely understood to encompass or at least involve all these realms. The word also provided the best way of referring to competing tendencies of thought and practice, and it was the closest available analogue to Western ideas such as "religion" and "philosophy."

In lieu of a survey of the full range of early Chinese views of the *Dao*, I intend here only to give a sense of shared early Confucian presuppositions about the Way, and of how this overarching term of art shaped Xunzi's conceptions of human life and personal formation.[1] As a word, *dao* refers primarily to a "path" or "way," as noted above; but by the Warring States era (403–221 BCE), *dao* had acquired more extended senses, such as the manner or method for doing something (e.g., the "way" to cook), a very broad sense of the "way the world is" or should be, and the teaching or guidance that can show one "the way" in any of these senses. *Dao* can also be used verbally to express the activity of guiding others along a path, or of following such a way oneself.

Early Confucians regarded the *Dao* in its largest sense as "nothing less than the total normative sociopolitical order with its networks of proper familial and . . . sociopolitical roles, statuses, and ranks, as well as the 'objective' prescriptions of proper behavior—ritual, ceremonial, and ethical—that govern the relationships among these roles."[2] And yet it was just as much a way of life for individuals, relating one's inner life to the broader life of the community and the natural environment, and even the cosmos as a whole. One crucial difference from the way of life promoted by Augustine must be noted immediately. For Augustine, as the next chapter discusses in more detail, the ultimate telos of the Christian life is a perfected, eternal life with God after the final resurrection of the dead. For Xunzi and other early Confucians, the Way is its own goal—there is no ultimate telos beyond living out the Way in the world that all can readily observe. Though there were widespread early Chinese beliefs in some sort of spiritual afterlife (although still in communion with the living generations of a family line), early Confucians tended to downplay such speculation, and Xunzi explicitly rejects it.[3]

For Xunzi, the Way is a path *through* the world we presently inhabit, which is our true and only home. The intrinsic goods made available by following the Way are their own "rewards," regardless of whether less important goods such as wealth and public acclaim accompany them or not.[4] So Xunzi claims that the *Dao* itself simply *is* the practice of Confucian virtues of ritual propriety, justice, deference, yielding, dutifulness, and trustworthiness (16/77/5–6). The Way is very much a way of life for Xunzi, that mode of existence lived by the noble man (8/28/16) and above all the sage (8/31/5). The *Dao* is the sort of thing one must *ti* 體, "embody," which consists of both deep understanding and practical mastery of the Way (21/104/6).[5]

This sense—that the Way itself, if properly followed, provides the best human life and is not ordered or validated by some further ultimate destination at which it aims—was widespread in Warring States China, even among rather different ideological antagonists. Thus it is somewhat surprising to find Xunzi arguing for the superiority of his vision of the Confucian Way by stressing that his Way leads somewhere, in fact to an end or "stopping place" that is worth arriving at after long, sustained effort (2/7/8–17). He employs this novel rhetorical strategy to make three points, some of which will be further developed below: first, that sustained effort over a long period of time is necessary to reach a fully flourishing state of life; second, that concentration on that goal is necessary to ever attain it, given the difficulty of the task of self-cultivation; and third, that other purported *daos* cannot lead to such a state because they misunderstand both the goal and the path, and so lead people astray into endless disputation and fruitless practices. We should note, however, that the "goal" or "end" Xunzi here describes is still the Way itself, fully enacted in the person of the sage who spontaneously and effortlessly accords with the true Way. Xunzi is keen to encourage his readers not to give up part way along the long road of self-cultivation—but where that road leads is to the full and perfect embodiment and performance of the Way itself.[6]

One of the most famous passages in the *Xunzi* provides a wealth of evocative imagery for understanding his sense of the Confucian life. He writes:

> Those who cross water mark the deep places; if the markers are unclear people will drown. Those who govern the people mark out the Way; if the markers are unclear there will be social chaos. The rites are the markers. To go against ritual is to darken the age, and a benighted age is one of great chaos. Thus when the Way is completely clear, the difference between outside and inside is marked, and the hidden and the manifest become constant, people will at last avoid drowning. (18/82/22–18/83/1; cf. 27/127/4–5)

Lamenting his own confused and benighted age, Xunzi imagines life in the Warring States as a treacherous river or swamp, which can only be navigated via the trustworthy signs left by past Confucian sages. In his context of confusion and disagreement, Xunzi yearns for clarity regarding what is within the boundaries of the Way and what outside it, so that people can see and avoid the greatest dangers, and also find and stay on the one true path. For Xunzi, Confucian ritual provides the trustworthy guidance human beings need to navigate life successfully, by clearly marking the boundaries of the Way.

Xunzi thinks following the Way will feel very different depending on how long one pursues it, because one's mastery of it will slowly and steadily increase over time. Xunzi's gradualist conception of moral improvement is reflected in his discussions of "accumulation" and eventual "transformation" on the Confucian Way, as well as his central trope of "artifice" as the engine for personal change. These themes are integral to his sophisticated theory of ethical development, which in turn helps justify his advocacy of the spiritual exercises of study, ritual, and music.[7]

Xunzi's metaphors for this process are revealing. Instead of speaking of cultivating "sprouts" of morality into full-fledged plants, as his predecessor Mencius does, Xunzi favors tougher images:

> A warped piece of wood must wait until it has been laid against the straightening board, steamed, and forced into shape before it becomes straight; a piece of blunt metal must wait until it has been whetted on a grindstone before it becomes sharp. [Similarly,] since humanity's innate endowment (*xing* 性) is bad it must wait for [the guidance of] a teacher and the model before it becomes upright, and get ritual and justice before it becomes well ordered. (23/113/9–10; see also 1/1/3–5, 23/115/16–18)[8]

For Xunzi, the process of learning from a teacher (*shi* 師), internalizing classical models (*fa* 法), and thereby *de* 得, "getting" ritual and just social norms (*liyi* 禮義), is most akin to the work of artisans practicing constructive crafts.[9] We must be forcibly conformed to an external model (the "straightening board"), and this requires processes akin to steaming wood and grinding metal.

In other words, Xunzi pictures moral change as a slow, arduous process of personal reformation in which we must rely for an extended period on external forms and guides to achieve what flourishing is possible for us. Xunzi here consciously articulates the example of Confucius, who is described in *Analects* 2.4 as narrating his own progress along the Way as follows: "When I was fifteen I set my heart/mind on learning, at thirty I was established [on this Way], at forty I had no confusions, at fifty I understood Heaven's decree, at sixty my ear complied, and at seventy I followed my heart's desires without overstepping the bounds." Though fully plumbing the historical and philosophical issues raised by this passage is beyond the scope of this chapter, one should note that Xunzi adopts the same view that the Confucian path is lifelong (1/3/8), that it contains different stages of achievement (which are treated in more detail in the final section of this chapter), and that progress through the stages is slow.

Situated within this temporal frame of reference, elements of Xunzi's psychology take on a new light, and their interrelations and roles within personal reformation become clearer. As discussed in chapter 3, Xunzi thinks it takes time to develop the mind's capacities to become empty, unified, and tranquil, and only after long practice of study, ritual, and music can these grow into the "great pure illumination" that he lauds as sagely. He writes:

> One who seeks the Way but has not yet attained it should be told to make emptiness, unity, and tranquillity his precepts. If one who would seek the Way becomes empty he will enter into it. If one who would serve the Way attains unity he will exhaust it. If one who would ponder the Way attains tranquillity he will discern its details. One who understands the Way with discernment and puts it into practice embodies the Way. Emptiness, unity, and tranquillity are called "Great Pure Illumination." (21/104/4–7)

In this description, there is at least a hint of sequential ordering: Becoming empty, and thus open to new ideas and practices, is crucial for learning to even get off the ground. Unity seems necessary for a full appropriation of the Way in one's own existence. Tranquillity appears to be a later achievement that supports the development of a truly sagely understanding that has mastered the details of the Way.

Xunzi particularly emphasizes the cultivation of unity or oneness as part of the process of personal formation. He ties this to *jing* 精, "concentration," a word he uses repeatedly in "Dispelling Obsessions," his chapter on the heart/mind. In one typical passage, farmers concentrate on their fields, merchants on their markets, and artisans on their products, but the noble man concentrates on the Way. This allows him to unify his attention, and eventually his entire being, on enacting the Way. By means of this, he can be correct and discerning in his handling of all things, and he may be entrusted with political authority over those with more specialized skills (21/104/16–21/105/3).

In his explicit discussions of personal reformation, Xunzi also touches on this concentration of attention that allows unification of a person's being on the Confucian Way. In a memorable passage, Xunzi writes:

> If you start cutting but put it aside, [even] rotten wood will not be broken; if you cut and do not put it aside, [even] metal and stone can be carved. Though the earthworm has neither the sharpness of claws and teeth nor the strength of muscles and bones, above it eats dusty earth and below drinks from the Yellow Springs, because it uses its heart/mind in a unified way. The crab has six legs and two claws, but if there is no hole made by a snake or an eel, it will have no place to live, because it uses its heart/mind impetuously. For these reasons if there is no dark obscurity of intent, there will be no shining brightness of illumination; if there is no quiet, unknown service, there will be no glorious achievement. One who walks two roads will not arrive; one who serves two lords will not be tolerated. The eye cannot see two things and be clear, the ear cannot hear two things and be acute. . . . Therefore the noble man is tied to unity. (1/2/11–1/3/1)

Unifying one's attention on the task of self-formation, and sustaining that attention over time, are for Xunzi critically important. In the slow process of personal reformation, one needs "dark obscurity of intent" and "quiet, unknown service" truly to improve oneself, and reach the understanding and efficacy that follow from this. Xunzi favors imagery of carving and polishing difficult materials like jade as a metaphor for this process (17/82/4, 27/134/6–7), and he explicitly likens human instincts to "raw material" that must be properly shaped to become fine (19/95/1). Everything hinges on whether the process is continued steadily over time: Even if one is as talented as a team of thoroughbreds is powerful and fast, but does not resolutely pursue the Way, one will fail to improve. Conversely, even if one is as "slow" as a "lame turtle," through steadfast dedication to Confucian practices, one will eventually perfect oneself (2/7/12–15).

Xunzi once describes this process of self-unification in terms of concentrating the mind and unifying the *zhi* 志, "intent." This occurs in an important passage on how even "a person in the street" can become a sage king. Xunzi writes:

> Now if a person in the street were made to yield to the techniques and engage in study, concentrate his heart/mind and unify his intent, think and probe [until he is] steeped [in the Way] and discerning [about it], add up the days over long distance and time, accumulate goodness and not rest, then he would comprehend with numinous illumination and form a triad with Heaven and Earth. Thus sagehood is something people attain after [such a process of] accumulation. (23/116/13–14)

Concentration and unity are again linked; unifying one's intent is parallel to concentrating the mind. Note that one begins by yielding to the (Confucian) techniques of personal reformation, especially study. The central motif is one of Xunzi's favorites: *ji shan* 積善, the "accumulation of goodness" through artifice, leading to the great Xunzian themes of "forming a triad with Heaven and Earth" by "comprehending with numinous illumination," that is, reaching a sagely comprehensiveness of vision and understanding so impressive that it seems superhuman.[10]

Before going on to examine "accumulation" in more detail, a few words are in order about Xunzi's concept of *zhi* 志, "intent" or "intention." *Zhi* is often translated without comment as "will," as in Watson's frequently used translation of the *Xunzi*, but this obscures important issues that this study hopes to bring more fully to light. As Bryan Van Norden has argued in relation to Mencius, *zhi* is the orientation of the heart/mind itself, rather than any faculty or power within it, whether of decision or anything else.[11] (This is perhaps why Xunzi does not bother to include *zhi* in either of his lists of the important elements of human beings, psychic and otherwise; it is derivative of the concept of the heart/mind.) *Zhi* is closer to "aspiration" or "goal" than to "will"; for Xunzi, it tends to mean the settled focus of one's attention and consciousness, which one steadily seeks (e.g., 8/34/2, 20/100/7), although in a few ambiguous cases he may be using it to refer to particular intended goals (e.g., 12/60/2). It is frequently part of a binome, *zhiyi* 志意, that means "intention and purpose," or just "intentions." He occasionally uses it verbally to mean "set one's attention and aspirations on" some object or goal (e.g., 5/17/20, 12/59/2). The word has an objective flavor, in that it refers both to the intentional orientation of the heart/mind and to the object that the heart/mind seeks (these two aspects are stressed at 8/28/8 and 12/60/2, respectively); it is thus not a purely psychological phenomenon but a linkage between inner (the heart/mind) and outer (what it attends to and seeks). Also, *zhi* characteristically combines both of these latter, potentially distinguishable elements, that is, attention to something and seeking it.

Thus "concentrating the mind and unifying the *zhi*" are two ways of saying the same thing: Xunzi is counseling students to focus their attention and aspirations on the Way alone, so that they will not be distracted by secondary considerations, (literally *qing* 傾, "tilted," (8/31/3–5, 21/105/5–8), nor will they become obsessed by wrong or merely partial doctrines (21/102/5–21/103/13). They should emulate the focused earthworm rather than the scattered crab that depends on the kindness of its enemies.

An underappreciated passage in chapter 8, "Confucian Achievements," goes into more detail about how unification of attention relates to some of Xunzi's other important technical terms. He analyzes the psychological mechanisms of gradual character change as follows (note the contrast between what one has and receives on the one hand, and what one does and makes on the other):

> If a person lacks a teacher and model then he will exalt innate endowment; if he has a teacher and model then he will exalt accumulation. Now, teaching and modeling are gained through accumulation, not received from the innate endowment, which is insufficient to allow one to establish oneself and become well ordered. I cannot make my innate endowment, and yet it can be transformed. Accumulation is not what I have, and yet it is possible to do it. Focus attention and arrange things [in order to] practice your customs: this is how to transform your innate endowment. Uniting into one so that you are undivided: this is how to perfect accumulation. Practicing your customs shifts your intent (*zhi* 志); maintain this for a long time and it shifts the substance [of your innate endowment]. If you unify so that

> you are undivided, then you will comprehend with numinous clarity and form a triad with Heaven and Earth. Thus if you accumulate earth you will make a mountain; accumulate water and you will make a sea. . . . If a person in the street, one of the common people, accumulates goodness and completely exhausts it, call him a sage. (8/33/18–8/34/9)[12]

Uniting one's heart/mind and focusing its attention on the Way are the means to perfect one's accumulation of goodness; this, then, is what Xunzi means by "artifice." Through this conscious, goal-oriented work one's "customs," that is, habits, change to become consonant with ritual propriety, and in parallel the orientation of one's heart/mind gradually shifts, even in its very "substance" (*zhi* 質). This seems to be a reference to the *qing* 情, "dispositions," which Xunzi regards as the "substance" of the innate endowment (22/111/14). In other words, if practiced assiduously, Confucian spiritual exercises will reshape what is innate so thoroughly that one's dispositions shift, and thus one's largely chaotic innate desires eventually become consonant with the Way; for Xunzi such a state of developed Confucian virtue is genuine human flourishing. In the end, this shifting of intent and disposition is so complete and far reaching that Xunzi can only call it *hua* 化, a "transformation" (8/34/1); the path of Confucius is a "transforming Way" (1/1/9).

One of the intriguing ironies of Xunzi's preference for craft metaphors for self-formation concerns the roles of authority and agency in the process. Who exactly is playing the part of craftsman, and who the raw material? As explored further in the next section, Xunzi emphasizes the necessity of good teachers for self-formation to be possible. Thus it might seem that the teacher is the one who "hammers" and "steams" the student, so that over time the student takes on the objective shape or character of the ideal human standard. Stated so baldly, this cannot be right. Such a picture appears indistinguishable from "brainwashing" and coercion, and it is hard to fathom how such processes could lead to anything like genuine self-mastery or virtue.

Xunzi clearly views the human heart/mind as the "craftsman" in the process of self-formation, and our impulses, thoughts, and practical abilities as the "material" to be shaped. He describes the heart/mind as a "lord" and "ruler" that issues orders but receives none without itself choosing to follow them (21/104/10–12). At another point, he describes the heart/mind as the *gongzai* 工宰, the "artisan master" of the Way, who can represent the Way with skillful and accurate discriminations and arguments (22/110/7).[13] Xunzi reaches for this pregnant image in the midst of one of his most abstract and comprehensive discussions of language, argument, and theoretical understanding, but it has broader significance for his thought. Humans have created and continue to extend the Way through purposeful "artifice," but the recurrent locus of this artifice is the transformation of individuals. Given the powers of even an ignorant and undeveloped heart/mind, however, such transformation can only take place through the slow accumulation of new understanding, sensitivity, and skill in conscious submission to an external authority, one's trusted teacher.

Thus the model of the teacher as the artisan retains a certain relevance, and bite. For Xunzi, only if we become convinced that we need external help to become truly human will we be in a position to acquire what we need. We will only succeed if we are able to find the right sort of teacher and follow him diligently, from ignorance, anxiety, and questioning, through difficulties we only slowly come to grasp, to deeper understanding, commitment, and tranquillity.

SPIRITUAL EXERCISES

As discussed above in chapter 2, for present comparative purposes, I borrow and adapt Pierre Hadot's concept of spiritual exercises derived from ancient Greek and Roman contexts. Recall that for Hadot, spiritual exercises are effective practices that engage thought, imagination, and sensibility, and that have a significant ethical component, yet also aim at a complete transformation of vision, a metamorphosis of the whole personality.

Xunzi definitely advocates some analogous practices as part of the version of the Confucian way of life that he propounds. He sees these various disciplinary exercises as different elements of the unified project of *xiu shen* 修身, customarily translated as "self-cultivation." What the proper methods of *xiu shen* might be was a widely debated topic in early China, particularly in the fourth and third centuries BCE. An astonishing variety of practices were advocated by various "masters": breath control meditation to regulate the flow of *qi* 氣, fasting and dietary controls, yogic physical exercises, sexual disciplines, various sorts of "spirit flight" around the cosmos, withdrawal from public life to an eremitic existence, lesser withdrawal to a simple life centered on farming, study of and reflection on classic texts, a variety of ritual and sacrificial practices, musical performance and appreciation, and various sorts of self-examination.[14] Followers of different traditions argued the merits of these exercises, upholding the efficacy and importance of their own and denigrating others'.

Xiu shen clearly covered quite various orientations and ways of life in early China. Although most students of Chinese thought are content to use "self-cultivation" as a placemarker translation for this variety, this standard rendering has some drawbacks, particularly in Xunzi's case. In general, *xiu* means to "improve," "set in order," or even "repair," although it can also mean to "adorn" or "beautify." It is occasionally used to describe enacting, following, or imitating a model or method (e.g., *Xunzi* 2/5/3, 8/30/15). It can also be used adjectivally to describe something that has become well ordered, complete, and beautiful (e.g., 8/31/1). The primary meaning of *shen* is the body. Derived from this is a sense of the word as referring to something "itself" or a person "himself" or "herself."

Xunzi, however, is at pains to distance himself from the agricultural model of self-development championed by Mencius, and so the very word "cultivation" might suggest a picture Xunzi thinks is dangerously misleading. (Indeed, *xiu* is not typically used in agricultural contexts, in the way that *yang* 養 may be used for animal husbandry, so the metaphor of cultivating naturally growing plants is neither primary nor even present in the Chinese.) Furthermore, the presence of the word *shen* does not suggest that what Chinese thinkers were discussing was primarily the development of a unique sense of self, of individual distinctiveness; nor does it suggest that the sort of development they were discussing was primarily accomplished alone or through introspection. As discussed below, introspective self-examination is one spiritual exercise that Xunzi does suggest, but only one, and not one of the central ones that he examines in detail. Nevertheless, *xiu shen* does carry the implication that what is at issue is improving oneself, considered as a whole being, rather than improving other people through teaching or good government.

"Self-cultivation" is certainly a serviceable category for analyzing Chinese ethical thought, precisely as a way to address debates about *xiu shen* as a general process of regulating and rectifying embodied persons and their movements, judgments, and responses. And it is certainly clear that the early Confucians were deeply concerned with personal commitment to the Way, and an awareness of oneself as someone striving to become a *junzi* 君子, "noble man," or at least an educated one (*shi* 士), someone who "desires when alone to improve himself" (2/7/5–6). "Spiritual exercises," then, is not a radically superior term, sweeping the field of scholarship clear; it is, however, a good way to highlight a related but different set of issues, which suit the purposes of this study.[15] Most important, attending to disciplinary exercises encourages a closer focus on the specific practices that Xunzi saw as making up the general process of *xiu shen*, thus providing a more nuanced structure for presenting both Xunzi's specific prescriptions for, and general theory of the efficacy of, practices of personal transformation.

What I am calling "exercises" Xunzi refers to in terms of the late Warring States vocabulary of *shu* 術, "arts" or "techniques," generally of personal discipline or of government. Xunzi contrasts the "techniques of the Ru [i.e., Confucians]" that lead to societal and personal flourishing and abundance, with those of the Mohists, which lead to poverty and disorder (10/45/16–10/46/4). And in his critique of the divinatory practice of physiognomy, he begins by arguing that in discerning a person's future:

> Divining from the physical form is not as good as evaluating the heart/mind, and evaluating the heart/mind is not as good as selecting techniques. The physical form does not triumph over the heart/mind, and the heart/mind does not triumph over techniques. If the techniques are correct and the heart/mind complies [with them], then although one's body and face are ugly, if the techniques for one's heart/mind are good there will be no harm to one's prospects for becoming a noble man. (5/17/11–13)

Clearly, for Xunzi, spiritual exercises are the key to human flourishing in the Confucian mode, capable of overcoming ugly bodily, emotional, and intellectual endowments. Indeed, Xunzi claims rather grandly that by "holding on to the [correct, Confucian] techniques," the noble man is able to see what is near yet know what is far away, separate right from wrong, extend the guiding principles of ritual and justice, and order all the world's people as if employing a single servant (3/11/14–18).[16]

Study

These Confucian techniques are primarily classical study, ritual practice, and the performance and appreciation of music. Concerning *xue* 學, "study" (and also "learning"), Xunzi writes:

> Its techniques begin with reciting the Classics and conclude with reading the Rituals. Their purpose in the beginning is to make an educated man, and in the end to make a sage. If you truly accumulate effort over a long period then you will enter [the Way]. Study continues until death and only then ceases. Thus, though the techniques of studying come to an end, the purpose of learning must never be put aside, even for an instant. Those who undertake learning become human; those who cast it aside become beasts. (1/3/7–9)[17]

For Xunzi, humanity worthy of the name rests on an assiduously accumulated foundation of study and learning. Xunzi is a defender in changed social and intellectual circumstances of the continued vitality and relevance of a particular tradition of thought and practice: the Way of the Zhou Dynasty revered and expounded by Confucius. Xunzi is the first person in ancient China to see this tradition as being transmitted by texts that are properly understood as "classics," *jing* 經. He is also the first to specify his own lineage of predecessors back to Confucius, to contrast it with other lineages or subtraditions that in his view had gone astray.[18] For Xunzi, only by hearing the words left by the Zhou kings will one realize the greatness of learning, just as one will not grasp the expanse of Heaven without climbing mountains, or the depth of Earth without peering into gorges. Xunzi continues: "The sons of Han, Yue, Yi and Mo [southern states and 'barbarian' tribes] make the same sounds at birth, but grow up with different customs, because teaching has made them so" (1/1/7–8). For Xunzi, teaching makes us what we are as human beings, and so the methods used and goals sought in that teaching are of paramount importance. Only the proper Confucian tradition that Xunzi sees himself as passing to posterity can serve as a firm foundation for human flourishing, in his view.

Xunzi uses a variety of parables to express the point that where one takes one's stand with respect to education and personal development is of the utmost importance, governing honor and disgrace, and even life and death. He discusses the southern "dunce dove" that builds beautiful nests among the reeds, only to have them destroyed when the winds come, because they are attached to the wrong base. He tells of miniature trees that despite diminutive size have spectacular views because they grow on top of mountains. And even delicacies, if they are soaked in the wrong liquid, will become disgusting. "Thus," Xunzi concludes, "some words call down disaster, and some actions summon disgrace, so the noble man is cautious about where he takes his stand" (1/1/17–1/2/7).

What exactly is this classical tradition that Xunzi reveres? For Xunzi, the most apparent objects of study are a set of crucially important ancient texts (1/3/9–12). The *Documents* purports to record various consultations and pronouncements by kings and ministers from the founding era of the Zhou Dynasty; some version of the text existed in the time of Confucius, although the currently existing versions are problematic in various ways.[19] The *Odes* are a collection of poems on quite various subjects, ranging from folks songs to hymns to political poems concerning the Zhou overthrow of the Shang Dynasty. Xunzi quotes the *Odes* frequently, and the extant version of this text derives from a redaction by one of his students. As with the *Documents* and the *Odes*, the texts Xunzi refers to as the *Rituals* and the *Music* no longer exist in the form that he used. The extant *Liji*, the "*Record of Ritual*," is a Han Dynasty text that incorporates an uncertain amount of Warring States and earlier material; the *Yili*, *Da Dai Liji*, and *Zhou Li* are similar ritual miscellanies. There is no single surviving text on music; the chapter in the *Liji* titled "Yueji," the "Record of Music," is highly dependent on Xunzi's own writings in his "Discussion of Music" chapter. The *Spring and*

Autumn Annals is an exceptionally terse record of events, mostly political and occasionally environmental, that occurred in Confucius's home state of Lu between 722 and 481 BCE; it is customarily read in conjunction with commentaries that give the spare text lengthy exegesis to discern the judgments of its author, traditionally taken to be Confucius himself.[20]

Xunzi reveres this group of texts because he sees them as collecting the lessons of the past, and in particular, recording the highest achievements of human civilization as he knew it: the political wisdom to be gleaned from the most successful government yet known, which oversaw centuries of peace and prosperity; and the artistic products exemplifying the goodness, beauty, and refined form that made such peace and harmony possible. The connection between these points requires some unpacking. For Xunzi, as for other Confucians, *wen* 文 is a cardinal value. The word refers in its most basic sense to patterns or designs, but can also refer to writing, written texts, or humane culture generally. It connotes beauty, refinement, and wise and humane judgment across all aspects of human existence. Xunzi is thus not a Kantian, in the sense that he fails to recognize fundamental categorical distinctions between aesthetic, moral, and scientific realms; from our vantage point in the modern West, the notion of *wen* especially crosses the first two realms, and through its association with *li* 理, "pattern" or "order," encompasses the third as well.[21]

The purpose of studying these classics that collect the highest *wen* from the past, Xunzi writes, is to make one's understanding "clear and bright," and one's conduct "faultless" (1/1/5); in other words, one aims to make one's whole person (i.e., *shen* 身) "fine" or "beautiful" (*mei* 美), despite the ugliness of one's innate endowment (1/3/17; 1/4/16).

Xunzi thinks a problem looms, however. He writes:

> The *Rituals* and *Music* present models but no explanations; the *Odes* and *Documents* concern ancient matters and are not always relevant; the *Spring and Autumn Annals* is terse and cannot be quickly understood. If one orients oneself by means of the practices of the learned and the explanations of the noble man, then one will be venerated for being unbiased, with a comprehensive understanding of the world. Thus I say: when studying, nothing is better than being close to the learned. (1/3/20–21)

One cannot just read the classics alone and gain all the benefits of study, or even grasp the texts' import. Without a learned teacher to guide one's study and offer exegesis of the often opaque classical texts, at best one will arrive merely at a command of disconnected facts, afflicted with jumbled intentions, able to offer quotations of the *Odes* and *Documents* but without a sense of their import. Xunzi calls such failures "vulgar" and "scattered" Confucians

(1/3/23–1/4/4). In other words, the Confucian tradition is not just a collection of books handed down but also a living lineage of teachers who pass along the deeper understanding of life that accompanies and is supported by the texts.[22]

We are now in a better position to examine the Xunzian course of instruction. As noted above, according to Xunzi, Confucian study commences with a lengthy process of reading and memorizing the various classics. Xunzi describes this first step as *song* 誦, "reciting" or "chanting." One can speculate that the teacher or master, *shi* 師, would recite a given section of text to a group of novices, thereby showing them the basic syntactical patterns in the text, as well as the pronunciation of difficult or ambiguous characters; this would have been a more significant step than it might appear, because literary remains excavated from Xunzi's era show that such texts were typically unpunctuated, presenting a seemingly endless string of characters, and were inconsistent at best in their recording of the "radicals" that govern precise meaning in later writings.[23] Such practices of textual production place high stress on authoritative exegesis for even basic understanding to be possible, as anyone who has attempted to read excavated texts in the absence of any commentarial tradition knows only too well. Xunzian novices would most likely have begun by simply echoing their master's words, to grasp the basic structure of each day's text, and attended to his explanations of difficult passages to gain some understanding of their meaning.

While this sort of imitation, if given a sufficiently full sense, can serve for Xunzi as a paradigm for successfully transmitting traditional wisdom and skill (2/8/1–3), he hastens to distinguish what he has in mind from rote memorization, and from a disembodied or uncommitted intellectual acquisition. He writes:

> The noble man's learning enters through his ear, is recorded in his heart/mind, spreads throughout his four limbs, and takes shape in his activity and repose. The beginnings of his speech, his slightest movement—even one of these can serve as a model and standard. The petty person's learning enters the ear and emerges from the mouth. Since the distance between mouth and ear is only four *cun*, how could this be sufficient to make beautiful [*mei* 美] a seven *chi* body? Those who studied in antiquity did it for themselves; those who study today do it for [other] people. Through his studies the noble man makes his own person beautiful; through his studies the petty person [merely] becomes an animal. (1/3/14–17)

Xunzian study is not the "petty" exercise of learning classical allusions in order to win admiration and influence. It is the integral pursuit of deeper intellectual understanding, developing in tandem with a thorough practical and bodily appropriation of a whole ethico-religious way of life, that is, the Confucian Way.[24] The ideological import of various Confucian doctrines cannot be grasped apart from this deeper appropriation, such that even single words and slight movements are perfected and can serve as models to be emulated. And although, to borrow some terminology from Alasdair MacIntyre, Xunzi thinks certain goods external to Confucian practices will probably accrue to the earnest student, such as prestige and official posts, these are emphatically not the purpose of his Confucianism, which aims at the transformation of individuals and society via the accumulation of goods internal to Confucian spiritual exercises, such as the virtues of wisdom, humaneness, justice, and trustworthiness.[25]

For Xunzi, the goal of studying is complete, sagelike perfection of both understanding and practice (e.g., 1/4/12–14). Xunzi describes how this process of appropriation should go, at least in its higher reaches, as follows:

> The noble man knows that what is incomplete and impure does not deserve to be judged fine [*mei* 美]. Thus he recites and investigates [the classics] in order to become familiar with them, thinks about and probes into [them] in order to comprehend them, makes himself a learned man in order to dwell in it [i.e., the Confucian Way], removes what harms it [from himself] in order to cleave to and nurture it. He makes his eyes be without desire to see what is contrary to it, makes his ears be without desire to hear what is contrary to it, makes his mouth be without desire to say what is contrary to it, and makes his heart/mind be without desire to reflect on what is contrary to it. When he reaches its highest point, he delights in it. His eyes like it more than the five colors, his ears more than the five sounds, his mouth more than the five flavors, and his heart/mind gains greater benefit from it than by possessing all under Heaven. (1/4/16–19; cf. *Analects* 12.1)

Xunzian study aims at a transformation so complete that one's whole person becomes *mei* 美, "fine" or "beautiful," with learning that is pure and perfect, able in life to hit one hundred targets out of a hundred, not just ninety nine (1/4/12). What necessarily begins with the rudimentary exercises of imitative recitation and attentive listening to a teacher's explanations slowly grows. As the student gains understanding, both practical and theoretical, of the Confucian Way, he investigates and ponders the Way so as to understand it more deeply and eventually come to "dwell" in it and even delight in it. Xunzi also thinks the noble man exercises a rigorous self-discipline, retraining his senses so that they accept only the delights of the Way, which are considerable, and which if fully appreciated outshine all other pleasures of the senses and even the greatest political power. He regulates his speech and action in accord with the proximate model of his teacher and the more distant sages of the past. He focuses his thought so that he will not be distracted by what is contrary to the Way, and he concentrates on the task of study.

Although self-regulation becomes progressively more important in Xunzian ethical development, its role in the process should not overshadow the critical importance of the group setting he envisions for the practice of Confucian spiritual exercises. Xunzi suggests that the quickest route to learning is to admire and draw close to others who study, who certainly include one's teacher but also his other students (1/3/23). This vision of a community of learners is based on the need to put one's learning into practice, and the need for help from others when doing so. In the "Improving Oneself" chapter, Xunzi begins by writing:

> When you see goodness, diligently be sure that it will exist within you; when you see what is not good, with apprehension be certain to examine yourself for it. When there is good in you, steadfastly be sure to delight in it; when there is bad in you, be certain to hate it in yourself as if it were a disaster. Thus one who chastises me and is right is my teacher; one who approves of me and is right is my friend; one who flatters me is my enemy. Therefore the noble man exalts his teacher and cherishes his friends, but thoroughly hates his enemies. Delighting in the good yet never satisfied, accepting admonition and able to take precautions accordingly—although someone like this has no desire to advance, how could he fail to? The petty person is just the opposite. (2/5/3–6)[26]

Xunzi counsels constant alertness to the qualities and flaws of both ourselves and others, linked always to an earnest passion to imitate and appropriate any good we come across and eliminate what is vicious from ourselves. Daily self-examination is essential, according to Xunzi. In the very first paragraph of the *Xunzi*, we are told that "the noble man studies broadly and each day examines himself in three ways" (1/1/5; cf. 2/5/3ff., 2/6/12, 11/54/13). This is a reference to a tradition started by Confucius's disciple Zengzi, recorded in *Analects* 1.4:[27] "Zengzi said, 'Every day I examine myself in three ways. Have I not been faithful in what I seek for others? Have I not been trustworthy in my dealings with friends? Have I not practiced what I transmit?'" Xunzian self-examination, then, is a self-interrogation concerning one's treatment of close and distant human beings, and whether one has conscientiously enacted what one teaches and purports to follow. And yet individual people are always liable to blindness and self-deception, particularly in their ethical self-assessments. Thus a community of likeminded students of the Way can provide the support and admonition necessary to slowly develop a more accurate view of oneself and of others, whittling away at greed, envy, and self-justifying illusion. Our choice of friends and teacher is critical on such a view, and extreme caution needs to be exercised with those who would feed our selfishness through flattery; such people are our true enemies, Xunzi thinks, more than the inhabitants of any antagonistic foreign state.

Xunzi even thinks our companions will spontaneously and unconsciously affect our developing habits, regardless of our conscious efforts to emulate them. He writes that no matter how talented someone is,

> he must seek an excellent teacher and serve him, select worthy friends and act as a friend to them. If he finds an excellent teacher and serves him, then what he hears will be the Way of [the sage kings] Yao, Shun, Yu and Tang; if he gets fine people to be his friends, then what he sees will be faithful, trustworthy, respectful, and deferential conduct. He [lit. "his body"] will make daily progress towards humaneness and justice without him realizing it—the "rubbing" [by others] makes it so. Now if he dwells among people who are not good, . . . [what he sees and hears will be vicious, and rubbing will daily lead him closer to disgrace]. A tradition says: "If you do not know your son watch his friends; if you do not know your lord watch his attendants." This is nothing but rubbing, nothing but rubbing! (23/117/16–23/118/1)[28]

For Xunzi, we *mo* 靡, "rub" against others in numerous ways each day, who subtly polish us into virtue or abrade us into vice. We absorb the words and conduct of those around us without even realizing it is happening. Thus having good friends to help one along the path is critical to spiritual progress, perhaps second only to having a good teacher.

Xunzi describes in some detail the need to restrict one's discussions with certain sorts of people, particularly ones who are *ku* 楛, "coarse," and those who argue angrily, presumably so as not to be swayed from the true Way before one has mastered it sufficiently to defend it and stick with it when difficulties arise. Students should receive and talk only to those who have followed the Way to achieve whatever position they have attained, and who demonstrate this through ritually appropriate bearing and conversation (1/4/6–9; see also *Analects* 16.6). In general, Xunzi thinks one should be guarded in one's discussions of the Way, making sure only to discuss what is appropriate to the level of understanding of one's interlocutor. And even the noble man does not bother with the truly coarse, elsewhere called "vulgar," for their lack of personal development (1/4/1, 4/15/22ff).

Xunzi's concern for the proper discussion partners of both beginning and advanced students of the Way stems from the already long-standing Confucian tradition of philosophical dialogue, which Xunzi certainly continued with his own students. By "philosophical dialogue," I mean thoughtful discussion, questioning, and argument premised on a shared love for wisdom and the good life within a self-conscious group of teacher and students who were all committed to such a reflective way of life. It seems to have been common early Confucian practice that students as they progressed would question or even dispute with their master about the main and secondary points of his teaching. Similarly, the teacher would ask his students questions to provoke deeper understanding and practice.

In Xunzi's time, debate was an established practice in the courts of aspiring rulers, and the vigor of this sort of controversy enlivened and made more sophisticated the exchanges over ideas that apparently went on in Xunzi's circle.[29] Chapter 15 of the *Xunzi* includes a lengthy, idealized retelling of a debate about military affairs between Xunzi and the Lord of Linwu before King Xiaocheng of Zhao. After this concludes, it includes records of shorter exchanges between Xunzi and two of his students, Chen Xiao and Li Si. These latter records are of more interest, because they show something of the quality of discussion in Xunzi's group. Chen Xiao questions Xunzi about the very possibility of a true king's use of military force, given his commitment to humaneness and justice, defined in terms of loving the people and following good order. Xunzi responds with what in comparative perspective is a variety of just war argument, justifying the use of force by wise and benevolent rulers for legitimate purposes, that is, the defense of humaneness and justice against those who would destroy the people and good societal order (15/71/21–27). Li Si's question is somewhat more poignant, showing him considering the ideas that would later lead him to leave the Confucian fold. Li questions Xunzi about the state of Qin's evident military successes, which seem to be based not on humaneness and justice but on "relying on opportunities and following along with events," that is, the pragmatic use of power in whatever circumstances present themselves. Xunzi counters that these are only apparent opportunities; the real opportunities, for a strong, unified, harmonious state and populace, and for the military and diplomatic successes that follow from this, are presented only by humaneness and justice when practiced as the foundation of governance (15/72/1–7).

It is clear from this that Xunzi encouraged his students to fully engage their intellects in their studies, absorbing the classical heritage and using questioning and discussion as a tool to deepen their understanding of the

Confucian Way. What begins with memorization and recitation slowly flowers into a reflective commitment to the Way, a commitment so strong that a noble man will follow this Way unto death (1/4/19–20). Thus whereas ritual reconditioning of habits is an important element of Xunzian personal transformation, he is not proposing a behaviorism that leaves consciousness and conscious assent out of the picture. Quite the contrary, Confucian personal development will only be successful if one comes to understand and assent to the Way as part of this larger process of ritual reformation (21/103/18–19).[30]

Ritual

Li 禮, "ritual," is many things for Xunzi. On the individual and familial levels, it is a method for personal formation; this is the aspect of ritual upon which I focus below. Ritual is also the source of genuine state power and authority, Xunzi thinks, much more effective at knitting the people and government together and generating political and military force than weapons and defenses, commands and punishments. Such tools obviously have their uses, but Xunzi finds them to be decidedly secondary to the quality of government, which rests primarily on ritual (15/72/9–12ff.). Ritual is even the key to the harmonious interrelationship and flourishing of Heaven, Earth, and humanity; it is the linchpin of what P. J. Ivanhoe has called Xunzi's "grand ecological vision."[31] Xunzi writes:

> Through [ritual] Heaven and Earth come together, the sun and moon shine, the four seasons follow each other, the stars and planets move, the great rivers flow, the myriad things all thrive, love and hate are moderated, and delight and anger made appropriate. If through ritual one is below, then one will be compliant; if through ritual one is above, then one will be enlightened. [Through it] the myriad things change but do not become chaotic. (19/92/4–6)

Although this might seem a burst of wild exuberance from Xunzi, verging on the magical, it should be read as a poetic evocation of what I discussed in chapter 3 as Xunzi's ritualized conception of the cosmos. Different elements of the universe each have their appropriate roles, which the heavenly bodies fill with admirable regularity. The human role is to order both the human and natural worlds so that inevitable ebbs and flows do not result in chaos. This can be accomplished both through agriculture that magnifies and orders natural fecundity, and through what might be called public works projects, such as the dredging and diking of the Yellow and Yangzi Rivers, traditionally credited to the sage king Yu, in order to stop destructive flooding.[32]

For Xunzi, ritual is the key to harmonious and flourishing life, both human and nonhuman. It is thus his general prescription for the misrule, unrest, and chaos of his age.[33]

It should be noted that Xunzi's term *li* 禮, translated here and by most others as "ritual" or "rites," has both narrow and wide senses. Its narrow sense covers the sorts of practices generally referred to by the English "ritual"—for example, sacrifices, mourning rituals, and rites of passage into adulthood marked by ceremonial donning of the appropriate hat. His more common meaning is very wide, far beyond the usual sense of "ritual," including all matters of personal appearance, deportment, dress, speech, action, and internal and external discipline, and all interpersonal etiquette and even morality. He writes:

> When all uses of blood and *qi*, intention and purpose, understanding and reflection, follow ritual, then order will permeate [you]; if they do not follow ritual, then you will be agitated and chaotic, [or] slack and lazy. If your eating and drinking, clothing and dwelling, and movement and stillness follow ritual then they will be harmonious and moderate; if not they will be offensive and excessive, producing illness. If your expression and appearance, bearing and deportment, approaches and withdrawals, and walk follow ritual, then they will be elegant; if not they will be arrogant and obstinate, low and wicked, common and wild. Thus people without ritual will not live, affairs without ritual will not be completed, and states and families without ritual will not have peace. An Ode says: "Rituals and ceremonies completely correct, laughter and talk completely appropriate." This expresses it. (2/5/12–15)

It is hard to overstate how alien such a sensibility is to modern America with its vendors of "lifestyle choices" and "personal style." For Xunzi, what to us seem optional matters of style and aesthetics are bound up in an integrated order encompassing personal and communal life, and the ecology of our environment as well. Clear and correct standards for such things are available and can be known: Human existence should be *ya* 雅, "elegant," and manifest *wenli* 文理, "refined form and good order."

But how can this be? How could anyone think that attending to one's manner of walking, one's clothes and abode, could be so essential that without it we cannot live as human beings? Obviously, Xunzi recognizes that many in his own day did not have correct ritual deportment and yet survived. He does appear to think that the moderation essential to a ritualized existence is much healthier, in a psychophysical sense, than a life without ritual, which would be marked by erratic excesses and deficiencies. His deeper point, however, is more subtle. He thinks that to have a truly humane existence—that is, one properly regulated by and as far as possible incarnating ideals of goodness and beauty—we must have ritual in his wide sense. To be human in this fuller sense, we need, Xunzi thinks, to live in community with others. To achieve this, we must have social order, which to be orderly must involve hierarchy. In order for such an arrangement to be based on more than fear and intimidation on the one hand, and/or greed on the other, it needs to develop and rely on other emotions: respect and reverence for the truly worthy, love for one's family and relatives, loyalty to good rulers. But because our raw dispositions are relatively better suited to being ruled by fear and greed, work must be done to heighten other sensibilities and reshape our dispositions.

This is where ritual as spiritual exercise fits into Xunzi's view. By imitating classical models in the details of life, both personal and interpersonal, Xunzi thinks we can cultivate the refinement, sensitivity, and subtle judgment of the sagacious Zhou kings. When such a large part of existence is ritualized in this way, we are then sharing a far superior form of life. Our every gesture and word is pregnant with meaning, beautiful, and appropriate. This may seem counterintuitive, but when expectations for behavior are so far reaching, greater possibilities for meaningful interaction open up, because the shared background of expectations against which people interpret each other is much fuller, allowing a wider range of variation in communication through more subtle shifts in expression, deportment, and spoken language.[34] At the same time, this habitation of classical forms serves as a training in virtue, by developing one's "taste" for the delights of good form in many aspects of life, and slowly retraining one's disposition accordingly. I explore this "virtuous circle" in Xunzi's thought between visible, outward form and inner emotional reality more fully below.

Authoritative teachers are crucial to Xunzi's account of ritual practice, perhaps even more so than in his account of studying. He writes:

> Ritual is the means by which to rectify yourself. A teacher is the means by which to rectify [your practice of] ritual. . . . When what ritual requires you make so [in your actions], then your dispositions will be at peace in ritual. When what your teacher says you say also, then your understanding will be like your teacher's. When your dispositions are at peace in ritual and your understanding is like that of your teacher, then you have become a sage. Hence to oppose ritual is to be without a model; to oppose your teacher is to be without a teacher. To refuse to accept your teacher and the model and instead prefer to govern yourself: this is like relying on a blind person to distinguish colors, or relying on a deaf person to distinguish sounds; you have no way to abandon chaos and foolishness.

> Hence to learn is to take ritual as your model. And as for a teacher, he makes of himself a correct standard, and cherishes those who find peace in him. (2/8/1–4)

Ritual serves as the model for human action, both in its basic orientations and its subtle refinements. As with studying the classics, a teacher is necessary, although in this case what is acquired is at least as much physical and emotional, in our terminology, as intellectual. The student aims to internalize the ritual skills that the teacher embodies, so that he may flourish as a human being, and as part of this flourishing, to continue the Confucian tradition by becoming a teacher himself. Lest the description of tradition as essentially being a matter of repetition seem too shallow or mechanical, we should recall Xunzi's cautions against rote memorization, and his view of the generally recalcitrant character of human *qing* 情, dispositions, which necessitates a long process of reformation. Most crucially, without reliance on a teacher and external model, we have no way to gain a sense of what is truly good—at first, we are all morally "blind" and "deaf," Xunzi thinks. Only with carefully guided practice will we develop a taste for the Way.

Xunzi sees certain general themes running throughout the whole body of Confucian ritual precepts. He says that ritual has three "roots": "Heaven and Earth are the root of life, ancestors are the root of family lineage, lords and teachers are the root of order. . . . If any one of these three were lost, there would be no peace for human beings. Thus above ritual serves Heaven, below it serves Earth, and it reveres ancestors and exalts lords and teachers" (19/90/20–22). Ritual orients us to what is most important in life, and in particular to those powers upon which we rely for our existence, and its quality. It thus reorients us from our immediate, generally selfish desires to a larger, more realistic understanding, as we serve, revere, and exalt the roots of human life.

Ritual also, Xunzi argues, serves to differentiate, especially between different types of people, such as noble and base, old and young, poor and wealthy, humble and eminent (19/90/10–11). Different members of the social hierarchy perform different sacrifices, and people in different roles or positions are accorded different degrees of respect; all this serves to distinguish different degrees of accomplishment among various people, and makes visible and tangible the hierarchy of excellence that Xunzi thinks the social hierarchy should reflect (19/91/1–5). Thus ritual clarifies degrees of status, and the duties of people toward those in different positions, including the duties of the living toward the dead to "send them off" appropriately and respectfully (19/95/16–19). As we saw above, Xunzi thinks such harmoniously interrelated differentiation is essential to a flourishing society, that is, one that can provide abundantly for all its members, not just the strong and the rapacious.

Xunzi summarizes this general role of ritual as humanizing and enriching communal life by saying in the introduction to his essay on it that "ritual is *yang* 養, nurturing." This has several aspects. He writes:

> Ritual is nurturing. Grain-fed and grass-fed animals, millet and wheat, properly blended with the five flavors—these are what nurture the mouth. The odors of pepper, orchid, and other sweet-smelling plants—these are what nurture the nose. The beauties of carving and inlay, embroidery and pattern—these are what nurture the eyes. Bells and drums, strings and wind instruments—these are what nurture the ears. Spacious rooms and secluded halls, soft mats, couches, benches, armrests and cushions—these are what nurture the body. Therefore ritual is nurturing. . . . Who knows that the means by which to nurture life is [being willing] to go out and suffer death because one sees propriety to be crucial? Who knows that external expenditures are the means by which to nurture wealth? Who knows that loyalty and respect, politeness and courtesy are the means by which to nurture peace? Who knows that ritual and just norms, refined form and good order, are the means by which to nurture the disposition? Thus a person who sees only life will certainly die; one who sees only profit will certainly suffer disasters; one who finds peace only in laziness and weakness will certainly be endangered; one who finds joy only in pleasing his disposition will certainly be annihilated. Thus if people unify themselves on ritual and just norms they will attain both; if they unify themselves on their disposition and innate endowment they will lose both [i.e., both pleasant satisfaction and the flourishing and security provided by ritual]. Thus Confucians will lead people to attain both, and Mohists will lead them to lose both. (19/90/5–8, 14–18)[35]

Ritual nurtures human life on several levels: It trains our senses so that we can appreciate the beauties of refined form and good order; it broadens our attention so that we can see beyond narrow and immediate perceptions of danger and benefit; by "nurturing the *qing* 情, disposition," it teaches us to extend ourselves in certain ways for higher goals; and it thereby supports a mode of life that is more satisfying as well as more moral. On the community level, ritual nurtures life, wealth, and peace; Xunzi thinks his Mohist enemies argue for a foolish frugality that leads only to poverty and contention, by cutting out the most important tools of civilization in the quest for a humane existence.[36] Truly, Xunzi thinks, Confucian ritual is the way of human flourishing in the widest sense of that term. It is the "ridgepole of the human Way," and it provides humans with much-needed *fang* 方, "orientation" in life (19/92/15–17).

Let us look more closely at what Xunzi means by "nurturing the *qing* 情, disposition." Recall that the word *yang* 養, translated as "nurture," "rear," or "nurse," normally refers to the proper treatment of domesticated animals, which need to be fed, cared for, and trained for useful work; it is also a word for "treating" an illness.[37] In other words, considered as a spiritual exercise, ritual practice is a tool for training and properly reforming the *qing*, in the same way that a compass and balance are tools for the constructions of carpentry (19/92/13–16).

Ritual reshapes the *qing* so that it is disposed toward desires and actions that accord with *wenli* 文理, "refined form and good order" (19/92/21–19/93/1). Xunzi writes that "ritual cuts what is long and stretches what is short, eliminates surplus and supplements insufficiency, extends the refined forms of love and respect, and develops and completes the beauties of right conduct" (19/94/8). Xunzi goes on to make the connection with *qing* explicit later in the paragraph as follows:

> People definitely have the beginnings of these two *qing* [joy and sorrow] from birth. If these *qing* are cut off and stretched out, broadened and narrowed, increased and diminished, analyzed and completely extended, made abundant and beautiful, so that root and branch, end and beginning are all appropriately linked and elegantly complete, sufficient to serve as a model for ten thousand generations, then this is ritual. (19/94/19–21)

By imitating classical forms in our external presentation and interactions, we do a certain amount of violence to our spontaneous promptings and desires, and we slowly reshape our disposition over time as we adjust to these respectful, deferential modes of life. Eventually, our disposition is transformed, and it becomes the model we have been imitating, spontaneously tending toward Confucian ritual propriety. It is worth noting that Xunzi thinks we should make our *qing* "abundant and beautiful." His Way relies on stimulation and heightened responsiveness at least as much as on the restraint of chaotic impulses.

We can explore the dynamics of this more fully by considering what may be called the consensus view of Xunzi's account: that he provides an expressive theory of ritual.[38] By "expressive," several commentators mean that Xunzi thinks ritual expresses inner emotions in visible external form. Stated so generally, this is a reasonable interpretation; but it needs to be filled out to capture the nuances of Xunzi's understanding of *li*.

A "romantic" reading that might be suggested by such a summary is that Xunzi thinks we have powerful emotions welling up within us that need to be expressed and dissipated, or else they could become destructive, either to our inner emotional equilibrium or to self and others through some sort of fit of passion; Xunzi's account of death rituals might be enlisted as evidence for this. This interpretation is not wrong but incomplete, and it slights ritual's role as a spiritual exercise that shapes and generates emotions, as well as merely shunting their flow as part of a "hydraulic" theory of inner forces.[39]

The key to interpreting Xunzi on this point is to see what exactly he says about ritual's effect on the *qing* and cognate notions. As noted above, his general description is that ritual *yang* 養, "nurtures" the *qing*. He suggests that ritual *jie* 節, "moderates" love and hate and *dang* 當, "makes appropriate" delight and anger (19/92/4–6). He says that the particularly strict treatment ritual gives to matters of birth and death "satisfies human yearnings" (足以為人願) when these beginnings and endings are treated "as one" (19/93/12–13). He justifies the tradition of letting the dead body of one's parent or lord lie in state for three months by contending that "it is done because of the duty to call forth and heighten longing and remembrance" of the dead (是致隆思慕之義也) (19/94/1). In discussing the mourning rites, he argues that the corpse must be properly adorned or else it will become repugnant, and mourners will not feel the appropriate sorrow; it must also be slowly moved further away so that it does not become the object of contempt and loathing, which lead to forgetfulness and lack of respect. All these natural failures of proper emotion are shameful and even bestial, Xunzi thinks, and need to be avoided by proper ritual observance, which makes possible the appropriate emotions (19/94/3–6). Shortly thereafter come the passages quoted above about ritual cutting and stretching, broadening and narrowing, increasing and decreasing various *qing*, as appropriate (19/94/8, 19–21). In between these two passages, Xunzi explains various ritual observances as "the emotions of joy and sorrow from auspicious and inauspicious events emerging through (*fa yu* 發於)" facial expression, sound, food, clothing, and dwelling, in turn (19/94/14–19). These various sorts of observance, depending on their nature and purpose, are "the means by which to sustain (*chi* 持) tranquillity and serve auspicious occasions" or "the means by which to sustain anxiety and serve inauspicious occasions" (19/94/10). Later, Xunzi suggests that the many ritual observances concerning the dressing of the corpse and the arrangement of the tomb are "all means by which to make grief heavier (*zhong ai* 重哀)" (19/95/13). Immediately thereafter, he says that in all rites "serving the living adorns (*shi*

飾) delight; sending off the dead adorns grief; sacrifices adorn reverence; and military troops adorn majesty" (19/95/14). Xunzi twice says that the mourning period extends for twenty-five months in order to "suit (*cheng* 稱) the emotions [aroused by the death of one's parents] and establish refined form." This is necessary because on such an occasion the pain of grieving is at its height. However, after twenty-five months, "[although] one's grief and pain have not yet ended, longing and remembrance are not yet forgotten, nevertheless ritual cuts them off here (*duan zhi* 斷之), for otherwise there would be no end to sending off the dead, no time to return to life" (19/96/4–8). Thus ritual cuts off the observance of mourning before it becomes excessive and destructive, even though one's grief would tend to continue (19/96/18–21). And last, in a passage that will be discussed at greater length below, Xunzi writes that "sacrificing is the concentration of intentions of fond longing" (19/97/20).

Thus, when looked at as a group, Xunzi's statements tend predominantly in one direction. Although he does mention "satisfying human yearnings" and "suiting the emotions" that are present after the death of a parent or lord, as well as "adorning" various emotions that are presumed to be present, all the other passages concern the reshaping of emotions—whether stretching some and cutting others off (three times); "nurturing," "moderating," "making appropriate," "calling forth," "heightening," "making heavier," and "sustaining" (twice); as well as generating the appropriate emotions by proper handling of the corpse and "refining" or "concentrating" the intention to have certain emotions through the act of sacrifice. The one other reference, to *qing* dispositions/emotions "emerging through" various ritual observances, points toward Xunzi's theory of inner and outer harmonization, his sort of "expressiveness."

Xunzi theorizes the "emergence" and "adornment" of the *qing* by again relating *qing* and *wen* 文, "refined form." His first run at this topic is elliptical: "The highest completeness [in ritual] is when emotion and form are both exhausted; second to this is when emotion and form prevail in turn; below this is when one returns to emotion in order to revert to the grand unity" (19/92/3–4). The word often translated, as above, by "exhaust," *jin* 盡, is quite multivalent, and it can also mean to finish, complete, or reach the limit or pinnacle of something; Xunzi's point is not yet clear. But he shortly returns to the issue in more detail:

> Ritual uses valuables and other goods for offerings, relies on distinctions of eminent and humble for its forms, employs more and fewer for differences [of status], is plentiful or sparse to show [the degree of] importance. When form and pattern are abundant and emotions and offerings

> reduced, this is the plentiful height of ritual; when form and pattern are reduced and emotion and offerings abundant, this is the sparse reduction of ritual. When form and pattern, emotions and offerings mutually serve as inner and outer, exterior garment and lining, moving together and united, this is the middle course where ritual flows (是禮之中流也). Therefore the noble man above reaches up to its plentiful height, below exhausts its sparse reduction, but in the middle dwells in its middle [course]. . . . He never departs from this, because it is the noble man's altar and dwelling, his palace court. (19/92/21–19/93/1)[40]

Rituals vary in their degree of lavishness, but whether ornate or minimal, subdued or very moving, Xunzi thinks the ideal is when emotions and appearances match each other throughout the sequence of ritual actions. In this way, emotions "emerge" and are "adorned" by action and observance; but the reverse is just as true: The forms and patterns of ritual cut and stretch the emotions, pushing and pulling our disposition into a new form that will more spontaneously tend toward humaneness, reverence, and justice. Indeed, on this second formulation, the height of ritual is when form predominates, whereas the lowest point is when emotion and offerings predominate; it would seem that formation is primary for Xunzi, even though the telos of ritual remains harmonious synchronization. The image of the "middle course where ritual flows" suggests the ease and grace that can be attained as ritual practice grows more expert, and the harmony between what one feels and wants and what one should do becomes greater. For the sage, this harmony of inner and outer is sustained through all variations in circumstances (19/93/2–3).

Xunzi's conception is thus not so much that humans have irrepressible eruptions of emotional fluid that must squirt out, and which he is concerned might disrupt good order. Rather, he aims to shape the combination of inner and outer, of emotions and outward signs, into a pleasing and appropriate form, which is both beautiful and proper. This is why when he discusses the mourning rites he shows how they manipulate reality to generate and heighten certain emotions, such as reverence and longing, while guarding against others, such as disgust. Xunzi is concerned to form and order inner and outer experience together, and bring harmony and beauty to what can be chaotic and even violent. He wants us to rely on ritual to modulate our emotions and actions into satisfying, orderly forms that both signify and reinforce our commitment to humane values.

Consider Xunzi's closing reflections on sacrifices for the dead, which are often translated as if they straightforwardly support a romantic expressive reading, despite textual problems with the passage that make such a reading unlikely. Given the significance of this discussion to the current argument, I quote it in full. He writes:

> Sacrificing is the concentration[41] of intentions of fond longing. At times [after the death of a parent or beloved lord] one cannot avoid the arrival of strange changes [of heart and appearance], breath catching in anxiety and grief. Thus at times of shared delight and camaraderie, even the dutiful minister or filial son will have occasions when strange changes arrive. This sort of arrival is extremely moving; if pressed down [so that it] ends hollowly, then he will find the concentration of his intentions to be dissatisfying and insufficient, and will see his ritual practice as empty and incomplete. Thus the former kings pressed it down so as to make of it an established form to fulfill the duties of honoring the honorable and showing affection for those who deserve affection. Thus I say sacrificing is the concentration of intentions of fond longing; the height of loyalty, trust, love, and respect; and the flourishing of ritual practice and refined demeanor. None but a sage is able to understand this. The sage understands this with clarity, educated and noble men find peace in enacting it, ministers work to preserve it, and the hundred clans regard it as established custom. Noble men see [sacrificing] as the Human Way; the hundred clans see it as serving ghosts. Thus bells and drums, flutes and chimes, stringed and wind instruments, . . . [and eight kinds of musical performance] are the means by which the noble man makes these strange changes into the refined forms of happiness and joy. The mourning garments and staff, dwelling in a hut and eating gruel, using twigs as a mat and earth as a pillow, these are the means by which the noble man makes these strange changes into the refined forms of sorrow and pain. That military expeditions have restrictions, that punishments and laws have grades, such that each equals the crime committed, these are the means by which the noble man makes these strange changes into the refined forms of deep hatred. One divines to discern the [proper] day, fasts and prepares the road, sets out the tables and mats with the offerings and informs the invocator as though someone were going to accept them; takes up the goods and sacrifices all of them; the server does not lift up the wine cup, but the host himself has this honor, as though someone would drink it. When the guests leave the host bows and escorts them out, returns and changes clothes, adopts his position and cries, as if someone had departed with them. Such grief! Such reverence! [The sacrifice] serves the dead as one serves the living, serves the departed as one serves those who remain, gives an outline to the shapeless and shadowless, but nevertheless it completes refined form. (19/97/20 to 19/98–110)[42]

The sacrifice at the ancestral temple is the culmination of the twenty-five-month mourning period. It is, Xunzi suggests, the *jing* 精, "concentration," "refinement," and "essence" of the mourner's "intentions of fond longing," that is, the emotionally charged attentive focus on the deceased parent or lord. Although understood more or less adequately by different sorts of people, the sacrificial ritual itself is a reliable kind of catharsis. It purposefully calls forth and generates intense feelings of grief and reverence in a communal context of shared concern and regret, but it shapes and forms these emotions in an ordered and fitting, even beautiful, manner. This is what Xunzi means by his earlier reference to *qing wen ju jin* 情文俱盡: The intensity of full and correct ritual brings the emotions to their height but also their completion, their ending, by exhausting them appropriately. The question for Xunzi is not whether emotions should be "pressed" in certain ways, but in which ways; he thinks they can be supported and shaped in ways that are finally satisfying and appropriate, instead of frustrating and alienating. Clearly, Xunzi thinks the death of a loved parent or lord is a moving event, which agitates and disrupts our *qing*; such deaths generate "strange changes" in us that distract and upset us—although note well that he does not specify that these are emotional rather than having to do with demeanor or appearance.[43] Note also that he thinks such changes occur in a variety of situations, including the administration of criminal justice and war.

The sacrifice for one's dead parent or lord, then, is for Xunzi a manner of enacting appropriate grief and reverence; mourners not only express the grief they naturally possess but also call up the appropriate emotions in turn to navigate a difficult passage in life and demonstrate their profound commitment to the duties of filial son and/or loyal minister (19/93/9–10). The Confucian Way—with its virtues of loyalty, trust, love, and respect, and its duties to "honor the honorable and show affection for those who deserve affection"—sets the standard and makes possible full human flourishing, in the context of shared human frailty and mortality.[44]

Music

The third principal technique of personal formation that Xunzi promotes is the playing and appreciation of music.[45] Music for Xunzi is based on a classical repertoire instituted by the ancient kings, and it includes the entire ritual performance in multiple media: playing instruments, singing, and sacred dance. The bulk of Xunzi's chapter on music is an indignant defense of Confucian practices in the face of Mohist attacks. Mohists considered musical performances wasteful and pointless, but Xunzi sees music as one of the crucial "arts of civilization," in Knoblock's well-turned phrase,[46] without which human life would not just be poorer but also savage and despicable.

He begins by exploiting a peculiarity of the Chinese language, suggesting what to his readers would have been intuitively appealing, that "music is joy" (20/98/14). In classical Chinese, the word for music, *yue* 樂, is written with the same character as the word for joy, *le* 樂. Little argument is necessary to establish what is already taken for granted in one's language.

Xunzi moves from this opening observation to another statement of his "expressive" understanding of ritual and music. He writes:

> Music is joy, the human emotion that is certainly unavoidable, and thus people cannot be without music. When one feels joyful then it must emerge through sounds and tones, take shape through movement and stillness, and [thus] the human Way—sounds and tones, movement and stillness, and the changes wrought by the techniques for living—is exhausted through this [i.e., music]. Therefore people cannot be without joy, and when there is joy it cannot fail to take shape, but if it takes shape contrary to the Way then they cannot avoid chaos. The former kings hated such chaos, and thus established the sounds of the *Odes* and *Hymns* in order to guide them, made their sounds sufficient for joy but not to overflowing, made their forms sufficient to mark distinctions but not induce anxiety, made their directness, complexity, intensity, and rhythm sufficient to arouse and move people's good hearts, and made it so that evil and stagnant *qi* would have no way to enter them. This was the method of the former kings in establishing music, and yet Mozi opposes it—what is to be done about him? (20/98/14–19)[47]

In structure, this is partially similar to Xunzi's justification of ritual: Music both prevents the chaos that would result if people's tendencies to joy were wrongly directed and also promotes full human flourishing by guiding us to more edifying forms of emotion and practice consistent with the Way. Here Xunzi straightforwardly postulates a human need for joy, as well as a need for it to emerge and take shape, and yet he also clearly sees music as a way to "guide" people, generate and support the right kind of joy in the proper measure, and "arouse and move people's good hearts."

Referring to human beings' "good hearts" is one of Xunzi's most serious breaches with his doctrine of the badness of our innate endowment, but I think we should see this as a rhetorical flourish that shows his very high opinion of music's transformative power. He thinks music can draw us out and inspire us like nothing else. A later review of these points makes this clear:

> Music is what the sages delighted in, and can be used to make the hearts of the people good; it arouses people deeply, and alters their manner and

> changes their customs. Thus the former kings guided them with ritual and music, and the people became harmonious and amicable. If the people have the dispositions of love and hate yet lack [a way to] respond through delight and anger, then there will be chaos. The former kings hated their chaos, and thus improved their conduct, corrected their music, and all under Heaven became compliant through this. (20/99/24–26)

Music makes our hearts good by deeply arousing us and altering our manner and customs, whether we participate or merely watch and are moved as spectators. Xunzi thinks music makes people "harmonious," "amicable," and *shun* 順, "compliant," a word that is one of his favorite attributes of good people yet is hard to convey cleanly in English. It is usually translated rather starkly as "submissive" or "obedient," but for Xunzi it also carries overtones of agreeableness and sociability, and interest in and concern for others, in contrast to people who are arrogant, rebellious, or resentful. As Xunzi points out in the first quote above, the human Way is *jin* 盡, "exhausted," "fulfilled," and "completed" in music, just as human *qing* are in ritual. These passages show that Xunzi considered music to be essential to a humane way of life, that is, one that does not radically truncate our existence by suppressing or amputating our tendencies to feel, desire, and act but uses these tendencies and shapes them into better and more fulfilling forms.

Among spiritual exercises, music is perhaps the most straightforwardly efficacious, and also the easiest and most delightful. Xunzi writes that "sound and music enters people deeply, transforms people rapidly, and therefore the former kings were careful to give it refined form" (20/99/15). Music produces these effects by working on and eventually transforming the *qing* 情, "disposition," and *zhi* 志, "intent." Music shapes and inspires harmonious fellowship between people, uniting them through shared feelings of reverence, familial love, and compliance, according to the occasion and type of music (20/98/21–22). Listening to the *Odes* and *Hymns* broadens our intentions, taking up shields and battle-axes in the war dance makes our personal presentation more vigorous, coordinating our movements with others while dancing corrects our conduct and timing, all of this inspiring us equally well to go on military expeditions, or to be polite and yielding, depending on the music and situation (20/99/4–7). Xunzi writes:

> The noble man uses bells and drums to guide his intentions, uses zithers to bring joy to his heart. He is moved by shields and battle-axes, adorned by feathers and yak tails, and yields by means of chimes and flutes. . . . Hence when music is performed so that intent becomes pure, when ritual is developed so that conduct becomes complete, then ears and eyes

> become acute and clear; blood and *qi* become harmonious and even, manner is altered and customs changed, and all under Heaven is at peace, the beautiful and the good mutually giving joy. Thus it is said, "music is joy." The noble man finds joy in attaining the Way, while the petty person finds joy in getting what he desires. If you use the Way to regulate desires then you will be joyful and not chaotic, if through [following] desires you forget the Way then you will be deluded and not joyful. Thus music is the means by which to guide joy, and metal, stone, silk [strings], and bamboo are the means by which to guide music.[48] When music is performed the people will turn to face in its direction. Thus music is the flourishing of human governance. (20/100/7–11; cf. 20/99/15–22)

Music brings joy to the heart/mind while guiding one's *zhi* 志, intentions, that is, the goals and aspirations upon which one's attention is habitually focused. The substance of this guidance is that the right sort of music reorients people's manner, customs, and intentions to the pursuit of the Way above all. It even provides benefits to perception and physiological function, Xunzi thinks. Only through the Way and the music that is a part of it can we attain true joy, and peace in our life together; otherwise people are condemned to a deluded and restless race to satisfy endlessly shifting desires. Xunzi thinks the right sort of music is critical and helps all people be pleased with their role in the social whole, whether exalted or lowly; good music is thus an essential part of good public policy, "the beginning of true kingship" (20/99/15–18). Dissolute music leads to discontent, strife, and even chaos, weakening a state and making it susceptible to conquest (20/99/18–22). Joy makes it possible, emotionally, for people to live with the restraints on their immediate desires imposed by Confucian disciplines.

Xunzi theorizes this power of music to influence our heart/minds in terms of *qi* 氣, roughly translatable as "vital energy."[49] He writes:

> In general, treacherous sounds arouse people so that they respond with deviant *qi*; if deviant *qi* achieves full representation disorder is generated. Correct sounds move people so that they respond with compliant *qi*; when compliant *qi* achieves full representation good order (*zhi* 治) is generated. There is a responsiveness when a leader sings and others accompany him: good or bad are mutually represented [depending on the leader's song]. Thus the noble man is careful about what [music] he rejects and accepts. (20/100/4–5)

Apparently, the harmonies present in music and its shared performance resonate with human social harmonies, calling up similar responses from our dispositions. Depending on the music and the master presenting it, vastly different desires can be called forth as different sorts of *qi* permeate the group and are reinforced in song and movement. Although this may sound somewhat dubious to those unfamiliar with practices based on theories of *qi*, similar experiences can be readily achieved in musical performances of different sorts, whether in a concert hall or nightclub, especially if one is part of a large group; if anything, Xunzi's understandable concern to remedy the horrifying social disorder of his time leads him to oversimplify the range of emotions and desires that music can generate. These possible criticisms aside, Xunzi is much more concerned with how to discern and properly harness music's classical forms than with developing a general theory of music's effects on the human heart.

Because music is such a nearly automatic source of human inspiration, Xunzi thinks, it is a very powerful tool for humane government, and it is uniquely suitable for affecting the masses of people who will never be able to undertake the full range of Confucian disciplines, especially those dependent on literacy. This power, however, makes the choice of music absolutely crucial: One must rely on the *Odes* and *Hymns* of Zhou rather than, for example, the "lewd" music from the states of Zheng and Wei (20/99/24–20/100/1).

Xunzi briefly relates ritual and music. He writes that the harmonies in music, just like the patterns of ritual, cannot be changed. He goes on: "Music unites what is the same; ritual distinguishes what is different. The principles of ritual and music are the pitchpipe directing the human heart/mind. The essence of music is to exhaust the root and reach the limit of change, while the constant standard of ritual is to manifest sincerity (*cheng* 誠) and get rid of hypocrisy (*wei* 僞)" (20/100/14–15). Presumably, he means that music tends to unify people as a group by providing similar, deeply rooted inspiration to all, while ritual often differentiates people according to their positions within a group. This general contrast can easily be overstated, however. For Xunzi, many sorts of ceremonies include some sort of musical performance, and music playing of even the most casual sort does not supersede basic ritual propriety, which intrinsically includes a vigorous sense of differentiated social hierarchy.[50] Furthermore, ritual is not a purely negative constraint, as was shown above. It provokes and inspires various emotions through the beauty, and ugliness, of its required forms, and it provides paths for people's emotions and desires to take shape and issue in action. As Xunzi says above, perhaps to our surprise, ritual aims to "manifest sincerity and get rid of hypocrisy." If it were only and always a constraint on our impulses, such a statement would be unthinkable.

This close interplay of ritual and music can be seen in Xunzi's account of the *xiang* 鄉, or village drinking ceremony. He writes, "When I examine the *xiang* I understand how gentle and easy is the Way of the true king" (20/101/6). The ceremony consists of a host welcoming a chief guest, his retainers, and other guests. This welcoming involves repeated exchanges of bows, polite refusals, and entreaties to come ascend the steps and partake, which are most elaborate with the chief guest, less so with the retainers, and minimal with the others. A singer and mouth organ player arrive and perform songs alone and together, then retire. The final formal element consists of rounds of toasts with a shared tankard of liquor, passed in order from the most senior to the most junior, with none left out.[51] After this, all descend from the main ritual space and remove their sandals, then return and drink together without such careful protocol, although not to such an extent, Xunzi assures us, that they endanger their fulfillment of the next day's responsibilities. At the conclusion of the evening, the host sends off the guests with a final bow, so that restraint and good form prevail at the end (20/101/8–19). Xunzi sums up the import of this as follows: "Illuminating noble and base, distinguishing exalted and lowly, being harmonious and joyful but not overflowing, with young and old together so none are left out, peacefully feasting without disorder: these five forms of conduct are sufficient to correct oneself and bring peace to the state, and if the state is at peace then all under Heaven will be at peace" (20/101/21–22). In this case at least, music and ritual work together, lifting people up with joy and harmonious fellowship while distinguishing different roles within the community.

At the end of a difficult passage likening different musical instruments to natural phenomena, presumably to illuminate their characters within various pieces of music, Xunzi closes by discussing *wu yi* 舞意, "the purpose of the dance." He writes:

> How can we understand the purpose of the dance? I say the eyes by themselves do not see it; the ears by themselves do not hear it. Nevertheless, when every lowering and raising of the head, every bending and straightening, approach and withdrawal, slowing and quickening, are governed so that they are precisely regulated, using up the full strength of muscles and bones so that what is important is the rhythm of bowing together with the bells and drums, and no [movement] clashes [with them], the group accumulates this purpose again and again! (20/101/2–4)[52]

The purpose of the dance is not merely a visible, audible display but also the repeated, splendid coordination in time of movement, voice, and instruments. This shared exertion, as long as it continues, incarnates the beauty, goodness, and harmony of the Way in a profoundly satisfying performance of perfection. I take this to be a reference to music as a spiritual exercise, the repetitive, shared practice of which fills people with joy while knitting them together as a community in the pursuit of the Way. Thus, as Xunzi says earlier in the paragraph, "the purpose of the dance pairs with the Way of Heaven" (20/100/20), just as the human Way should harmonize with the rest of the cosmos.

Summary on Spiritual Exercises in Xunzi

Xunzi gives detailed, careful accounts of three spiritual exercises central to his Confucianism. *Xue* 學, which includes both "study" and "learning," is a combination of textual study, focused on the classical *Documents*, *Odes*, *Rituals*, *Music*, and *Spring and Autumn Annals*; and the bodily, emotional, and intellectual appropriation of the lessons of the past into students' daily existence. It is highly dependent on authoritative teachers and a shared community of learners. Study includes wide-ranging reflection and philosophical dialogue as parts of the process of appropriation, leading ideally to deep intellectual and personal commitment to the Confucian Way.

Li 禮, "ritual," covers both specific ceremonial observances and a very wide range of the details of daily life, from appearance and deportment to etiquette and interpersonal morality. Ritual reorients human beings to those roots of their shared existence—Heaven and Earth, ancestors, and lords and teachers—which are not the immediate objects of our innate dispositions. It also clarifies and strengthens just social norms by highlighting social distinctions, and thus, perhaps somewhat paradoxically, reinforcing social harmony and unity in the community as a whole; this point becomes more comprehensible when we attend to Xunzi's view that ritual propriety enacts the *mutual* duties between superiors and inferiors, not merely duties of loyalty and obedience from below (e.g., 11/54/11–13). Ritual as a spiritual exercise shapes human *qing* 情, "dispositions," so that they match *wenli* 文理, "refined form and good order." This process of cutting and stretching, calling up and tamping down, aims to eventually produce a state Xunzi calls "the middle course where ritual flows," where emotions and external observances are in perfect harmony with each other, and people gracefully perform their commitments to the Confucian virtues of humaneness, justice, trustworthiness, loyalty, and reverence. But even before this state is achieved, and even without perfect understanding, ritual allows people to navigate life's transitions, however joyful or traumatic, with dignity, so that community life can continue to flourish and all enjoy peace.

Yue 樂, "music," is also *le* 樂, "joy," for Xunzi. Music has a unique power to inspire people in any number of directions, and so the sage kings carefully composed the *Odes* and *Hymns*, which use this magnetic influence in the service of refined form. By broadening and purifying listeners' intentions, and enlivening them by generating harmonious and orderly joy, music moves human beings of all sorts relatively quickly and easily to feel the rightness of the Confucian Way and develop its virtues. To discard it because of its expense would be a colossal miscalculation, Xunzi thinks, and impoverish our life together in every way.

XUNZI'S THEORY OF THE STAGES OF PERSONAL FORMATION

In comparison with Augustine, Xunzi's choice of emphases in his account of personal formation is striking. Xunzi focuses so resolutely on the ongoing, cumulative *process* of self-improvement that conversion to the Confucian Way barely registers as an issue for him. We can begin to unravel this apparent mystery by examining Xunzi's account of the stages of personal development. Although he occasionally presents other schemas (8/32/16–8/33/9, 8/34/14–18), his most dominant model is fourfold: the "petty person," the educated man, the noble man, and finally the sage.

In this process, we start as if blind and deaf to what we most need to know (2/8/3–4). We need a teacher to present to us the model of past exemplars and the Way that they followed. Xunzi writes:

> From birth human beings are certainly petty people. If they are without a teacher and the model, they will see things only in terms of personal benefit. Since human beings are certainly petty from birth, if they should moreover meet with a chaotic age they will gain chaotic customs; this is using the petty to deepen the petty, using the chaotic to attain chaos. . . . Now as for a person's mouth and stomach: How can they know ritual and justice? How can they know declining and yielding? How can they know honesty and shame, and accumulate [all] the corners [i.e., the different aspects of the Way]?[53] They merely suck and chew away, feast and enjoy until full. If a person lacks a teacher and the model then his heart/mind will be just like his mouth and stomach. (4/15/14–17)

Without thorough education, people act in all areas as if they were thinking with their stomachs. This is what Xunzi means by the "small" or "petty" person, *xiao ren* 小人: Such people, who Xunzi thinks represent most of humanity in his chaotic age, move immediately toward what they desire, stopping only when satiated, with no thought to the nature or consequences of their actions. Such a person hates any reproof to his or her behavior, preferring comforting illusions about the quality of their character (2/5/6–8). Common people unreflectively follow custom and seek primarily to accumulate material goods, all with an ultimate purpose of keeping themselves alive (8/30/12). The petty person is thus "a servant to things," following their lead, and subject to the fear and anxiety that dependence on them brings

(2/6/12–13, 22/112/9–16). Pettiness of this sort seems to cover a fairly broad range for Xunzi, from those who have simply not had any chance to improve themselves yet, to those that have deepened their pettiness into real viciousness through repeated aggression or dishonesty. Xunzi's account of unreconstructed humanity thus echoes Augustine's on some significant points: Especially as human beings "deepen their pettiness" by avidly pursuing their immediate, instinctive desires, we become prone to self-aggrandizing self-deception, which becomes increasingly ironic as we simultaneously assert our goodness while becoming more and more enslaved to physical goods and social acclaim, and consequently wracked by fear and anxiety about reversals of fortune. This adds welcome notes of psychological depth and sophistication to Xunzi's account of "obsession," especially as this applies to fixation on our seemingly natural category of evaluation, *li* 利, "profit" or "benefit."

If such malaise prompts a person to seek greater wisdom from a Confucian teacher, he or she may have the good fortune, from Xunzi's point of view, to hear about the Way of the Zhou and become exposed to the classic texts and ritual practices of a Confucian community. Xunzi does not even have a name for this stage, in contrast to the attention Augustine, as a late antique Roman Catholic bishop, lavishes on the ritual, moral, and religious progression of the catechumenate toward baptism and full church membership.[54] "Conversion," as such, is not a topic that Xunzi self-consciously articulates and analyzes, so interpreters impressed by the Augustinian narrative of Christian selfhood must piece together various elements from Xunzi's texts to construct a suitable object for comparison.

Xunzi thinks anyone who is exposed to Confucian practices will find them strange at first, but if they go ahead and try them, they will recognize their beauty and excellence and will be attracted to them, just as an impoverished rustic would, after initial bewilderment ("What is this strange stuff?") come to love fine food if he could only have some, because of his attraction to its flavor, fragrance, and healthfulness (4/15/14–4/16/3). On Xunzi's account, such attraction is not overwhelming, however. It would not guarantee acceptance if other forces intervened, such as a particularly arrogant or obstreperous disposition, or any sort of material or social disruption, such as famine or war.

In a similar vein, Xunzi argues that the *de* 德, "virtue" or "moral charisma," of the noble man and sage is spontaneously attractive to all people, even the uncultivated.[55] There seem to be two aspects to this. On the one hand, as Xunzi argues when explaining that even among "barbarians" the noble man will be honored and appreciated, "If you are the first to undertake hard work and can leave ease and enjoyment to others, if you are honest and trustworthy, persevering and meticulous in your job, then you can travel all over the world and, though you choose to live among barbarians, everyone will want to employ you" (2/6/16–17). It seems clear that even petty and ignorant people will see the benefits of having a highly cultivated, energetic, public-spirited Confucian around, simply because they get so much socially beneficial work done. Moreover, as the passage goes on to relate, barbarians detest vicious conduct even if they lack the categories to make such a judgment fully articulate (2/7/1–3). Such recognition and reaction require no deep understanding of the Way; they rest at least in part on the calculation of likely gain. Second, and a bit more mysteriously, however, Xunzi believes with other Confucians in the inspiring power of true moral authority, so that a leader's moral charisma may *yin* 音, "sound" forth, and call up resonant echoes in all who hear (10/43/20, 11/55/23). The attractiveness of true virtue for Xunzi seems to go well beyond its evident social benefits. "Petty people" will feel not just gratitude but real admiration for any noble man with whom they interact.

Xunzi thinks sufficient exposure to the *mei* 美, "beauty" or "fineness," of noble Confucian conduct will likely kindle a desire to possess such attractive qualities. When combined with fear of the dangers of petty behavior, and prudential judgments about which mode of life would more likely lead to comfort and honor or pain and disgrace (4/15/4–5), Xunzi apparently thinks it will be fairly likely that human beings will embark on the Confucian Way, if they have the good fortune to come across and seriously consider an exemplification of it. Thus Xunzi does not view "conversion" per se as a deep existential problem to be unraveled.

Truly becoming a student of the Way, however, requires submitting oneself to a teacher and the classical models preserved and passed down in conjunction with the classic texts. This is the beginning period Xunzi seems to be pointing toward with his craft metaphors of straightening crooked wood and grinding dull metal. Here one begins to learn about the Confucian Way, and one struggles to assent to it when it comes into conflict with one's immediate desires. This is where significant problems begin to appear, according to Xunzi, and thus he dedicates much of his moral psychological analysis to the difficulties of the aspiring Confucian.

It is striking, at least in comparison with Augustine, that Xunzi does not even give a name to this "beginner" stage but leaves it within the catchall category of "pettiness." For Augustine, as I discuss more fully in the next chapter, there are monumental differences between those who have never heard of the divine law, those who are "under the law" but not yet "under grace," and finally those who have been effectively called back to God through the gift of His grace (who are of course still far from perfect). To preview one of the arguments from chapter 8, in comparison with Augustine's sense of radically different possible existential stances (toward self in the "city of man," or toward God), which can be changed for the better only via a decisive, transformative conversion, Xunzi sees a more subtle set of distinctions between animalistic, shortsighted selfishness, more prudential concern for long-term benefits, and a gradually deepening appreciation of the Confucian Way, which is indeed the most beneficial way of all, at least on balance for whole societies, although what makes it so is precisely its demotion of profit in favor of other, genuinely ethical motivations that govern our desires for physical satisfaction and gain.

Eventually, a Confucian beginner may become what Xunzi calls a *shi* 士, often translated as "knight" or "scholar," but probably closer in Xunzi's time to "educated man," that is, someone fit for government service through intelligence, literacy, and dependability.[56] In Xunzi's hands, these men are distinguished primarily by their ethical qualities. He writes: "Those whose enactment of the model has reached a steadfastness such that they do not let selfish desires disorder what they have heard [from their teacher] can be called a forceful *shi*" (8/30/12–13). In contrast to beginners, who apparently are still easily swayed and confused by their wayward desires, an educated man has learned enough to have a basic commitment to the Way. An educated man desires to develop himself (2/7/5–6), despite many remaining misguided desires, and is capable of following the classical Zhou models as long as he has support from others around him. In Aristotelian terms, Xunzi's educated man is continent, at least when he can rely on a supportive community around him, but not yet truly virtuous, although he genuinely aims to become so. He is convinced of the goodness of the Way, even if he has only begun to truly embody it, and so is still vulnerable to deflection from it.

After a long period of assiduous practice of Confucian disciplines, a *shi* may become a *junzi* 君子. This term literally denotes the son of a lord, but Confucianism transmutes this marker of elite birth into a sign of high ethical character, and *junzi* becomes one of the more resonant terms in the classical Confucian conceptual repertoire. Thus, throughout this study, I translate *junzi* as "noble man." Xunzi discusses the noble man repeatedly as one of the primary exemplars of his views, second only to the sage. He writes in one such passage:

> Those whose enactment of the model has reached a steadfastness such that they like to imitate and correct what they have heard in order to rectify and adorn their disposition and innate impulses, such that their speech is mostly appropriate but they do not yet fully understand, their conduct

> is mostly appropriate but they are not yet at peace, their understanding and reflection is mostly appropriate but they are not yet comprehensive and settled, for those above them they are able to glorify what they exalt, and below they are able to open up the Way for those not equal to themselves—if they are like this, then they may be called a strong and solid *junzi*. (8/30/13–15)

The noble man has internalized the Way to such an extent that he has begun to like the process of personal improvement, even if it is not yet finished and his speech, action, and thought are not yet perfect. His ambitions have become clear and unified, even if he is not flawlessly virtuous. He is at ease in the moral hierarchy of the Confucian social group, delighting in those superior to him, helping those less accomplished, solidly committed to the Way, even if his disposition has not yet been completely transformed, and he still must battle internally at times with selfish desires so that broader concerns of justice win out in his action (2/8/16). The noble man develops himself internally while yielding externally, accumulates *de* 德 ("virtue" or "moral charisma") in his person, and has a reputation, Xunzi contends, that rises like the sun and moon. Despite his yielding demeanor, he triumphs in his exquisitely polite dealings with others, because all are spontaneously moved to echo him like a clap of thunder (8/30/1–2). The noble man's commitment to the Way is so thorough that he will follow it through poverty and ignominy, even unto death, without faltering (1/4/16–20).

The sage (*sheng ren* 聖人) is the pinnacle of Xunzi's hierarchy of personal development, and the ultimate telos of Confucian learning. Xunzi writes:

> If someone imitates the model of the hundred kings as easily as he distinguishes white and black; if he responds appropriately to the changes of his age as easily as he counts one, two; if he enacts the essentials and details of ritual and is at peace with them just as he has been born with four limbs; if his skill in establishing accomplishments at the crucial time is like calling forth the four seasons; if his excellence at making the people peaceful, upright, and harmonious is such that he can gather the myriad crowds as if they were a single person; then he may be called a sage. (8/30/15–17)

A sage has assimilated the ancient models into his being so thoroughly that he has himself become the ultimate model, with his ritual propriety as perfect and natural as his full human form, his timing and judgment unerring, his leadership wise and powerfully effective. The sage has thoroughly regulated himself with good order, and thus he can "follow his desires and fulfill his dispositions" (21/105/18), because they have been transformed. The sage has no need for the preservative or corrective virtues of lesser people, who depend on strength and watchfulness as they try to unify themselves on the Way; in a sense, he has *become* the Way, because he enacts it without effort (21/105/19).[57] The sage is distinguished by his comprehensive understanding of all phenomena relevant to the human Way; he is free from obsession, and he can smoothly handle whatever changes arise without endangering his emptiness, unity, or tranquillity (21/104/7–10). The sage is joyful, delighting in the Way and its fruits (8/31/1).

It is worth asking to what extent Xunzi believed sagehood was really attainable. His descriptions of both the noble man and the sage are rich and resonant. Yet while the noble man often sounds heroic but is always recognizably human in his continued striving for goodness, the sage often sounds superhuman in his perfection. But Xunzi is quite clear in his claim that it is possible for a "person in the street" to become a sage if he or she accumulates goodness without ceasing. Anyone, in other words, has the capacities, at least in the abstract, to come to understand and enact the patterns of humaneness and justice that are transmitted within the Confucian Way. Nevertheless, Xunzi thinks a developed *ability* to be sagelike is not already present in us, and it can only become a real possibility after enormous work in submission to Confucian disciplines, as part of the right sort of community of learners (23/116/6–23). Furthermore, Xunzi thought there had been at least a few sages in the past, and he clearly hoped that others would arise and guide the peoples of the central states back to the harmonious flourishing first achieved by the Zhou Dynasty. The rare possibility of perfection, then, is real for Xunzi. This possibility serves to chasten the virtuous to remain dissatisfied with themselves and continue striving to enact the Way flawlessly, not just well. The universality of this potential also gave Xunzi hope as he tried to persuade the warlords of his age to adopt a more humane way of governance, and thereby eventually end the savagery afflicting everyone.

NOTES

1. The best such surveys are Schwartz 1985 and Graham 1989.

2. Schwartz 1985, 62.

3. On early Chinese views of the spirit world, see Poo 1998 and Puett 2002. For Xunzi's views, see especially *Xunzi* 17/82/6–8, and chapter 17 generally. I discuss his use of the rhetoric of *shen* 神, "spirit," in Stalnaker 2003. On the dangers of an "otherworldly" reading of Augustine, see chapter 5, note 4.

4. I do not mean to imply that Augustine counsels a way of life focused on external rewards of some sort, which would be a grotesque reading of his understanding of life after the resurrection. Eternal life in the presence of God fulfills and perfects the highest goods of the Christian life here on Earth, according to Augustine (*civ. Dei* 22.29–30).

5. Xunzi also speaks of the Way as something that can be known in such a way that it can serve as the "scales" in which diverse alternatives may be "weighed" and properly assessed (21/103/16–22). Rather than being a vague stab at some model or calculus for practical rationality, Xunzi seems to use this metaphor because it allows him to sum up the comprehensiveness of the Dao, which unites and properly relates all significant values within a single vision that can correctly guide anyone in any situation.

6. I discuss Xunzi's account of the stages of personal development in the third section of this chapter. For a fine account that analyzes his various metaphors for this process with insight, and that also stresses the effortless, *wuwei* character of Xunzi's fully realized sage, see Slingerland 2003b, 217–64.

7. There are several excellent studies of Xunzi's views of these topics. Probably the best are Ivanhoe 1990, 1991, 2000b [1994]; Kline 1998; and Schofer 2000 [1993].

8. Translation adapted from Watson 1963, 157–58.

9. For insightful discussion, see Kline 1998, 205–50; and Slingerland 2003b, 217–64.

10. For fuller historical and philosophical analysis of Xunzi's talk of "numinous illumination," see Stalnaker 2003.

11. Van Norden 2000 [1992], 172–73.

12. For a pithy summary and accurate assessment of the textual problems in this paragraph, see Knoblock 1988–94, vol. 2, 289–90, nn. 104–6. All emendations follow Lau 1996.

13. I owe this apt rendering to Slingerland 2003b, 231. I discuss this passage and some of the broader issues in Stalnaker 2004. The best larger treatment of Xunzi's views of the heart/mind is Hutton 2001.

14. On breath and dietary controls, see the "Neiye" chapter of the *Guanzi*, translated in Roth 1999. Yogic practices are mocked in the *Zhuangzi* and advocated in some of the texts excavated at Zhangjiashan and Mawangdui, which also discuss sexual techniques and a variety of other practices of "macrobiotic hygiene"; on these topics, see Harper 1987, 1995, 1997. Spirit flight practices seem to be behind certain stories in the *Zhuangzi*, and the *Chuci* (Qu et al. 1985); for a discussion of such practices in context, see Puett 2002, 201–24. Withdrawal is advocated in different ways in the *Zhuangzi*, and by followers of Shennong, such as Xu Xing in *Mencius* 3A4, who advocated a simple life of farming by all. The last four practices are all Confucian, and Xunzi's views of them are discussed below.

15. "Spiritual exercises" on the face of it might suggest an even more wrongheaded emphasis on developing or strengthening one's "spirit," considered as a nonphysical, vivifying, immortal substance, but I hope to have ruled out such misimpressions through my discussions above of Hadot's use of the term; Hadot does not intend such

a sense either, not even in Roman contexts. Some sinologists might worry that using Hadot's terminology even in the way I propose inevitably brings along wisps of Western metaphysics or even "onto-theology" that are foreign to early Chinese thought; such a worry seems to me to be seriously misguided, and to underestimate our ability to use technically delimited stipulative definitions of terms for analysis. For a learned critique of Hadot that argues for an opposing conclusion, that Hadot is unjustly prejudiced *against* Neoplatonic metaphysics and practices in a way that skews his account of ancient and medieval spiritual exercises, at the expense of Christianity, see Hankey 2003. I thank Robert Dodaro for this reference.

16. For an alternative reading of this passage, see Cook 1997, 20, n. 50.

17. I follow Yang Liang, who glosses *shu* 數, "amount," as *shu* 術, "technique" (Xunzi 1988a, 11). This is a sufficiently common loan character that it shows up as a definition of *shu* 數 in many dictionaries.

18. See Knoblock 1988–94, vol. 1, 50–53.

19. The textual history of the *Shujing* (also called *Shang Shu*) is extraordinarily tangled. For discussion, see Shaughnessy 1993.

20. For discussion of all of these texts, see the relevant articles in Loewe 1993.

21. On *li*, see Stalnaker 2004.

22. On these points, see Kline 1998, 205–50.

23. For a well-produced reproduction of such texts, see *Guodian Chumu Zhujian* 1998. Homophonous loan characters are common in excavated texts from this period.

24. See also 8/33/11–14: "Not to hear something is not as good as to hear it; to hear something is not as good as to see it; to see something is not as good as to understand it; to understand something is not as good as to put it into practice. Study extends until it is put into practice and then stops." Note also the very first words of the *Analects*: "The master said: 'To study and at the proper time practice what you have learned—is this not a joy?'" (1.1)

25. On goods internal and external to practices, and the importance of this distinction to traditions of virtue ethics, see MacIntyre 1984, 181–203.

26. For discussion of a minor textual problem (one excrescent character in the edition upon which Lau 1996 is based), which does not affect the overall sense of the passage, see Stalnaker 2001, 167–68 n. 35.

27. Goldin 1999, 15 n. 31, notes this connection.

28. See also 8/34/4–12 for a passage that relates this "rubbing" to Xunzi's terminology of "accumulation" and "unification" with regard to the Way.

29. For a general history of Warring States thought that traces the theme of debate through the period, see Graham 1989.

30. Robert Eno (1990) reflects on Xunzi's fascination with ritual, and on the general integration of intellectual understanding and ritual practice in early Confucianism. Eno's attention to the social context and ritual practices of Confucians is an important contribution, and has strongly stimulated my own reflections on the *Xunzi*. Nevertheless, I disagree with him on significant issues. Eno seems to conclude that the early Confucian commitment to ritual was essentially ideological in a pejorative sense,

a philosophical slide into group solipsism and away from political commitment. I think this interpretation distorts crucial aspects of early Confucianism, especially regarding their concern for and involvement in politics. I am also less suspicious than Eno of Xunzi's attempt to transform people's awareness and evaluations through disciplinary exercises, which seems to me to be a process typical of all significant education.

31. Ivanhoe 1991.

32. For a brief discussion of Yu's achievements, see Knoblock 1988–94, vol. 2, 13-14.

33. Epstein (n.d.) helpfully discusses this aspect of Xunzi's view of ritual.

34. A classic, although in certain respects deservedly controversial, statement of the meaning of ritual in Confucianism is Fingarette 1972. A fine discussion of ritual in Xunzi is Yearley n.d., which has appeared in somewhat different form as Yearley 1996a.

35. The translation is adapted from Watson 1963, 89.

36. Xunzi elsewhere makes this argument explicitly in the context of political economy, where he contends that only Confucianism can provide both the moral vision and community resources, including the accumulated wealth and political power, to protect the vulnerable and include everyone in the Confucian "Great Society." For this argument, see 10/45/6–10/46/4; this passage and its relevance to my argument were pointed out to me by Eric Hutton. For a good summary of Xunzi's political views, see Rosemont 2000 [1970–71].

37. Yu 1997, 74 n. 74. For fuller discussion, see chapter 3.

38. See, e.g., Yearley n.d., Watson 1963, Knoblock 1988–94, and Irene Bloom's translation, in de Bary 1999, 174–77. Note also Campany 1992, esp. 206–8; Campany remarks that Xunzi thinks ritual not only expresses but also reshapes our *qing*, although he makes little of this insight. Of all Western commentators on Xunzi, Slingerland (2003b, 234–35) has written most insightfully, although briefly, on this aspect of Xunzi's view of ritual.

39. I am thinking here of the suggestive and insightful account of Xunzi's ritual theory put forth by Lee Yearley (n.d.; see also 1996a). I have learned much from this piece, but nevertheless think it needs to be supplemented to bring out other aspects of Xunzi's account. On Xunzi's supposed "hydraulic" model of the self, see Yearley 1980, 475.

40. This passage begins: 禮者, 以財物為用, 以貴賤為文, 以多少為異, 以隆殺為要. The Sibu Congkan edition, which Lau (1996) uses as the basis for his concordance, has 用 for the seventeenth character in the first sentence, making the sense of the clause and its relation to its surroundings obscure. Wang Xianqian (Xunzi 1988a) and Liang Qixiong (Xunzi 1983) both have 異 here in the same position without comment. Yang Liang's commentary also explains the sense as if *yi* rather than *yong* were the word in question. I thus follow Yang, Wang, and Liang, and emend Lau's text.

41. The received text uses the word *qing* 情, "emotion" or "disposition," here. Wang Niansun argues that it is impossible for there to be a *qing* of *zhiyi* 志意, "intentions," because these words are nearly synonyms, and proposes that *qing* is a graph-

ical error for *ji* 積, "accumulation," based on a passage in chapter 8 of the *Xunzi*, where such an error occurs twice (8/33/19–20). Lau 1996 follows Wang on this point (19/97/20 n. 10). I would suggest the problem lies not in the terms' closeness in meaning so much as that the set of a person's *qing* does not include their *zhiyi*, as best we can reconstruct Xunzi's psychology. P. J. Ivanhoe has proposed an even better emendation in conversation. Instead of *qing*, the word *jing* 精, "concentration," seems to link together the three somewhat disparate uses of the character in this paragraph best, especially the last one which includes a parallel list of nouns denoting the extremity of sacrifice's excellences, while making sense of the psychological uses earlier in the paragraph, and linking the points made to Xunzi's broader doctrines about ritual development of persons. Furthermore, it is an emendation only of the radical, which were not yet standardized in the Warring States period, and so may have been added incorrectly in Han editions of the text. As with Wang's suggested emendation, this exact error (of *qing* 情 for *jing* 精) occurs elsewhere in the *Xunzi*, at 21/104/13 (as argued by Lu Wenchao and seconded by Wang Xianqian). Even if my proposal were not acceptable, Wang Niansun's emendation leads to essentially identical conclusions about Xunzi's point. And last, contra Knoblock 1988–94 and Watson 1963, this passage has nothing to do with the general origins of ritual, which Xunzi treats at the beginning of the chapter.

42. Some descriptions in this quotation are adapted from Watson 1963, 110.

43. Yang Liang takes Xunzi to be referring to "the appearance of changing emotions;" Xunzi 1988a, 376.

44. My account is further supported by Xunzi's discussion of deviations from the "middle course" in mourning. He considers both excessively sparse and brief funerals, in roughly the manner suggested by the antiritual Mohists (19/93/15–17), and extravagant mourning that goes on interminably and leads people to harm their own well-being through competitive fasting and other exertions (19/96/15–21, 19/94/10–14). Sparse funerals have limited grave goods, occur under cover of darkness, and then are over as if nothing had happened. "This is the ultimate disgrace," Xunzi suggests, and in his view is fit only for "castrated criminals." Both excessive and sparse funerals deform human emotions (although perhaps in cases involving criminals shame would counter or even outweigh grief, in a Xunzian world), but also and equally importantly they distort ritual forms and thus fail to properly demonstrate and dramatize basic Confucian commitments to a humane existence. (Another condemnation of excessive burial practices, in this case including human sacrifice, occurs at 19/96/1–2.)

45. A good discussion of Xunzi's views on music, along with a comparison to ideas in the *Liji*, may be found in Cook 1997.

46. Knoblock 1988–94, vol. 2, 53.

47. I follow Watson's (1963) compression ("directness, complexity, intensity, and rhythm") of Xunzi's somewhat opaque technical terms for the various aspects of the music of the *ya* 雅, *Odes*, and *song* 頌, *Hymns*, which form different parts of the *Shijing*, the *Classic of Poetry*, itself frequently translated as the "*Odes*."

48. I emend *de* 德, "virtue," to *yue* 樂, "music," following Knoblock (1988–94, vol. 3, 326 n. 24), who follows the reading in the rare early Xishu and Erzhe editions, as discussed by Qian Dian in his study of variant readings in the *Xunzi*.

49. See chapter three for fuller discussion of *qi* in the *Xunzi*.

50. For the blending of musical performance and ritual, see the "village drinking ceremony" discussed below as Xunzi's main example of appreciating music (20/101/6–22). See, e.g., *Analects* 11.26 for a relaxed scene involving music (and where hopes for another such event are expressed), which is nevertheless fully proper in terms of ritual behavior. For a reading of ritual and music in Xunzi that stresses rather than downplays this contrast, see Cook 1997.

51. It seems clear, however, from the context and Xunzi's general views (e.g., 20/100/2) that "no one being left out" applies only to men; women appear to be barred from participation.

52. My rendering follows Liang Qixiong's reading of the last phrase (Xunzi 1983, 283). See also Xunzi 1988a, 384, for more discussion, and a similar interpretation by Lu Wenchao.

53. As Wang Xianqian points out (Xunzi 1988a, 64), this calls to mind Xunzi's discussion of *bi* 蔽, "obsession," as holding up only one "corner" of the Way and mistaking it for the whole, in contrast to Confucius, who understood all and had perfected his accumulation as a consequence (21/103/8–15).

54. For ample discussion, see Harmless 1995.

55. For an insightful interpretation of Xunzi that accents the role of moral charisma, and from which I draw in this paragraph, see Kline 2000, esp. 167ff.

56. For a discussion of the rise of this class of people, and of the social context generally, see Hsu 1965. See also, for brief but more recent accounts, Loewe and Shaughnessy 1999, 583–86, 641–45. On the sexism of Xunzi's outlook, see chapter 2.

57. For a discussion of Xunzi and other major figures in early Chinese thought that highlights this mode of life as a widely shared if differently understood spiritual goal, see Slingerland 2003b.

CHAPTER SEVEN

Crucifying and Resurrecting the Mind

✦

Augustine's vast literary output encompasses so much, it is inevitable that a particular era's fascinations bring certain aspects to the fore and leave others less widely known. At least since the Reformation, the intellectual anxiety provoked by Augustine's doctrine of predestination has led to intensive critical scrutiny of this and related themes, especially in his late, anti-Pelagian writings. It might seem that if the number and identity of the elect have been known since the founding of the universe, and salvation is not in our power but in God's, then we humans are puppets in the hands of the Lord,[1] and there is nothing people can or should do to improve themselves, because all rests with God.

Augustine would vigorously dispute this counsel of passivity. Contrary to common perceptions, he passionately advocates what in this study I am calling "spiritual exercises." This can hardly be surprising, given the role ascetic literature and exemplars played in his conversion to Catholic Christianity.[2] Indeed, as noted in chapter 2, his conversion issued not only in study as a Catholic catechumen but also in philosophical retreat from the ambitious world of Milanese society and patronage. He continued to organize and lead a sequence of monastic social groupings, and he risked forcible recruitment to be a presbyter in Hippo only in order to interview a prospective monastic "brother." This led to his ordination by Valerius, the bishop of Hippo, who honored Augustine's wish to continue living as a monastic by permitting him to.construct and head a monastery adjoining the basilica.[3] He lived for the rest of his life in a community of likeminded *fratres*, all embracing individual poverty, communal property, celibacy, daily prayer and study, and manual labor. He wrote the first monastic rule in Western Christendom, and he founded other monasteries for monks and nuns.[4]

Looking simply at Augustine's views of monasticism, however, especially when contrasted implicitly or explicitly with his expectations for lay

Christians, unnecessarily truncates an account of his normative ideas about practices of personal formation, which he did not think were reserved only for a few (see, e.g., *s.* 301A.8).[5] It would not be overstating the case to say that Augustine views the Christian life, in lay, clerical, and monastic forms, as consisting essentially of the practice of spiritual exercises. At various times, to various audiences, Augustine recommends practices such as sexual restraint or renunciation, voluntary poverty, almsgiving, communal ownership of property, fasting, self-examination, private and public confession of sins, various kinds of prayer, Bible study and other sorts of learning (including the traditional liberal arts), philosophical dialogue, brotherly rebuke, and various forms of penance. And in his capacities as priest and bishop, Augustine of course led many through catechesis, baptism, and shared worship, which included scripture recitation, preaching, music, and celebration of the Eucharist. Examining Augustine's account of each of these individually, as well as their relations to each other and the Christian life as a whole, would require a rather considerable volume of its own, and probably several, judging by the fruitfulness of one recent work focused solely on Augustine's ideas about reading.[6] The problem of selection is compounded, moreover, because Augustine wrote no single, comprehensive work on personal formation,[7] and his ideas on the subject are scattered throughout his vast corpus.

In this chapter, I examine Augustine's account of a few of these practices in sufficient detail for my larger comparative purposes, although certainly not in a manner intended to be encyclopedic and final. I first survey Augustine's general understanding of ethico-religious development, examining some of his numerous metaphors for this process, as well as his understanding of *exercitationes animi*, "exercises of the soul," and *disciplina*, "teaching" or "training." I then briefly summarize Augustine's account of the preconditions for gaining anything from spiritual exercises, most notably catechesis and baptism into the church. The third and longest section analyzes Augustine's accounts of several particular exercises: the classical liberal arts, reading and listening to scripture, literal and symbolic practices of eating (including both fasting and the Eucharist), and various types of prayer. In the last section, I return to Augustine's account of progress in righteousness, attending to his mature theory of stages of spiritual development, correlated to Isaiah 11:2–3 and the Beatitudes, which culminates in full "adoption" by God and "deification" after the resurrection.

FROM DEATH INTO LIFE: THE SHAPE OF AUGUSTINIAN CHRISTIANITY

Augustine uses a variety of highly suggestive traditional metaphors to convey his understanding of the Christian life. According to Augustine, for humans here on Earth "the whole of our lifetime is nothing but a race towards death, in which no one is allowed the slightest pause or any slackening of the pace" (*civ. Dei* 13.10).[8] This is so in both literal and spiritual senses: We all will weaken and die physically, and in our fallen condition we are also dying spiritually, headed for the everlasting second death of divine condemnation (*civ. Dei* 13.10–11). He sometimes goes even further, saying that the unchristian life *is* death, in both soul and body, because of sin and sin's punishment; before conversion to Christianity "both soul and body [are] in need of healing and resurrection, in order to renew for the better what [has] changed for the worse" (*Trin.* 4.5).[9]

Unsurprisingly, Christ serves for Augustine as the primary model for our passage from this living death to true eternal life and felicity. More specifically, Christ is a "*sacramentum* for the inner man and an *exemplum* for the outer one" (*Trin.* 4.6).[10] By *sacramentum*, Augustine does not mean "sacrament" in any post-Tridentine sense but rather a sacred sign, something that signifies an important religious or spiritual reality (*doc. Chr.* 3.19.31; *civ. Dei* 10.5; *ep.* 138.7).[11] In a passage larded with scriptural allusions, Augustine explains what he means:

> As a symbol of our inner man [Christ] uttered that cry, both in the psalm and on the cross, which was intended to represent the death of our soul: "My God, my God, why have you forsaken me" (Ps 22:1; Mk 15:34)? To this cry there corresponds what the apostle [Paul] says, "Knowing that our old man was crucified together with him, in order to cancel the body of sin, that we might no longer be the slaves of sin" (Rom. 6:6). By the crucifixion of the inner man is to be understood the sorrows of repentance and a kind of salutary torment of restraint, a kind of death to erase the death of ungodliness in which God does not leave us. . . . It all takes place within, this process that the apostle refers to in the words, "Strip off the old man and put on the new" (Eph 4:22). (*Trin.* 4.6)[12]

Being carnal rather than properly spiritual—that is, oriented toward love and delight in things instead of God—our inner man must be "crucified," and so suffer a "kind of death" as its carnal impulses are slowly annihilated inwardly via repentance and the "salutary torment" of restrained Christian practices. Christ's resurrection is equally a *sacramentum* "of our inner resurrection" as well, to which Augustine correlates Paul's admonition (Col. 3:1) that "if you have risen with Christ, seek the things that are above, where Christ is seated at God's right hand; set your thoughts on the things that are above." Augustine explains that to rise with Christ means "not to think carnally about Christ" (*Trin.* 4.6).[13] In other words, we are to rise with Christ and contemplate eternal realities, principally God, instead of directing our attention primarily to earthly things.

Christ's death and resurrection are also *exempla* of the outer man, that is, "patterns" or "models" for imitation. His death, Augustine thinks, encourages us not to fear those who kill the body but not the soul (Mt 10:28), and his resurrection is a "preenactment" of the resurrection of the bodies of the elect at the eschaton (*Trin*. 4.6).

Although the metaphor of Christlike resurrection is Augustine's dominant one, he uses many others frequently as well. A recurrent image is that of Christ as the true doctor, healing and strengthening sick, injured humanity in the wake of our disastrous fall. In a representative passage from one of Augustine's sermons, he writes:

> So when Peter was still seeing things in a carnal sort of way, he was troubled by the serving maid's questions and denied the Lord three times. The doctor had warned the sick man beforehand what was going to happen with him. The sick man did not know how dangerously ill he was, and sick as he was, he had every confidence in his good health; but the doctor saw the truth of the matter. He had said he would die with the Lord and for the Lord, but he was unable to do so yet, because he was ill. Afterward however, when the Holy Spirit came, sent from heaven, and strengthened those it came upon, Peter was filled with spiritual confidence and now began truly to be ready to die for the one he had previously denied. (*s*. 4.2; cf. *s*. 346A.8)[14]

Fallen humanity suffers from an illness so profound its sufferers cannot recognize its severity without divine illumination, which sometimes comes via tests or "exercises," to be discussed more fully below. We are all gravely ill, and need the medicine of grace, which is reliably present in the "wholesome treatment provided for the faithful" by and in the church, "whereby the due observance of piety makes the ailing mind well for the perception of unchanging truth" (*Trin*. 1.4). This *medicina* or "treatment" builds up our true strength, filling us with "spiritual confidence" even to the point of martyrdom, rather than puffing us up with the vanities of worldly knowledge. Christian faith is the "medicine to heal the tumor of our pride" and "break the chains of sin" that bind us (*Trin*. 8.7).[15]

Augustine also frequently uses the vocabulary of cleaning and purification to evoke his sense of the Christian life. To contemplate and gain full knowledge of God's substance, "it is necessary for our minds to be purified," and "in order to make us fit and capable of grasping it, we are led along more endurable routes, nurtured on faith as long as we have not yet been endowed with that necessary purification" (*Trin*. 1.3). Later Augustine continues: "Our enlightenment is to participate in the Word. . . . Yet we were absolutely incapable of such participation and quite unfit for it, so unclean were we through sin, so we had to be cleansed" (*Trin*. 4.4; cf. 4.24).[16] We can be cleansed from our sinfulness only by Christ, not only through His resurrection, but through baptism, to be discussed more fully below. Christ is our intercessor and mediator, the way by which we may "participate" in God's divinity.

This process of healing, strengthening, cleansing, and purification may be seen as the obverse of the "crucifixion of the inner man." Augustine summarizes this healing as the "renewal" of the inner man, or more specifically the renewal of the image of God in the mind. In an important passage, he writes:

> To be sure, this renewal does not happen in one moment of conversion, as the baptismal renewal by the forgiveness of all sins happens in a moment, so that not even one tiny sin remains unforgiven. But it is one thing to throw off a fever, another to recover from the weakness which the fever leaves behind it; it is one thing to remove from the body a missile stuck in it, another to heal the wound it made with a complete cure. The first stage of the cure is to remove the cause of the debility, and this is done by pardoning all sins; the second stage is curing the debility itself, and this is done gradually by making steady progress in the renewal of this image. . . . About this [second stage] the apostle speaks quite explicitly when he says, "Even if our outer man is decaying, yet our inner man is being renewed day by day" (2 Cor 4:16). . . . So then the man who is being renewed in the recognition of God and in justice and holiness of truth by making progress day by day, is transferring his love from temporal things to eternal, from visible to intelligible, from carnal to spiritual things; he is industriously applying himself to checking and lessening his greed for the one sort and binding himself with charity to the other. But his success in this depends on divine assistance; it is after all God who declares, "without me you can do nothing" (Jn 15:5). When the last day of his life overtakes someone who has kept faith in the mediator, making steady progress of this sort, he will be received by the holy angels to be led into the presence of the God he has worshipped and to be perfected by him and so to get his body back again at the end of the world, not for punishment but for glory. For only when it comes to the perfect vision of God will this image bear God's perfect likeness. (*Trin*. 14.23)[17]

This passage may be Augustine's best general description of the process of Christian discipleship he envisions. By a variety of means, we are to "make progress day by day" in the renewal of the inner man, which essentially consists of the "transference" of love from earthly and temporal to heavenly and eternal things. This process is only possible on the basis of divine assistance through the many forms of grace, and it is the "second stage" of healing and strengthening the Christian believer, after baptism's new beginning. The "complete cure" is received only in person before God at the resurrection, when the divine image is reformed to a final perfect likeness, and one finally moves beyond faith to the "perfect vision of God."

A rather different but still very common metaphor Augustine uses is the familiar Platonic image of ascent. As a general theme, the movement upward from material things to God provides the basic structure for such important works as the *Confessions* and *On the Trinity*. It also provides the explicit form of human attempts to know God in this life via intellectual analysis and contemplation, as for example when we "climb up inward . . . through the parts of the soul by certain steps of reflection," making our way to eternal truths and God by stripping away our misguided attachment to things (*Trin*. 12.13).[18] This process of interior ascent to the unchangeable is also famously described by Augustine as the way by which he arrived at a momentary vision of God in Milan (*conf*. 7.17.23); the same motif occurs as well in the other mystical visions he describes in the *Confessions*, including the vision with Monica at Ostia (7.10.16; 9.10.24–25).

The last common metaphor I will examine here is that of life as a voyage, with Christians seeing themselves as sojourners on the way back to their heavenly home. Augustine writes:

> Suppose we were travelers who could live happily only in our homeland, and because our absence made us unhappy we wished to put an end to our misery and return there: we would need transport by land or sea which we could use to travel to our homeland, the object of our enjoyment. But if we were fascinated by the delights of the journey and the actual traveling, we would be perversely enjoying things that we should be using; and we would be reluctant to finish our journey quickly, being ensnared in the wrong kind of pleasure and estranged from the homeland whose pleasures could make us happy. So in this mortal life we are like travelers away from our Lord: If we wish to return to the homeland where we can be happy we must use this world, not enjoy it, in order to . . . derive eternal and spiritual value from corporeal and temporal things. (*doc. Chr*. 1.4.4)[19]

Augustine sees believers as wayfarers far from home, on a quest to return.[20] From this point of view, any delights peculiar to the journey are snares, and should be used only as tools or means to the end of final beatitude. Augustine continues later: "Let us consider this process of cleansing as a trek, or a voyage, to our homeland; though progress towards the one who is ever present is not made through space, but through zeal for the good and through good mores" (*doc. Chr.* 1.10.10). Linking the metaphor of voyage with those of purification and cleansing, Augustine underscores the gradual nature of progress in the Christian life, as well as the centrality of ethical improvement to his vision. He also points out that although wisdom itself, that is, God, "is actually our homeland, it has also made itself the road to our homeland" (*doc. Chr.* 1.11.11).[21] Christ is the way, as well as the truth and the life, for Christians on their slow journey home.

Whatever the metaphor Augustine chooses in any particular situation—whether it be crucifixion, healing, strengthening, purification, cleansing, renewal, ascent, voyage, or other tropes—he generally suggests that the true and good Christian life is one of gradual progress in righteousness, supported and guided by grace as the inner man is renewed day by day. Augustine is quite clear, however, about the primary agency implied in his metaphors. He attacks Neoplatonic philosophers for thinking they can purify themselves sufficiently to contemplate God by their own power; in fact, Augustine argues, they are defiled by pride (*Trin.* 4.20). Against this, Augustine contends, human beings are "incapable of grasping eternal things, and weighed down by the accumulated dirt of our sins," caked on by love of temporal things, "so we need purifying" via faith in the humility and mercy of God's incarnation and self-sacrifice (*Trin.* 4.24).[22]

This implied combination of primary divine agency and secondary or derived human agency recurs in Augustine's occasional references to *exercitationes animi*, or "exercises of the soul," and his much more frequent references to *disciplina*, usually "instruction," "teaching" or "training," but sometimes "discipline" in the senses of a branch of knowledge, and of training in self-restraint. Before exploring these relatively less well-known aspects of Augustine's theory of personal formation, however, I must briefly address his approach to the received Roman terminology for speaking of excellent character, that is, *virtus* or "virtue."[23]

Augustine famously rejects classical Stoic and Platonic accounts of virtue as rational self-mastery, substituting instead an account of virtue as *ordo amoris*, "rightly ordered love," in his pithy and influential definition (*civ. Dei* 15.22). This right ordering of love reflects the divinely ordained hierarchy of nature, with God at the apex; indeed, Augustine in 387 can speak of *virtus* as "nothing else than perfect love of God" and go on to define the four classical virtues of fortitude, temperance, justice, and prudence as forms of this love of God (*mor.* 1.15.25).

In lieu of a fuller treatment, because excellent accounts have already been offered by others,[24] I simply register the aspects of Augustine's account that are most significant for present purposes. By defining *virtus* in terms of correct love, Augustine makes it into a divine gift, rather than a human achievement. Indeed we can even say that for Augustine "true virtue resides in God and is not proper to the soul," so that true human virtue is always a "participation" in the divine via the mediation of Christ (*civ. Dei* 22.30).[25] Virtue is thus thoroughly and continuously dependent on grace.

This means that there is a categorical difference between true virtue, based in God's "pouring" love into human souls, and apparent self-control based on any other love (*civ. Dei* 19.25). Though it is certainly true that on Augustine's account pagan "virtues" are superior to pagan vices, such "virtues" remain always at bottom counterfeit, based on self-assertion and the all-too-human yen for glory.[26] The creeping subterranean tendrils of *superbia*, "pride" or perhaps better "arrogance," can choke the growth of virtue even in serious Christians. Prime examples, according to Augustine, would be the Pelagians, who are like the five foolish virgins who are continent and do many good works but still are lacking inwardly. They have let the oil filling their lamps burn down to nothing, meaning that they have forgotten that the source of their virtue is God's interior grace transforming their minds, and so "want to attribute not to God but to themselves the fact that they are good." Their hearts have become vain and dark, forgetting that only God gives continence, or any virtue. Having become foolish and proud, "they will deservedly remain outside [when the bridegroom comes, i.e., at the resurrection], because they do not bring with them the disposition of internal grace" (*ep*. 140.83–84; see Mt 25:1–13).[27] Although Augustine is notably unsystematic in his discussion of *virtus*, especially when compared with Aquinas, he is clear in his insistence that true human virtue can only come from inward conversion, understood as an unmerited gift of God, and manifest in obedience to God (*civ. Dei* 14.12), faith (*nupt. et conc.* 1.4.5), and humble acknowledgement that our only glory is the extent to which we can perfect and manifest our status as images of God (*Trin*. 12.16).

This concentration of the ground of virtue in God's gift of divine love unifies all particular virtues in the one virtue of love, which serves as the root of all other particular excellences. Thus whether Augustine speaks of *iustitia*, "righteousness" and "justice," *sapientia*, "wisdom," or *caritas*, "Christian love," among other possible summaries for human goodness, each of these formulations points equally to God's gift of love poured into our hearts. True human agency is always empowered by divine grace, for Augustine; anything else is a vain, counterfeit existence. But due to the pervasive effects of sin in human life, on Augustine's account, our virtue in this life will never be perfect, and it will always consist in part in struggle against continuing sinful impulses. It is also worth recalling Augustine's insistence on the unity of the mind, so that his talk of virtue as love should not be seen as somehow separate from the intellectual apprehension of God, nor as undercutting the use of understanding when deliberating about action in a fallen, frequently ambiguous world. He means only to undercut the pretensions of rational human discernment on the way back to the heavenly city.

Let us return now to Augustine's understanding of *exercitationes* and *disciplina*. *Exercitatio* sometimes refers merely to physical exercise (*civ. Dei* 5.2), but sometimes to a more spiritual exercise (*qu. Hept.* 1.69) or to a trial or hardship to be endured (*ep.* 167.2.8). In 419, Augustine writes that although "exercises of the soul" are sometimes classed as a fault, they are generally regarded as a good thing throughout the scriptures, and the expression seems to him "to signify a striving of the soul thinking most zealously about something with delight in the thinking" (*qu. Hept.* 1.69). This suggests passionate attention or meditation on some datum of Christian teaching. In other passages, exercises are presented instead as "salutary torments" to be endured, which in the case of insults from one's enemies can "shake my eye, perturb my light, grab at my heart, destroy my soul" (*en. Ps.* 54.8). Perhaps Augustine's best general statement is the following: "Let us go forward then, walking in hope, hoping for what we do not yet possess, believing what we do not yet see, loving what we do not yet embrace. The exercise of our souls in faith, hope, and love makes them fit to grasp what is yet to come" (*s.* 4.1). This sort of exercise frees us from slavery to temporal pleasures, so that we "should become instead the master of the body and slave of the creator, and so keep the path of God's commandments" (*s.* 4.1).[28] Whatever they are, Augustine clearly thinks such exercises contribute to Christians' progress in the renewal of the divine image in the mind, properly reorienting us to the divine order of the universe. However, both the rarity and variety of these references to "exercises of the soul" suggest that it would be unwise to make this phrase the basis for a broader interpretation of "spiritual exercises" in Augustine's thought.

Disciplina, conversely, is a more central and pervasive concept for Augustine. The word and its cognates appear approximately 850 times in his agreed-upon corpus of writings, and it is common from the beginning to the end of his literary career; he even devotes a medium-sized sermon to it (*s.* 399). As noted above, in Latin generally *disciplina* is polysemous, meaning "instruction," "teaching," "training," "education," a branch of knowledge, or "discipline" in the sense of order-giving restraint and chastisement. Augustine uses it at various times in all these senses. He suggests that *disciplina* is a difficult topic. It is "the medicine of the soul," by which its health is restored, and on the basis of its use in the scriptures, includes two aspects: "restraint and instruction. Restraint implies fear, and instruction love, in the person benefited by the discipline; for in the giver of the benefit there is love without the fear." Moreover, fear of God should come first, and then love of God (*mor.* 1.28.55–56).[29]

This twofold conception stays more or less constant throughout Augustine's writings, although the theme of restraint becomes increasingly prominent. Augustine suggests *disciplina* has been used to translate both Greek *paideia*, meaning "training" or "education" (*en. Ps.* 118, s. 17.2), and *epistêmê*, meaning "knowledge" (*Trin.* 14.1), because it derives from the Latin word *discere*, "to learn," and so can mean knowledge or instruction; but *disciplina* can also mean "the pains a man suffers for his sins in order to be corrected," as in Hebrews 12:7–11 (*Trin.* 14.1).[30]

At one point, Augustine suggests that the Son's mode of being pertains especially to *disciplina* and a "certain art" by which people's "minds are molded in their thoughts," and that Christ's assumption of human existence effectively presented an education or *disciplina* in the right way of living and an exemplification of Christian precepts. Christ thus answered a deep human need, because "*disciplina* is necessary for people, in which they might be steeped, and by which they might be formed after a model" (*ep.* 11.4). In other words, *disciplina* is the means by which we can be modeled after Christ, the absolute moral exemplar.

In a classically ambivalent presentation, Augustine in the *Confessions* discussed his own literary education as a youth. He loved the "fabulous poems" in Latin, such as the *Aeneid*, filled with romantic travels and other "vanities," while hating the numbing recitation of arithmetical rules. He especially hated learning Greek, despite similarly fabulous tales, because he "did not know any of the words, and violent pressure was imposed on me by means of fearful and cruel punishments." This he contrasted sharply with his easy and pleasant learning of Latin, without threats or punishment, simply by listening to people talking (*conf.* 1.13.22–14.23).[31] He comments,

> This experience sufficiently illuminates the truth that free curiosity has greater power to stimulate learning than rigorous coercion. Nevertheless, the free-ranging flux of curiosity is restrained under your laws, God. By your laws we are restrained, from the canes of schoolmasters to the ordeals of martyrs. Your laws have the power to temper bitter experiences in a constructive way, recalling us to yourself from the pestilential life of easy comforts which have taken us away from you. (*conf.* 1.14.23)[32]

Augustine goes on to pray to God that his soul may not "collapse under your *disciplina*," and that he may turn what he learned in school, pursuing fictions, to God's service. Although Augustine's suspicion of *curiositas* as an aspect of destructive concupiscence is well known,[33] he here seems to recognize it as a power to be harnessed and restrained by God's *disciplina*, so that it might be reformed into a true love of learning and knowledge. Augustine commends this sort of love highly in *On the Trinity* (10.1ff.), and this holy curiosity seems to undergird not only that work as a whole but also Augustine's own intellectual quest to understand God and the soul.[34] For Augustine, then, divine *disciplina* restrains us through suffering, sprinkling gall on what seems but is not truly good, so that we might be recalled to the love of God from love of things (e.g., *conf*. 3.1.1). It also leads us on, step by step, into greater righteousness and purer love, by instructing us positively in the ways of God.

At least partly in response to the controversy with the Donatists, Augustine's conception of *disciplina* became more forceful later in his career as bishop. In a sermon preached on Matthew 18 in 408 or 409, he says that "undisciplined" children, seeking to avoid a beating, will plead and plead for forgiveness each time they sin, again and again. He writes:

> If the strictness of good discipline is to be lulled to sleep by this rule [of indefinitely repeated forgiveness], then with discipline held in check wickedness will rampage unpunished. So what's to be done? Let us reprove with words, and if necessary with a cane; but let us forgive the wrong and rid our hearts of all thought of blame. You see, that's why the Lord added "from your hearts" [Mt 18:35], so that even if love requires the imposition of discipline, gentleness should not depart from the heart. What after all could be more considerate than the doctor bringing his scalpel? The patient due to be cut open cries—and is cut open, cries at the prospect of cauterization—and is cauterized. That's not cruelty. God forbid we should charge the doctor with ferocity. He's ferocious against the wound, in order to cure the person, because if the wound is just fondled, the person's finished. (*s*. 83.7.8)[35]

For the mature Augustine, sin is a terminal illness, a mortal wound, and so it often requires dramatic curative action, not fumbling counterfeit tenderness. Hating the sin but loving the sinner, although only in his or her potential to be finally free of sin (*Trin*. 1.21), God imposes appropriate *disciplina* on human beings, as harshly as necessary to conduce to reorienting life and love to God. This sort of teaching is delivered with and on account of love. God is the ultimate agent of such *disciplina*, sowing seeds of righteousness over all the Earth, with helpers such as Augustine serving as "cheap baskets" for the priceless seeds that are scattered widely (*s*. 399.1; cf. Mk 4:3–8). This view comports easily with Augustine's final position on religious coercion; as many have argued, the social results of later applications of these ideas have been bitter indeed.

PRECONDITIONS FOR EFFECTIVE PRACTICE

Augustine is quite clear that personal effort alone is insufficient to attain beatitude, but where and how grace enters in on his account is a very complex question. Many students of Augustine focus on the inward drama of conversion, especially as this is represented in Augustine's own *Confessions*, and such attention can be revealing. But, as James Wetzel has argued, for Augustine the absolute beginning of faith leaves a vanishing trace, as the story of grace preparing the will to turn to God can be tracked further and further back behind conversion.[36] In the end, Augustine would say, we have each been in God's care from the moment we began to exist (e.g., *spir. et litt.* 34.60).[37]

If we look beyond the *Confessions* account, however, and especially at Augustine's sermons, it becomes clear that in comparison with the "moment" of conversion, he saw the event of baptism as having equal or in all likelihood greater importance.[38] Baptism for Augustine marks the forgiveness and washing away of all previous sins, and the beginning of membership in the church, the "body" of Christ here on Earth, oriented toward its heavenly "head," that is, Christ. Without this cleansing bath, humans are still trapped in sin, justly merit eternal condemnation, and will receive no real benefit from any of the spiritual exercises Augustine advocates for the faithful. Thus, in this section I give a brief summary of Augustine's views of the necessary preconditions for successful progress in righteousness: catechesis, baptism, and membership in the Catholic Church.[39]

The first stage in church membership was becoming a catechumen. This commenced with an interview to discern the motives of a potential church member, followed by an introductory exposition of the Christian faith crafted to speak directly to the situation and concerns of the listener (*cat. rud.* 5.9; 3.5, 6.10ff.). At the conclusion of the address, the hearer was asked whether he or she believed and desired to observe these things. If so, then brief guidance was given on the spiritual symbolism of Christian ritual and how to understand allegorically passages in the Bible that might seem immoral or carnal (*cat. rud.* 26.50). The ceremony was concluded by receiving the sign of the cross on the forehead, a taste of salt, and the laying on of hands, along with a prayer (*conf.* 1.11.17, *pecc. mer.* 26.42). The listener at this point became a catechumen and was entitled to be called a Christian and church member, even if this preliminary sanctification was insufficient for final salvation (*s.* 301A.8, *pecc. mer.* 26.42).

This stage could last an indefinite period of time. Augustine regularly exhorted the catechumens in his congregations to apply for baptism (e.g., *en. Ps.* 80.8, *s.* 132.1, 260C.1). They received no further special training, but they attended worship with the baptized *fideles*, or faithful. Catechumens were barred only from the mysteries of baptism and the Eucharist, "that [these rites] may be as passionately desired by them, as they are honorably concealed from their view" (*Jo. ev. tr.* 96.3).

When catechumens felt ready, they would "petition" for baptism, and they were then known as *competentes* or "petitioners" (*s.* 216.1). Although baptism could happen at any time of year to persons of any age, if circumstances warranted, it was normally a practice engaged in by adults in conjunction with the Lenten season and Easter. Petitioners engaged in a full range of Lenten renunciation, fasting every day until supper, abstaining from meat and wine, "moderating" marital sexual relations, refraining from bathing until the day before baptism, attending overnight prayer vigils, and giving alms to the poor (*s.* 207, *ep.* 54.9). At some time before Easter, the *competentes* underwent a public exorcism where they renounced evil and the sinful heritage of Adam and were finally exorcised by being blown on by the leader of the ritual (*s.* 216.6, 227, 229.1, 398.2). Starting two weeks before Easter, they received instruction in the creed, and they were expected to memorize it in a week's time; in the final week before Easter, this process was repeated with the Lord's Prayer, and the *competentes* were to recite both in a week's time before the assembled congregation of the faithful (*s.* 213.1, 11, 58.1, 59.1; cf. *conf.* 8.2.5).

This ceremony marking the "handing back" of the creed by the petitioners was a crucial element of the Easter vigil, in which the whole congregation participated. Everyone stayed up all night in the basilica, which was lit by numerous lamps, listening to scripture readings and sermons, meditating on Christ's resurrection (*s.* 219–22; see also 223A–K). Augustine regarded the vigil itself as a spiritual exercise: "By keeping vigil it's as though we were re-enacting the Lord's resurrection by the residue of thought [i.e., memory], while by thinking more literally and realistically we confess that it happened only once" (*s.* 220).[40] Holy vigils are practice in living like the angels, rebuking the "earthly burden" of the "weakness of the flesh" that restricts heavenly desires; "by longer vigils they are exercising their spiritual muscles against this deadly dead weight, in order to gain themselves merit in life everlasting. . . . So . . . that's the explanation why Christians should frequently exercise their minds by keeping awake in vigils" (*s.* 221.3).[41]

Before dawn, the petitioners and the clergy would process to the baptistery, with Psalm 41 being chanted (*en. Ps.* 41.1). The water of the baptismal font was consecrated in the name of Christ and with the sign of the cross (*s.* 352.3). The baptism itself was conducted "in the name of the Father, and of the Son, and of the Holy Spirit" (*bapt.* 3.14.19–3.15.20), and it was followed by chrismation, an anointing of the heads of the baptized with consecrated oil (*c. litt. Pet.* 2.105.239). After these rites, all returned to the basilica to be greeted by the faithful as *infantes*, as Augustine now called them, and to witness and partake in their first Eucharist (*s.* 227). For the next week, the *infantes* would wear white robes, signifying the "splendor of their minds," which had been "cleansed and purified," their sins "washed clean in the bath of amnesty" (*s.* 223.1). They would attend church daily for the next week, listening at close range to sermons on the resurrection and the meaning of Easter for Christian living (e.g., *s.* 227).

For Augustine, baptism is above all the way in which God's grace acts on us to forgive our sins. He writes:

> If the forgiveness of sins were not to be had in the Church, there would be no hope of a future life and eternal liberation. We thank God, who gave his Church such a gift. Here you are; you are going to come to the holy font, you will be washed in saving baptism, you will be renewed in the bath of rebirth, you will be without any sin at all as you come up from that bath. All the things that were plaguing you in the past will there be blotted out. Your sins will be like the Egyptians, hard on the heels of the Israelites; pursuing them, but only as far as the Red Sea. (*s.* 213.9)[42]

Like the Egyptians pursuing the Israelites, our sins are overwhelmed and blotted out by divinely directed waters (see also *s.* 363.2). Though Augustine is perhaps more widely known as an observer of the subtle workings of grace within the depths of the heart, he is most definitely also committed to the reality of the Catholic Church's social role as divinely ordained custodian of grace on Earth, administering efficacious rituals of purification such as baptism that provide the only hope of human salvation (e.g., *doc. Chr.* 1.18.17).[43]

It is difficult to overstate the extreme seriousness with which Augustine and his North African neighbors took baptism. For him, it is the only way to escape the dragging weight of original sin: "No one of those who have come to Christ through baptism has ever been excluded from the grace of the forgiveness of sins, and . . . no one can possess eternal salvation apart from his kingdom. . . . All those who have a share in this life will be brought to life only in Christ, just as they have all died in Adam." Moreover, "there is no middle ground, so that one who is not with Christ must be with the devil," definitely including unbaptized infants (*pecc. mer.* 1.28.55).[44] Regardless of the moral quality of the officiating priest, according to Augustine the baptism is necessarily holy and efficacious, because the "spiritual virtue of the sacrament" passes through the officiant like fluid through a channel (*Jo. ev. tr.* 5.15; see also *bapt.* 3.10.15). This holy power makes a permanent change in the recipient, making and marking them a Christian in a way analogous to foot soldiers in Roman legions being branded, so that even if they deserted it was still obvious they had been a soldier (*bapt.* 1.4.5, *Jo. ev. tr.* 6.15).

Despite all this, Augustine does not overstate the transformation accomplished in baptism. It does not remake new Christians into morally perfect beings. It breaks the fever, it removes the foreign object stuck in the wound, but it does not immediately convey full-strength or complete healing (*Trin.* 14.23). Augustine criticizes those who overemphasize the curative effects of baptism, saying:

> For they do not notice that people become children of God to the extent that they begin to exist in the newness of the Spirit and begin to be renewed in the inner man according to the image of him who created them. All the old weakness is not done away with from the moment of one's baptism. Rather, the renewal begins with the forgiveness of all sins and is realized to the extent that one who is wise is wise about spiritual things. But the other things are realized in hope, until they are brought about in reality as well . . . [at the resurrection]. (*pecc. mer.* 2.7.9)[45]

Baptism gives us a real, new start on the way of salvation, but it is by no means already the completion of that way. Augustine recognizes that for some baptism is just an interlude before even greater sinning, when it is received wrongly (*Jo. ev. tr.* 6.15). The full renewal of the image of God within our minds can begin after baptism, but it is only completed in the afterlife.

SPIRITUAL EXERCISES

In this section, I examine Augustine's accounts of a few of the spiritual exercises he advocated at various times in his life: traditional study of the liberal arts; reading and listening to scripture; fasting and eating, both literal and symbolic, including consideration of the Eucharist; and various types of prayer, especially petitionary prayer, confession, and contemplation of the eternal. As with so many aspects of his theology, Augustine's thought in this area moves from an initial, highly philosophical account to a more explicitly Christian conception that retains and adapts some lineaments of his early views while rejecting others.

Liberal Arts

When Augustine was himself a catechumen awaiting baptism in 386–87, he lived in philosophical retreat at Cassiciacum, near Milan, in the villa of a wealthy friend, Verecundus. He lived with his mother and a few younger men, engaging in conversation and debate about many topics, and he produced a number of books in the form of dialogues, both external and internal, some of which purport to be records of actual discussions among the residents, including Augustine (*ord.* 1.2.5). He refers to this gathering as a "school"; and beyond their discussions, he would lead the other men in reading half a book of Virgil before dinner each day (*ord.* 1.3.7, 1.8.26).

During this period, Augustine wrote a treatise *On Order*, which treats the problem of order first at a metaphysical level, examining divine providence, good, and evil, then moves to a full-blown theory of an "order of study" in the liberal arts, "whereby one can proceed from corporeal to incorporeal things" (*retr.* 1.3). He planned to write individual treatises on grammar, dialectic, rhetoric, music, geometry, arithmetic, and philosophy, but he completed only two, on grammar and music, leaving only the beginnings of the later volumes, which he later lost (*retr.* 1.5). He soon abandoned this Christianized vision of study in the liberal arts as the pathway to true knowledge of God, but not before leaving a fairly clear account of what he had in mind as a new convert.

Augustine sees his program of learning, that is, his presentation of the *disciplinae liberales*, as that "by which the rational soul, heretofore in no way fitted for a divine planting, is cleared and cultivated" (*ord.* 1.2.4). He tells one of his students that "instruction in the liberal arts, if only it is moderate and concise, produces devotees more alert and steadfast and better equipped for embracing truth . . . so that they more ardently seek and more consistently pursue and in the end more lovingly cling to that which is called the happy life" (*ord.* 1.8.24). Augustine thinks the liberal *disciplinae*, or branches of learning (e.g., *ord.* 2.5.15), directly contribute to the quality of the Christian quest for love and knowledge of God, which is the essential core of the *beata vita*, the "happy" or "blessed life," for Augustine. Indeed, he goes even further, saying that no matter how holy and upright someone's mode of life, if "they condemn the liberal arts, or are incapable of being well-instructed in them—I know not how I could call them happy as long as they live among men," although he hastens to add that such righteous but unlearned people will be liberated after death in accordance with their virtue (*ord.* 2.9.26).[46] In his *Reconsiderations*, Augustine singles out such statements for censure, suggesting that many saintly people are completely ignorant of the liberal arts. This judgment seems to rest mainly on a change in his understanding of the blessed life, which in 386 he still held to be possible for a few in this life (*ord.* 1.6.16, 2.9.26). His later rejection of this possibility seemed to him to require a corresponding denigration of the value of liberal learning (*retr.* 1.3.2).

The young Augustine saw his order of studies as justified on the basis of his discernment of "the law of God . . . transcribed, as it were, on the souls of the wise," which imposes a twofold order on all who wish to know it, regulating life and directing studies (*ord.* 2.8.25). The regulations he suggests are staples of late antique Roman wisdom, and he spends little time on them, before moving on to the order of instruction, which itself proceeds on the twofold basis of authority and reason. Authority may be prior in time, and especially suited for the instruction of the multitude, Augustine assures us, but reason is prior in reality, is "more highly prized as the object of desire," and is better for the further development of the educated. Authority alone opens the door, but "after one has entered, then without any hesitation he begins to follow the precepts of the perfect life," having been made docile by following them (2.9.26). One should note, however, that concomitant with this sunny outlook on rational human striving, Augustine is even more confident in the sacred rites of the church into which he is being initiated: "Therein the life of good men is most easily purified, not indeed by the circumlocution of disputation, but by the authority of the mysteries" (2.9.27).[47]

Augustine outlines a theory of two levels of learning, matching the trajectory of reason's own passionate quest to ascend to contemplation of divine things (2.14.39). On the first are grammar, the study of language in a very full sense, including literature and even history as part of the study of "letters" (2.12.35ff.); dialectic, the "discipline of disciplines," which covers reason itself, including how to think, teach, and learn; and because people generally follow their feelings and habits rather than truth, rhetoric is added, to charm the crowd and move them to action for their own good (2.13.38).[48] Next come those disciplines leading directly to contemplation of eternal truth, specifically the mathematical disciplines of music, the study of rhythm in language and sound, and therefore of numeric proportion (2.14.39–41); geometry, the study of dimensions and thus number; and astronomy, the study of distance, dimension, and number in the heavenly realm (2.15.42–43). These seem to be crowned by mathematics, the study of numbers themselves, which holds the key to the study of metaphysics, which in turn is necessary to successfully investigate basic questions about God and the soul, that is, the subject matter of philosophy. To become learned enough to see the unity in these branches of study, so as to be able to use them well, and to know and contemplate divine things, not merely believe in them, "is very difficult except for some very gifted person who even from boyhood has earnestly and constantly applied himself" (2.16.44; cf. 2.18.47).[49]

For the Augustine of 386, any investigation of divine matters must be according to this order of study, or not at all; no one should aspire to divine knowledge without grasping dialectic and mathematics (2.17.46–18.47). Augustine writes, near the end of the book:

> Indeed, it is not by faith alone, but by trustworthy reason, that the soul leads itself little by little to the best mores and life. For, to the soul that diligently considers the nature and the power of numbers, it will appear manifestly unfitting and most deplorable that it should write a rhythmic line and play the harp by virtue of this knowledge, and that its life and very self—which is the soul—should nevertheless follow a crooked path and, under the domination of lust, be out of tune by the clangor of shameful vices. But when the soul has properly adjusted and disposed itself, and has rendered itself harmonious and beautiful, then will it dare to see God. (2.19.50–51)[50]

As a new convert and eager catechumen, Augustine is confident in the soul's power to reason its way to a vision of God and attain beatitude, just as it can learn to produce beautiful poetry and melodious music. By studying the liberal arts, it seems, at least a few can learn how to "adjust and dispose" themselves into good order, in perfect harmony with the eternal and divine order "transcribed . . . on the souls of the wise."

Learning from Scripture

Augustine's ardor for beatitude does not cool, but it is rather thoroughly reshaped over the course of the next ten years. The distance between *On Order* and *On Christian Teaching*, for example, which was written in two chunks, mostly in 396 but finished only in 426 or 427, is considerable.[51] Augustine's mature view of reading and listening to scripture may be read as proposing an alternative *disciplina* to his early account of the liberal arts.

Augustine makes quite explicit his sense of his own break with "pagan" learning and the Roman schools in which he had taught rhetoric, although in terms that suggest his continued debts to these traditions. In a sermon preached around 398 or slightly later, he says that the "house of learning is the Church of Christ" (*s.* 399.1).[52] The Catholic Church, this house of *disciplina*, is a "school," with free enrollment, and a master whose chair is in Heaven, that is, Christ, who is the real teacher for true Christians, who are his students (399.1, 9, 15). What they learn is "how to live a good life," so that they can live for ever. Though some seek to avoid the Lord's discipline, not only at home but even in the house of *disciplina* itself, true Christians hear the word of God and accept it like the seed sown on good soil, and they yield an abundant crop (399.1). Christ is the true sower, his Word is his seed, and Augustine's role as preacher is merely to serve as the humble basket for the priceless seed (399.1; cf. 399.14). Augustine regarded himself and all other clergy, like all believers, as "fellow students in the school of the Lord," and argued that "we are all to be educated under this master [Christ], whose chair is in heaven, from his writings" (270.1).[53] "His school is on earth, and his school is his own body [i.e., the church]. The head is teaching his members, the tongue talking to his feet. It is Christ who is doing the teaching; we hear; let us fear, let us act" (399.15). In a reversal of his habitual imagery, Augustine suggests that those who "hear, and hear well, both fall away and make progress; they fall away from iniquity, make progress in the truth; fall away from the world, make progress in God" (399.14).[54] Hearing the Word spoken by Christ is the true *disciplina*, and is crucial to "making progress in God" toward final perfection and beatitude.

The graced engagement with scripture leading to a reformed life is clearly the centerpiece of Augustine's mature view of *disciplina*, of teaching, learning, and discipline. For Augustine, scripture carries great authority: We should treat it as if it were God speaking directly to us, with the boundaries of the canon set by the Holy Spirit acting through the church (162C.15). Repetition of the encounter with scripture, both directly and through explanatory sermons, is critical and can even be pleasant (*s*. 5.1, 125.1). Developing a daily habit of listening to Bible readings serves to cultivate the initial planting of the divine seed in the heart and to ward off destructive competition from worldly weeds: "Anybody who wishes to make progress has the means of doing so. When you assemble in church, put aside silly stories and concentrate on the scriptures" (227.1).[55]

Augustine harps on the necessity of really learning the lessons of scripture, not just listening to but hearing the divine Word. On his account, true Christians "join their hearts to their ears," reforming inwardly to match the divine teaching (*s*. 399.1). He counsels rigorously skeptical self-examination to root out pride, envy, and love of possessions and money, because our neighbor love is only true if it is ordered to God; otherwise, we draw our neighbors into our own carnal loves, our own false self-love (399.4–8, 10–11). After a long discussion of worldly loves, especially the love of possessions, he says:

> At least let us be ashamed, and confess, and beat our breasts—but not just so as to tamp down a solid floor on top of our sins. I mean if you beat your breast without correcting your way of life, you are just tamping down your sins, not removing them. So let us beat our breasts, and beat ourselves, and be corrected by ourselves, or else the one who is the master here will beat us later on. (399.11)[56]

Without true inward reformation, halfhearted displays of contrition only cement us in hypocrisy, with a compressed and hardened locus of sin still within us, a repressed but still pernicious habit.

Because of the possibility of counterfeit virtue, Augustine advocates a disciplinary severity to match the gravity of the illness of sinning. This should be directed both toward ourselves and those in our care, and modeled on the loving severity of God. Speaking about the need to forgive our enemies without a reserve of inward bitterness, he suggests that even seemingly cruel actions may be loving, depending on the intention. In a sermon that quite clearly shows his late Roman social location, he asks, "When you beat your son, is your heart full of hatred for him? That's why I said it is a matter of what is in your heart. Only God sees if there has been forgiveness" (*s*. 5.2). He considers the general case as follows:

> There are those who appear as it were to give tit for tat outwardly, but that sort of physical reproof is really love. He wants him to attain a good life, and all the more does he want him reproved the more he loves him. That's what God is like. . . . But let's look around us, brothers; does this [God's overflowing love for humans] mean he doesn't scourge them? Does it mean he doesn't reprove them? If he doesn't reprove them, how do you explain famine, how do you explain sicknesses, epidemics and diseases? They are all God's ways of reproving us. If then he loves and yet reproves, do likewise yourself; if you have anyone under your authority, while you maintain your feeling of love for them do not deny the rod of correction. If you do refuse it, you will not be maintaining your love. He dies in his sins, and he might perhaps have given them up if you had corrected him; and what you are really guilty of is hating him. (5.2)[57]

Failure to wield the "rod of correction" aggressively is a failure of love, for Augustine, presuming of course that one is properly motivated by Christian love for the neighbor's true best interest (i.e., salvation). Earthly sufferings are one of God's ways for reproving the righteous, as well as punishing the wicked. This is another aspect of divine *disciplina*, mixing gall in with the sweetness of earthly pleasures to orient us to the abiding joy of loving God (*conf*. 3.1.1).

Despite such passages, Augustine does not dwell morbidly on the need for physical punishment to help the work of grace.[58] The goal of Augustinian *disciplina* is always primarily learning, learning to love in the right way, and daily meditation on scripture is one of the most important means to effect such learning. Augustine advocates practices of solitary reading, oral reading to groups, and oral and written commentaries on scripture in a variety of genres, both spoken and written; he also uses the imagery of both reading and listening to make broader points about all facets of personal religious development. These practices are hardly the only spiritual exercises he recommends, however, as I am trying to show in this chapter. Moreover, Augustine recognizes the possibility of completely dispensing with scripture, if God grants faith, hope, and love sufficient for salvation, as with numerous solitary ascetics, some of them illiterate, who made a deep impression on him (*doc. Chr.* 1.39.43, *conf.* 8.6.14–8.8.19).

For the serious student, Augustine counsels reading the entire range of canonical scriptures and committing them to memory as much as possible, but at least becoming familiar with them. Then one should carefully examine the clearest passages, which straightforwardly express central truths about faith and the moral life (*doc. Chr.* 2.9.14). Besides the central truths about Christ and our human condition, Augustine thinks we need in particular to learn how and what to love, according to the different sorts of love appropriate to God above us, ourselves, other human beings, and what is beneath us, including not only things but our bodies as bodies. In brief, all love should be oriented ultimately toward God, and "any other object of love that enters the mind should be swept towards the same destination as that to which the whole flood of our love is directed" (1.23.22, 1.22.21).[59]

In general, passages should be studied until they can be connected with divine love or the love commandments, either literally or figuratively (3.15.23). Augustine describes scripture as a vast collection of treasure, which has been kindly summarized in the command by Christ to love God above all and one's neighbor as oneself; this is the "pearl of great price," he suggests, which should guide both interpretation and personal reformation (*s.* 399.2–3). Augustine writes: "Scripture enjoins nothing but *caritas*, and censures nothing but *cupiditas*, and molds men's minds accordingly. . . . It asserts nothing except the catholic faith, in time past, present, and future. It narrates the past, foretells the future, and demonstrates the present, but all these things serve to nourish and strengthen this *caritas*, and to overcome and annihilate *cupiditas*" (*doc. Chr.* 3.10.15).[60] The relation between these two internal maneuvers is quite direct: "As much as the reign of *cupiditas* is destroyed, so much is that of *caritas* increased" (3.10.16). Harsh or even cruel words or deeds attributed in the Bible to God or his servants signify this destruction of *cupiditas*, which we should all practice through the "crucifixion" of carnal impulses (3.11.17).

Augustine's final guideline for understanding scripture, which is "paramount and absolutely vital," is to pray for divine illumination to further one's understanding (3.37.56).[61] Augustine himself made this a part of his habitual practice, before and even during any commentary on scripture, whether oral or written. As he became more confident in his exegetical and theological understanding, he also relied more confidently on spontaneous inspiration from the inner teacher, Christ, who gave what seemed to him to be plentiful insights into the signification of scripture (e.g., *s.* 6.1). People should not, however, haughtily demand direct illumination from God in all matters; God uses humans to minister to humans, and we should humbly accept instruction from other people concerning what must be learned from them, such as the alphabet, and certainly regarding the scriptures where possible. Augustine even suggests that without human teaching and interchange there would be no way for love to tie us together in bonds of unity, making souls overflow and intermingle with each other (*doc. Chr.* preface par. 1, 11–15).

A paradox of Augustine's account of reading (or listening to) scripture is that in the end only God effects any benefits of human-delivered teaching on the soul, making the listener directly responsive to Himself (4.16.33). As Stock puts it, "An act of reading is the vehicle rather than the cause of conversion. . . . The final lesson of Augustine's education as a reader is that nothing is learned from reading itself."[62] This thesis is overblown, because for Augustine the keys to properly understanding human life are to be learned from the Christian scriptures, either directly or indirectly.[63] Nevertheless, it does helpfully reemphasize the crucial role of grace and divine illumination, occasioned by repeated encounters with scripture, in intensifying our virtuous loves, so that we might "fall away from the world, [and] make progress in God" (*s.* 399.14).

Feeding Body and Soul

To focus on this transference of love that grounds Augustine's understanding of the Christian life of striving for holiness, one might turn to his frequently criticized account of sexual desire.[64] But I would suggest that we can learn more about basic issues in his view of desire by focusing on his less frequently discussed accounts of hunger and eating.[65] In this section, I examine Augustine's views of fasting and eating, both as religious practices of personal reformation, and as symbols for addressing what they are meant to regulate, that is, the flow and direction of human loves. Perhaps the most important constituent of this symbolic field for Augustine is the Eucharist; I will thus treat it in this context, adding a brief excursus on his understanding of Christian worship and ritual. Attending to the Eucharist, which for him is a blessed occasion for the potentially positive experience of desire, contributes to a fuller account of his theology of personal reformation, by reading his emphasis on the renunciation of certain desires in combination with his counsel to heighten others.

In his sermon on the value of fasting, Augustine notes the condition of angels, who experience total and eternal satiety in the presence of God, who directly fills their minds with Himself and keeps them whole. In contrast to this, human beings must eat earthly food to support their flesh and survive; sadly, though it nourishes, it also diminishes us, reinforcing our carnality. Against this carnal hunger, Augustine points out,

> Christ instructed us to hunger for this [heavenly] food, when he said, "Blessed are those who hunger and thirst for justice, since they shall be satisfied" (Mt 5:6). So it's the business of human beings living this mortal life to hunger and thirst for justice; but to be filled with justice belongs to that other life. The angels have their fill of this bread, this food; human beings, however, in being hungry for it stretch themselves; in stretching themselves they are enlarged; in being enlarged they increase their capacity; through increasing their capacity, they will be filled in due course. (*s*. 400.1)[66]

Augustine counsels us to intensify our spiritual hunger for justice, and he promises that this yearning will be satisfied in the end. Although we get a taste of this divine justice on the Christian way, we should be like Paul: "He says he is not yet perfect. . . . He is on the way; he's hungry, he wants to be filled, he's busy about it, he longs to arrive, he's simmering with impatience, nothing seems to him to be so long delayed as 'his casting off and being with Christ' (Phil 1:23)" (*s*. 400.1).[67] Fasting, like the rest of the Christian life, is according to Augustine a training in yearning.[68] We learn to stop desiring earthly goods in themselves, even food, and learn instead to crave the presence of God. Thus: "Let us imitate [Christ's] cross, pacifying and nailing our lusts with the nails of abstinence" (207.2).[69]

Augustine himself apparently fasted daily, eating one simple meal each day, with no particular dietary restrictions, in contrast to the Manichees; the key was to restrict and as much as possible eliminate carnal delight in food (*conf*. 10.31.43–46; *s*. 207.2). All his monastic brothers and sisters fasted during weekdays, resting on Saturday and Sunday, with everyone redoubling their efforts during Lent (*ep*. 36.8, *s*. 205.2).[70]

Augustine understands this traditional and widespread ancient practice as follows. Being suspended, as it were, between Heaven and Earth, believers are to do all they can to stop bending down, burdened by carnal desires, to Earth, and are instead to reach up to eternal and heavenly goods, "eagerly panting to be joined to the angels." He continues:

> So what good does it do us to abstain a little from the nourishment and the joys of the flesh? The flesh is dragging us down to the earth, the mind is tending upward; it is snatched up by love, but held back by weight. . . . So if the flesh . . . is a load on the soul, and a burden weighing down the

> soul as it tries to fly ahead; the more you delight in your higher life, the more ready you are to lay down your earthly burden. (400.2)[71]

This is the crux of the matter, for Augustine: Eating is a prime element of our carnal existence, and to the extent we can subdue our fleshly cravings in this area, the more steadily we may rise up with free and unburdened spirit to God. Fasting, for Augustine, is a key element of the righteousness possible on our journey through mortality, and it refers not only to the restriction of food intake but also to "the whole chastisement of the body" (*perf. just*. 8.18). Bringing the body into submission, so that the mind itself will submit to God, here seems to be a particularly radical preparatory training for death, in Hadot's sense, so that earthly life will be seen as a burden restraining us from our true homeland.

Why exactly is fasting effective as a spiritual exercise? Augustine seems to believe that satisfying our desires only makes them stronger, at least in the long run. According to Augustine, heavenly food feeds the loving kindness of the mind, while earthly food nourishes the weakness of the flesh (400.2). We might also recall in this context his sense of the astonishing power of carnal desire to seize and "enchain" a person's will after even a single instance of satisfaction (e.g., *conf*. 6.8.13). Thus we should frustrate and stunt our carnal desires, while carefully nurturing our nascent spiritual ones.

One might object that such a reading is false to Augustine's own sense that desire is stoked by the appeal to fallen souls of what is forbidden, because this presents an ideal scenario for the delusional assertion of self-centered autonomy, as with Augustine's own youthful pear theft (*conf*. 2). Such a presumption even underlies the restriction of the Eucharist to baptized Christians, on Augustine's account (*Jo. ev. tr.* 96.3). I think Augustine would respond, at least with regard to food, that there is a difference between restriction and absolute prohibition—the point of minimizing our eating is precisely to deaden our "taste" for the pleasures of the table. This also explains why, for Augustine, no particular foods were forbidden, in conscious contrast to his earlier Manichean practice, which centered on a complicated set of prohibitions. An obvious objection to this line of response would start from Augustine's own discussion of celibacy, which seems to require just this sort of categorical prohibition. However, Augustine is quite clear that celibacy can only be attained by means of unusual grace. Suffice it to say that prohibition for Augustine does heighten desire, unless that desire is gratuitously blotted out by God's gift of holy love. His deeper point about spiritual exercises is similar: Restricting pleasurable consumption will cause desire to slowly burn out, rather than causing it to flare up even more strongly, if and only if our fundamental orientation is already to love God more than self. This deep orientation, which can only be attained through grace, is what allows fasting to quell carnal desire rather than refine it.

The thought that we are merely torturing ourselves to please a cruel God is a temptation, to which we should respond as follows: We are hurting ourselves, but for a good end, that our flesh will "exert less pressure" on our mind. Augustine provides the following evocative metaphor:

> Suppose you were going to mount . . . a horse, and it looked as if it might throw you with its friskiness, wouldn't you make sure of having a safe journey, by cutting the rations of the unruly beast, and taming it with hunger, since you couldn't curb it with the reins? My flesh is my mount. On my journey to Jerusalem it frequently runs away with me, and tries to make me lose my way, and my way is Christ; so since it capers about like that, shouldn't I restrain it with fasting? (*s*. 400.3)[72]

Fasting tames our flesh, making it docile and obedient, or at least more so, sufficient to get us where we should go on our journey. Following Paul, we should chastise our bodies and reduce them to slavery (1 Cor 9:26–27), so that we might reintroduce the proper order of obedience into the order of nature, just as Adam introduced disobedience. God is above us, our flesh "below" (at least below our souls), and we are the disobedient servant faced with disobedience from our own servant. However, God turns all things to good, and so even though in this life we never regain perfect control over our bodies, God "is often using your servant to train and exercise you, so that because you have often ignored the Lord, you may be suitably corrected through your servant" (*s*. 400.5).[73]

The efficacy of fasting as a spiritual exercise thus rests on the intimate connection between flesh and spirit, body and soul, in Augustine's theology. Though soul and body are on different metaphysical levels, and "flesh" and "spirit" sometimes serve as stand-ins for these ideas, they are at a deeper level about types of desire: "After all, the flesh does not desire without the soul, though we say that the flesh desires, because the soul desires in a carnal manner" (*perf. just*. 8.19).[74] The flesh as body is not the enemy of the spirit, and comes from the same creator, although they lust against each other (Gal 5:17). After all, Augustine says, quoting Paul, "nobody ever hates his own flesh; but he nourishes and cherishes it, just as Christ does the church" (Eph 5:29, *s*. 400.4). Far from being enemies, flesh and spirit are joined by a kind of marriage bond, and they only have opposed desires because of punishment for the Fall. The body, as flesh, is emphatically not a chain, a prison, or a punishment (*s.* 400.4). Thus our fasting should never become excessive, and turn into hatred of the flesh, which Augustine in any case seems to think is impossible: "However much . . . you may be a tamer of the flesh, however great the severity you enthusiastically treat it with, I imagine you shut your eye if something or someone is about to hit it" (400.4).[75] We lust against the flesh, Augustine says, to discipline (*dare disciplinam*) and tame it; in an alarming sequence of images, he suggests we should treat the body in the same lovingly severe way he thinks his fellow fifth-century Christians should discipline their wives, sons, and slaves, where occasional violence within the household was completely ordinary (400.5).

How exactly was this "marriage" to be conducted? Augustine counsels that we are "not to give the flesh its head in the pursuit of unlawful pleasures, and to rein it in to some extent even from lawful ones," or else we will be always on the verge of slipping over into unlawful delights (400.6). We should be temperate, in questions of both food and sex (if married), and be aware always of why we restrain ourselves: to "abstain from the joys of the flesh and obtain the joys of the mind" (400.6).[76] Over time, Augustine thinks, we can induce what amounts to a good habit of submission in our flesh (although he usually reserves *consuetudo*, "habit," for the nearly unstoppable momentum of carnal concupiscence), because "the flesh will readily submit to you in not sticking to what belongs to others, if it has got used to being held back even from what is its own" (207.2).[77]

In this life, however, the joys of the mind are only occasional because worries over the joys of the flesh too often crowd them out, if we are to believe Augustine's accounting in the *Confessions* of his personal regimen to discipline himself. This program combats the three main types of concupiscence he finds still rampant in his soul, even as a mature bishop: the lust of the flesh (sensory delight in things), the lust of the eyes (misguided curiosity), and worldly ambition (pride and the lust for acclaim) (*conf.* 10.30.41–10.41.66, following 1 Jn 2:16). He describes his existence as a "total temptation," one still regularly assailed by the "temptations of fleshly concupiscence" (10.32.48, 10.34.51). Focusing only on eating and the pleasures of the palate and stomach, we can still get a sense of the outlines of his concerns and methods of addressing them. He confesses that "at the present time the necessity of food is sweet to me, and against that sweetness I fight lest I become captive." He "wage[s] a daily battle in fastings," and he fears not the impurity of food "but that of uncontrolled desire," that is, *cupiditas* (10.31.43, 46).[78] Augustine has learned from God to think of food as medicine for his earthly condition; a certain amount is necessary to keep the illness in check, but he should take no more than that. For Augustine, the danger lies in the eating:

> But while I pass from the discomfort of need to the tranquillity of satisfaction, the very transition contains for me an insidious trap of *cupiditas*. The transition itself is a pleasure, and there is no other way of making that transition, which is forced upon us by necessity. Although health is the reason for eating and drinking, a dangerous pleasantness joins itself to the process like a companion. Many a time it tries to take first place, so that I am doing for pleasure what I profess or wish to do only for health's sake. . . . What is enough for health is too little for pleasure. And often there is uncertainty whether the motive is necessary care of the body seeking sustenance or the deceptive desire for pleasure demanding service. . . . [The unhappy soul] is delighted not to be clear how much is sufficient to maintain health, so that the quest for pleasure is obscured by the pretext of health. Every day I try to resist these temptations. I invoke the help of your right hand and report to you my impulses, because in this matter my mind has not yet achieved a settled pattern. (10.31.44)[79]

The danger in eating is the inevitable pleasure (*voluptas*) afforded our concupiscence when we meet our bodily needs. This pleasure clouds sober commitments to health in a fog of pleasure, giving earthly lust a continuously open door to disrupt the soul striving for God. This is the deeper temptation, to please ourselves alone apart from God, *delighting* in something we are only meant to *use* on our journey home (e.g., *doc. Chr.* 1.3.3–1.5.5).

Augustine's intense suspicion of sensory pleasure puts him in an almost insoluble bind. Though the pain of abstinence is safer, and accompanied by a certain "joy of the mind," it is unsustainable, and the pleasure of God's presence is intermittent at best in this habitually carnal life, hoped for but not yet fully present: "Here I have the power to be, but do not wish it. There I wish to be, but lack the power. On both grounds I am in misery" (*conf.* 10.40.65). Augustine's only hope is to rely on God's kindness, confessing inwardly and outwardly his wayward impulses and his earnest attempts at self-improvement. He writes: "Anyone who could change from the worse to the better can also change from the better to the worse. There is one hope, one confidence, one reliable promise—your mercy" (10.32.48).[80]

If eating in the usual sense is so fraught with the danger that pleasure will pollute our souls with unnatural desire, where else can we turn, according to Augustine? Besides direct prayer, to be treated more fully below, we can enact the mysterious *sacramentum* or "sacred sign" of the Lord's Table, the central symbol of Augustinian Christianity, that is, the Eucharist.[81] Indeed, this is Augustine's own conclusion to book 10 of the *Confessions*. He casts his anxiety on the Lord that he might live; he prays that God teach and heal him; he reflects on the sacrifice of Christ, redeeming Augustine by his blood on the cross; and he concludes the book: "For I think upon the price of my redemption, and I eat and drink it, and distribute it. In my poverty I desire to be satisfied from it together with those who 'eat and are satisfied' (Ps 61:5). 'And they shall praise the Lord who seek him' (Ps 21:27)" (*conf*. 10.43.70).[82] Although this *sacramentum* is only of minor nutritive significance in a fleshly sense, it answers human spiritual hunger perfectly as people celebrate and reflect on it. For Augustine, the Eucharist is the true and purely vivifying food available to Christians, satisfying at the deepest possible level our desire to cleave to God. Unsurprisingly, the first food actually taken on fast days in Augustine's church was the Eucharist.[83]

Although such a practice seems to rest on the idea that merely physical hunger can be enlisted to bolster spiritual desires, Augustine never seems to recognize such a possibility. Instead he focuses on the dangers of a merely "carnal" reception of the bread and wine. In a sermon on the Lord's Prayer, Augustine explicates "Give us this day our daily bread" as follows. We need both physical and spiritual nourishment, and so the prayer refers to both, to give us support on the way to the kingdom of God. The Eucharist in particular provides us with necessary daily spiritual nourishment: "So the Eucharist is our daily bread; but we should receive it in such a way that our minds and not just our bellies find refreshment. You see, the special property to be understood in it is unity, so that by being digested into His body and turned into His members we may be what we receive. Then it will really be our daily bread" (*s*. 57.7).[84] We are to receive and reflect on the Eucharist so that our minds are refreshed in their divine love. In this way, as we digest the bread, the church will digest us, turning all recipients throughout the world into members of the body of Christ, unified in their love for God and neighbor.

In other words, according to Augustine, through the Eucharist Christ is making us into Himself, reforming the image of God in our minds. God not only became man in Christ, "he also presented us in this sacrament with his body and blood, and this is what he even made us ourselves into as well" (229.1). Strikingly, through the Eucharist believers are to "be what [they] can see," and receive themselves as the body and blood of Christ (*s*. 272; see also 227, 229, 229A). As Augustine says: "There you are on the table, and there you are in the cup" (229.2).[85]

Although for Augustine the ritual on its own does seem to carry and transmit a salvific power, exactly how this should be understood is less clear than in the case of baptism, where he employs the imagery of grace as a fluid coming directly from Christ through the priest, as discussed above. Augustine's most theoretical statement of the operations and significance of the Eucharist occurs in *City of God*, as part of a discussion of sacrifice and worship.

Augustine thinks that sacrifice is due to God alone, but that it is foolish to think sacrifice is necessary or even beneficial to Him (*civ. Dei* 10.4–5). Instead, "it is man, not God, who is benefited by all the worship which is rightly offered to God" (10.5). Thus the previous regime of sacrifice, involving killing animals, has been superseded by the current, much simpler rituals, even if the intention symbolized by them remains the same: to cleave to God and seek the good of our neighbor in the same end. "Thus," Augustine continues, "the visible sacrifice is the *sacramentum*, the sacred sign, of the invisible sacrifice" (10.5). The invisible sacrifice is internal and spiritual: The Christian believer's contrite and humble heart, filled with mercy and love, is the one sacrifice God truly desires (10.5). The Christian path of purification and consecration to Christ, fruitfully issuing in love of God and neighbor, so that each does all he or she can to bring others to love God—according to Augustine, "this is the worship of God; this is true religion; this is the right kind of devotion; this is the service which is owed to God alone" (10.3). Thus a true sacrifice is offered in every act aiming to unite people in holy fellowship with God, every act of compassion with God as its ultimate end. One's body is a sacrifice when disciplined with continence, its capabilities offered to God as "instruments of righteousness." Even more so is one's soul, "when it offers itself to God, so that it may be kindled by the fire of love and may lose the 'form' of worldly desire, and may be 're-formed' by submission to God as to the unchangeable 'form,' thus becoming acceptable to God because of what it has received from his beauty" (10.6).[86] This internal reformation to God's form—that is, to the image of God obscured within the mind—is what God desires and commands.

Augustine hastens to underline the absolute centrality of the communal aspect of this reformation. It is not merely the reformation of individual believers that is at stake (10.6). The Eucharist, or "sacrament of the altar," is the ritual locus of Christian devotion, wherein believers communally incarnate Christ, serving as His sacrificial body on Earth while He reigns in Heaven. As the God-man, Christ thus offers, receives, and is the sacrifice: "He is both the priest, Himself making the offering, and the oblation. This is the reality, and He intended the daily sacrifice of the Church to be the *sacramentum* of this; for the Church, being the body of which He is the head, learns to offer itself through Him" (10.20).[87] The church, as a communal entity of human beings, learns from Christ, its head, to offer itself as a suffering but eager servant to God, to do the works of love that He desires and commands. Through daily repetition of the Eucharist, Christian believers have the spectacle of obedience unto death before them and hear the call to "be what you can see, and receive what you are."[88]

For Augustine, then, a ritual that is itself a sacred sign provides through the power of symbolic association the daily bread to sustain and enliven us as spiritual beings, helping our souls to become more Christlike. Repeated reflection on the Eucharist satisfies our minds and, perhaps paradoxically, over time leaves our souls longing for even more divinity. At the same time, frequent fasting allows us to "crucify" the carnal impulses still rampant in our souls, and bring our unruly "inner man" to heel. By quelling our fleshly desires and stretching and expanding our desires for Christlike love, we undergo a two-sided training in longing, reforming our bestial desires so that we might become worthy to join the angels who eat and drink their fill in the contemplation of God.

Before going on to examine prayer, another crucial Augustinian exercise, we should pause to consider an intriguing ambivalence in his account concerning the intrinsic efficacy of both fasting and participation in the Eucharist. At least partly in response to the Donatist schism, Augustine frequently returns to the need to receive the bread and wine worthily, with love of God and all neighbors, rather than unworthily, with enmity toward some members of the body of Christ. He even calls the Eucharist "the sacrament of unity." Whoever receives it without peaceful love in their heart does not benefit from it but receives it as a testimony against them (*s*. 272). All of this suggests that for Augustine spiritual exercises are not automatically efficacious. On the contrary, even the Eucharist needs the catalyst of proper understanding and love in order to transmit its saving effects. This is a massive Augustinian caveat to the very idea of spiritual exercises, and it is continuous with his insistence on conversion, baptism, and church membership as preconditions for making ethico-religious progress. Though these "prerequisites" might appear to be the most vulgar sort of in-group/out-group thinking dressed up in distinguished traditional robes, Augustine has a real anthropological basis for his insistence: Without a contrite and humble heart fired by divine love, he thinks spiritual exercises will simply refine our pride and thereby give greater subtlety and strength to our habitual sinning, masking it in a Christian guise.

In what sense, then, do spiritual exercises differ from any other action motivated by divinely given love of God and neighbor? In terms of their motivational basis and goal, they do not differ at all. On Augustine's account, every properly motivated Christlike action is a spiritual exercise, at least in a broad sense, because it conforms us to God. Nevertheless, traditional practices such as the Eucharist serve as reliably potent if not irresistible vehicles for inspiration, because of the way their symbolism "feeds" our minds. Furthermore, exhortation to properly understand and receive the Host helps to ward off corruption of this central practice, as well as inspire the faithful in their yearning to be conformed to the divine pattern.

Prayer

So far, then, Augustine recommends three basic types of spiritual exercise: learning (via listening to and reading scripture, along with secondary explanations like sermons); restriction and renunciation of sources of carnal pleasure, such as food and sex; and inspiring symbolic actions manifest in various liturgical settings. Augustine appears to conceive of these practices as influencing all three aspects of the triune human mind, that is, memory, understanding, and will or love. Given his emphasis on the unity of the *mens*, it is unsurprising that the practices I am surveying here do not correlate in any exclusive way with particular aspects of the mind. So, for instance, genuine learning must issue as much in change of heart, in our terms, as in change of mind. Even in the case of fasting, the exercise as Augustine understands it involves not only practice in quelling certain loves by directly constraining behavior but also maneuvers to revise self-interpretation. If any aspect of the *mens* might seem relatively shadowed in the account provided so far, it would be memory. To remedy this deficiency, while still emphasizing the underlying unity in Augustine's conception of both the psyche and the processes of character formation, I turn now to Augustine's account of prayer.

Augustine recommends three main types of prayer: petitionary, confessional, and contemplative.[89] His most sustained analysis of *oratio* or petitionary prayer occurs in Letter 130, to Proba, a rich Roman widow who had fled Rome with a retinue of women and was allowed to found a nunnery for them in Carthage. For Augustine, prayer is a matter of great importance, and after the love commandments he treats it before all other issues in the part of his *Rule* on monastic order (*ep*. 130.1.1, *reg*. 2.2). In the darkness of this world, walking by faith and not sight on our pilgrimage, "the Christian soul ought to regard itself as desolate, so that it does not cease to pray, and it should learn to turn the eye of faith to the words of the divine and holy Scriptures," as on a light in the darkness (*ep*. 130.2.5).[90] Prayer is thus an aspect of our earthly life, which is beset by temptation, suffering, and weakness, and it will pass away, as will faith in deference to actual sight, in the life to come (130.2.5). In this life, however, all should pray to Christ as if they were poor, bereaved, and desolate widows, supplicating God night and day (130.3.7, 16.30).

We should pray above all for beatitude; this is an absolutely trustworthy and blameless goal, and it should be the end of all our desire and striving (130.4.9, 14.27). Although the safest course, because of the corrupting influence of earthly pleasures, is to look upon possessions and worldly comforts with contempt and to give all that we have to the poor, it is still permissible according to Augustine to pray for temporal goods such as food, shelter, and clothing, for ourselves and all others, because such things are necessary for human life (130.3.7–8, 5.11, 6.13). Somewhat surprisingly, Augustine goes on to suggest that as long as we ultimately subordinate everything to the love of God and the desire to cleave to Him, it is even permissible to desire and pray for honor and worldly power, and clothes and housing suitable to a high social station, as long as they are for a good end (even a subsidiary one like the welfare of offspring); such prayers are only bad if such things are asked for in themselves, to gratify pride or envy (130.6.12). We often also pray for relief from some affliction, and this is proper as well, as long as we truly subordinate our own will to God's, as Christ did during his passion. Unpleasant as they often are, the trials of this world heal the wound of pride, exercise our patience, and punish or even eradicate sins; thus we should trust in God's mercy to discern what is truly most beneficial for us in the ultimate sense, and fear only that God will punish us by granting an unwise or vicious request (130.14.25–26; cf. *Trin*. 13.20). Thus there is a certain "learned ignorance" in prayer as we wait patiently for the great blessing to come and in the meantime learn patiently to trust the God who transcends human understanding, however inscrutable His decisions with regard to our petitions may be (*ep*. 130.15.28).

For Augustine, prayer is fundamentally a matter of desire or, more precisely, of reshaping desire. We should pray with and for only one desire: to spend eternity in the presence of God (130.8.15). God asks us to pray our wishes to Him, although He already knows everything, so that "our desire by which we may receive what He prepares to give is exercised through prayers" (130.8.17). In other words, prayer does not benefit or illuminate God in any way, but serves as an exercise for human beings to increase their holy desire for God. We ought to "pray always," not in the sense that we are murmuring or speaking words ad infinitum, but rather that "we cherish uninterrupted desire [for God] with faith, hope, and love." The effect of prayer correlates directly to the fervor of the desire behind it, and in a sense our desire itself is our prayer (*ep*. 130. 9.18, *en. Ps*. 37.14). We should, however, use words to pray at various set hours and seasons to admonish ourselves, and to check our progress in holy desire; in this way, we can "arouse ourselves more intensely to increase it" (*ep*. 130.9.18). Augustine writes:

> But at certain hours we recall our minds to the task of prayer from other cares and concerns, in which desire itself is in a sense cooled down, admonishing ourselves by the words of our prayer to aim at that which we desire; otherwise our desire that had begun to cool might become

> altogether cold, and be entirely extinguished, if it were not inflamed more frequently. (130.9.18)[91]

Prayer, then, is a way of fanning the flames of holy desire, which are all too frequently weakened by the distractions of secular existence. A "watchful and keen intention" is "indispensable in prayer," according to Augustine, and we should pray in whatever manner, long or short, with many words or few, that supports this state of alertness stretching out toward divine illumination (130.10.20). In general, "to petition much is to knock with a long and pious stirring of the heart towards Him to whom we pray. For this task is often carried out more with sighs than words, more with weeping than speaking" (130.10.20).[92]

Although God does not need human words, they are nevertheless as useful to people in prayer as they are in reading, listening, and preaching. Augustine writes: "We, then, need words by which we may be reminded and may consider what we ask for, not by which we believe that we should either instruct or persuade the Lord." And moreover, after considering the Lord's Prayer, he concludes, "For it was necessary that the truth itself be committed to our memory by these words" (130.11.21). According to Augustine, desire can precede the words of prayer, which give it form, or "come after them and attend to them, that it may increase in fervor" (130.12.22). By using the divine words of the psalms and the Lord's Prayer, especially, we admonish ourselves to desire what we must, for instance that God's name be seen as holy among people here on Earth, and by these words "stir up our desire for that kingdom [of Heaven] that it may come for us, and that we may be found worthy to reign in it" (130.11.21).[93] All Christian prayer is summed up in the Lord's Prayer, the paradigmatic petitionary prayer, and we should seek nothing beyond what can be subsumed under it (130.12.22). The right words, being divinely inspired, stir up the right desires in us and refresh our memories, so that our intention toward and desire for God may be constantly reinflamed by daily prayer.

"Confession," or rather the Latin *confessio*, carries a double meaning. It does include the sense of confessing one's sins or failures (e.g., *conf.* 5.10.18), but also of acknowledging the glory or mercy of God, and especially of acknowledging God's healing action within one's own life (e.g., 1.6.10). Confession, for Augustine, is very similar in form and purpose to petitionary prayer or *oratio*, but even more intimate, a direct address to God concerning the state of one's soul and God's relations to that soul. Augustine writes:

> Accept the sacrifice of my confessions offered by "the hand of my tongue" which you have formed and stirred up to confess your name. "Heal all

> my bones" and let them say "Lord who is like you?" He who is making confession to you is not instructing you of that which is happening within him. The closed heart does not shut out your eye, and your hand is not kept away by the hardness of humanity, but you melt that when you wish, either in mercy or in punishment, and there is "none who can hide from your heat." Let my soul praise you that it may love you, and confess to you your mercies that it may praise you. (5.1.1)[94]

Confession should be a prayer of honest self-examination directed to God, truth telling of the highest possible human order, based on a scrupulous accounting of inner impulses and thoughts (10.30.41ff.). God forms and stirs our voice, whether physical or mental, to acknowledge Him. Again, it is not a question of telling God anything He does not already know but of shaping our "inner discourse," to borrow Hadot's terminology, into the proper theocentric form. By reflecting on God's kindness to us, we realize how great God is and how much we owe Him; by praising God in prayer, we can increase our love for Him. And as the larding of the above passage with quotations from the psalms shows, a crucial aspect of confession for Augustine is to recognize how the Word of God in scripture applies to and illuminates one's past and thus one's self.[95] The habits of concupiscence live on in our memories (10.30.41–34.51), but so do recollections of moments when God has "melted" our carnal hardness of heart, freeing us from the weight of habit to soar up in love for Him (10.27.38, 10.36.58). By thinking about them as we confess them, as past still present to us, we reform our memories through concentrated attention and conscious rearrangement of elements of our self-narrative (10.11.18). Because we are a mystery to ourselves, this process is not easy, and it needs to continue throughout life, to persevere in some limited righteousness until the end, lest we cease to make progress but instead fall back into the abyss of sinful degradation (10.32.48, 10.35.57). And as we come to know ourselves better over time, Augustine hopes, we will come to know the God who knows us better than we ever will ourselves (10.1.1).

Occasionally, confession can be a public act as well, either as an element of penance for grave sins after baptism, or, as in Augustine's own case, for political and religious ends, which provoked him to write the *Confessions*.[96] Augustine's need to justify the reality of his conversion, both away from Manicheism and to Christianity, led him to confess not only inwardly in his heart but also outwardly before many witnesses with his pen (10.1.1). He hoped to provoke his readers as he had been provoked by the narratives of others' conversions, such as Antony's (8.6.14ff.). He aimed "to lift up human understanding and affection to [God]," and as an old man rereading his earlier work, he reported that both writing it originally and reading it again had had just this effect, although he recognized this was a matter of individual responsiveness (*retr*. 2.6.1). He reflected with some care about how to achieve this aim, despite human inquisitiveness and defensiveness, and in the midst of his analysis prayed to God for success:

> Nevertheless, make it clear to me, physician of my most intimate self, that good results from my present undertaking. Stir up the heart when people read and hear the confessions of my past wickednesses, which you have forgiven and covered up to grant me happiness in yourself, transforming my soul by faith and your sacrament. Prevent their heart from sinking into the sleep of despair and saying "it is beyond my power." On the contrary, the heart is aroused in the love of your mercy and sweetness of your grace, by which every weak person is given power, while dependence on grace produces awareness of one's own weakness. Good people are delighted to hear about the past sins of those who have now shed them. The pleasure is not in the evils as such, but that though they were so once, they are not like that now. (*conf*. 10.3.4)[97]

Understanding the need for and reality of grace induces a salutary dependence and humility, though conversely the reception of grace produces a new sort of loving power that overcomes despair and no longer seeks its own glorification, but God's. Augustine's soul and loves have been "transformed," if still incompletely before the final resurrection. He has come to trust that God can and will do the same for (at least some) others, and he attempts to be an instrument of this divine will.

Fittingly, the last type of Augustinian prayer I shall consider is contemplation. *Contemplatio* for Augustine is, properly speaking, the final goal and reward of a life of faith, which purifies the mind to behold God. It will be the sole activity of the beatified after the resurrection. That contemplation will be direct and total illumination by God, producing perfect knowledge and unending joy, as human desire for God is met, at last, by full divine presence (*Trin*. 1.17, 20; see also *ep*. 147). Martha's sister Mary is for Augustine not a figure for a fully contemplative life but of contemplation within our inevitably active life here on Earth: "A sort of picture of what this joy will be like was sketched by Mary sitting at the Lord's feet, intent upon his words; at rest from all activity and intent upon the truth, in such measure as this life allows, but thereby nonetheless foreshadowing that joy which is going to last for ever" (*Trin*. 1.20; see Lk 10:38–42 on Martha and Mary).[98] Contemplation in this life is but a foreshadowing of what will come, but it is nevertheless a great joy to be at rest from activity and intent on God's eternal Word (*Trin*. 13.2).

For Augustine, contemplation is the function of the higher application of the human mind, concerned with wisdom about eternal things, not knowledge of temporal matters (*Trin*. 12.4). He even suggests that the mind's being made in the image of God implies the "capacity to use reason and understanding in order to understand and gaze upon God," presumably within the limitations of different stages of our existence (14.6). Augustine seeks this intellectual ascent to God from the beginning of his authorship, from his early semimythological account of impersonal reason's own quest for understanding giving birth to the various liberal arts (*ord*. 2.36ff.), to his mature reflections on Christian faith seeking understanding of God and mind in *On the Trinity*. The latter half of *On the Trinity* is organized around "climbing up, step by step" through different levels of human activity to discern triune structures in each sphere, including various aspects of the "outer" and "inner man;" this process of reflection on one's self, and especially on the mind's action, Augustine calls "training the mind . . . to come in our own small measure to a sight of that trinity which God is" (*Trin*. 13.26; cf. 15.1, 10).[99]

There are two difficulties in this training: The first is the Platonic one, which Augustine realized throughout his authorship, of shearing away from the mind's habitual interest in physical and temporal things, which exert an almost overwhelming force on our attention, to focus on eternal and divine truths (14.7; 12.13–14). The second difficulty, however, is specifically Christian: Because we are in fact images of God in our thinking, we must understand ourselves as such to understand ourselves correctly (15.44), but are unable to come to such an understanding without divine aid (e.g., 15.10). Augustinian contemplation, then, is always a gift from above.

To come to understand ourselves as images of the triune God is to activate that image in ourselves by the mental act of focusing, not on the mind itself, which is in a preliminary sense the divine image, but on God per se. When this is done, the unified inner word of our *mens* matches the divine Word "just exactly as it is," and in this way created human imagehood "approaches as far as it can to the likeness of the born image," that is, Christ (15.20). Though we may be trained to do this, Augustine hopes, by reading his book, the actual work of contemplation will be done internally, as we seek in our minds this "contemplative wisdom" that consists in knowing Christ, "to become truly wise" by our minds "sharing in" Christ Himself, if we are granted this (14.26).[100] Augustine writes:

> But when the sight face to face comes that is promised to us, we shall see this trinity that is not only incorporeal but also supremely inseparable and truly unchangeable much more clearly and definitely than we now

> see its image which we ourselves are. However, those who do see through this mirror and in this obscurity, as much as it is granted to see in this life, are not those who merely observe in their own minds what we have discussed and suggested, but those who see it precisely as an image, so that they can in some fashion refer what they see to that of which it is an image, and also see that other by inference through its image which they see by observation, since they cannot see it face to face. (15.44)[101]

For Augustine, the intellectual apprehension of God and of one's own mind are mutually reinforcing. Self-examination leads to God, and the quest for God leads inward as well as upward, to the contemplation of divine truths not simply as eternal but also as ordained by the Christian God, creator, redeemer, and judge. Nevertheless, the fruits of such contemplation are in this life fleeting, only foretastes of what is to come when clear vision replaces faith, and the contemplation of God will be our whole existence.

Summary on Spiritual Exercises in Augustine

Augustine believes that the Christian life, following Christ as the way toward Christ the goal, is a collection of spiritual exercises. By this, I mean that he sees Christian practices and experiences primarily as means of purification and reformation of the soul, all in order to become actually rather than merely potentially capable of cleaving to God in beatitude after the resurrection, and to a limited extent in this life. After 396, however, he is adamant and consistent that human efforts alone, no matter how committed to the power of reason and earnest effort, are insufficient by themselves to effect this reformation. Spiritual exercises must be Christian, and thus they must be subsequent to baptism and performed as part of the church, joined in loving unity to other believers in submission to Christ, as body parts submitting to their head.

As noted above, Augustine thinks he has deep anthropological and theological reasons for his views of both the prerequisites and character of spiritual exercises, which follow from the essential nature of the human mind as a partly vitiated image of the divine. Unless we properly understand, remember, and love this derived, creaturely nature precisely in its relation to the divine, we will misunderstand ourselves and God. But if we overestimate the actual state of our mental kinship with God, we will misapprehend our own powers and debilities, our love of self will remain idolatrous, and our practice of self-formation will either be obviously ineffective or (even worse) will issue in counterfeit virtue of a particularly subtle kind.

Being created in the "image" of God, as argued in chapter 4, is therefore not simply an ontological status but also and primarily a charge, a calling, to be "refashioned to the image of God" (*Trin*. 7.5). Imaging God is not a state of being, but instead a lifelong process that essentially involves certain activities of the mind (7.12). As Rowan Williams argues, we "image" God when we understand ourselves as existing on the basis of the divine reality of love: "The image of God in us might be said to entail a movement into our createdness, because this is a movement into God's own life as turned 'outwards.' What this practically involves is . . . the life of corporate charity."[102] In other words, we are only truly human when we not only understand but also embrace our status as created beings, radically dependent on God, unable to will the good apart from Him. But with God, as one of His chosen, one can participate in the outflowing life of the divine, serving as an agent of graced love for others. Of course for Augustine, God does not need us to do His work, but He lovingly chooses to employ us, not as tools but as trusted servants. God includes us in the work of salvation through the activity of the body of Christ, that is, the church. The church may be the "house of *disciplina*," but what we learn in this school is how to further the work of redemption, the unmerited project of bringing good out of evil.

Christian spiritual exercises on Augustine's account may thus be best understood as responses to grace. Perhaps they should even be thought of as modes of grace, after an analogy to the Eucharist: Such practices may be relied upon as guides and supports for the faithful on their journey home. They are not attempts to storm the gates of heaven but to answer divine mercy and love with thankfulness, joy, and renewed commitment to the transference of love from earthly to heavenly things. All the different practices Augustine recommends, even beyond those discussed here, are oriented toward this movement from carnal to spiritual love. Such practices provide repeated occasions for grace to enter us, to "melt" our habitually hard hearts, and perhaps to even begin training the body to submit, as it should, to the soul and particularly the mind, as the mind is progressively refashioned in the image of God. This submission breaks our tendency to solipsistic unhappiness and delusion, and it draws us out of ourselves into loving (rather than manipulative or desperate) engagement with others, when they are at last properly understood as finite, mortal children of God.

The form of such practices reflects Augustine's psychology. Because of the unity of the *mens*, techniques for self-formation must engage our memory, understanding, and love together. Only in this way can we effect the sort of "transference" of love that Augustine expects. So, for example, even when we search our memories to confess God's care for us and our own defections from that care, we come to understand our situation better and love God more deeply. Perhaps most tellingly, when we articulate our wishes in petitionary prayer, we can only give shape to our yearning with words, the "inner words" that combine memory, understanding, and love.

Although the early Augustine, as noted above, conceives of Christian *disciplina* as involving both restraint, which relies on fear, and instruction, which relies on love (*mor.* 1.28.55–56), we have seen that these become relatively capacious categories for him, especially instruction. To put things schematically, three of the four main categories of Augustinian spiritual exercises discussed here should probably be seen as varieties of instruction: learning from scripture, grace-transmitting symbolic practices of the church such as the Eucharist and chrismation, and the various practices of internalizing Christian discourse that I grouped together under the heading of prayer—all these are fundamentally about instruction in the ways of God. Only the restriction of activities that might tempt us to indulge our own carnality, such as excessive eating or illicit sex, seems to fall under the rubric of restraint. So Augustine does advocate certain sorts of "ascetic" practices that startle contemporary readers, but these are only one part of the much broader regimen of personal formation that he favors. Looking at crucifixion alone, without resurrection, is to fundamentally misunderstand Augustine's vision of the Christian life.

Augustine's account of personal formation reflects his absolute commitment to the primacy of divine agency, and the secondary, derived status of capable human agency. Keeping this basic structure straight helps to explain Augustine's curious sense of "exercises" as both practices purposely engaged in to reform ourselves and as trials imposed by God to test, purify, and strengthen us. There is finally no categorical difference for Augustine between those traditional practices followed to purify us and those providential sufferings imposed directly by the "divine physician," that is, Christ, to minister directly to our unique needs in particular situations. Both serve to reform us to the image of God, to call us back to the object of our hearts' deepest yearnings. We should note, however, that Augustine never thought that suffering per se was intrinsically edifying, but only understanding and enduring suffering in certain ways and for the end of greater closeness with God. On this, Lawless points out Augustine's refrain in several of his sermons on martyrdom, partly directed against the Donatists, that "it is the reason for the suffering, not the suffering itself" (*s.* 275.1, 306.2, 306A, 327.1, 328.7).[103] For Augustine, proper understanding and intention are crucial in both traditionally sanctioned spiritual exercises like fasting and prayer and also in the unexpected and unique experiences, whether humbling and painful or thrilling and inspirational, that reflect divine care for each individual soul.

Augustine understands spiritual exercises, then, to be not so much the choreographed movements of divinely controlled puppets but persons' willing submission and obedience to God, invigorated by the spiritual gifts of faith, hope, and love. These gifts inspire us upward to God as counter-forces to habitual carnal concupiscence. But there is no question where the initiative lies, for Augustine, throughout the whole process of personal reformation: It is God who calls whom He will. Thus Augustine may provocatively say, "My entire hope is exclusively in your very great mercy. Grant what you command, and command what you will" (*conf.* 10.29.40).[104] For Augustine, we answer God's call. When God turns us around back toward Him, we can repay His kindness with eager obedience and can strive to make ourselves as pleasing to God as possible, and as fit for divine love as we would wish to be, so that we might someday enjoy true beatitude, with unfailing certainty.

AUGUSTINE'S THEORY OF THE STAGES OF PERSONAL FORMATION

Much of Augustine's general understanding of human reformation has been treated above, in the first section of the chapter. Nevertheless, as with Xunzi, to fully understand Augustine's account of personal formation, we must grapple with his more detailed notions of progress in righteousness, which he expresses as a theory of stages of religious development, often correlated to exegesis of Isaiah 11:2–3 on the seven gifts of the Holy Spirit, as well as other passages such as the Beatitudes (Mt 5:3–9).[105] Augustine develops this explicit itinerary of the human spirit very early, and his fullest statements display notable Platonic tendencies, which he will later rein in in other contexts. He seems never to have abandoned its basic outlines, although in dispute with the Pelagians later in life he often shifts his rhetorical emphasis toward the more explicitly Pauline scheme of the transition from being "under the law" to "under grace" (e.g., *spir. et litt.*). I discuss this familiar move briefly at the end of this section.

Perhaps the most straightforward exposition of Augustine's theory of religious development appears in *On Christian Teaching* (2.7.9–11); he also gives full discussions in his commentary *On the Lord's Sermon on the Mount*, where he relates it explicitly to Isaiah 11:2–3, as well as the seven blessings of the eight Matthean Beatitudes, and even the seven petitions of the Lord's Prayer (1.1.3–1.4.12, 2.11.38), and in Sermon 347, where he does much the same in correlating the stages to numerous scriptural passages.[106]

In this sevenfold scheme, the first "step" or "stage," *gradus*, is fear, *timor*. Augustine writes: "It is therefore necessary above all else to be moved by the fear of God towards learning his will: what he instructs us to seek and avoid. This fear will necessarily inspire reflection about our mortality and future death, and by nailing our flesh to the wood of the cross as it were crucify all our proud impulses" (*doct. Chr.* 2.7.9).[107] Fear is the hallmark of the "poor in spirit," who are not puffed up and proud but humble (*s. Dom. mon.* 1.4.11). Apparently, for Augustine, only mortal terror before our fate as fallen and unregenerate sinners will inspire us to quell our self-aggrandizing impulses and return humbly to God for help.

On the basis of this fear, we move on to the second stage, *pietas*, meaning "holiness" or "piety." Piety consists fundamentally in meekness or docility before the authority of holy scripture. A person at this stage realizes that "what is written there, even if obscure, is better and truer than any insights that we can gain by our own efforts" (*doct. Chr.* 2.7.9; see also *s. Dom. mon.* 1.4.11).[108] Whether some passage of scripture is understood or not, the meek person recognizes the fundamental need to submit to its authority as the surest path to understanding God.

The first two steps prepare the way for the third, which is *scientia* or knowledge. Here the student of scripture exerts himself or herself and learns from the Bible the fundamental Christian lessons, the commandments to love God with one's whole being and one's neighbor as oneself, for God's sake. Augustine continues:

> It is vital that the reader first learns from the scriptures that he is entangled in a love of this present age, of temporal things, that is, and is far from loving God and his neighbor to the extent that scripture prescribes. It is at this point that the fear which makes him ponder the judgment of God, and the holiness which makes it impossible for him not to admit and submit to the authority of the holy books, compel him to deplore his own condition. For this knowledge makes a person with good reason to hope not boastful but remorseful; in this state he obtains by constant prayer the encouragement of divine assistance, so that he is not crushed by despair. (*doc. Chr.* 2.7.10)[109]

Only the study of scripture, properly oriented by the love commandments, leads to true insight into the human condition. This knowledge leads to mourning, and even despair, unless through "constant prayer" God buoys us up with hope for the future possibility of redemption from our present carnal entanglements.

As knowledge is deepened, the Augustinian aspirant moves on to the fourth stage, *fortitudo*, meaning "courage" or "resolution," with a general connotation in Latin of manly strength. This "brings a hunger and thirst after righteousness. In this state he extricates himself from all the fatal charms of transient things; turning away from these, he turns to the love of eternal things, namely the unchangeable unity which is also the Trinity" (2.7.10).[110] As one's repeated prayers are answered, "the love of God is poured into [one's] heart," giving a new thirst for righteousness that begins to overwhelm the attractions of temporal things. This stage marks a new strength in Christian commitment and capacity, which seems to be mirrored by deeper understanding. The reference to "turning away" from transient things may indicate that Augustine thought this stage included the movement to public conversion and baptism, but he does not address this issue explicitly.

Beyond fortitude comes the fifth stage of *consilium misericordiae*, meaning compassionate judgment or counsel.[111] Augustine describes this as follows:

> When he beholds this light, as far as he is able to, shining as it does even into remote places, and realizes that because of the weakness of his vision he cannot bear its brilliance, he is at the fifth stage, that is of compassionate judgment, and purifies his mind, which is somehow turbulent and in conflict with itself because of the impurities accumulated by its desire for what is inferior. Here he strenuously occupies himself with the love of his neighbor and becomes perfect in it. (2.7.11)[112]

For Augustine, the purification of one's mind is inseparable from the purification of one's loves and conduct. Augustine prescribes strenuous focus on loving one's neighbor as a way to resolve the inner contradictions of *cupiditas* and *caritas* and to cleanse the memory of the "accumulated impurities" of carnal habits. Over time, the practice of mercy toward others, (i.e., "almsgiving" in the broadest sense) reorients our loves, deepens our understanding of the Christian way, and strengthens our interior sight so that we can more readily absorb divine illumination.

Needless to say, this rhetoric of perfected love and of gaining strength to bear full illumination clearly belongs to the young Augustine, who still trusts in the power of the liberal arts and similar exercises advocated by the philosophical schools and still hopes to attain perfect virtue in this life. His understanding of these stages will shift as he matures, but the basic pattern will remain, because he is confident in its scriptural basis. Nevertheless, I continue for now with his youthful descriptions, because they are the fullest and most explicit he provides.

"Full of hope now, and at full strength," capable of loving even an enemy, a Christian comes to the sixth stage, *intellectus*, or genuine understanding (*doc. Chr.* 2.7.11, *s. Dom. mon.* 1.4.11). This stage is marked by a purification of inner sight directed at eternal things, so God Himself may be seen, insofar as is possible in this life, insofar as the person of understanding "dies to this world." Such direct vision of God is, to be sure, "seen still obscurely and through a mirror," as we always rely more on faith than sight, but it "begins to appear more steady and not only more tolerable but also more pleasant" (*doc. Chr.* 2.7.11). Augustine goes on:

> At this stage he purifies the eye of his heart so that not even his neighbor is given a higher priority than the truth, or even an equal one; nor does he give priority to himself, since he does not give it to the one whom he loves as himself. So this holy person will have a heart so single-minded and purified that he will not be deflected from the truth either by an eagerness to please men or by the thought of avoiding any of the troubles which beset him in this life. (2.7.11)[113]

True understanding, for Augustine, means a thorough internalization of the two love commandments, in proper hierarchical order. (That pure love is the essence of *intellectus*, for Augustine, provides one more confirmation of my emphasis on reading his psychology in terms of the unity of the triune, God-imaging mind.) To the extent that this is done, one has attained purity of heart (see also *s. Dom. mon.* 1.4.11), and so will not be swayed to sinful action by desire for praise or fear of suffering.

When this purity of heart is truly attained, one ascends to the seventh and last stage of personal development, wisdom or *sapientia*. Wisdom is "enjoyed by those who are calm and peaceful" (*doc. Chr.* 2.7.11).[114] In terms of the Beatitudes, the wise are the peacemakers, according to Augustine, in whom everything is in proper order within their hearts and minds, because they are fully obedient to God; this apparently empowers them to extend their calm and peaceful influence to others (*s. Dom. mon.* 1.4.11).

As for the whole sequence, Augustine cites Psalm 111:10, "The fear of the Lord is the beginning of wisdom," and he comments that "these are the stages by which we progress from the one to the other" (*doc. Chr.* 2.7.11).[115] Nonetheless, it seems clear that he thinks the "stages" or "steps" are cumulative, not a matter of complete succession, so that even those, for example, who have attained true understanding might still be puzzled by particular scriptural passages and so continue to seek knowledge by interpreting them. Furthermore, certain early stages can be deeply changed over time as higher stages are attained, as for example the root fear of God, which moves from a basically carnal fear of punishment to an abiding "chaste fear" of iniquity lest one's soul be forsaken by God (*s.* 348.4).

As Augustine matures, he purges from this scheme of the seven gifts of the Holy Spirit all hope for the complete purification of intention within earthly life. Augustine is quite clear in his anti-Pelagian treatises that although sinlessness is a logical possibility, given the power of God's grace and our capacity to choose freely (in service to our loves), it is despite this never an actuality, excepting the unique case of the sinless Christ. In other words, all people—even the holiest—continue to sin throughout their lives. Daily recitation of the Lord's Prayer, including praying for forgiveness, is thus a reasonable devotional practice, as Augustine never tires of repeating against the Pelagians. We are being adopted as children of God, but this adoption is only partial in this life, as full as our wisdom in spiritual matters grows through the renewal of the image of God in our minds, and will be completed only after the resurrection of the body (e.g., *pecc. mer.* 2.6.7–10.11). In his accounts of the seven stages, Augustine does correlate wisdom, as the ultimate stage of human religious development, to adoption as "sons" or "children" of God (*doc. Chr.* 2.7.11, *pecc. mer.* 2.7.9–8.10), but it would seem that this adoption is only completed in the final "divinization" or "deification" that the elect shall experience after the resurrection, when the divine image is completely reformed in them and they are totally healed from sin, and even from the possibility of sinning (*civ. Dei* 22.30).[116] Augustine also moves from categorical talk of the "fruits" of the Holy Spirit to speaking more carefully of the "first fruits" (e.g., *pecc. mer.* 2.7.9–8.10), which implies that these are all the sorts of gifts Christians receive in the present life of faith, and all will either pass away or be perfected in the life to come.

Later in life, in the midst of controversy with the Pelagians, Augustine seeks out a terminology of spiritual attainment that will be less amenable to being coopted by what he perceives as misguided self-reliance. He settles on the Pauline terminology of grace and the law as the vocabulary most suited to driving a wedge between Pelagius's understanding of personal formation and his own, and he develops this in works such as *On the Spirit and the Letter*.

The overly sharp distinctions that make up this map of both religious history and the Christian life are well known.[117] Before receiving the law (*ante legem*), human beings simply follow our sinful desires, unaware that we are contravening divine requirements. Once we have received the preliminary revelation of this divine law, however, we move to a new stage, "under the law" (*sub lege*). In this condition, we recognize that certain desired things are sinful, but we are unable to meet God's requirements and so feel wretched and fearful as we struggle fruitlessly to meet what seems to be an impossible standard. When God mercifully pours His grace into our hearts, however, we are powerfully changed by the possession of God-given delight in justice. Now "under grace" (*sub gratia*), this delight makes it possible for us to refuse consent to our still-troubling sinful desires, so that we are in effect engaged in "Christian combat" internally as we struggle more successfully against our remaining concupiscence. Only in the final stage, "in peace" (*in pace*) after the resurrection, will our internal struggle cease as our desire for God at last completely predominates within us, and we suffer no further resistance to God's righteous will (*ex. prop. Rm.* 13–18; *div. qu.* 61.7, 66.3; *ex. Gal.* 46–47; *ench.* 31.118–19).

The distinctions are too sharp, for reasons already discussed; most crucially, for Augustine we are in God's care, and thus in some very important sense "under grace," from the time we are born. The utility of the central distinction between law and grace is precisely to hammer home the necessity of grace for any sort of progress in righteousness, indeed for any righteousness at all.

When combined with Augustine's more subtle analysis of the seven gifts of the Holy Spirit, we see that the crucial point remains the emphasis on grace, reflected in the explicit terminology of "gifts" or "first fruits." Also noteworthy is the sequential accumulation of the gifts, each of which transforms the earlier ones. Though a contemporary ethicist might wish for a carefully organized schema that relates the gifts to various sorts of virtues, after the manner of Aquinas, Augustine provides nothing of the sort. His reasons for this relative obscurity in his charting of the stages of religious development, especially when contrasted with Xunzi's straightforward clarity, will be treated in the next chapter.

NOTES

1. On humans as "puppets," see Rist 1969 and Rist 1994, 133–36.

2. Lawless 1987, 10, 57, and throughout.

3. Lawless 1987, 29–57; *s.* 355.2.

4. Lawless 1987, xii, 62.

5. Lawless 2000, esp. 148–52. This is the best recent essay on "asceticism" in Augustine's thought and life.

6. Stock 1996.

7. The *Confessions* is probably the closest, although focusing solely on this work would leave much of significant interest to the side.

8. As translated in Bettenson 1984, 518.

9. As translated in Hill 1991, 155.

10. As translated in Hill 1991, 156.

11. For discussion and a fuller bibliography, see Cutrone 1999. Note especially the excellent recent treatment of *sacramentum* and *exemplum* in Dodaro 2004, 147–59. As Edmund Hill points out (1991, 178 n. 18), Augustine frequently sees Christ as the deeper signified reality pointed to by the many *sacramenta* of the Bible and church, but he here interprets Christ Himself as the sacred sign, one who suggests hidden truths about human salvation.

12. Translation adapted from Hill 1991, 156–67.

13. Translation adapted from Hill 1991, 157.

14. Translation adapted from Hill 1990–97 (*The Works of Saint Augustine*), part III, vol. 1, 185–86. The sermons will be cited below as date, WSA part/volume, page.

15. As translated in Hill 1991, 67 (adapted), 247.

16. As translated in Hill 1991, 66, 154–55.

17. As translated in Hill 1991, 389–90.

18. As translated in Hill 1991, 329.

19. As translated in Green 1995, 15–17.

20. This motif has Christian and Plotinian antecedents, certainly, but also recalls Virgil's *Aeneid* and the tradition of which it is a part.

21. As translated in Green 1995, 23 (adapted), 23.

22. As translated in Hill 1991, 169.

23. For a helpful survey of the cultural and philosophical background to Augustine's usage of *virtus*, see Johnson 1975.

24. The best comprehensive account of virtue in Augustine is now Dodaro 2004. See also Rist 1994, 148–202.

25. Dodaro 2004, 111. Although helpful, Dodaro's statement is potentially misleading when taken out of the context of his larger study. For Augustine, our love is our own, motivating us directly, and so in this crucial sense our virtue is always our own as well as God's—it is not an imposition from outside that seizes control and rules as an alien force within. Habit as a chain that binds is Augustine's closest approximation to this picture of hijacked agency.

26. On the question of "pagan virtue" in Augustine's thought, see Dodaro 2004, esp. 111, 184. Note also Wang 1938, Irwin 1999b, and Osborne 2003. The latter two argue that common contrasts between Augustine and Aquinas on pagan virtue are overdrawn, and in the process helpfully relate the two figures.

27. As translated in Teske 2003, 288, 289.

28. Translations adapted from Hill 1990–97, WSA III/1, 185.

29. Translation adapted from Stothert 1979 [1886], 56.

30. As translated in Hill 1991, 370.

31. As translated in Chadwick 1991, 17.

32. Translation adapted from Chadwick 1991, 17.

33. See, e.g., *ep*. 118.1ff. O'Donnell 1992, vol. 3, 223–24, provides discussion, numerous textual citations, and more bibliography.

34. Conversation with Albert Raboteau and Jeffrey Stout has helped to clarify my thinking on "curiosity" in Augustine.

35. Translation adapted from Hill 1990–97, WSA III/3, 385–86.

36. Wetzel 1992, 166–68.

37. I will not enter the debate about Augustine's various views on the origins of the soul. For discussion, see O'Connell 1968, 1987.

38. See, e.g., *s*. 324, where Augustine breathlessly narrates the story of a dead baby, whose mother beseeched St. Stephen for aid at the martyr's own shrine, who was revived just long enough to be baptized, and then died again, but whose pious mother was completely tranquil and content, knowing that the infant's salvation was assured. Augustine concludes: "The woman's faithful heart was tried and passed the test."

39. In what follows, I have been greatly helped by the writings of William Harmless, S.J. For brief discussion, see Fitzgerald 1999, 84–91, 145–49. For a full account, see Harmless 1995.

40. As translated in Hill 1990–97, WSA III/6, 201.

41. The *Patrologia Latina* contains only fragments from this sermon. Text from *Miscellanea Agostiniana* 1930, 458–59. As translated in Hill 1990–97, WSA III/6, 203–4.

42. As translated in Hill 1990–97, WSA III/6, 145–46.

43. This statement needs to be qualified. Augustine did think that baptism, for instance, was performed efficaciously by Christian schismatics such as the Donatists (*bapt*. 3.10.15).

44. As translated in Teske 1997, 65. Augustine was certainly troubled by the force of this logic, although not as much as ancient and modern critics of his thought. In *ep*. 166.10, as part of a broader set of questions on the origin of the soul, he makes an anguished plea to Jerome for help in unraveling what kind of justice allows so many thousands of babies to be damned only because they have not yet been baptized, Jerome chided Augustine for bothering him when he was so busy and never responded substantively (*retr*. 2.45).

45. Translation adapted from Teske 1997, 86.

46. Translations adapted from Russell 1948, 242, 261, 304.

47. As translated in Russell 1948, 301, 303, 305.

48. As discussed in chapter 5, n. 7, this apparent holdover from classical traditions of rhetoric, relying on a view of the soul in which reason tries to rule the passions that oppose it, leads Augustine occasionally to say things that conflict with his mature view of the unity of the *mens* in all its aspects of understanding, loving, and remembering.

49. As translated in Russell 1948, 321.

50. Translation adapted from Russell 1948, 327–28.

51. Green 1995, ix–xiv.

52. As translated in Hill 1990–97, WSA III/10, 458. This sermon, number 399, is also known as the *Sermon on Christian Teaching*, or *Sermo de disciplina christiana*. For discussion of its date, see Hill 1990–97, WSA III/10, 468–69 nn. 1–2.

53. As translated in Hill 1990–97, WSA III/7, 288.

54. As translated in Hill 1990–97, WSA III/10, 468.

55. As translated in Hill 1990–97, WSA III/6, 254. He immediately goes on to say to the illiterate in the audience that he and the other clergy can serve as their books, by reading and talking about scripture to them.

56. As translated in Hill 1990–97, WSA III/10, 465.

57. Translations adapted from Hill 1990–97, WSA III/1, 217.

58. As George Lawless (2000) argues, Augustine is suspicious of extreme ascetic exertions, fearing a mindset of competitive achievement that is intrinsically prone to pride and antagonistic to Christian love. See also Leyser 2000, 3–32.

59. As translated in Green 1995, 31.

60. Translation adapted from Green 1995, 149.

61. As translated in Green 1995, 195.

62. Stock 1996, 125.

63. On this point, see Cavadini's (1999) insightful review of Stock.

64. The most sensitive and sympathetic treatment of these issues, with more extensive bibliography, is Cavadini 2005. See also Brown 1988, 387–427.

65. For a similar maneuver, at least initially, see Meilaender 2001. As will become clear, however, I think Meilaender understates Augustine's worries about pleasure.

66. As translated in Hill 1990–97, WSA III/10, 471.

67. As translated in Hill 1990–97, WSA III/10, 472.

68. I owe this felicitous way of framing the issue to Charles Mathewes, who coined this phrase in conversation to summarize his reading of Carol Harrison's fine recent book (2000).

69. As translated in Hill 1990–97, WSA III/6, 110.

70. For fuller discussion of Augustine's practice of fasting, see Sage 1990, 48–54.

71. As translated in Hill 1990–97, WSA III/10, 473.

72. Translations adapted from Hill 1990–97, WSA III/10, 473.

73. As translated in Hill 1990–97, WSA III/10, 475.

74. As translated in Teske 1997, 297.

75. As translated in Hill 1990–97, WSA III/10, 474.

76. As translated in Hill 1990–97, WSA III/10, 475.

77. As translated in Hill 1990–97, WSA III/6, 110.

78. As translated in Chadwick 1991, 204, 206.

79. As translated in Chadwick 1991, 204–5.

80. Translations from Chadwick 1991, 218, 207 (adapted).

81. I have no interest in contributing to the long-standing and anachronistic debate, along predictable lines, between those who would enlist Augustine on the side of Christ's "real presence" in the Eucharist and those who see him as advocating a "purely symbolic" reading of the Eucharist. For an example of evidence seemingly supporting both interpretations side by side, see *ep.* 98.9. For a "Protestant" reading, see *doc. Chr.* 3.9.13, for a "Catholic" one, *s.* 229.1.

82. As translated in Chadwick 1991, 220.

83. Sage 1990, 51. It would seem, on the basis of passages such as *en. Ps.* 42.1, that fasts were not broken before church, and therefore the first food of the day would have been the Eucharist.

84. As translated in Hill 1990–97, WSA III/3, 112. Augustine goes on to list sermons, Bible readings, and hymns as other spiritual types of daily bread necessary for this life.

85. As translated in Hill 1990–97, WSA III/6, 265. The *Patrologia Latina* has only a fragment of this sermon.

86. As translated in Bettenson 1984, 377, 377, 376, 379.

87. Translation adapted from Bettenson 1984, 401.

88. This was not a part of the actual eucharistic liturgy, but the force of the presentation, combined with Augustine's explanatory sermons, would suggest the incarnational imperative (*s.* 272; also 227, 229, 229A).

89. I thus under the heading of "prayer" survey Augustine's accounts of *oratio*, *confessio*, *contemplatio*, and their cognates. Augustine at times also highlights the impor-

tance of *laus*, or "praise," in prayer, as an expression of our love for and hope in God, and as a pleasant foretaste of the activity of the redeemed in Heaven, who will praise God unceasingly (*s*. 252.9, 255.1).

90. As translated in Teske 2003, 186.

91. Translations adapted from Teske 2003, 192.

92. Translations adapted from Teske 2003, 193.

93. Translations adapted from Teske 2003, 194, 194, 193.

94. As translated in Chadwick 1991, 72.

95. On this theme see Stock 1996, 207–32, 273–78.

96. On the immediate reasons for Augustine's writing of his *Confessions*, see Chadwick 1991, ix–xiii; and Brown 1967, 158–81.

97. As translated in Chadwick 1991, 180.

98. As translated in Hill 1991, 79–80.

99. As translated in Hill 1991, 374, 364.

100. As translated in Hill 1991, 410, 391.

101. Translation adapted from Hill 1991, 429.

102. Williams 1990.

103. Lawless 2000, 146.

104. As translated in Chadwick 1991, 202.

105. An exhaustive account of this theme and the relevant textual evidence in Augustine is van Lierde 1935 [1994].

106. For a fuller list of relevant Augustinian passages, which span most of his adult life, see van Lierde 1935 [1994], 7–13.

107. Translation adapted from Green 1995, 63.

108. As translated in Green 1995, 65.

109. As translated in Green 1995, 65.

110. As translated in Green 1995, 65.

111. This might also be rendered as a determination or resolution to be merciful and compassionate; this is the way Green 1995 takes the phrase. The corresponding passage in *s. Dom. mon.*, 1.4.11, however, as well as other passages on the gifts of the Holy Spirit (see van Lierde 1935 [1994]), suggest the reading I give here.

112. Translation adapted from Green 1995, 65.

113. As translated in Green 1995, 65, 67, 67.

114. As translated in Green 1995, 67.

115. As translated in Green 1995, 67.

116. On these issues, see the excellent article by Gerald Bonner (1986).

117. For discussion, see Babcock 1979, 1994; and Fredriksen 1988.

CHAPTER EIGHT

Reformations: Spiritual Exercises in Comparative Perspective

✦

Augustine and Xunzi both aim ultimately at perfection, although how they conceive of such a state differs dramatically. They also focus on rather different issues as they chart the path toward this perfection, which reflect their distinctive worries about the gravest spiritual dangers. Examining their differing interests in mapping these "stages of development" helps to prepare the way for comparing their complex regimes of personal formation. As outlined in chapter 7, early on in his authorship, Augustine develops his sequential account of the seven gifts of the Holy Spirit, but under the pressure of his debate with Pelagianism he later submerges this account in favor of the simpler scheme of law and grace that he discerns in Paul's epistles. Xunzi, for his part, appears not to change his conception of a ladder of ethical development that stretches from the vast category of "pettiness" up through becoming "educated" and then "noble," to the final goal of sagehood.

As I implied in the last chapter, over the course of his embattled episcopate, Augustine becomes more and more convinced that the dangers of spiritual elitism and religious arrogance generally outweigh the goods to be attained through in-depth analysis of the real differences between beginning and advanced believers. He thus gravitates toward a scheme that draws a sharp line between those true believers who are "under grace" and those "pagans" and "heretics" who are outside the fold, still "under the law," whether they realize it or not. This scheme also draws a second sharp distinction between the living and the dead: It places all good Christians into the same fundamental status, dependent "under grace" on God's mercy, continuing to yearn for a time when their inner struggles will cease and they will be fully healed for eternal life "in peace." Xunzi, by contrast, gives all his attention to this period of religious discipleship, which Augustine seeks to level out.[1] Why this difference?

Augustine's growing resistance to distinguishing a hierarchy of spiritual achievement stems from his alarm over the extreme danger posed by *superbia* or "pride" to all who attempt to make progress in righteousness.[2] Such arrogance afflicts not only proud Roman traditionalists but even some outwardly exemplary Christians, such as Pelagius. Augustine's scheme of law and grace underlines the absolutely fundamental distinction he sees between a life rooted in love of self and one rooted in love of God.[3] Even the distinction between being "under grace" and "in peace" serves to cultivate humility in believers by reminding them that perfection is impossible in this life, no matter how great their efforts to avoid sin and cleave to God. All aspects of the schema are designed to prod Christians to cast their hopes on God, instead of relying on their own strength. For us in this life, according to Augustine, no one can know his or her own spiritual state with perfect clarity, although presumably one can discern evidence of the presence of grace whenever one is genuinely moved to take some holy, loving action. But beyond such wondrous signs of new life growing in the wake of baptism, even those who have been given the grace of a superior calling such as virginity have no way of knowing if their hearts have become pure enough to willingly accept martyrdom, the ultimate test of faith for Augustine, which is most certainly open to those who are married, if God grants it (*virg.* 44.45, 47).

Xunzi shares this concern about arrogance only in the derivative sense that it conflicts with his central virtues of benevolence, ritual propriety, and justice. Pride is not a special or uniquely potent danger, in Xunzi's reckoning. The most obvious human difficulties stem from ignorant impulse-following and the chaos and misrule that stem from and exacerbate this sort of life. The more subtle danger of obsession shares some similarities with *superbia*, at least in the aftereffects of self-satisfaction and preference for illusion over uncomfortable truth. But instead of being centered on the "mimetic desire" for Godlike sovereignty provoked by Satan's promise to Adam and Eve that "you shall be as gods," Xunzian obsession must be a partial apprehension of the truth, wrong only in its limited scope and failure to comprehend the larger patterns of existence.[4] Xunzi, in fact, thinks that every person desires to have the authority and lavish pleasures of an emperor, but he seems to see this as fundamentally a point about the strength and range of human desire, not its secret deviousness in deflecting moral self-cultivation into self-aggrandizement.

Indeed, Xunzi appears to use the prospect of becoming a glorious emperor as rhetorical enticement in recommending Confucianism to the aspiring rulers of his day. This at least implies that the pursuit of such a vision will not automatically plunge a ruler into evil; it also implies that

Xunzi is quite confident in his abilities as a wise counselor, and in the power of virtuous ministers to steer an ambitious king rightly (11/53/12–25; note also 4/16/18ff.). Despite this seeming nonchalance about the dangers of the quest for supreme power and position, Xunzi's own program of ritual reformation centers on the need for aspiring Confucians to incessantly practice their deference as a corrective for human self-assertion, which suggests that he takes the ethical problem of arrogance more seriously than it might at first appear.

These differences in their estimation of human desires for power and mastery point toward deeper differences concerning proper subjection. By subjection, as discussed in chapter 2, I mean the sense of human agency as ordered toward and in important respects constituted by some authoritative standard or entity. Both Augustine and Xunzi are too frequently saddled with rather stupidly authoritarian interpretations, wherein the "best" human life is the one marked by the most thorough groveling before extant religious and even political powers.[5] Both do reject untutored self-guidance as profoundly misguided, but much of their respective bodies of work can be read as efforts to explain the sort of "tutoring" necessary for a truly humane and just life to be possible. Augustine and Xunzi are concerned to make true human moral agency possible, despite difficulties, not to derail or jail it.

For Augustine, the ultimate authority is of course God, and more specifically the triune Christian God as properly understood by the Catholic Church. As outlined in chapters 4 and 7, human beings cannot properly understand themselves, nor live well, unless they understand themselves in relation to God, Christ (including his body here on Earth, the church), and the Holy Spirit (e.g., *en. Ps.* 121.8). Such a relation must be subordinate, in the sense that Christ's word to believers, "even if obscure, is better and truer than any insights that we can gain by our own efforts" (*doct. Chr.* 2.7.9). Such subordination and dependence is distasteful to fallen humanity, precisely because we have been rendered rebellious, riven internally by lusts for dominance, covetous possession, and selfish enjoyment. In our zest to "be like gods," we create prisons for ourselves out of habit, making ourselves ever more wretched. "Conversion" is the process of breaking these chains, of a gain in freedom, power, and even self-control; and the ongoing process of "making progress in righteousness" continues this increase in true agency. For Augustine, then, agency that is derived from and appropriately dependent on the divine is true, good, and potent; all other "agency" is in the end only a simulacrum, still subject to God's authority but struggling fruitlessly against this fact rather than accepting and indeed loving it.[6]

Turning to Xunzi, the situation is not quite as clear, at least at first. *Tian* 天, or "Heaven," does occupy the supreme ritual position in the cosmos. But it is not the sort of entity that issues moral commands or ensures the ultimate justice of events, nor is it the source of the authority of the *Dao*, for Xunzi. On his account, we must be careful not to confuse the human Way with the very different Way of Heaven, each of which involves quite distinctive tasks. It might appear that Confucian tradition, especially as accumulated in the classics, would be the ultimate authority for Xunzi, but he makes it clear that the real authority rests with the human beings who carry on the Confucian tradition. Only they know how to interpret the classic texts, which are confusing and opaque to the uninitiated, Xunzi thinks (1/3/20–1/4/4). Moreover, only the best and wisest human beings have fully mastered Confucian ritual in such a way that they may teach it to others. This practical, fully articulated ritual mastery is the ultimate ground of their authority, and the ultimate source for aspiring Confucians. As Xunzi says:

> Ritual is the means by which to rectify yourself. A teacher is the means by which to rectify [your practice of] ritual. . . . When your dispositions are at peace in ritual and your understanding is like that of your teacher, then you have become a sage. Hence to oppose ritual is to be without a model; to oppose your teacher is to be without a teacher. To refuse to accept your teacher and the model and instead prefer to govern yourself: this is like relying on a blind person to distinguish colors, or relying on a deaf person to distinguish sounds; you have no way to abandon chaos and foolishness. (2/8/1–4)

Without reliance on a teacher and the external models he provides, people have no way to gain a sense of what is truly good. At first, we are all morally "blind" and "deaf," Xunzi thinks. Only with carefully guided practice can we develop an understanding of and taste for the Way, which is what the rituals themselves "mark out" (17/82/22–17/83/1).[7] And eventually, as discussed in chapter 6, after many years of practice, our tastes or desires will become "transformed," Xunzi thinks, so that we can continue the tradition ourselves without painful strain and without error. Thus for Xunzi true human agency is found in service as the "ministers" or indeed "agents" of the *Dao*, that is, in actively governing themselves and the world so that justice and beauty might prevail everywhere.

Clearly both Augustine and Xunzi require individually chosen subordination to just authorities as the necessary precondition for true human agency, although they conceive the particulars rather differently. Before moving on to more specific comparisons, however, we can sharpen some of the differences between them by noting the distinctive "spiritual geographies" imagined by Xunzi and Augustine as the spaces defining human agency.

As noted in chapter 5, Augustine conceives of desire, and indeed all love, as having a vertical dimension that relates it to God, presumed in this image to be "above" us and other worldly things. The *voluntas*-aspect of each of our mind's "inner words" is striving either "up" toward God or "down" toward various changeable physical realities. This radical disjunction explains many very basic features of Augustine's understanding of the religious life. First, it means that at the basis of any human life is a fundamental orientation, either correctly ordered toward God, or incorrectly away from him, which in this spatial scheme must be an opposite orientation. Second, this explains Augustine's strong interest in conversion—literally, "turning around" to face God as one should. Sin is not missing the target occasionally, as implied by Xunzi's formulation of fine character as "hitting the target" one hundred times out of one hundred (1/4/12); for Augustine, sin does not even aim at the target but away from it. Augustine does have a variety of goal or target metaphor operating, in the sense that beatitude in the presence of God is the end of all of our striving; what is unique is his insistence on how radically misguided sin must be, as well as the difficulty implied by the image of rising up to the heavens against the pull of our carnal "gravity" dragging us back to Earth.

In contrast to this picture, the space implied by Xunzi's conception of moral agency is, first of all, fundamentally horizontal: We are lost, and we seek a way through the world, with travel through space serving as an image for travel through time. There is no different realm to ascend to in Xunzi's Confucianism. Xunzi does use the metaphor of a fork in the road to underline the gravity of choosing the right path to follow, and he insists that a seemingly small error at the start can lead to terrible results later on (11/53/25–26). And as noted in chapter 6, he yearns for a clear distinction between what is "within" the Way and what is "outside" it. But his conception of obsession as focused on partial truths that obscure our awareness of broader issues suggests that it is at least logically conceivable for Xunzi that even non-Confucians might make "errors" without being radically misguided. Of course, Augustine distinguishes between more and less serious sins, as does Xunzi, and Xunzi does not hesitate to denounce the grievous errors of numerous opponents, including fellow Confucian Mencius, so it would be easy to overstate their differences here. The key issue is simply to note that Augustine's imagination of moral space drives him frequently to quite radical diagnoses of sin and evil, as in his disputes with, for example, the Donatists and Pelagians.

This difference in imagining the nature of the moral life also plays out in Xunzi's lack of interest in conversion, discussed above in chapters 5 and 6. According to Xunzi, we start out lost and ignorant, lacking reliable orientation. Our "bad" innate impulses do misguide us, but mostly because they overreach and thereby conflict with important values (to which we start out insensible), not because they direct us absolutely contrary to the good. Xunzi's followers, at least, seem to have thought that lifelong Confucian education, beginning in childhood, was the ideal (27/134/16). There would in any case seem to be no religious use, on Xunzi's account, in going wrong by following one's own devices, in order to see the bankruptcy of one's own resources for self-direction and to turn dramatically back to God, as with Augustine.

In the rest of this chapter, I explore some of the details beneath these broad differences, examining several issues raised by comparison of their views of the "will," as well as their differing emphases in the practice of personal formation, as these are illuminated by and speak to some aspects of modern virtue theory. I then pursue a constructive point that grows out of these comparisons, developing enduring similarities between Augustine and Xunzi as a general moral psychological outlook that I call "chastened intellectualism."

VIRTUE AND "THE WILL"

In chapter 2, I argued for a comparative conception of "the will" (a "bridge concept," in this study's lexicon) that was in effect an umbrella covering several related topics treated by both Xunzi and Augustine: their accounts of human action; their assessments of human capacities for choice and decisive commitment; and any characteristic limitations, flaws, or dangers they think afflict human decision and action. After elaborating and beginning to compare their theories of human nature and personal formation, it is now possible to give a much more precise account of "will" as a psychological term covering a more tightly integrated set of ethical issues, while still remaining attentive to broader concerns about human agency and its characteristic afflictions. Specifically, we can now say that "will" as a bridge concept between Xunzi and Augustine should include four related areas of ethical concern that both men share: first, more or less enduring dispositions to think, feel, and act in particular ways; second, more momentary feelings, desires, and aversions that move us to act in specific situations; third, intentions and goals, both proximate and ultimate; and fourth, whatever capacities humans may have to consent, assent, or dissent from particular actions, that is, the capacity to choose to do or refrain from doing something. This more precise set of distinctions and topics invites deeper specific comparisons, which I pursue in the rest of this chapter. We should note that seeing these areas as closely related, deserving joint analysis, shows how deeply Augustine has influenced the West, because Xunzi does not group these concerns into one named system like "the will." Nevertheless, he does treat each of them in varying degrees of detail, and we can reconstruct their logical relations to each other within his psychology and ethics.

This set of topics also allows me to relate comparative study of "the will" to what has come to be called virtue ethics. My goal in doing this is not to add even more complication to the current project, but to articulate some of my main arguments in a vocabulary familiar to contemporary ethicists. Indeed, "virtue" is the most common contemporary way of talking about growth in moral discernment and excellence, even if that development, the main subject of the current study, is not made central to most inquiries into virtue ethics.

"Virtue" is famously ambiguous between a general sense of fine character, and more specific excellences that together make up such a character, such as courage and wisdom. A virtue in the latter sense may be understood as a good disposition, that is, "a disposition to act, desire, and feel that involves the exercise of judgment and leads to a recognizable human excellence or instance of human flourishing."[8] Both Xunzi and Augustine have well-developed understandings of what might count as general human excellence, although I hope to have shown in this study how moral formation may rest on rather different sorts of virtues, reflecting different stages in this ongoing process, so that looking only at perfected virtue would miss much of importance. This point is clearest with Xunzi, who as just argued above makes sharper distinctions among aspiring Confucians than Augustine often wishes to draw among aspiring Christians.[9] (I discuss this issue further below when comparing their accounts of continence.) And although only Augustine, who draws on the massive tradition of Greco-Roman ethical philosophy, has the terminology to speak of particular excellences as distinct "virtues," Xunzi also discusses several specific excellences that fit together in systematic ways, including the most important: *ren* 仁, "benevolence" or "humaneness"; *yi* 義, "justice"; *li* 禮, "ritual propriety"; *xu* 虛, "emptiness" or "intellectual openness"; *yi* 一, "unity"; and *jing* 靜, "tranquillity."[10] Although to consider their differing lists of particular virtues in detail would require another book-length study, over the course of this chapter I do address Xunzian analogues to Augustinian continence, and I comment further on what is implied by Xunzi's consideration of ritual propriety as a crucial ethical virtue.

Virtue, then, is a matter of having well-formed dispositions to think, feel, desire, and act—presuming, of course, that life is complicated and that wise practical judgment will be essential to good human action, so that such dispositions are not mere reflex actions or thoughtless habitual responses. Stated so generally, it seems clear from the interpretations offered here that, broadly speaking, both Augustine and Xunzi are concerned that human beings come to possess true virtue. In Augustinian terms, *virtus* is primarily a matter of love or *voluntas*, but it always involves all aspects of the triune mind (memory, understanding, and will) and reflects the degree to which the mind conforms to and relies on God. In Xunzian terms, Confucian virtues involve both our relatively settled dispositions or *qing*, which account for the desires and emotions we feel, and also our patterns of assenting (*ke* 可) to an articulate understanding of the *Dao* as one's ethical standard and way of life. As always, however, the most intriguing points develop when we consider the details.

As noted in chapter 5, Xunzi has an ethical vocabulary that allows him to clearly mark the distinction between longer-lasting if still changeable dispositions (*qing* 情) and more momentary desires (*yu* 欲). He also, less fortunately, uses *qing* to refer to our more transient emotions or feelings. For his part, Augustine uses the same words interchangeably for both dispositions and desires or emotions—that is, he refers to all of these as forms of love, whether properly ordered to God as the divine love *caritas*, or not, as covetous *cupiditas*. This ambiguity suits his religious purposes, however, by calling into question some aspects of the very idea of a virtue as a long-lasting, dependable disposition toward the good. For Augustine, this idea of a steady, powerful inclination to goodness presents a temptation to human beings to defect once again from God and to prefer our own seemingly good self-command to obedience to the Lord. Nevertheless, Augustine's psychology of delight does rest on the idea of underlying dispositions, of both *caritas* and *cupiditas* considered as deep inclinations, which inflame us with desires both holy and profane. And his account of "progress in righteousness," especially in practices like fasting, seeks directly to change the ratio of these underlying dispositions to each other.

Where Augustine and Xunzi differ is in their estimation of habituation as a means of effecting this transformation. Xunzi understands ritual in particular as being primarily a method of re-habituating human "customs" or practices; he talks of this in terms of the gradual "accumulation" of goodness, via repetitive Confucian disciplines, into the deeper "artifice" of a reconstructed character. As argued in chapter 5, Xunzi recognizes the possibility of "deviant" and "chaotic" customs, but he thinks such things can generally be restrained and even reformed by good government, and so are above all a political problem. In his account of personal formation, Xunzi attends almost exclusively to the power of habit formation for good. Augustine, however, reserves *consuetudo* or "habit" almost exclusively for evil, misguided dispositions, those "chains" of perverse love that drag us away from God. Most important, according to Augustine, even the best Christians are always capable of willing evil, of defecting from God's providential order. In the wake of the Fall, even the elect are incapable, without grace, of fully and completely willing the good. Concupiscence continually besets us, tugging our souls away from spiritual matters to the concerns of "the flesh."

Why this difference? As noted above, Augustine conceives of most spontaneous human desires as results of our concupiscence, that is, of covetousness as a deep disposition within the mind. Thus habits formed on the basis of these loves cannot be for good. Conversely, our genuinely good dispositions are fundamentally gifts from God, always a matter of inspiration. The most helpful spiritual exercises provide occasions for this inspiration to occur. Augustine's view of concupiscence leads him to suspect "delight" in any earthly thing, even those things used in holy worship, which makes it nearly impossible for him to conceive of habituation as good, because it seems to trade on our fondness for pleasure. Indeed, the only sort of habituation Augustine seems to countenance is that of restraint, which quells carnal pleasure to make room for God-given delight in the good to burst forth. This suggests that the thoughtlessness of habituation as a sort of conditioning strikes Augustine as dangerous, especially if used to reinforce pleasures. But habituation seems dangerous to him even if used for what might seem like good ends, because whatever independent effectiveness it might possess as a technique of self-shaping makes it usable for human projects of defiance. For Xunzi, though, this "directionless" quality of habituation is no problem at all—at least it does not automatically lead us away from the *Dao*, and more to the point wise teachers can enlist it to lead earnest students to the *Dao*. As noted, in contrast to Augustine, Xunzi thinks desire has only one form, and that it cannot be destroyed but only redirected, and to a certain extent heightened or suppressed.

This disagreement about the manipulation of desire through repeated practices reflects another aspect of what I called above their differing spiritual geographies. One could reasonably say that Augustine thinks habituation is both stronger and weaker than Xunzi contends, depending on whether it goes along with or thwarts our spontaneous carnal impulses. On Augustine's account, sinful habit can take hold of us instantly, as when Augustine's friend Alypius "drank in savagery" during one forced trip to the gladiatorial shows (*conf*. 6.8.13). Or it can never really take hold at all, if it aims to thwart our concupiscent desires all by itself, because it will merely end up refining them by cloaking them in the subterfuges of pride. By contrast, Xunzi's craft metaphors of reshaping stiff, difficult materials into a beautiful form suggest that although our dispositions will tend to remain as they are, they are adaptable to changes in circumstances, and to growth or contraction in response to consciously contrived experiences, at least when repeated sufficiently.

Although Augustine is doubtless correct to say that pleasure can move us strongly, this is not really what is at issue between the two figures; at the most obvious level, the question concerns whether everyday pleasures of food, sex, and personal contact are as potently habit forming, and potentially soul destroying, as drugs like methamphetamine, and therefore need to be very carefully regulated. Put this way, it seems obvious that Xunzi is right to say that, except in unusual cases, pleasures move us strongly but not overwhelmingly, and even our real delights need practice to become refined and strong. But Augustine's account is more insightful when considered below the surface implications of his extreme remarks on habit: His point is that even after honestly dedicating ourselves to goodness, with real desire for that prospect, we remain prone to self-deception precisely because at a very deep level our minds remain inclined to seek our own pleasure regardless of any other considerations, and this tendency (*concupiscentia*, *cupiditas*) always threatens to undermine and corrupt our ongoing efforts at personal formation.

To engage these issues further, we need to examine how Augustine and Xunzi conceive of what is often called the "divided self." To get at least the lineaments of their positions before us, we should briefly review their understandings of intention and consent, as analyzed in chapters 5 through 7. Augustine makes a distinction between "proper" or immediate ends and "final" ends that motivate more specific *voluntates* or "wills" in the plural. The final end of the *voluntas* as a whole is its settled, long-range intention, and this corresponds strikingly well to Xunzi's predominant sense of *zhi* 志 as a settled intention, our ultimate aspiration or goal. (Although Xunzi sometimes speaks of it in the sense of proximate intention as well, *zhi* for him generally reflects the fundamental orientation of the heart/mind.) For both of them, intention overlaps with our dispositions in complex ways: Ultimate intentions seem to reflect our second-order judgments and desires about what is of the very highest worth, and for both seem to reflect a genuine yearning for that goal. But at the same time, those intentions may be self-deceptive and reflect more than we care to admit our less-than-perfect dispositions and desires. Although Augustine is much more alert to and concerned about this possibility than Xunzi, Xunzi does recognize it at various points, as I discuss more fully below. Both of them also think that a central aspect of spiritual exercises is the project of unifying our proximate intentions around the ultimate intention of following God or the Way—and, indeed, uniting and purifying that ultimate intention itself. "Purity of heart is to will one thing" is a slogan both could happily embrace, although they would explicate it quite differently.

Significant differences emerge, however, in their accounts of choice and its relation to intention and desire, as discussed especially in chapter 5. According to Augustine, consent and dissent from possible actions "belong to the will (*voluntas*)"; by this, he means that *arbitrium*, that is, choice or decision, is a subsidiary power of *voluntas* (*spir. et litt.* 34.60). In other words, on Augustine's account, we follow what we love, because it delights us, and our *consensio* "agreement" or "consent" to those delights is our freely given decision to pursue them in particular circumstances. We are not constrained by any outside forces in our deliberations about how to satisfy our wishes, but the basic orientation of our loves remains relatively impervious to reflective choice, in Augustine's picture. As I put it in chapter 5, for Augustine our second-order choices to assent or dissent from particular courses of action are only logically superior to our desires, and before God's saving grace allows us to convert to Christianity we will not infrequently find ourselves "consenting" to habitual activities that we find loathsome, and that we ineffectively wish to stop doing. Only God can pour Christian love into our hearts in sufficient amounts to outweigh our carnal predispositions and fire our imaginations with a truer understanding of the beatitude we have mistakenly sought in worldly goods. We can contribute to the consolidation of God's gifts through eager Christian service, but this is always a response to prior divine initiative.

For Xunzi, however, even the uncultivated have full possession of the innate power to assent or dissent from particular desires, although such "petty" people analyze and evaluate the world only in terms of what will benefit them by satisfying as many of their desires as possible. Thus they will not in fact dissent from their desires very often—presumably only in cases of immediate physical danger. When such people experience the anxiety and fear that stem from the social chaos of unrestricted interhuman conflict over goods, they may search out some better way of life. They are capable of assenting to the idea of learning a new way of life, and putting themselves before a teacher—if they are lucky enough to come across one who seems to promise a better Way. They are incapable of acting like a noble man, let alone a sage, but if offered the chance they can at least begin the long journey necessary to reach such goals.

As noted in chapter 5, however, these sketches leave to the side some of the most interesting issues regarding conflict within the self, to which we now turn. A striking similarity in Xunzi's and Augustine's views is their distinction between positive and negative kinds of personal disintegration. Both see the unredeemed or uncultivated person (perhaps after a brief "happily vicious" initial period) as torn between conflicting first-order desires, which tend when followed to produce profoundly harmful consequences for both individuals and the community. And yet to escape such dissipation both suggest that an even more profound internal chasm needs to open, as people begin to recognize qualitatively higher values that overrule immediate desires, to use Charles Taylor's language, although what they think these are certainly varies. For Augustine, we need to turn away from our "carnal" orientation of private delight in lower, earthly goods, and turn toward God, the supreme good. For Xunzi, we need to be exposed to the excellences of the Confucian Way, which will attract many people sufficiently for them to commit to the more onerous program of cultivation he advocates, which in turn can slowly strengthen their commitment to that Way until it is indestructible. For both of them, then, the second disintegration is salutary because it leads eventually to a unified focus on the good that transcends all confusion, vacillation, and personal disintegration. Put in modern terms, both seek a state of perfect virtue wherein all internal conflict disappears and we freely, effectively, and capably will to live righteously. Of course, Xunzi thinks that such a state can be attained by at least a tiny number in this life, who can share the benefits of sagehood with others through teaching and good government, whereas Augustine argues consistently that no one will be free from uncertainty and internal conflict until the resurrection, and that earthly peace is always flawed and fragile, whereas eternal peace will be untroubled and absolutely secure.

Augustine and Xunzi seem to agree in large measure in their low estimate of the wretchedness of unregenerate humanity, caught between desires for pleasure, dominance, and safety that seem to preclude mutual satisfaction. They both portray the self-restraint of such impulses as crucial to at least some spiritual exercises that will help us make progress in virtue, and they conceive of this restraint as part of a two-sided training process that restrains some desires but heightens or magnifies others. But here their differences over consent loom large, even if we restrict ourselves to comparing the situation of Christians "under grace" and of aspiring Confucians, whether "petty" or more accomplished.

We can focus the issues by considering one of the few virtues to which Augustine devotes a freestanding treatise, *continentia* or "continence."[11] According to Augustine, continence is a "spiritual virtue" that is "a gift" from the Holy Spirit, "whereby we control and rule and conquer carnal desire" (*cont.* 1.1, 5.12). Though it certainly refers to the ability to preserve sexual chastity, its deeper meaning concerns the ability to stop the inward consent of the heart to any sinful desire, precisely by putting a "gate" on the "inner mouth" of the heart to stop it from uttering sinful "words" internally (1.1–2.3). The ambiguities of Augustine's discursive model of the psyche have already been addressed in chapter 5, where I developed a slightly revised Augustinian account of inner discourse that includes "words" we do not consciously consent to, precisely in the form of the fleshly temptations of concupiscence. Continence, then, refuses to agree to follow such words, which bubble up within us from the fault in our human nature, as exacerbated by past sinful habits but also diminished by the grace of baptism and Christian worship (7.18–8.19). Thus continence is a virtue found only in Christians under grace, who have been inspired by God to fight inwardly in a ferocious struggle against concupiscence, as they "crucify" fleshly desires in Christian "combat" (3.6–9, 8.20, 7.18). In other words, for Augustine continent dissent from sin is the engine that makes practices such as fasting and sexual restraint possible as true spiritual exercises, which over time cause not only our sins to decrease but even our carnal desires themselves (8.20). However, given the conflict of the different sorts of delight that make up our *voluntas*, this refusal of consent to sin is only made possible when "the Lord gives a sweetness that is beneficial, making continence more pleasurable," to counter the sweetness of satisfying sinful desire (3.7).[12]

So continence is a virtue that presupposes both a delight in sinning that must be restrained, but also a stronger delight in goodness that is given to us by God, and that makes possible our refusal to consent to sin.[13] Thus Augustine's account of the Christian life of inward struggle presupposes not the grim refusal of all delight but the earnest preference for a superior delight to an inferior, for the "gentle joy of sanctity" over lingering carnal temptations (14.31). Augustinian continence both reflects and heightens the increasingly strong love for God that motivates Christian believers who are progressively purifying their imaging of God.[14] But in this life, even under grace, this inward combat is tinged by fear and uncertainty (11.25) and the alarming possibility of relapse, because despite all our new and holy inclinations, we might reenact the Fall yet again, more horribly. Augustine writes that in Christians "base carnal impulses" are "being continually suppressed by continence to prevent them from rising up again. If anyone ceases to put them aside in this way, as though safe from them, they will launch themselves at the stronghold of that person's soul, and overthrow it and make it their slave again, a foully mutilated captive" (14.31).[15] Thus continence is an ongoing necessity; it can never be forgotten or neglected for an instant. Augustine's insistent language of struggle, combined with his urgent pleas to trust in God, not in oneself and one's own powers of self-restraint, which are bound to fail (5.12), all suggest that Augustinian virtue is best understood as continuous striving for something higher, not repose in dependable excellences of character. Augustinian virtue risks the self by trusting entirely in God's power and mercy, carefully retaining a humble, expectant, obedient inward posture.

In comparison with this full Augustinian treatment, which places continence at the center of the Christian life of spiritual exercises, Xunzi's treatment is strikingly thin. He seems to have a similar concept, but the idea appears to be relatively uninteresting to him theoretically because he thinks the power of assent is common to all humans, and so he is much more concerned with how we might learn to what we should assent. This is fundamentally an intellectual and even epistemological problem, which motivates his thorough treatment of learning and the virtues of the heart/mind.[16]

Xunzi speaks of something analogous to continence in two places: his discussions of unity as a virtue and goal of the heart/mind that should guide ongoing Confucian practice; and his discussion of the lower levels of Confucian ethical achievement, especially surrounding the transition from pettiness to becoming an "educated man."[17] In the first area, unity implies "dark obscurity of intent" as one struggles as an uncelebrated, unskilled beginner to follow the Way. If my intention is unified, then I will be steadfast in my pursuit of the Way, like the single-minded earthworm rather than the *zao* 躁, "impetuous" or "scattered" crab (1/2/13). In the second area, we hear that educated men are those "whose enactment of the model has reached a steadfastness such that they do not let selfish desires disorder what they have heard" from their teacher (8/30/12–13). This implies that aspirants who have not yet reached this stage still allow "selfish desires" to disorder their moral deliberation, and it implies further that their intellectual grasp of the *Dao* is still relatively tenuous—it is something they have heard about but have not yet truly made their own through deep understanding and practice.

So far, this might seem hard to distinguish from Augustine's picture, but Xunzi's psychological model implies a very different treatment of such "disunity" and disordering conflict within the self. Most crucially, Xunzi's deep distinction between, on the one hand, our initially innate system of spontaneous responsiveness to our environment that includes our dispositions and desires and, on the other hand, the reflective and deliberative desires that consist in our judgments of assent, implies a localization and domestication of conflict within the self. Such conflict is always between our considered, reflective judgments and our spontaneous impulses. This is so because, according to Xunzi, the actual power to assent to particular courses of action is never lacking, even in beginners; when I stray from the *Dao*, I have made some sort of error, whether of evaluation or perception, about what the *Dao* is or how it relates to the situation before me. If we just learned more, or thought through the implications of what we had learned, or more creatively drew analogies from it, we would not err so badly again. Crucially, Xunzi seems to think that "selfish desires" can "disorder what [aspirants] have heard" by "pulling" and "tilting" our perceptions so that we are blind to anything but our own immediate benefit or pleasure (21/105/7–8). Indeed, his stress on how desire can constrict and skew our perceptions, and thus undercut our capacities to deliberate from the very start, is essential to the plausibility of his psychology of assent and desire. Unless we actively address such difficulties, our vulgar innate desires will not only "tilt" our perceptions but also incline us toward corrupt interpretations of the Way, in which personal benefit or pleasure play too large a role, rather than an appropriately limited one. This means that internal conflict tends in the end for Xunzi to be a relatively simple and clear phenomenon: our impulses are bad; but if we understand things properly, we will be reflectively moved to restrain and eventually reshape them. At least for aspiring Confucians in a good environment, Xunzi in effect localizes, delimits, and demystifies our impulses to evil by making them strictly a matter of our spontaneously reactive disposition.[18] A Xunzian Confucian can then think of himself as fundamentally what he assents to, with a holdover of first-order desires that are no longer truly his own, because he decisively rejects them, and that he can patiently work on like a steadfast artisan working on a grand work of art. The larger and growing portion of first-order desires he does approve of will slowly and steadily eclipse the rest, until there are no more misshapen desires left within him and his self-crafting will at last be completed.

Xunzi's treatment of unity as both goal and virtue implies two main existential worries: first, the possibility of "obsession" derailing continued learning about and appropriation of the Way; and second, the very alarming (to Xunzi) possibility that someone might begin Confucian study and then give up because it was too frustrating or slow, or simply because they got distracted from it somehow and stopped paying attention to the task of self-improvement. This helps to explain his stress on communal support, which leads him to coin a seemingly unique idea of proto-continence: Educated men can command themselves well enough to follow the Way, as long as they are part of a dependable Confucian grouping that can keep pressing and guiding them onward and correcting their errors on specific points. Only when such people are truly dependable when alone or in antagonistic circumstances have they become noble men, who seem more than continent in their delight in "the [Confucian] model" of conduct, but not yet perfectly, effortlessly virtuous.

This is still considerably less radical, however, than Augustine's conception of the inner conflict within good, aspiring Christians "under grace." As William Babcock writes, Augustine's anti-Manichean account provides no localization of differing centers of desire but instead develops a way "to portray a true internal struggle of the self against itself."[19] Both our carnal and spiritual desires are our own desires, our own "inner words" within our own minds that battle for supremacy. This implies that for Augustine the mind's resistance to itself will always retain an element of mystery in the negative sense, of incomprehensibility, just like the Fall. Inner conflict cannot be quarantined by placing sinful impulses only within the body, or a lower part of the soul, when our own inner discourse is divided against itself.

Not only that, but according to Augustine even when grace has provided that superior delight in the good that makes continence possible, our minds may still "defect" from this stronger yearning by consenting to sin (*cont.* 5.12–13, 8.20, 14.31). If such consent is given to a sufficiently serious offense, a lifetime of continence can be destroyed in an instant, if God has predestined such a catastrophic warning to others (*persev.* 22.61).

For Xunzi, by contrast, the vigilant attention to pursuing unity that is appropriate to aspirants and even educated men slowly fades out as our dispositions are more and more thoroughly reshaped through steady Confucian practice. Though unity remains as a virtue, "dark obscurity of intent" eventually gives way to the "shining brightness of illumination" (1/2/13–14), when what we would call continence is no longer necessary. Even for the noble man, who still must practice self-overcoming of a sort, the fundamental battle has been won. Although noble men still make occasional mistakes of speech, conduct, and understanding, they have nevertheless fundamentally settled their new orientation to the Way, so that there is no reason for them to *fear* their remaining imperfect impulses or misjudgments, even if they might be cause for shame (8/30/13–15). For Xunzi, if the Way prevails in society at large, such men can only be considered happy, as they continue their pursuit of sagehood. The real danger concerns aspirants who might overestimate their grasp of the Way, or give up on it foolishly, or simply become distracted by enticing possibilities that they do not even recognize as temptations.

To sum up the discussion so far, Xunzi and Augustine are proposing two intriguingly different accounts of the long quest for the ethical perfection that each enjoins. Each of their distinctive ideas of such perfection (effortlessly splendid sagehood for Xunzi, and eternal beatitude in perfected relation to God for Augustine) stands in sharp contrast to the petty or sinful state of normal human beings, and serves to goad and entice aspirants further along their respective paths. These ideals, in other words, are meant to induce passionate striving within the religious life, and a sense of dissatisfaction with one's current state of existence, perhaps even a sort of positive anxiety to be transformed.

Xunzi's account of this striving is relatively more straightforward. Throughout the process of moving from pettiness to nobility, we have a humbling awareness of how far we remain from the ideal of the sage, who spontaneously desires to follow the Way alone, and who is so skillful in his ritualized interpersonal mastery that he has no trouble responding well to any unusual person or situation. But if we remain steadfast in our practice of Confucian spiritual exercises, according to Xunzi, we will gradually notice the change in our desires, in concert with the increasing depth of our understanding. It would seem, then, that practice is initially quite difficult but becomes noticeably easier as we progress for Xunzi, although I suspect that Xunzi and other Confucians proffer the sage ideal at least in part to keep those who perceive themselves to be noble from overestimating their mastery of self and the arts of the Way. But even so, it would seem that a noble man would be right to feel growing self-assurance and ease, even as he continues to strive for greater creativity, flexibility, and insight in his ritual practice, and his teaching of beginning Confucians.

For Augustine, however, his teachings about the inevitable imperfections of personal cultivation in this life, as compared with the beatitude that is our true goal as human beings, combine to lead to what might be called a double ideal: one suited to our present existence under grace, and another more ultimate one. Though in the next life we will enjoy perfect, untroubled rest and the barely imaginable joy of having our greatest desire eternally satisfied, in the current life our situation is fundamentally one of expectation. This means that in a certain sense, even as our loves become more integrated through Christian discipleship, our yearning and striving only increase in intensity—as long as we are still pilgrims on the way home to the heavenly Jerusalem. Augustine writes: "Our task lies in desiring. Holy desire is the whole life of good Christians. . . . Thus God, by deferring [what we yearn for], stretches our desire; by the desiring, stretches the soul; by stretching, makes it more capacious. Let us therefore desire, brothers, because we shall be filled" (*ep. Jo.* 4.6).[20]

Augustine suggests that we should work to increase our spiritual hunger and even dissatisfaction, that we might strive all the more and become inwardly capable, through greatness of love, for true beatitude. Though increasingly intense *caritas* may be satisfied in part through regular prayer and worship and the practice of other spiritual exercises, it demands as well vigorous striving to love other human beings through active, extensive benevolence. In this sense Paul, rather than Christ, becomes the model for

Christians in this life, according to Augustine: Paul forgets what lies behind, stretches out to what lies ahead, and presses on intently toward the ultimate union with Christ in beatitude (Phil 3:13, *Trin*. 9.1; see also *s*. 400.1).[21]

In other words, Augustine counsels an ideal that continues to fascinate many in the West, although often in a radically altered, Nietzschean form: a life of ever-increasing passion, which is marked by increasingly intense yet disciplined striving for spiritual perfection. This heroic striving seems to require continuing antagonistic contests, with significant challenges and resistance to be overcome, where great acts and great passion incite each other in turn. Of course Augustine undoubtedly also questions this heroic tendency, most notably via his skeptical interrogation of *superbia*, and he suggests that genuine perseverance against the ongoing threats of concupiscence is the finest achievement believers may reasonably hope for in this life. But the basic structure of continuing struggle, effort, and impassioned striving is present nonetheless.

In contrast, Xunzi imagines that the ideal human state is one of "effortless action," in Edward Slingerland's apt phrase.[22] In such a sagely state, one's desires, thoughts, skills, and actions are all perfectly integrated in "the middle course where ritual flows." As Slingerland argues, this vision reflects a shared early Chinese ideal of effortlessly skillful mastery as the ultimate human state.[23] Though Xunzi undoubtedly pictures the Confucian path as an extremely demanding endeavor in its earlier stages, the sense of struggle and striving that are essential to any movement from pettiness to higher stages of life gradually dissipates as one's dispositions are reformed into the proper shape. The Way gets easier as one walks it over a lifetime, until one may skip along it with unselfconscious delight. But unlike Augustinian beatitude, which is essentially contemplative, Xunzian sagehood is fundamentally a matter of active engagement with the world as a preternaturally capable moral leader. (The Augustinian life of inspired corporate charity within and beyond the church, however, is equally active and engaged, although it eschews hope for perfect peace or flawless moral leadership here on Earth.)

The extreme difficulty of actually living this sort of sage-leader ideal, however, suggests that Xunzi is trying to ward off the self-satisfaction that would ordinarily come with high rank, an ample salary, and social influence, if our dispositions are not fully transformed (23/116/25–23/117/1). Even the internal rewards of a fully ritualized life are obviously insufficient by themselves, in this sort of vision, without political effectiveness in ushering the Way more widely into society. In other words, for Xunzi, the extremity of the ideal makes the pursuit of perfection asymptotic, with significant further progress possible for even the highly virtuous and very capable. As

Confucius's celebrated disciple Yan Hui is reported to say of the Way in *Analects* 9.11, "The more I look up at it the higher it seems; the more I delve into it, the harder it becomes. Catching a glimpse of it before me, I then find it suddenly at my back. The Master is skilled at gradually leading people on, step by step. He broadens me with culture and restrains me with the rites, so that even if I wanted to give up I could not."[24] For Xunzi, as with other early Confucians of his outlook, following the *Dao* with sagely perfection is a vast challenge, and it requires a lifetime of commitment to master.

Augustine goes even further, however, undercutting the pretensions of human virtue decisively. In this life, everyone still has far to go, according to Augustine. Though believers should have confidence in the Lord, pride is always a dangerous, devious enemy.

For both figures, long-term or even unceasing striving is necessary in part because aspiring Christians and Confucians, on their accounts, are seeking to live an ideal that they only dimly and partially understand. As with many of the most important endeavors in life, both Augustine and Xunzi think that personal formation is a long-term project to which we must commit ourselves before we fully understand it, in part because its difficulties would terrify us if we knew them in advance.

SPIRITUAL EXERCISES AND THE MANIPULATION OF INNER AND OUTER

One of the striking similarities between Augustine and Xunzi is their shared conviction that learning is a foundational spiritual exercise. People cannot flourish without learning. Put another way, we do not innately possess the resources necessary to live a good life, and so we must learn from others the most important, indeed salvific, facts about human existence. Moreover, learning must continue throughout our lives. It is not as if there are a few earthshaking truths we must grasp, after which all is resolved. It might seem, then, that both Xunzi and Augustine would insist on the necessity of external assistance because of the paucity of internal resources available to uncultivated people. Though this is true in a general sense, it obscures important differences in their treatments of what is "inner" or hidden and what is "outer" or visible, differences that help explain many of the dissimilarities between their overarching accounts of spiritual exercises. (I return to their shared emphasis on learning in the third section of this chapter.)

So far, much of this chapter has focused on moral psychology, but to grasp the deeper organizing principles in Augustine and Xunzi's regimes of personal formation, we need to note as well their partially divergent conceptions of a related topic: what is morally required of human beings. In other words, what counts as a good or right action, for each of them? On this issue, Augustine sits squarely within a central stream of western ethical reflection, which he helped shape. For Augustine, the crucial issue in evaluating human actions is whether they stem from a rightly directed will. This means they must be properly motivated by *caritas*, and properly "referred" to the right ultimate end, beatitude with God (*Trin*. 11.10). The notion of reference at play here concerns the reason or end for which an action is taken, and Augustine envisions logical links between immediate proximate intentions, intermediate goals, and the ultimate ends of beatitude, glory, or pleasure, which determine the moral quality of every particular *voluntas*, no matter how minor. This means, crucially, that for Augustine actions that seem to perfectly fulfill the requirements of some duty, at least outwardly in terms of performance, can still be fundamentally evil if they are ultimately motivated by and "referred" to some wrong end, such as personal glory.[25] An example would be doing some visibly good deed, such as helping the proverbial old lady across the street, for an ultimately selfish reason, such as gaining a good reputation so that one might be entrusted with responsibility and thus power.

A corollary of this conception is that the actual outcome of one's efforts is secondary at best, for Augustine. Indeed, because God uses all things for good, even the evil wills of sinning humans, according to Augustine *every* action will in some objective, external sense become part of God's providential design, and thus be just and right. If one's own aims in action are thwarted, one may still rest assured that God has justly and wisely overruled one's efforts. For Augustine, in sum, moral evaluation hinges fundamentally on individual intention and motivation. As Augustine famously counsels, "Love, and do what you will. . . . Let the root of love be within. From such a root nothing but good can come forth" (*ep. Jo.* 7.8).

For Xunzi, the situation is more complicated. On his account, right action must be manifest in correct outward form, although to be perfect such action must be matched by appropriate emotions and desires; such is the "middle course where ritual flows." In his criticism of Mencius, Xunzi defines *shan* 善, "good," and *e* 惡, "bad," as follows: "From antiquity to the present, what all under Heaven have called good is what is correct, properly patterned, peaceful, and orderly. What is called bad is what is slanted, vicious, perverse, and chaotic" (23/115/1–2). The root meanings of goodness for Xunzi seem to concern publicly observable states of affairs, mostly involving proper social order. But the context in which this remark is made is the debate over the character of human *xing* or instincts, which suggests that the quality of human impulses is also at issue. Moreover, badness for Xunzi seems to include certain qualities of volition, such as viciousness and perversity.

To grasp what Xunzi has in mind, recall that for him the Way is "marked out" by the rituals (18/82/22–18/83/1). As discussed in chapter 6, to follow the Way one must behave in a ritually appropriate manner, which requires a certain sort of personal demeanor as well as a wide range of specific behaviors, across all spheres of human activity, including but going well beyond particular important ceremonies. Moreover, the minute details of ritual incarnate general norms of justice (*yi* 義), and so they are crucial to the right ordering of society. Indeed, Xunzi says at one point that the Way is essentially a matter of creating community, by properly ordering, harmonizing, and nourishing people, so that they may flourish together (12/59/11–16). All of this suggests that right actions, on Xunzi's understanding, both *aim at* and *successfully achieve* the outward manifestation of a properly patterned society.[26]

This insistence on excellent observable form might suggest that Xunzi does not care particularly much about proper motivation and intention, but this would be mistaken. (It would also make rather mysterious his insistence on spiritual exercises designed to reform our dispositions and desires.) It is clear that Xunzi thinks we must possess the proper emotions and dispositions to fully exemplify the Way. One of his more general ways of making this point is his insistence that right action (i.e., action in accord with ritual and justice, and thus the *Dao* as well) must manifest the virtue of *ren* 仁, which for him means something like "benevolence," "caring," or "humaneness" (8/28/15). Indeed, he explicitly rejects actions that are not based on ritual and justice but that accidentally hit on what is outwardly fitting, because he thinks such actions are not truly benevolent and will thus necessarily "fail," perhaps because they will fail to move their recipients appropriately (8/33/14). For him, it appears that fully good actions must both be motivated by and manifest the benevolence, justice, and beautiful propriety characteristic of the Confucian Way.

This generates an interesting complication, given Xunzi's account of assent overruling our inadequate emotions and desires. To put the point briefly, his psychology and personal formation program suggest that most people, not being sages, will need to frequently push themselves toward proper outward observances of ritual and just action in ways that pull back from or go beyond their felt emotions and desires. Such actions, for him, must in some significant sense be good, because their ultimate goal is enacting the Way, even though they are imperfect in their flawed motivation. He thus prioritizes correct outward form and performance, but he relates this in complex ways to our considered intentions manifest in what we assent to, and to our initially misdirected dispositions and impulses.

These differences in their conceptions of what counts as genuinely good or right action play out in the regimes of spiritual exercises that Augustine and Xunzi each recommend, especially those that go beyond textual study and serve to help internalize or genuinely realize the lessons learned in such study. Xunzi's overarching concern with proper social order and beautiful outward form (*wenli* 文禮, "proper form and good order") leads him to devote much of his attention to what may be called performative practices like ritual and music. Such practices order persons in terms of not only their appearance and positioning but also their interrelations within groups, aiming throughout to create forms and patterns that are *mei* 美, "fine" and "beautiful," as well as just. In this sort of practice, individuals are pulled outward—their attention is focused on timely and appropriate interactions with others. They thus cultivate alert awareness of others and their actions, and sensitivity to the numerous moral and aesthetic distinctions that ritual forms create and enforce.

When Augustine moves beyond study, by contrast, he advocates turning primarily to symbolic activities such as the Eucharist and discursive practices such as petitionary prayer, contemplation, and confession. Even practices of self-restraint such as fasting and celibacy are repeatedly understood symbolically, and he clearly envisions them as being simultaneous with more positive, articulate practices of prayer, mutual exhortation, and self-examination, as in the annual Easter vigil. All these exercises encourage what Foucault has called a "hermeneutics of the self," wherein one carefully scrutinizes one's inner impulses and thoughts, even when these concern seemingly outward activities such as partaking in the bread and wine, or refraining from eating for a period of time.[27]

Because the mind for Augustine is a trinity of memory, understanding, and will/love, which exists as an ongoing stream of "inner words," the crucial issues in personal formation are to discern the quality and "direction" of one's inner discourse at any given moment, and to do all one can to reshape it and properly direct it toward its true end. These goals may be accomplished by refusing consent to sinful internal words before they issue in action, by as it were "reciting" inwardly the discourse one wishes to adopt, and by using the proper terms to analyze and articulate one's own conception of self and world. Instead of finding one's rightful place in beautiful and just harmonization with other ritual actors, for Augustine we are to find our true self by correctly discerning our own deep inner relation to God.

By locating and relying on this divine fountain within, we may confidently go forth to love neighbor and even enemy; but without it, we are lost, both inwardly and outwardly.

To put the contrast schematically, Augustine pursues an "inside-out" model of personal formation, while Xunzi pursues an "outside-in" model.[28] In other words, Augustine's exercises focus as much as possible on the mysterious source of our actions in our inward "heart of hearts." By working to restrain concupiscent impulses so that God's love and wisdom may enter in and inspire us to righteous action, spiritual exercises *directly* address what is most inward to change what generates our outward behavior. Xunzi instead suggests that the most potent strategy for effecting lasting inward change is to focus on what we can control reasonably well—our outward movements, gestures, and speech—and by working to perfect these observable actions, slowly and *indirectly* reforming the impulses that move us spontaneously, until at last they lead just as surely to outwardly perfect action.

This contrast helps to explain some of the striking differences between Augustine's and Xunzi's programs for personal formation. Xunzi gives remarkably little attention to the sorts of meditations that seem so integral to the various forms of Augustinian prayer, for instance. Xunzi makes exercises such as the memorization and recitation of classical poetry subsidiary and introductory parts of his account of Confucian study and learning, and he explicitly warns against making them more central than ritual practice under the personal guidance of a wise teacher (1/3/7–1/4/4). And though Xunzi does mention self-examination occasionally in his writings, it occupies nothing like the central place confession and self-scrutiny do for Augustine (1/1/5, 1/4/16–19, 2/5/3–6, 2/6/12, 11/54/13; cf. 1/1/12–15). As argued in chapter 6, Xunzian self-examination seems to be a self-interrogation concerning one's treatment of close and distant human beings, and whether one has conscientiously enacted what one teaches and purports to follow, rather than a careful sifting and interpretation of thoughts and desires to ferret out hidden sinfulness.

Furthermore, in contrast to the relatively direct pageantry of Xunzian ritual, Augustinian rituals such as the Eucharist are shot through with symbolism, and they are meant to be occasions for the contemplation of symbols. As Robert Dodaro has argued, "Behind [Augustine's] enthusiasm for liturgical symbolism lies a Platonic sensitivity to the movement from visible to invisible orders of reality."[29] According to Augustine, as we move mentally from the physical reality of the bread and wine to their Christian symbolic meaning, to their *spiritus* or inner meaning, our minds are excited and drawn "upward and inward" to God's eternal truths in a way that would be difficult to achieve without allegory and symbolism (*ep*. 55.21). For Xunzi, the details of the rituals he discusses have meaning in that they are commonly understood to express certain feelings and thoughts; yet the mode of this meaning is not in any obvious sense symbolic but rather conventional and somewhat literal, as when the grave goods are all in some way incomplete or unusable, to mark the fact that, although mourners wish the dead person were simply moving to a new abode, he or she will not actually be using any of these implements (19/95/6–13).

Let us pursue one such issue in greater depth. The basic contrast between inside-out and outside-in strategies of personal cultivation helps explain an intriguing and deep disagreement between Augustine and Xunzi concerning the value of pretence in self-formation. Consider first Augustine's absolute proscription of lying, which he discusses in two separate treatises, and which was a departure from earlier, somewhat less strict Christian reflection on the topic (*mend.*, *c. mend.*).[30] For Augustine, lying appears to be essential to most forms of sin, which except in unusual cases (e.g., the unevangelized who are "before the law") require that we lie to ourselves about the relative goodness of the end we pursue, such as human companionship, by semiconsciously overvaluing it relative to God's unchanging hierarchical ordering of reality (e.g., *conf.* 2.3.7, 2.6.14, 2.8.16, *Gn. litt.* 11.42.59). Because God for Augustine *is* the Truth (*conf.* 3.6.10, *c. mend.* 40), lying is at root a defection from God and God's ordering of reality, and so it may never be excused under any circumstances, no matter what other evils might be avoided by doing so (*mend.* 42). Indeed, for Augustine, the worst sort of deception is a lie about matters of religion; he views any sort of lying in the midst of religious instruction or training, purportedly for someone's spiritual good, as particularly heinous (*mend.* 17).

This absolutist conception of truthfulness leads Augustine to exalt a vision of the religious life as a continuing confession of the truth, both inwardly and outwardly, so that the Christian life can be seen as a contest between truth telling and lying as general modes of existence. According to Augustine, "Every proud person is an impostor. . . . Any proud person pretends to be what he is not; he cannot do otherwise." In contrast to this, the "true Israelite" or genuine believer who "ascends to Jerusalem" is one "in whom no guile (*dolus*, lit. 'artifice') is to be found." Augustine concludes: "Why do they ascend? How do they ascend? To confess to your name, oh Lord. It cannot be more splendidly said. Just as pride presumes, humility confesses. The presumptuous wants to appear to be something they are not; just so someone who confesses does not want to appear other than they truly are, and loves what He [i.e., God] is" (*en. Ps.* 121.8). On Augustine's account, it appears that pretense or outward artifice is always a mark of human pride, which seeks to dissemble about its true state as subject to God. This world-oriented guile is radically opposed to the truth-confessing love of God. The need for humble confession of dependence on God becomes only greater when one takes up exalted positions within the community, such as ecclesiastical office or consecrated virginity. Indeed, a great danger in such a state is pretending to be humble outwardly, while inwardly one begins to revel proudly in the graces one has already been given, which destroys from within like a spiritual cancer (*virg.* 43.44).

Needless to say, such a vision of the dangers of pretense is dramatically opposed to both the rhetoric and, to a lesser degree, the real position of Xunzi, who provocatively chooses *wei* 偽 or "artifice" as his summary term for both the process of personal formation and good character itself (22/107/24). On Xunzi's account, we must meet objective moral standards, which often take the form of observable public performances, despite the fact that our inadequately cultivated dispositions do not spontaneously make us feel like doing so. We thus, in a very real sense, pretend to be more virtuous than we yet are, by imitating the clothes, gestures, words, and general demeanor of a noble man, even though this does violence to our true feelings.

Is Xunzi guilty of advising all aspiring Confucians to lie about their true character? The charitable answer must be no, because a Xunzian aspirant is not deceiving himself, or even others, about what he is doing, which is learning to become good by trying to act the part. More precisely, when someone engages in "artifice" in Xunzi's technical sense, they are *ke* 可, "assenting," to some particular plan of action based on preceding *lü* 慮, "deliberation," about what is best, that is, what matches the Way in the current situation; or if they are true beginners, by assenting to directions given by their teacher, whom they respect and trust even though they do not yet understand him well. Though the aspirant will suffer the frustration of thwarting some of his desires, he will be achieving, however clumsily and imperfectly, what he aims for, which is a ritually correct performance. Even in the case of an educated man, Xunzi's partly cultivated Confucian, who assents to acting properly in public on the basis of his own assessment of some matter despite his countervailing desires, this cannot really be counted as deception, because of the essential role of his assent in making such an action possible. Such Confucians are neither deceived about their own internal states, because they overrule their inappropriate desires and emotions, nor do they deceive others, because they honestly cherish the values conveyed by their performances.

Xunzi's psychological separation of assent from the responsive system of dispositions governing spontaneous desire and emotion thus makes possible a fundamentally different form of pretence from anything envisaged by Augustine. But even a very charitable Augustinian might wonder why exactly Xunzi thinks "acting the part" of goodness will eventually make one good.[31] Might it not simply cultivate acting skill, while leaving one's heart and mind as corrupt as ever?

Xunzi's reply to such a query would be multifaceted. First, there are very important dissimilarities between "acting" as a contemporary artistic practice and Xunzian ritual as a spiritual exercise. Acting does not intrinsically relate to some higher goal, and it can be pursued for any number of reasons, in pursuit of goods internal to the practice such as producing splendid dramatic performances, or further cultivating one's skill as an actor; or goods external to the practice, such as earning a paycheck, becoming famous, or running away from one's own troubled existence.[32] By contrast, Xunzian ritual is supposed to be performed in order to follow the Way by making just and beautiful both everyday existence and important occasions. Moreover, acting covers any and all sorts of behavior—perfect mimicry, or at least believable simulation, of the full range of human conduct included. But Xunzian ritual is focused on only one sort of character, that of the ancient sages, and it is meant to encode and vivify their mode of life in as much detail as possible, so that the aspiring Confucian is not learning to imitate in general but to imitate the mode of life of the wisest and best human beings.[33] Thus the skill at ritual an aspirant cultivates by following the advice of his teacher would be skill only at acting like a sage. Moreover, skill at acting in the contemporary sense is a specialized craft that one might exercise or not exercise whenever one felt like it. But for Xunzi, and for Confucians generally, "skill" at ritual is equivalent to increasing mastery of the overarching art of living as a human being, which covers all aspects of life and is not something one sets aside, or even could set aside if sufficiently cultivated, based on whim or circumstance.[34] In other words, for Confucians like Xunzi, genuine skill at ritual is identical to virtue itself, in their conception.

Moving to the vocabulary of "skill" recalls Aristotle's famous discussion of cultivating virtue through practicing it, where he distinguishes sharply between virtue and skill in order to defeat the objection that one could not learn to be virtuous by doing virtuous actions, because such actions must already have the proper intention to be truly virtuous.[35] Aristotle suggests that though excellent outward form is sufficient to judge the goodness of craft products, it is not enough to judge the skill of the artisan. Moreover, it is insufficient for virtuous actions to merely possess the right qualities; such actions must be done by a person in the right state, that is, one who knows what he is doing and why (something good, because it is good), and furthermore does it out of a "firm and unchanging" state of character. On this basis, he distinguishes between just actions, which are the sort that a just person would do, and performing such actions in the right way, in the manner that a truly just person would. Aristotle at this point simply asserts that the only way one can move toward actually possessing steady states of virtuous character is to frequently perform actions that outwardly manifest the good ("just actions"), as a way of practicing the deliberation that decides on what is good for its own sake, and of training emotions, desires, and discernment in order to see and judge in a consistently just manner.

Xunzi, however, can go well beyond this sort of account, given his view of the centrality of ritual skill to moral virtue. For him, this special sort of skill is much closer to virtue, and indeed is essential to its full possession. Where Aristotle distinguishes sharply between virtue and skill, Xunzi conspicuously fails to make such a sharp distinction, although we should note the disanalogies mentioned above between acting and ritual mastery.

Although the two sorts of practice do differ, Xunzian personal formation seems to share significant commonalities with the process of becoming an excellent musician or dancer.[36] In such practices, one must learn many basic rules and also learn how to actually execute certain sorts of movements and, eventually, performances, so that they are beautiful and good, according to the standards of the practice in question.[37] Several related things happen as practice deepens. As one gains greater expertise, one begins to understand the rationale for aspects of the practice that initially seemed arbitrary, painful, or irritating. Skill of this sort, however, is just as much physical as mental—one learns how to play the violin beautifully with one's fingers and hands as much as one's mind; one learns with both body and mind how to move smoothly and easily through various sorts of ritually regulated interactions. One also comes to better appreciate the subtleties that differentiate poor, middling, and fine performances. In tandem with this growing sensitivity, one gradually develops what can only be called artful style in one's own practice, although here there would presumably be room for a range of achievement. Indeed, Xunzi's near-assimilation of virtue with a certain sort of skill at living extends to his treatment of the sage, who may be distinguished from the noble man not only by his greater understanding of the Way and his perfected dispositions but also by his extraordinary skill at politically effective moral leadership (8/30/15–17). Perhaps most crucially, as ritual mastery increases, one gradually delights more and more in the beauty of the art one is creating through performance, and in one's own and others' abilities to perform so well.

This last point is essential to the plausibility of Xunzi's Confucianism. At the end of chapter 5, I questioned whether Xunzi could adequately explain how petty people might come to be motivated by love for the Way itself rather than the benefits they might perceive to "playing along" with it. Xunzi's ritual reformation model hinges on the characteristics of performative skill training just discussed, combined with the process of Confucian learning. As this regimen is pursued over time, one will become aware of new sources of satisfaction, new values, that will relativize all that went before and will show that one's previous concerns were indeed "petty" or "small," as Xunzi puts it. Profit or personal benefit is not evil, on Xunzi's reckoning, but it is dramatically less important and valuable than the Confucian form of life marked by social justice, benevolent communal harmony, and the ritual and aesthetic culture that makes these possible. Confucian learning, ritual, and musical practice thus promise to transform our understanding and scheme of evaluation, our sensibilities, our capabilities and habits, and our tastes and desires. Xunzi's Confucianism is a comprehensive art of living well, shorn of the contemporary associations of that phrase with self-indulgent pleasure seeking.

On Xunzi's account, almost everything that makes life good grows on the basis of learning, considered broadly. In the same way that we might justifiably say that someone who never learned to read at all has missed all that comes from loving literature, and lived a stunted and deprived existence, Xunzi thinks that the culture of Confucian learning and practice opens up the most important human goods, without which human beings are barely distinguishable from animals.[38]

A critic could certainly persist, however, and question whether this has just moved the problem of "faking it" to a new level. Why could one not view the whole Confucian system as merely an excellent method for personal advancement, as many throughout premodern Chinese history undoubtedly did? Xunzi, like the circle of Confucius's followers who produced the *Analects*, is fully aware of this problem, and in the end he thinks there can be no foolproof certainty that going through the "wood-straightening" process of submitting to a Confucian teacher will automatically lead to true inner goodness. Only if that process genuinely opens new horizons of life, which kindle awareness of and taste for previously unimagined goods, will Xunzian virtue become possible. A story in one of the late chapters of the *Xunzi* probably put together by his students presents Confucius talking to a duke about how to choose worthy ministers. Confucius first suggests choosing those who follow the ancient ritual codes, including dress and demeanor, to which the duke responds: "Is anyone who dons court robes and court shoes and tucks an official tablet into his sash a worthy person?" Confucius replies that this is not necessarily so, and then he clearly relates the excellence of Confucians to the way they focus their *zhi* 志, "intentions" (i.e., direct their heart/mind) on the ways of the ancients and care little about food, which seems to stand in here for personal interests in pleasure and advancement. He concludes, "Even if there should be some who abide by these [ways of the ancients] and still do wrong, they would be few indeed, would they not?" To which the duke can only reply: "Well spoken!" (31/144/27–31/145/5).[39]

The idea seems to be that it would be extraordinarily difficult to pursue Confucian training long enough to become observably excellent at ritual without being changed inwardly. If one never came to delight in the Way, one's dedication would flag and one would simply give up, or one would betray continuing pettiness through "slips" of the tongue or body. (This suggests that corrupt, lazy, or irreducibly "petty" students would eventually by expelled from a Xunzian teaching group.) Xunzi thinks that the practices of learning, ritual, and music are themselves very potent, and when guided by a capable teacher and accompanied by other serious students, one will be "rubbed" daily by good influences that only heighten these exercises' effectiveness—but because the root issue is the transformation of the self-commanding human heart/mind, Xunzi must allow for all-too-explicable failures of cultivation, due to the intransigent pull of instinctive desires. Such failures may take the form of "apostates" from Confucianism who advocate some other Way, or the *su Ru* 俗儒, "vulgar Confucians," whom Xunzi describes with scorn as those who ape the manner of a true ritualist and spout pointless quotations from the *Odes*, all for the purpose of enriching themselves at the expense of others (8/32/17–21).

Might the aesthetic delights of Confucian ritual become a sort of idol, so that the adept who sees and enjoys his growing mastery of ritual could fall prey to a final sort of immoral seduction, caring only about the beauty of ritual performance and forgetting the value of justice and benevolence? Though Xunzi does not explicitly entertain this possibility, it seems clear that he could understand this as a case of obsession by ritual. And though ritual is a fine thing, essential to personal formation and the conduct of a good life, for Xunzi, it is not the only or uniquely supreme human value. Apparent "mastery" of ritual without a deeper understanding and love for the Way, manifest in the equal possession of the virtues of benevolence and justice, would be rigid and misguided (2/7/18–19). In other words, it would be merely counterfeit propriety.

To sum up, Xunzi thinks "artifice" is both necessary and saving because it allows us to learn, as embodied actors, how to live like sages. Such artifice is more like learning an art of performance than it is like pretending to be something one is not, because beginners cannot effectively pretend to be ritual masters, any more than I can pretend to be a concert violinist. Early-stage Confucians aspire to ritual mastery, but they only gradually approach such a state. In so doing, they are genuinely transformed, as long as they persevere with a heart/mind focused on the Way, because ritual for Xunzi is not something that one engages in occasionally but rather a style or mode of existence that permeates all our activities and social interactions. As one gradually grasps what is truly at stake, one will even *shen qi du* 慎其獨, "be watchful over oneself when alone," so that one never departs from ritual even for a moment (3/11/7).

One might say, then, that Xunzi allows for something like inspiration—and even demands it. Where Augustine solves the problem of sincerity and moral purpose decisively by insisting on the primacy of divine agency in enabling true human agency and virtue, Xunzi "solves" the problem with much less finality. For Xunzi, we come to experience a new sincerity, if we ever do, when we find ourselves to be changed by our ongoing practices of learning and performance, when the Way we sought in order to find safety and a more impressive and pleasant form of life turns out to be something altogether richer than we had initially imagined possible, and we find that the desires that once moved us have been joined by new desires, subtly changing the whole constellation of our emotional life, in gradually better accord with our increasingly sophisticated understanding of what life is about.

CHASTENED INTELLECTUALISM

As noted at the beginning of the previous section, perhaps the most arresting and significant commonality between Xunzi and Augustine is their shared stress on the need for study, learning, and reflection as the backbone of their respective programs of spiritual exercises. In this section, I argue that despite their very significant differences, this shared emphasis marks out their religious programs as variants of a common sort of ethical position, one that is quite powerful and attractive, which I call "chastened intellectualism." Such a position affirms the value of intellectual apprehension and reflection, but it questions the neutrality and absolute sovereignty of thinking.

Augustinian Christianity and Xunzian Confucianism are "intellectualist" because they think text-based learning and intellectual reflection on this learning are prerequisites for living well as human beings. (And although Augustine, as noted in chapter 6, recognizes and respects illiterate holy people as heroes of the faith, he thinks that even such people have had to learn a web of crucial truths, stories, and symbols from someone, via language, in order to be saved and live righteously.) The common elements here stretch across anthropology, personal formation, and ethics itself. Augustine and Xunzi both believe that human beings have much to learn, that we come into existence ignorant of the most important truths, so that we must learn at least these facts about our condition to live decent human lives, and much more to be capable of wise and just leadership in a community.

These views lead both Augustine and Xunzi to strongly emphasize education and to generate integrated accounts of its intellectual, moral, somatic, and aesthetic aspects. For both of them, proper understanding is essential to right living; progressively deeper wisdom is a concomitant of growth in virtue. Both think that the mastery of certain received texts helps us immensely toward these goals of understanding and virtue. These goals are not easy to achieve, but are needed nonetheless, because life is complicated and the best course of action is frequently unclear. This implies that some form of thoughtful deliberation, guided by traditional categories and modes of analysis assimilated through reflective practice, will often be required in order to choose and live well in a confusing and often disordered world.

This sort of position therefore judges ethical theory to be indispensable to living rightly. Ethical theory plays several important roles in this sort of vision, most notably description, guidance, and inspiration. It describes the ethically ideal form of life, and it justifies its superiority on the basis of an overarching account of both human beings and the world we inhabit. Theory explains how and why this better mode differs from typical human existence, and it at least in part guides us to this new form of life. Though the task of mastering ethical theory is therefore essential to living well, without teachers, practice, and various forms of transhuman aid, theory will be insufficient by itself to lead us to goodness. Guidance, then, includes not only the more familiar problem of sorting out which sorts of actions are typically forbidden or required by various moral considerations but also a full response to the problem of personal appropriation of a new way of life. And to the extent that it can make compelling its analysis and contrast of typical human life and the perfected, flourishing life, ethical theory is thereby inspiring to its students, although this sort of contrast is most often made vivid through more traditional rhetorical arts such as storytelling and drama.

Augustine and Xunzi are each, however, "chastened" in their intellectualism. This makes their positions more sophisticated and promising than the kind of modern philosophical ethics that concentrates only on theories of the right or the good, leaving the question of how to actually appropriate and live such theories to the side as a nonissue—a maneuver that seems to presuppose a naive voluntarism, as well as an unreasonably benign account of human nature.

There are several aspects to this chastening. The most obvious aspect is the highly critical accounts of elements of human "nature" offered by Augustine and Xunzi, as discussed in chapters 3 to 5. Although they differ in their analyses, the basic point is that good human agency is an achievement, something that does not come "naturally" (i.e., spontaneously and easily) to us in our current state, whether this is conceived as fallen from some earlier, better form of life or not. We need significant outside assistance in order to live well, often taking the form of sustained, benevolent action from other people who help us escape our initial, rather bestial, existence and move toward something better.

Neither Augustine nor Xunzi could ever be accused of propounding a philosophy of bootstrapping or rugged individualism in moral development. According to Augustine, we need not only to hear from others the "good news" about Jesus Christ and the way he provides for humans to return to God; we also need direct intervention from God to move us toward Him. Furthermore, the only means of gaining forgiveness from our sins and the potential for a new start in life is through baptism into the church, a human collective and institution that points beyond itself to its heavenly head, Christ, who has deputized his human members as parts of the *totus Christus* or "whole Christ." Reformation and eventual beatitude are only possible through participation in the common life of the church and the practices that its members share, including scriptural study and the Eucharist.

Even on Xunzi's account, however, individuals are not in a position to save themselves from their misguided desires purely on their own power. Only when frustrated and afraid will people look for guidance beyond their instinctive urges. They need a teacher and fellow students to make any ethical progress. But if they turn to the wrong teacher or are afflicted with bad friends, they are just as likely to exacerbate the problems generated by their bad impulses. According to Xunzi, the tradition of the Zhou sages, preserved and developed by Confucians, holds the unique keys to resolving the dilemmas of the human condition. Without exposure to this tradition, humans remain "vulgar," dangerous to each other and everything else.

Although both thinkers clearly believe human assistance is required for anyone to progress in righteousness, it might seem that only Augustine thinks we need transhuman aid as well, in the form of divine grace. Xunzi is commonly read as a "debunker" of traditional Chinese religious beliefs, and he is beloved by some moderns (including many in the People's Republic of China) as a protosecularist. Though a full consideration of the aptness of this judgment is beyond the scope of this chapter, I would argue that Xunzi does rely on the efficacy of at least one transhuman power, specifically the interactions of *qi* with and between human beings.[40] Particularly in his discussions of music, Xunzi attributes almost magical power to singing and listening to classical Zhou poetry (with musical accompaniment), which can evoke responses in us that draw out properly humane emotions and desires, contributing very quickly to our transformation. By causing us to take joy in the Way, music quite literally energizes us to follow it, building up our strength and commitment. Nevertheless, it must be noted that these effects are still predictable, almost technological, and are produced within human practices devised by past sages; such a picture is a far cry from Augustine's account of a transcendent God with perfect knowledge and an eternally unwavering will, who nevertheless enters time and supports and oversees every aspect of temporal existence.

A second, more subtle aspect of the chastening I am discussing is Augustine and Xunzi's shared tendency to combine what are often called "cognitive" and "affective" dimensions of human action. In Xunzi, we can see this in his accounts of the interpenetration of perception and interpretation with desire and emotion, as well as the very idea of "assent" to the Confucian Way, which implies both deliberative reflection and a motivating recognition of action-compelling factors in some complex situation. For Augustine, we can see such a conception quite clearly in his account of the integration of memory, understanding, and forms of will or love in the mental "word" that is the beginning of any human action.

This shared tendency to integrated models of thought, emotion, and action helps show why spiritual exercises might be necessary, and how they might work: It is naive to think that we can just decide one day, having been convinced by an argument, to transform our lives and change who we are. The interplay of settled conviction and emotional responsiveness, and thus of habitual inclinations to action, can only be changed by reforming all these elements in tandem. Conscious exercises seem perfectly suited to this task, because they require reflective commitment, however minimal, to a set of forms or rules for behavior that guide us in the repetitive practice of alternative behaviors, and they prescribe alternative emotions as well. As practice continues, and reflection on it deepens, intellectual commitment and inclinational tendencies will, at least ideally, gradually increase together. It is thus unsurprising that one of the central aims of learning, and indeed of all spiritual exercises for Xunzi and Augustine, is the reformation of human emotions and desires.

This sort of picture provides a corrective to Hadot's stress in his accounts of Hellenistic spiritual exercises on universalizing reason restraining the passions; I would argue that both Augustine and Xunzi have more subtle models of the human person, and especially the psyche. They both reject the thought that we could or should ever be free of our emotions, and they also reject the view that emotions are essentially disruptive of good judgment and action; instead, they insist on the crucial importance of emotions and their reformation within the moral life. Indeed, on such a view, "understanding" without the properly correlated dispositions and emotional responses to situations would be either immature or counterfeit. In any case, commitment to spiritual exercises clearly does not rest on a simplistic rationalism, even though reflection and intellectual assent do seem to be essential to them.

Their views are chastened in another sense. On Xunzi's and Augustine's accounts, true understanding can only be attained in the context of a shared practice aimed at assimilating the correct view of human life in community, and in the cosmos. This implies that commitment to an only partially understood path of personal formation is required for full understanding to ever become possible. Detachment is thus less a precondition to genuine knowledge than an obstacle to it. Both promise an eventual return to a comprehensive and tranquil perspective after sufficient personal development, although such a perspective is largely constituted by its passionate assent to the universal order, so it could hardly be considered detached or neutral. Put another way, Augustine and Xunzi insist on the need for faith in the efficacy of a chosen religious path, because deep and universal understanding arrives only late in life for a few, on Xunzi's account, or in the presence of God after the resurrection, for Augustine.

As a type of practice, chastened intellectualists therefore view personal formation as voluntary submission to an authoritative teaching. Submission to a position recognized as authoritative is critical, in order that the dictates a practitioner tries to assimilate will be seen as binding, standing in judgment over any and all impulses she or he might feel. Without this, the whole project of trying to attain a definite intellectual, emotional, and moral shape would be unjustified. Conscious assent to a regimen of formative practices differentiates spiritual exercises from the use of propaganda or coercive programs of "thought reform." However, spiritual exercises do make use of what could be called "conditioning," through the repetition of rituals, meditations, readings, and other practices designed to affect our habitual responses to situations, or our "inner discourse" of reflection and evaluation.

This need for voluntary, conscious assent underlines the extent to which this sort of position is still intellectualist, and it also helps qualify and flesh out the sort of subordination to authority each envisions. Without first-person experience of actual improvement—combined with an increasingly compelling understanding of the justification, nature, and goal of one's religious practices—spiritual exercises would cease to appeal to the considered, critical judgment of practitioners. Both Augustine and Xunzi clearly view questioning and debate as central to the process of the thoroughgoing education they propose, at least for those literate elites who pursue the ideal sort of personal formation.

Being a chastened intellectualist means that one views the task of learning not merely as gaining new information but primarily as the task of assimilating transformative knowledge into one's mode of existence. Looking specifically at Augustine's and Xunzi's accounts of learning, it is remarkable how similar they are. As noted, both insist on the authority of teachers over students, and of a unique and comprehensive set of classic texts, although exactly how they understand this varies. Both urge a rigorous program of assimilation of those texts, starting with as much memorization as possible, but accompanied by deepening practice in interpretation, which is essential to proper understanding. The final goal is correct understanding, which intrinsically includes "practical" understanding of how to implement traditional teachings in one's own life. For Augustine, true knowledge reaches the heart; for Xunzi, it permeates the whole body, including the heart/mind.

Subtle differences regarding the process of learning separate their views, however. For Augustine, as noted at the beginning of this chapter, the triune God is the ultimate authority. The Bible as the words of God directed to humans is thus also absolutely authoritative, with every word a significant source of meaning, and the whole serving as an inexhaustible storehouse of information about God's will; Augustine thus invests the Bible with an intrinsic authority that goes far beyond Xunzi's respect for the Confucian classics. Nevertheless, although some of the Bible is very simple and clear, expressed so that anyone can understand it and grasp the essentials of Christian teaching, significant portions are quite difficult to understand and challenge even the greatest exegetes. Here learned teachers play the role not only of conveying clear truths to a wider, often illiterate audience but also of explicating difficult passages and resolving apparent conflicts as they extend the range of shared understanding of the text.[41] Despite the importance of teachers, and the necessity of obeying their direction, particularly in matters of ethics and spiritual exercises, Augustine's anthropology places God at the root of each person's soul and mind. His doctrine of direct illumination adds an ambiguous element that at least potentially undercuts the authority of teachers and their interpretations.[42]

For Xunzi, though the classics are the authoritative teachings of the ancient sage-kings, as noted above, they are themselves so hard to understand that the authority of the teacher becomes paramount. Only the person-to-person transmission of wise insight and interpretive skill can lead to true learning. The inherent difficulty in understanding the classics also leads Xunzi to highlight the value of a good community of learners, without which it is impossible to reorient oneself fully to the Way. Though a shared community of learners is the normal state of affairs for Augustine, and is generally helpful, for example in monastic and congregational settings, unlike Xunzi he not only recognizes but also highly respects supposedly solitary ascetics who serve God by reforming themselves alone, often without access even to the Bible itself, but sufficiently illuminated and inflamed by God directly.

Xunzi, then, is confident in the power of human teachers to impart both basic knowledge and real wisdom, and he is also confident in the power of learners to absorb such teaching. For Augustine, however, though thinking that real learning can be and usually is occasioned by human teaching, the crucial agent is always Christ, the "interior teacher" illuminating our minds. For Augustine, human teaching can and often does fail, when the "seed" of divine *disciplina* is tossed on rocky ground or partially accepted and then choked by the weeds of concupiscence. Xunzi, by contrast, despite the infamous defection of two of his most famous students, remains convinced of the efficacy of Confucian communities of learning when they are led by a truly virtuous teacher.

This general way of looking at moral development can help resolve basic conundrums about character development generated by the abstract models of a person advocated by Harry Frankfurt and Charles Taylor, which were discussed in chapter 2. To review, Frankfurt proposes a picture in which persons are defined as beings who not only have desires in the normal sense ("first-order desires"), but also "second-order" desires about which first-order desires they want to have. Despite the real utility of this basic distinction to studies such as the present one, Frankfurt's larger position on agency is inherently flawed, as Gary Watson and more recently James Wetzel have argued.[43] Frankfurt, at least in the original formulation of his ideas, is caught between two unpalatable options: first, an infinite regress of competing desires about one's desires, which would vitiate the entire point of the move to have some desires trump others; or second, making "second-order volitions," that is, effective second-order desires, the result of a mysterious, ungrounded, and voluntaristic personal commitment to "identify" with some desires.

However, "identification" in this sense is hardly a simple matter, as both Xunzi and Augustine show us. To take an extreme example, it is radically insufficient for a repentant pedophile to simply "not identify" with his sexual desires for children; long-term work at personal reformation would be necessary to even have a chance to change such impulses, and even this appears frequently to be insufficient.[44] For almost everyone, a mental effort of "identification" with some of our desires rather than others will quite often be fruitless if those desires are even moderately strong; instead, some therapeutic strategy will be required for substantive change. Both Xunzi and

Augustine provide much fuller pictures of how, via spiritual exercises, the gradual development of reflective commitment, in tandem with the reform of emotions and desires, can make considered evaluations of the good one's central motivation—without seeming to make such judgments a matter of brute, sovereign choice.

Taylor's related view of "strong evaluations" as the constituents of "moral frameworks" which give structures and ends to human lives, has the virtue of reintroducing social life and history into Frankfurt's general picture. However, Taylor in the end underplays the power of reflection on inherited and/or unfamiliar moral frameworks, as well as the effectiveness of personal decision and intentional character formation, shrinking these to the "articulation" of the "moral sources" within the West that determine our moral horizons. Both Xunzi and Augustine make room for the recognition and pursuit of an integrated comprehensive good amid conflicts and disagreements. They also provide models that show how practice leads to the assimilation and deepening of such recognition, whether it be of the triune God or the human Way. And even though they disagree on precisely how assent or consent function, they provide subtle and believable accounts of both the difficulties and possibilities of personal decisions.

When considering the full range of both figures' programs of personal formation, we can see several basic differences separating their two versions of chastened intellectualism. As argued in the previous section, their subtly differing conceptions of the nature of moral requirements, when combined with their more obviously differing anthropologies, lead Xunzi to advocate an "outside-in" model of personal formation that supplements learning with pervasively developed practices of performance; and lead Augustine to advocate an "inside-out" model of moral change that centers on discursive and symbolic practices that aim to assimilate Christian truth by reshaping the "inner discourse" of our triune minds.

Leaving aside global theological judgments as either quixotic, if pursued from putatively neutral grounds, or unilluminating, if they simply reflect previous confessional commitments, what can a contemporary student of these ancient ethical vocabularies conclude about their strengths and weaknesses, with regard to the main themes of this study? Numerous arguments are possible here, but I concentrate on only a few, and even these can only be sketched rather than fully developed. Xunzi's account seems particularly capable of addressing the everyday struggle to domesticate and train our first-order desires, and thus better illuminates gradual progress in cultivating virtue; he also, for related reasons, articulates a fuller and more positive role for human embodiment in the moral and religious life. Augustine's ethical vocabulary, conversely, seems better suited to addressing our ongoing, second-order tendencies to rebel against the very idea of this sort of work on ourselves. He also provides a much better account of what can be called radical evil as a continuing human potential.

As argued in chapters 3 and 6, Xunzi's psychological model makes a rather sharp distinction between two kinds of motivation. The first and most basic type is desire, *yu* 欲, which he conceives as a spontaneous reaction of our relatively stable disposition, *qing* 情. The second is assent, *ke* 可, which is fundamentally a form of judgment about what is possible, permissible, or best in some situation. This two-source model makes it rather easy to envisage how second-order evaluations of our first-order desires could be brought to bear on those desires, at least insofar as Xunzi thinks assent always trumps desire when the two come into direct conflict, although we noted in chapter 5 some complications to this seemingly simple position that make it more believable. The crucial point here is that Xunzi's moral psychological vocabulary makes it easy to theorize the common human phenomenon of impulse control, simply by separating a controlling power from our spontaneous impulses. Moreover, the terminology of "dispositions" gives him a straightforward way to fill out the psychology of long-term character formation, which he describes metaphorically as "artifice," and the "accumulation" of many actions consciously assented to over time, which slowly "cut" and "pull" our dispositions into new and better forms. Like crooked wood that has been steamed and forced to become straight, after the process has been completed, our dispositions have taken on a new form, which means that we no longer desire the "petty" things we once craved; instead, we genuinely delight in good actions and find them as satisfying as a fine meal.[45] "Virtue" in the fullest sense, for Xunzi, would then seem to imply both a wise grasp of the *Dao* considered as a comprehensive "scale" for evaluating possible actions, which allows the good Confucian to deliberate well, and also as a refashioned set of dispositions, both achieved through persistent Confucian practice of study, ritual, and music.

Part of what makes this seem achievable for Xunzi is the nature, and not just the form, of the moral demands he thinks are imperative. Xunzi thinks it is impossible for anyone to extirpate basic desires for food, sex, safety, rest, and respect, so the ethical challenge is to create a form of life that can satisfy everyone's desires in a beautiful, harmonious, and just way—this grand cultural achievement is the *Dao* itself, the artful creation of past sages who have properly discerned the best way to order human life. It is no small matter that Augustine thinks the best Christian life is celibate, with very restricted food intake, and this leads him to experience the continuing presence of sexual desire and hunger in the way he does. Xunzi never even entertains celibacy as a desirable option, let alone a possibility, and he makes lavish feasting a central religious ritual (cf., of course, the Eucharistic "meal" of small amounts of bread and wine). As argued previously, Xunzi understands ritual as to some extent a restraint, but just as much it is a way of "nourishing" and "adorning" our desires so that they take on the proper forms—forms that lead to social harmony rather than destructive competition and mutual predation. The degree of change to our dispositions that Xunzi aims for is considerably less radical than Augustine's "crucifixion" of our carnal loves, and so his expectation of the possibility of success in this endeavor, at least for some, seems achievable.

Xunzi thus possesses a relatively benign characterization of the nature of spontaneous human desires as blind and ignorantly selfish, not to be trusted to guide the self alone, but still aiming at basic human goods in a way that needs to be reshaped and ordered but not razed and recreated. This conception relates rather directly to his anthropology, which conceives of us as our bodies in their entirety. He thinks the *xin* 心, "heart/mind," is the ruler of the self and needs to be well trained to fulfill this function properly, but he never imagines that there might be some locus of the self that is separable from the body. In other words, he does not identify with a soul, let alone an immortal soul, that vivifies the body and is categorically superior to it, in the way Augustine does, like almost everyone in the ancient Mediterranean world. Not surprisingly, then, the role of embodiment in full ethical personhood for Xunzi is rather different than it is for Augustine. Although Augustine's most considered image of the soul–body relation is of a marriage, understood of course in a late antique Roman way as a relationship of stark inequality that ought to be characterized by strict obedience of lower to higher, he can also imagine our bodies as an "unruly mount" that is being ridden against its will toward our true goal, beatitude. Augustine's sense of the body as at least partly "other" to ourselves, as something that needs to be ruled because it can never be trusted, is considerably more extreme, and even self-alienating, than Xunzi's views.[46] For Xunzi, the body should be beautifully adorned in appropriate clothing, and it should also be trained to become an expressive medium almost equal to our own voice, through the performative "language" of Confucian ritual, which allows us to express our concern for each other in every daily interaction, no matter how minor. Bodily skill is essential to ethical virtue, for Xunzi.

This may all have a surprising whiff of Apollonian confidence, at least from an Augustinian point of view. Xunzi's account of steady work to reform oneself seems to presume both the desirability and the possibility of achieving transparent self-understanding, so that we can work steadily on our weak points to slowly but surely whittle them away. In particular, Xunzi's vocabulary and ethical theory seem relatively limited in their resources for articulating ongoing resistance to self-formation as anything other than frustrated first-order desire. At best, Xunzi can speak about using the wrong ethical categories to guide our deliberations, as for instance the way "petty people" "see things only in terms of personal benefit" (4/15/14). This would be one very common form of "obsession" with one consideration to the detriment of many others that form part of the Way. But these sources of vicious behavior are not cases of internal resistance to self-formation so much as misguided self-formation, which are so dangerous precisely because of our long-term capacities to reshape ourselves.

In comparison with this, Augustine's starkly antagonistic account of good and evil, as manifest in what I called above his "spiritual geography" of desire and intention, helps him to articulate resistance to personal formation as something more fundamental and deep within human beings. Even more important, as argued earlier in this chapter, his structurally unified account of the *mens* or mind makes the contest between divergent desires, both first- and second-order, a real case of self-division, of vacillation, and even personal incoherence as competing inner discourses swirl within us, debating or talking past each other. What is truly striking in Augustine's account, in comparison with Xunzi's, is how this incoherence can be mitigated with divine aid but not finally resolved until the "complete cure" that comes with resurrection. Self-knowledge, like the knowledge of God, remains elusive and imperfect for human beings in this life, according to Augustine; God always knows us better than we know ourselves.

Because he thinks self-preference, and the grasping, covetous desires it spawns, remain as active potentials within our minds, whispering tempting inner words that continence must vigilantly reject, Augustine is also much more capable than Xunzi of articulating a robust account of corruption and self-deception. Augustine's vocabulary makes it easy to speak about how rebellion against the good can start in seemingly innocuous ways. Loving a friend, seeking to govern justly as a public official, even striving for virtue can also serve as projects of human arrogance instead of divine service, and inward confusion about what I really intend can cover these beginnings of sin all too effectively.

Augustine thus views the challenge of personal formation as more daunting than even Xunzi; indeed, Augustine views it as completely unmanageable were it not for God's merciful love guiding us back to goodness. The success of the venture to live righteously remains unsettled throughout this life for Augustine; unless God grants us the grace to persevere to the end, we will not succeed. We simply do not know what tests we might be ready to pass, on Augustine's account, although we can trust that with God all things are possible. In contrast to this, Xunzi appears to believe that even before sagehood, which forms the distant summit of personal formation in any case, noble men can be sure of their own commitment to the Way. Inward struggles of a sort continue for such men, but these are much less grievous than those that can afflict the Augustinian believer, who continues to harbor at least occasional sinful doubts about the entire project of submitting to God.

This suggests that, on an Augustinian account, genuine evil remains a "live option" for everyone, even the holiest, who retain the possibility of defecting from God throughout earthly existence. Though Xunzi's understanding of human propensities for thoughtless self-gratification, avaricious personal aggrandizement, and the obsessive pursuit of a merely partial good together provide an account of how some humans commit truly horrible crimes, Augustine's account goes further, in several insightful ways. It rules out thinking of one's own group or even self as purely good, untainted by sin, and instead instructs us to searchingly question our own motives and plans to test their good faith and loving intentions. Falsely localizing evil in some other social group seems to be a precondition for true atrocities, such as genocide; but Augustine's anthropology and theology stop this move decisively, while giving as well an explanation for why it tempts us (we love to see ourselves in the best possible light, even if this is blatant self-deception). Moreover, his understanding of the continuing frailty and weakness of the seemingly law-abiding and even the genuinely virtuous suggests that his understanding of sin can account very well for the shocking but "banal" evils of the twentieth century, perpetrated in significant part by bureaucrats and functionaries who loved their families and home communities. Last, Augustine argues powerfully that the human lust for power manifests itself in a perverse imitation of divine omnipotence, which drives us to assert ourselves precisely through the manipulation and destruction of other things and people. This incisive charge provides a much stronger account of the sometimes baffling cruelty we routinely visit upon each other than is possible to construct out of Xunzian worries about bad impulses, distracting desire, and misguided self-formation.[47]

Although in certain respects it might be possible to combine the insights of both these figures while avoiding any respective difficulties—for example, by importing some of Augustine's points about the nature and dangerousness of the human will to power into a Xunzian ethical position—in other respects it is not clear how such a synthesis could ever be achieved. Beyond their obvious and fundamental disagreements over metaphysics, sacred history, and sacred texts, one basic problem of ethical theory is that Xunzi's separation of desire from assent proves powerful when addressing issues of the gradual formation of character through sustained practice but weak when trying to address deep self-division of the sort that Augustine charts. Conversely, Augustine's picture of a structurally unified but nevertheless disintegrated *mens*, which remains to some extent mysterious to itself, provides an excellent way of articulating the self's continuing resistance to its own highest aspirations. (This is only furthered by Augustine's contention that consent cannot overrule our strongest loves, unless we are defecting from God's providential order through sin.) But this same picture makes it relatively more difficult for Augustine than Xunzi to account for the gradual development of virtue over time. It appears that there is no easy way to harmonize these two types of moral psychological pictures.[48]

A more intriguing and less clear-cut challenge would be presented by an effort to integrate a Xunzian account of the positive role of embodiment, concerning both typical "desires of the flesh" and embodied ritual action as an expressive medium for human relations, into an Augustinian Christianity. Could performance practices as an "outside-in" approach to formation supplement Augustine's more familiar symbolic and discursive spiritual exercises? I pursue such speculations no further here, but instead turn in the final chapter to the broader issues they raise concerning interpretation, evaluation, and cross-traditional learning.

NOTES

1. On the ways in which Augustine does and does not engage in such "leveling" of believers, see Clark 2003.

2. Augustine does of course make such distinctions, e.g., between married and celibate, and clerical and lay Christians. He believes these differences are real and important but nonetheless tempt our tendencies to pride.

3. The classic studies of this theme in Augustine are Burnaby 1947 and O'Donovan 1980.

4. The term "mimetic desire" comes from Girard 1977, 145–49, and is applied fruitfully to Augustine in the sense I intend by Dodaro 2004, 68–69.

5. For an egregious example, see again Dubs 1956, 218. For a serious attempt to address concerns of some modern despisers of Augustine, and in the process to articulate an "Augustinian liberalism," see Gregory, n.d.

6. I address some complications to this picture in the final section of this chapter.

7. Note also the revealing discussion of the priority of wise people to good *fa* 法, "models" and "standards," which cannot implement themselves, and which are both created and "corrected" by those who possess an enlightened understanding of the *Dao* that lies behind all such models (12/57/1–7). See Hutton 2001, 82ff., for discussion.

8. Yearley 1990, 13. For brief but insightful discussion of this generalized conception, see Yearley 1990, 6–23, 95–111.

9. On this point with regard to Xunzi, see Schofer 2000 [1993].

10. For discussion of general issues, and of the interrelations of the last three virtues in particular, see Hutton 2001.

11. Augustine's *On Continence* appears to have been written during the Pelagian controversy, sometime around 418–20 CE. See Kearney 1999, 189, for discussion.

12. This suggests that although Augustine conceives of continence as a preservative virtue that restrains us from doing evil, in contrast to inclinational virtues like justice that positively move us to good acts (*cont.* 7.17), it functions on the basis of a powerful inclination toward goodness implanted within us. For brief discussion of the inclinational/preservative distinction, along with fuller bibliography, see Yearley 1990, 13–14, 16, 207 n. 13.

13. For insightful analysis, see Babcock 1994. The only flaw in Babcock's excellent discussion is his apparent reading of continence as in effect infallible, because our greater desire for righteousness overwhelms our lesser desire for sin, so that under grace "our spirits are fixed in the grace and love of God" and we "cease to sin" (1994, 188). But Augustine explicitly rejects the possibility of sinlessness throughout the Pelagian controversy; even the best Christians continue to sin daily (e.g., *cont.* 5.12–13, 8.20, 14.31).

14. On this, note especially Schlabach 1998.

15. Translations adapted from Kearney 1999, 215.

16. On Xunzi's epistemology see Hutton 2001.

17. Both of these issues are discussed in chapter 6.

18. This leaves to the side the dangers of *bi* 蔽, "obsession," which as discussed in chapter 5 can derail even passionate seekers of what is truly good by trapping them within a merely partial awareness of the Way—one that still misguides even though it is partly correct. Obsession does not really imply conflict within the self, but a lack of conflict where it should be present. One other important counterexample is the case of self-deceived counterfeit "Confucians," whom Xunzi labels *su Ru* 俗儒, "vulgar Confucians." Such people follow *miu* 繆, "mistaken" or more likely "fake," techniques and their learning is *za* 雜, "mixed up." Xunzi presents them as thoroughly corrupt and deeply deluded (8/32/17–21). This would seem to be, however, a rather extreme and even simple case of hypocrisy and corruption, rather than a more interesting case of a seemingly earnest misunderstanding of Confucianism leading to gross evil in the name of the good.

19. Babcock 1994, 194. For textual basis see, e.g., *conf.* 8.11.27.

20. See Babcock 1994, 190, for insightful discussion of this passage.

21. There are many rich issues regarding Augustine's use of Paul as an exemplar that I cannot pursue here. Two helpful recent discussions are Dodaro 2004, 183–95, and Martin 2001.

22. Slingerland 2003b, 3–19, 217–64.

23. A modern account of happiness as "flow" that bears intriguing similarities to this vision is Csikszentmihalyi 1990. Yearley 1996b gives a helpful general discussion of this sort of skill-mastery.

24. Translation adapted from Slingerland 2003a.

25. As Augustine writes: "You know, then, that the virtues are to be distinguished from the vices, not by the duties [performed], but by their ends. A duty is what one ought to do, but an end is that on account of which one ought to do it. Therefore, when persons do some action in which they seem not to sin, if they do not do it on account of that for which they ought to do it, they are found to be guilty of sinning" (*c. Jul.* 4.21). Translation adapted from Teske 1998, 393.

26. For Xunzi's "'success' conception of the virtues" see Hutton 2001, 180. (Note also his illuminating general discussion of the interrelation of benevolence, ritual propriety, and justice in Xunzi on pp. 168–79, from which I draw here). Hutton takes this term from Irwin 1988.

27. Foucault 1985, 6.

28. I draw these terms and the general sort of contrast from Kline 1998, 51–52, who uses them to contrast Mencius and Xunzi. Note also Slingerland's (2003b, 12ff. and passim) developed contrast between self-cultivation "internalism" and "externalism." As Slingerland rightly notes (2003b, 291 n. 32), this contrast is not to be confused with current philosophical debates over motivational and epistemological internalism and externalism. The danger of such general slogans is that they can run together certain topics that can and should be kept distinct, specifically: (1) having or lacking various internal moral resources; (2) whether, when, and why effort or striving may be required in the moral life; and (3) various approaches to spiritual exercises. Here I am using the terms "inside-out" and "outside-in" only to refer to two differing strategies of personal formation, exemplified by Augustine and Xunzi, that support different sorts of spiritual exercises, as detailed in the main text.

29. Dodaro 2004, 124, and 115–81 generally.

30. On the background to Augustine's treatment, see Ramsey 1999, 556.

31. For a thoughtful and perceptive essay that draws from Stoicism and attends to similar issues, framed in terms of the relation of good manners to good morals, see Sherman 2005. It is no accident that Sherman focuses on the military, one of the few strongly ritualized cultural realms in the United States. For fascinating depictions of U.S. Marine Corps boot camp as a carefully structured setting for the rapid, purposeful transformation of the hearts, minds, and bodies of raw recruits, see Ricks 1997 (for a more objective, analytical account) and Schaeffer and Schaeffer 2002 (for an evocative subjective account).

32. The distinction between goods internal and external to a practice comes from MacIntyre 1984, 187–91.

33. Hutton 2001, 221, makes this point nicely.

34. See Xunzi's contrast between the comprehensive skill of a noble man as political leader and *Dao* follower with that of various artisans with more specialized sorts of expertise (21/104/16–21/105/3). On this issue, see Kupperman 1968, 181.

35. Aristotle, *Nicomachean Ethics* 1105a16–1105b20. For insightful discussion, see Irwin 1999a, 22, 193, 195–96, who notes the logical parallel to the problem about how one could learn something one did not already know in Plato, *Meno* 80a–e. Pace Slingerland 2003b, 259–64, Aristotle thinks he has resolved the issues regarding the cultivation of virtue by distinguishing between outward form, intention, and stable

"state" or virtuous disposition. Xunzi too is much more successful in resolving these apparent difficulties than Slingerland allows.

36. These ideas are hardly original; on these issues, I have learned most from conversation with Jack Kline. For other accounts that make similar points, see, e.g., Lai 2003; Kline 1998; Ivanhoe 2000a, 6–7, 29–37; and Kupperman 1968, 2002.

37. On the relation of practices and virtue, see MacIntyre 1984, 181–203.

38. Counterarguments could certainly be provided to the literacy example, but note that it would be genuinely hard to imagine someone living without storytelling or significant shared human culture as living a good human life.

39. I owe this reference to Hutton 2001, 222, and adapt his translation.

40. Although other Confucians, such as Mencius, make relatively more of the doctrine of Heaven-given *ming* 命, "fate" or "destiny," it is less significant in Xunzi's thought.

41. This sketch skips over some very complicated issues in Augustine regarding the authority of Catholic Church officials over the explication of scripture and articulation of doctrine. Even these knotty topics are but a subset of the larger controversies over how best to read Augustine's attempts to flesh out the relation between the sovereignty of God with various sorts of human authorities. I hope to pursue all of these issues in future work, but cannot do justice to them here.

42. Later Christian history bears this out, particularly in the development of pietist and other sorts of "inner light" Protestant sects in the wake of the Reformation. For a classic survey that treats this theme extensively and well, see Troeltsch 1992.

43. Wetzel 1992, 222–35; Watson 1975. Note also Frankfurt 1999 for his more recent work on these issues.

44. Bergner 2005.

45. This is somewhat inexact. For Xunzi, the noble man no longer desires certain basic goods such as food or social acclaim in a petty way, but only as properly understood parts of the *Dao*.

46. Of course, Augustine is relatively positive regarding the body when judged in his own context, as many commentators have remarked, and he is notable in his insistence that the body will be fully redeemed at the resurrection, so that eternal life will be embodied, in some mysterious and flawless way. None of this, however, vitiates the comparison with Xunzi regarding our experience of the body in this life.

47. For a fine recent exploration of these and related themes, see Mathewes 2001. For a parallel argument comparing Augustine with the early Confucian Mencius, see Van Norden 2003a.

48. The challenging test case to this claim would be someone like Aquinas, who develops a faculty psychology much more complex than Xunzi's separation of assent from desire, yet still wishes to save central Augustinian insights.

CHAPTER NINE

Understanding and Neighborliness

✦

It should be clear by now that I am practicing a form of intellectual self-restraint in these pages, one with roots in the phenomenological tradition of religious studies.[1] By deferring global judgments of truth or superiority in favor of one or the other figure (although not eschewing specific criticisms and evaluative choices), I have built up detailed accounts of Xunzi's and Augustine's views of personal formation, articulated in relation to each other and to some modern ethical theory. The interpretations offered suggest that despite both their broad apparent similarities regarding the ethical dangers of human nature and the need for spiritual exercises, and their deep religious differences concerning the best way to live (following Christ or the *Dao*), they each provide accounts of personal formation that are powerful and suggestive, although with notable weaknesses as well as strengths.

One rhetorical and philosophical challenge of comparative works of this sort is to balance competing needs for generality and specificity, in both audience and treatment. In this final chapter, I pull back from the careful analysis of our subjects' prescriptions to address three broader implications of the current study. First, I argue that if any sort of chastened intellectualist view of human beings is correct, then in conditions of religious diversity we will need for the foreseeable future to operate with two-level theories of ethics and politics. Second, regarding "method" in religious ethics, I explore how the need for a certain sort of holism in interpretation complicates but does not ultimately undermine efforts at "retrieval" in studies of ancient ethics. And third, I outline a conception of "global neighborliness" as a regulative ideal for comparative studies.

THE VARIETIES OF MORAL AGENCY

I argued in the last chapter that Augustine and Xunzi both exemplify a laudable general view of human moral psychology, which I called "chastened intellectualism." Such a view suggests that "human nature," in its various registers as a family of related concerns, is sufficiently flawed that we humans are not spontaneously ethical in any full-bodied sense. Furthermore, on this sort of view, personal change is not easy and therefore not trivial. Human beings need significant education and formation to become moral, and they need to willingly assent to such formation if it is to be effective. Such assent is necessary for the requisite level of striving, and it will only be possible in the pursuit of a compelling vision of human existence.

All this implies that most people need the sort of fully worked out programs of character development provided by religious or quasi-religious traditions in order to cultivate dependable virtue, because we cannot simply "identify" with some of our desires or choose some new form of life, without real strain and likely failure. Trusted practices, articulate theories and justifications, socially recognized authorities, aesthetic and literary traditions, and communal and institutional support, especially when integrated together, all increase the possibility of successfully practicing spiritual exercises.

In contrast, despite the undeniable value of the basic distinctions drawn by Frankfurt and Taylor, their general theories of personhood and agency are so abstract and thin that they are finally inert and unhelpful as actual guides to self-formation. Of course, this was hardly their intent in producing such accounts, but it is still worthwhile to reflect on the gap between what can be compellingly argued for on such strictly limited general premises and the richness and complexity in fully realized ways of life.

Chastened intellectualism as I have articulated it here is in the end no different, except that it points beyond itself as a sort of general summary to the necessity of more fully specified versions of the approach (as, to be fair, does Taylor). But Taylor still seeks to provide an overarching synthesis of the "moral horizons" or "sources" of the West, whereas my view does not require the preexistence of any such shared horizon.

It makes a great deal of difference whether one regards oneself as a sick patient being healed of sinfulness by Christ, so that one might love God and neighbor rightly and eventually complete one's journey to beatitude after death, or a person aspiring to nobility by following the sagacious tradition of the Confucian Way, in hopes of properly harmonizing and ordering the human community and taking our appropriate place in the larger ecology of the cosmos. Although I think it is not outlandish to speak of these as varieties of a common sort of view, the differences in specific understandings, expectations, practices, and overall flavor or style are profound.

Several things follow from the distance between the relatively vague generalities of thin views aiming for universality and the precise but controversial accounts propounded by individual thinkers in particular traditions and contexts. First, agreement on general ideas shared in common can conceal disagreements just as it reveals similarities. Second, the spiritual exercises that are necessary on a chastened intellectualist view cannot be vague if they are to be effective; one will be praying to God for forgiveness or singing the hymns of Zhou, but not merely sitting around wishing for a stronger and better character. This would lead to a third point, that in order to be a chastened intellectualist, one would need to be more than that as well, whether a Christian, a Confucian, or something else. This something else could include a systematic synthesis of different religious and/or philosophical elements; I will return to this point below.

Both Xunzi and Augustine recognized a variety of competitors for people's allegiance, a variety of ways to be human, but they were each confident that they had found the one uniquely correct synthetic and comprehensive path. This chapter is not the place to rehearse current debates within the comparative philosophy of religions, nor to provide my views on the familiar trio of "exclusivism," "inclusivism," and "pluralism" in interreligious understanding. Probably in part because of its colonialist past and current global hegemony, the modern West has simultaneously developed traditions of attentive and empathetic attention to other religions and philosophical systems. Studies in these traditions, as well as recent immigration policies that have brought unprecedented religious heterogeneity to the United States, among other places, have made it much more difficult to conclude that any particular tradition is the unique path to virtue, leaving aside how such goodness relates to salvation, enlightenment, or other supranormal religious goals. On the contrary, pace both Augustine and Xunzi, it seems hard to deny that multiple traditions provide sufficient resources for cultivating recognizable moral virtue.[2]

It would thus seem inevitable that we are stuck for the foreseeable future with relatively messy two-level approaches to ethics and politics: On the one hand, we all need general but vague views upon which most can agree in order to facilitate political and diplomatic relationships. But on the other hand, we also need to nurture and follow more specific traditions of personal development in order to (1) follow with integrity our considered conclusions about ultimate value; and (2) have the rich philosophical, metaphorical, ritual, and artistic resources for personal formation that particular, historically extended traditions provide (even as this subjects us to the weaknesses, failings, and internal struggles of such traditions as they try to survive and improve).

Even restricting ourselves to the two cases studied here, simply because of the obvious disagreements between Xunzi and Augustine over metaphysics, history, and the character of the ultimate authorities they recognize, it would be impossible to create a supervocabulary of moral agency that would somehow harmonize their disparate ways of life. A fortiori, no one could create a "moral Esperanto" that could successfully articulate everything of moral (and cultural?) significance in one all-purpose vocabulary, and thereby supercede various religious and quasi-religious vocabularies for human life.[3]

What can be created are generalized vocabularies that address problems of coexistence amid social diversity. For example, the vocabulary of "human rights" has considerable utility in the contemporary world, because it makes it possible to articulate basic claims for justice to people around the world, despite our divergent specific moral vocabularies. Such claims are certainly not the whole of ethics, but they are still valuable. To live well as a human being requires being a citizen of a particular commonwealth, a rationally committed adherent of particular complex and conflicted traditions. Today, however, it also requires a tolerance for coalitions built around practical goals of justice that cannot be justified in the same way to everyone who values such goals. Even the most abstract lists of general goods in life will be hard to nail down to everyone's satisfaction, but this can no longer be surprising or even upsetting.[4]

"SPOILING THE EGYPTIANS": HOLISM, INTERPRETATION, AND THEFT

According to Augustine, all truth belongs to the Lord, wherever it is found, even in "pagan" traditions such as Stoicism and Platonism. Thus Christians should not hesitate to "spoil the Egyptians" as they leave the pagan world behind, taking whatever is good for Christian use, but being sure to "ceaselessly ponder" Paul's dictum that "knowledge puffs up, but love builds up" (*doc. Chr.* 2.18.28, 2.40.60–2.41.61).[5] Xunzi, too, did not hesitate to take good ideas from a variety of sources as he developed his understanding of Confucianism, as I have argued elsewhere.[6]

Contemporary debates about this sort of "borrowing" or "stealing" from sources outside one's primary tradition are usually cast in terms of "bricolage."[7] Though this word may unfortunately connote a haphazard, unsystematic, and merely pragmatic process of borrowing, the basic issues involved are both deep and old, as Augustine's statements above attest. Put simply, how might we best understand some unfamiliar ethical vocabulary, and how might we best learn something genuinely helpful from such study? I obviously cannot here give a full account of hermeneutics, nor a general theory of theory creation with a set of criteria to distinguish better from worse attempts. Instead, I address a particularly relevant and interesting claim in one of the most successful recent works of comparative ethics, Lee Yearley's *Mencius and Aquinas*.

In this book, Yearley argues for distinctions among what he (building on the work of the anthropologist Robin Horton) calls primary, practical, and secondary theory. On Yearley's account, primary theory concerns everyday empirical and technical matters and is widely shared across cultures; secondary theory concerns peculiar and distressing events, makes recourse to unobservable entities, and diverges strongly across cultures; and practical theory concerns how to live and what to do, and is partially shared across cultures. He suggests that partially overlapping practical theories are especially promising objects for comparison, and he uses this tripartite division to explain why he finds "real and textured resemblances" between Mencius's and Aquinas's conceptions of virtue, especially courage, while noting only "thin resemblances" and stark differences in other areas of their thought.[8]

Although this contention about fruitful comparison is borne out to some degree in the current study, I hope I have shown that it is not a waste of time to compare elements of "secondary theory." More important, I think my accounts of Xunzi and Augustine show that the strategy of isolating different "levels" of theory in order to compare only one of them is fraught with difficulty, because in most sophisticated thinkers "primary," "practical," and "secondary" concerns and ideas mix together into a generally coherent whole.[9] One cannot talk about their views of spiritual exercises without talking about their views of human nature and cosmology. Indeed, all three of these areas bleed across the boundaries of Yearley's schema.

More specifically, I disagree that secondary theory "may hinder" the analysis of human flourishing offered by sophisticated religious thinkers such as Xunzi and Augustine (as well as Mencius and Aquinas); on the contrary, such theories are essential and constitutive of that analysis.[10] In chapter 2 of the present study, I argued for a "weak holism" that views ethical "vocabularies" as generally integrated human constructions that enable particular forms of social and individual life. As we have seen in the cases of Xunzi and Augustine, their religious vocabularies as presented here reveal interrelated conceptions of metaphysics, history, recognized authorities, anthropology, general moral theory, and both theory and practices of personal reformation. Attempting to isolate the last three apparently "practical" considerations from the first three would eviscerate both figures' accounts of human life, robbing them in particular of those considerations that justify the character of the spiritual exercises they recommend.

More deeply, several of these interrelated realms seem to resist classification into primary, practical, and secondary. Xunzi and especially Augustine think that history, which would seem to be an example of primary theory, cannot be comprehended without reference to proper conceptions of metaphysics, anthropology, and what is truly authoritative. Holy texts, institutions, traditions, and people—about which our figures would disagree so absolutely—are certainly as present and obvious as the objects of primary theory, shape human life in a practical way, and yet are decisively shaped by secondary theory. Perhaps most important, both their anthropologies rely very strongly on secondary theory. This is particularly obvious with Augustine, who refers constantly in his analysis of human beings to grace, imaging God, and the difference between various positions in the divine metaphysical hierarchy, among other "secondary" topics. Even the metaphysically more austere Xunzi relies on notions of *qi* 氣, *li* 理, ("pattern"), and the distinction between the "heavenly" and the "human" to explicate his anthropology. All this suggests that merely talking about the "ethics" of ancient thinkers is descriptively misleading if done in abstraction from the rest of their views. It also suggests that it may be impossible to engage some important aspects of practical theory, such as spiritual exercises, without simultaneously addressing "secondary" theoretical conceptions of various sorts.

We cannot then hope to understand or adequately represent Xunzi's or Augustine's "practical" theories in isolation from their "secondary" theories. This stance complicates efforts to "retrieve" past practices, ideas, and theories, by showing how they interrelate with numerous elements of their lived context. Shorn of these mutual supports and dependencies, particular bits and pieces may be unpersuasive and apparently useless. However, a broadly based and subtle reading that does not slight the connections between different aspects of a thinker's views may also show which parts of a broader "system" of living do and do not depend on others, and in what ways. This charting of logical dependencies gives an opening, at least, to borrowing—and in any case, creative recasting is always possible in principle, even if one cannot imagine exactly how it might be done in advance.[11]

This holistic approach to ethico-religious vocabularies even helps explain why such transplantation works so frequently in practice: Intercultural borrowing is often successful because bringing practices and theories into "reflective equilibrium" is always a creative production, requiring serious work and rigorous discipline, whether one is following ancient practices from precursors of one's own group or taking "spoils" from someone else.[12] Successful borrowing can happen, even in unlikely places, because the disciplined work required is at least partially motivated by the formative practices themselves, which precisely in their difficulty call out for explanation and justification, and in their experienced effectiveness both inspire and strengthen practitioners to pursue such accounts. Simply as a matter of religious history, practices in particular seem able at times to float free of old justifications and to inspire new justifications in whatever vocabulary presents itself, if they are perceived to be effective. Models of personhood and "subjection" often seem to guide the incorporation of details, but perhaps even these could be borrowed or at least amended, once their distinctiveness is articulated in relation to other possibilities.

Of course, both Xunzi and Augustine would be deeply suspicious of beginners attempting to fashion their own religious way out of whatever techniques or ideas they might come across, given their analyses of the debilities of human nature. They felt licensed to engage in such borrowing only to the extent that they were confident they had grasped the essential elements, and a good bit of the details, of preexisting paths they judged to be superior to all other possibilities. They understood themselves to be engaged in the systematic elaboration of the truth, the outlines of which were already well in hand, allowing modest corrections to resolve particular difficulties. They engaged, in other words, in careful, systematic synthesis. The extent to which one sanctions this sort of experimentation, and by whom, will hinge largely on one's sense of the requirements of sufficient personal formation.

More generally speaking, even if one cannot honestly embrace an alien tradition via conversion, one can amend one's own tradition in small or large ways in response to the other tradition's strengths. Even the attempt to be scrupulously faithful to a complex historical tradition involves numerous evaluative choices in matters that are frequently difficult to grasp with confidence. This sort of elaboration and adjustment of one's own commitments as they continue to deepen seems to be essential to the process of learning that chastened intellectualists like Xunzi and Augustine advocate. Whatever the "sources" one might come across, if they suggest valuable new possibilities or promise resolutions to old difficulties, how could one refrain from making use of them? The borrowing involved might concern particular details of various issues, or it might even concern broader issues of overall architecture and approach—exactly what will prove helpful seems not to be limited necessarily to the realm of the "practical," in Yearley's sense, although he is surely right to suggest that concerns with how to live well as human beings recur in numerous cultures, promising ample material, at least, for engagement.

The process of comparison itself, as Yearley suggests, can also be helpful in this regard, by showing the distinctiveness and complexity of previously assumed ideas such as "human nature" and "the will," and also expanding the scope of other subjects, such as "spiritual exercises," by examining previously ignored conceptions and adjusting general accounts accordingly. Sorting the different and indeed competing strands in various accounts of "human nature" provides a new metric for analyzing the seemingly familiar accounts of both Augustine and Xunzi, as well as contemporary accounts that advocate or denounce versions of such an idea. Working out which aspects of the complex family of concerns amalgamated in the idea of the "will" are unique to the post-Augustinian West, and which are treated, in varying degrees of depth, in an unrelated tradition like classical Confucianism, helps us to understand the distinctiveness of each tradition without succumbing to simplistic "East versus West" dichotomies.

Regarding spiritual exercises, rather than dismissing non-western exercises as insufficiently cognitive,[13] attending carefully to Xunzi has helped expand the range of the idea beyond previous discussions focused on the Hellenistic world. For example, Hadot's classification of spiritual exercises into four types (disciplines of attention, meditations, other intellectual exercises, and active exercises intended to create habits) seems to presume a split between intellectual contemplation, to be governed by the first three, clearly superior sorts of exercises, and practical action, where habits of activity would be valuable as a sort of supplement. Xunzi recognizes no such distinction, and his exercises are tuned directly to his anthropological analysis of human beings as bodies ruled internally by the *xin* 心, or "heart/mind." His emphasis on practices of communal performance such as ritual and music is far from the typical range of discussions in the ancient Mediterranean world.

Augustine's emphasis on inward self-scrutiny, combined with his strong interest in discursive and symbolic practices designed to reshape our "inner discourse" of ongoing interpretation and deliberation, seems to put him squarely within the predominantly cognitive therapeutic traditions of the West, which stretch from the ancient philosophical schools and early Christian monastic movements to the various forms of "talking cure" practiced in contemporary psychotherapy. And yet his distinctive psychology, proposing a structurally unified mind involving memory, understanding, and *voluntas*, which is nevertheless divided in its ongoing stream of inner "words," along with his overarching account of the Christian life, changes the context and import of many of the exercises he adopted from extant traditions.

Moreover, both Augustine and Xunzi make study and learning foundational and central. In itself, this is hardly unique. But what I have called their "chastened intellectualism" leads them each to give distinctive interpretations of the subtle interplay between intellectual progress and emotional, moral, and even physical progress within the ongoing process of education, at least when compared with views that presuppose a strong distinction between intellectual virtue and character virtue, for instance.

Which of these points, or the many other specific ideas and practices discussed in this study, will be most striking or useful will of course depend on the commitments and views of particular readers. The sort of comparative religious ethics I have been practicing in this work is thus not antagonistic toward more confessional approaches, including varieties of self-consciously Christian ethics, but complementary to them. It is more exploratory and experimental, but this should not be read as a rejection of continuing attempts to articulate the kind of comprehensive visions of personal formation that Augustine and Xunzi created. Indeed, such a rejection would be self-contradictory, given my arguments about the character of chastened intellectualism.

GLOBAL NEIGHBORLINESS

To increase the possibility of learning from others, from both distant and resident aliens, I propose "global neighborliness" as a regulative ideal for comparative studies of religious thought and for relating to religious "others" generally.[14] This implies a conception of such neighbors as potential teachers, not merely potential converts. It also implies an openness that refuses to fear the neighbor as a potential or likely threat, unless proven otherwise—some apparent neighbors really are threatening, but mere difference and disagreement are not. Testifying, apologetics, debate, and even proselytizing all have their times and places, but if any of these comes first, before neighborliness, learning something new will be a surprise and an accident, rather than something sought.

This ideal has several facets. First, it implies attentiveness to and curiosity about the ideas, practices, and general mode of life of others. Obviously, the appropriate degree and extent of such an attitude will depend on a number of factors related to one's social position and responsibilities. This is not a blanket policy of affirmation or even toleration of all ways of life. Instead, it suggests alert openness and an eagerness to learn.

Second, global neighborliness implies a commitment to the widely lauded goal of charitable interpretation: the sustained presumption that one's interlocutors are neither fools nor villains, unless such a conclusion becomes inescapable. This implies real evaluative concern, not the lack or evasion of it. Charity requires postulating the strongest, most sensible interpretation of seemingly strange ideas or behavior, as a way of reaching deeper insight; and an interpreter cannot arrive at such judgments without attempting to see how someone else's views make sense, or occasionally fail to. By refraining from rushing to negative judgments about one's neighbor, charity requires patience, along with both moral and epistemological humility. The first sort of humility is justified by an awareness of our own faults, and the second by an awareness of the relation of sustained practice to real understanding—and both suggest the inherent difficulties in coming to grasp an alien tradition or person.[15]

A closely related third point is that neighborliness requires taking others' commitments seriously. This sort of maneuver is sometimes confused with an apparently nonjudgmental respect or admiration for any system of values (an ideal that seems self-contradictory). To the contrary, I would argue that serious consideration of others' views implies real critical engagement with them, as a corollary to charitable interpretation itself. Even if final judgments are deferred for some time, especially if they are strongly negative, working hypotheses about insight and confusion are essential to the process of gaining understanding. This process is ongoing, however, and needs to be sustained over time so that nuances and interconnections can be fully absorbed, precisely through the testing and revision of interpretive hypotheses, which cannot avoid being at least implicitly evaluative.

This critical engagement requires awareness of and attention to both differences and similarities between familiar theories or ideas and new, apparently strange ones. A rush to assimilate the new to the familiar is one of the easiest ways to miss any chance at learning something—indeed, it risks deceptively confirming the apparently impressive magnitude of our current wisdom. Yearley's insistence on sifting through "similarities within differences" and "differences within similarities" by drawing complex analogies and disanalogies between positions is particularly helpful here.[16]

This degree of careful engagement leads to the fifth characteristic of global neighborliness, which is alertness to complexity. Such alertness refuses to overgeneralize about whole "religions" or "traditions," and it recognizes that the range of views and practices in most social groups is large—not to mention in vast, historically extended traditions such as Christianity and Confucianism, let alone the cultural complexes associated with whole regions like East Asia or Europe. Any broad generalizations that comparative ethics might justifiably produce should not be about "mentalities" or "deep assumptions" of whole civilizations and/or eras but about the shaping of debates within and between religious traditions. This guards historical particularity, complexity, and conflict, while leaving room for comparing and contrasting different narratives of change over time. So, for instance, we can recognize the immense influence of Augustine's particular formulation of the idea of *voluntas*, which has guided so much inquiry and subsequent debate in the West. And although in the section above I stressed the carefully synthetic, even systematic character of Augustine's borrowing from his numerous sources, the influence of his ideas about the will stems at least as much from the inherent tensions in the idea—for example, between freedom and determinism, and between responsible choice and spontaneous, powerful desire. Noting that the *problématique* for inquiry created by such tensions is simply not present in the same way in Chinese intellectual history, we could investigate what *problématiques* have been present, and compare them with more familiar ones, if broad civilizational contrast is what is in question.

Last, the most obviously Confucian element of this conception would be the need for tact, precisely as an expression of, and guide to, the serious care essential to neighborliness. This sort of diplomatic discretion concerns when and how to ask questions and listen, to forthrightly report one's own differing convictions, to criticize, and to suggest possible alternatives or even improvements in someone else's conceptions. As Xunzi and the other Confucians teach us, such benevolent politesse is required at all times, even if it might seem to exceed what an interlocutor appears to deserve, in part because of the responsiveness of human beings to signs of respect and disrespect, and in part because neighborliness as an ideal simply demands it.

This sort of attentive, charitable yet critical, patient, subtle, and tactful neighborliness facilitates learning from others, as well as the self-scrutiny that accompanies such learning. Though the remarkable diversity of human cultures and traditions suggests that no particular mode of personal formation is either biologically or logically necessary, if a chastened intellectualist account is at least roughly on track, we each need some version of such formation to become ethical beings. If we truly aspire to goodness, and not merely to a distanced consideration of models of human goodness, than we could hardly do better than to investigate conceptions of personal formation, aiming thereby to develop and refine our own convictions—by practicing them.

NOTES

1. For a helpful overview, see Twiss and Conser 1992.

2. I think this aspect of John Hick's work (1985, 1989) is inescapable, regardless of his theory's failings.

3. Actually, in terms of this study's lingo, one could argue that modern moral theories such as utilitarianism and Kantian constructivism are attempts to create just this sort of "moral Esperanto" and are notably more influential than the actual language

of Esperanto. Many have learned to speak and even live these moral vocabularies, but I would wager that their numbers are still dwarfed by those who adhere to some form of religion, and those who have absorbed elements of such accounts into comprehensive religious visions.

4. My position on human rights has been influenced most by the works of Sumner Twiss, as developed, e.g., in Twiss 1998b.

5. On the Israelites stealing from the Egyptians as they left, see Ex. 3:21–22, 12:35–6. On knowledge and love according to Paul, see 1 Cor. 8:1.

6. Stalnaker 2003.

7. On "bricolage," see Stout 1988, 74–77; and Stalnaker 2005, 215–19. Contrast this with the common habit of treating the parallel issue addressed within one's tradition, considered sometimes very broadly, as the "retrieval" of one's own "moral sources."

8. Yearley 1990, 175–82, 169–75.

9. Yearley now seems to see the force of this sort of objection, and to be moving in a similar direction. See Yearley 1998, 124. And even in *Mencius and Aquinas* (1990), Yearley's methodological conclusions about comparison and types of theory do not seem to have precluded him from offering detailed descriptions of the views of his two subjects, which draw on ideas from their "secondary" theories such as grace and *qi*, for example, in the body of the work itself.

10. Yearley 1990, 180. But Yearley's contention does have real bite: One could certainly argue that Augustine's understanding of sin is radicalized by his theological commitments, e.g., regarding atonement and the proper reading of the Letter to the Romans, in a way that is ultimately unconvincing. But this position is so essential to his overall understanding of life that to reject it is tantamount to rejecting his broader religious vision, in favor of something more like that of his late antagonist Julian of Eclanum.

11. Indeed, one of the other purposes for which Yearley deploys the distinctions between levels of theory is to authorize and guide his constructive efforts in contemporary virtue ethics, which draw on both Aquinas and Mencius to develop general accounts of dispositions, virtues, and the virtue of courage.

12. The phrase "reflective equilibrium" comes from Rawls 1971, 20ff.

13. Compare Hadot 1995, 116 n. 79.

14. Although the rhetorical allusion to the Christian love command is intended, that is hardly this ideal's only source. Global neighborliness is not meant to be restricted to Christians or automatically governed by Christian norms, but is proposed for others as well. The particular elements of the conception owe much to reflecting on the comparative procedures of Frank Clooney and Lee Yearley, among others.

15. A critic might question whether such counsels of charity are compatible with skeptical accounts of human nature such as Augustine's or Xunzi's, which might instead suggest that we should be dubious about the professed intentions and aspirations of our interlocutors. But as long as one is equally skeptical of both the familiar and the strange, then this criticism has a hard time getting off the ground: If one refuses to presume one's own superiority, then there are no grounds for high-handed, insensitive interrogations to begin.

16. Yearley 1990, 4–6, 170–75.

References

Allen, Douglas, ed. 1997. *Culture and Self: Philosophical and Religious Perspectives, East and West*. Boulder, Colo.: Westview Press.

Ames, Roger T., Wimal Dissanayake, and Thomas P. Kasulis, eds. 1994. *Self as Person in Asian Theory and Practice*. Albany: State University of New York Press.

———. 1996. *Self and Deception: A Cross-Cultural Philosophical Enquiry*. Albany: State University of New York Press.

Antonaccio, Maria. 1998. Contemporary Forms of *Askesis* and the Return of Spiritual Exercises. *Annual of the Society of Christian Ethics* 18: 69–92.

Augustine. 1844–64a. *De baptismo.* In Migne 1844–64, vol. 43, col. 107–244.

———. 1844–64b. *De catechizandis rudibus*. In Migne 1844–64, vol. 40, col. 309–48.

———. 1844–64c. *De civitate Dei*. In Migne 1844–64, vol. 41, col. 13–804. [Trans. Bettenson 1984.]

———. 1844–64d. *Confessiones.* In Migne 1844–64, vol. 32, col. 657–868. [Trans. Chadwick 1991.]

———. 1844–64e. *De continentia*. In Migne 1844–64, vol. 40, col. 349–72. [Trans. Kearney 1999.]

———. 1844–64f. *Contra duas epistulas Pelagianorum*. In Migne 1844–64, vol. 44, col. 549–638. [Trans. Teske 1998, 116–219.]

———. 1844–64g. *Contra Julianum*. In Migne 1844–64, vol. 44, col. 641–874. [Trans. Teske 1998, 268–536.]

———. 1844–64h. *Contra Julianum, opus imperfectum*. In Migne 1844–64, vol. 45, col. 1049–1608. [Trans. Teske 1999a.]

———. 1844–64i. *Contra litteras Petiliani*. In Migne 1844–64, vol. 43, col. 245–388.

———. 1844–64j. *De diversis quaestionibus octoginta tribus*. In Migne 1844–64, vol. 40, col. 11–100.

———. 1844–64k. *De doctrina Christiana*. In Migne 1844–64, vol. 34, col. 15–122. [Trans. Green 1995.]

———. 1844–64l. *De duabus animabus*. In Migne 1844–64, vol. 42, col. 93–112. Paris.

———. 1844–64m. *Enchiridion ad Laurentium de fide spe et caritate*. In Migne 1844–64, vol. 40, col. 231–90.

———. 1844–64n. *Ennarrationes in Psalmos*. In Migne 1844–64, vol. 36, col. 37–vol. 37, col. 1966.

———. 1844–64o. *Epistulae*. In Migne 1844–64, vol. 33, col. 60–1094. [Trans. Teske 2003.]

———. 1844–64p. *In epistulam Joannis ad Parthos tractatus*. In Migne 1844–64, vol. 35, col. 1977–2062.

———. 1844–64q. *Expositio Epistulae ad Galatas*. In Migne 1844–64, vol. 35, col. 2105–148.

———. 1844–64r. *Expositio quarundam propositionum ex epistula Apostoli ad Romanos*. In Migne 1844–64, vol. 35, col. 2063–88.

———. 1844–64s. *De Genesi ad litteram*. In Migne 1844–64, vol. 34, col. 245–486.

———. 1844–64t. *De gratia Christi et de peccato originali*. In Migne 1844–64, vol. 44, col. 359–410. [Trans. Teske 1997, 403–63.]

———. 1844–64u. *In Johannis evangelium tractatus*. In Migne 1844–64, vol. 35, col. 1379–1976.

———. 1844–64v. *De libero arbitrio voluntatis*. In Migne 1844–64, vol. 32, col. 1219–1310.

———. 1844–64w. *De magistro*. In Migne 1844–64, vol. 32, col. 1193–1220.

———. 1844–64x. *De moribus ecclesiae catholicae et de moribus Manichaeorum*. In Migne 1844–64, vol. 32, col. 1309–78. [Trans. Stothert 1886.]

———. 1844–64y. *De natura boni*. In Migne 1844–64, vol. 42, col. 551–72. [Trans. Burleigh 1953, 326–48.]

———. 1844–64z. *De natura et gratia*. In Migne 1844–64, vol. 44, col. 245–90. [Trans. Teske 1997, 225–75.]

———. 1844–64aa. *De ordine*. In Migne 1844–64, vol. 32, col. 977–1020. [Trans. Russell 1948.]

———. 1844–64bb. *De patientia*. In Migne 1844–64, vol. 40, col. 611–26.

———. 1844–64cc. *De peccatorum meritis et remissione et de baptismo parvulorum*. In Migne 1844–64, vol. 44, col. 109–200. [Trans. Teske 1997, 34–137.]

———. 1844–64dd. *De perfectione justitiae hominis*. In Migne 1844–64, vol. 44, col. 289–318. [Trans. Teske 1997, 289–316.]

———. 1844–64ee. *Quaestiones in Heptateuchum*. In Migne 1844–64, vol. 34, col. 545–824.

———. 1844–64ff. *De animae quantitate*. In Migne 1844–64, vol. 32, col. 1033–80.

———. 1844–64gg. *Regula: Ordo monaserii*. In Migne 1844–64, vol. 32, col. 1377–84.

———. 1844–64hh. *Retractationes*. In Migne 1844–64, vol. 32, col. 581–656.

———. 1844–64ii. *De sancta virginitate*. In Migne 1844–64, vol. 40, col. 395–428. [Trans. Kearney 1999.]

———. 1844–64jj. *Sermones*. In Migne 1844–64, vol. 38, col. 23-vol. 39, col. 1638. [Trans. Hill 1990–97.]

———. 1844–64kk. *De sermone Domini in monte*. In Migne 1844–64, vol. 34, col. 1229–1308.

———. 1844–64ll. *De spiritu et littera*. In Migne 1844–64, vol. 44, col. 199–246. [Trans. Teske 1997, 150–202.]

———. 1844–64mm. *De Trinitate*. In Migne 1844–64, vol. 42, col. 819–1098. [Trans. Hill 1990–97.]

———. 1844–64nn. *De vera religione*. In Migne 1844–64, vol. 34, col. 121–72. [Trans. Burleigh 1953, 225–83.]

Babcock, William S. 1979. Augustine's Interpretations of Romans (A.D. 394–396). *Augustinian Studies* 10: 58–61.

———. 1988. Augustine on Sin and Moral Agency. *Journal of Religious Ethics* 16: 28–55. [Reprinted in *The Ethics of St. Augustine*, ed. William S. Babcock. Atlanta: Scholars Press, 1991.]

———. 1991a. *Cupiditas* and *Caritas*: The Early Augustine on Love and Human Fulfillment. In *The Ethics of St. Augustine,* ed. William Babcock. Atlanta: Scholars Press.

———, ed. 1991b. *The Ethics of St. Augustine*. Atlanta: Scholars Press.

———. 1992. The Human and the Angelic Fall: Will and Moral Agency in Augustine's *City of God*. In *Augustine: From Rhetorician to Theologian*, ed. Joanne McWilliam. Waterloo, Ontario: Wilfrid Laurier University Press.

———. 1994. Augustine and the Spirituality of Desire. *Augustinian Studies* 25: 187–96.

Baier, Annette. 1991. *A Progress of Sentiments: Reflections on Hume's Treatise*. Cambridge, Mass.: Harvard University Press.

BeDuhn, Jason. 2000. *The Manichean Body: In Discipline and Ritual*. Baltimore: Johns Hopkins University Press.

Bergner, Daniel. 2005. The Making of a Molester. *New York Times Magazine*, January 23.

Berkson, Mark A. 2005. Conceptions of Self/No-Self and Modes of Connection: Comparative Soteriological Structures in Classical Chinese Thought. *Journal of Religious Ethics* 33, no. 2 (Summer): 293–331.

Bernstein, Richard J. 1971. *Praxis and Action: Contemporary Philosophies of Human Activity*. Philadelphia: University of Pennsylvania Press.

Bettenson, Henry, trans. 1984. *Concerning the City of God Against the Pagans*. London: Penguin.

Bohman, James. 1991. *New Philosophy of Social Science*. Cambridge, Mass.: MIT Press.

Bonner, Gerald. 1986. Augustine's Conception of Deification. *Journal of Theological Studies* 37, no. 2 (October): 369–86.

Brandom, Robert. 1994. *Making It Explicit: Reasoning, Representing, and Discursive Commitment*. Cambridge, Mass.: Harvard University Press.

———. 2000a. *Articulating Reasons: An Introduction to Inferentialism*. Cambridge, Mass.: Harvard University Press.

———. 2000b. Vocabularies of Pragmatism: Synthesizing Naturalism and Historicism. In *Rorty and His Critics*, ed. Robert Brandom. Malden, Mass.: Blackwell.

Brown, Peter. 1967. *Augustine of Hippo*. Berkeley: University of California Press. [Expanded ed. published 2000.]

———. 1988. *The Body and Society: Men, Women, and Sexual Renunciation in Early Christianity.* New York: Columbia University Press.

Brown, Robert. 1978. The First Evil Will Must Be Incomprehensible: A Critique of Augustine. *Journal of the American Academy of Religion* 46: 315–29.

Burleigh, J. H. S. 1953. *Augustine: Earlier Writings*. Philadelphia: Westminster Press.

Burnaby, John. 1947. *Amor Dei: A Study of the Religion of St. Augustine.* London: Hodder & Stoughton.

Burnell, Peter. 1999. Concupiscence. In *Augustine through the Ages*, ed. Allan D. Fitzgerald. Grand Rapids, Mich.: William B. Eerdmans.

Burns, J. Patout. 1991. Augustine on the Origin and Progress of Evil. In *The Ethics of St. Augustine,* ed. William Babcock. Atlanta: Scholars Press.

Cabezón, José Ignacio. 1998. *Scholasticism: Cross-Cultural and Comparative Perspectives*. Albany: State University of New York Press.

Campany, Robert. 1992. Xunzi and Durkheim as Theorists of Ritual Practice. In *Myth and Philosophy,* ed. Frank Reynolds and David Tracy. Albany: State University of New York Press.

———. 2003. On the Very Idea of Religions (in the Modern West and in Early Medieval China). *History of Religions* 42, no. 4 (May): 287–319.

Carney, Frederick S. 1991. The Structure of Augustine's Ethic. In *The Ethics of St. Augustine,* ed. William Babcock. Atlanta: Scholars Press.

Carr, Karen L., and Philip J. Ivanhoe. 2000. *The Sense of Anti-Rationalism: The Religious Thought of Zhuangzi and Kierkegaard*. New York: Seven Bridges Press.

Carrithers, Michael, Steven Collins, and Steven Lukes, eds. 1985. *The Category of the Person: Anthropology, Philosophy, History*. Cambridge, Mass.: Cambridge University Press.

Case, Jennifer. 1997. On the Right Idea of a Conceptual Scheme. *Southern Journal of Philosophy* 35, no. 1: 1–18.

Cavadini, John. 1999. Review of *Augustine the Reader: Meditation, Self-Knowledge, and the Ethics of Interpretation*, by Brian Stock. *Journal of Early Christian Studies* 7 (Spring): 165–67.

———. 2005. Feeling It Right: Augustine on Sex and the Passions. *Augustinian Studies* 36, no. 1: 196–218.

Chadwick, Henry. 1986. *Augustine*. New York: Oxford University Press.

———, trans. 1991. *The Confessions*. Oxford: Oxford University Press.

Clark, Elizabeth A. 1986. Vitiated Seeds and Holy Vessels: Augustine's Manichean Past. In *Ascetic Piety and Women's Faith: Essays on Late Ancient Christianity*. Lewiston, N.Y.: Edwin Mellen Press.

———. 1999. *Reading Renunciation: Asceticism and Scripture in Early Christianity*. Princeton, N.J.: Princeton University Press.

———. 2003. Distinguishing "Distinction": The Uses of a Bishop's Authority. Paper presented at Reconsiderations: A Conference on Contemporary Augustinian Scholarship, Villanova, Pa., December.

Clarke, J. J. 1997. *Oriental Enlightenment: The Encounter Between Asian and Western Thought*. New York: Routledge.

Clooney, Francis X. 1993. *Theology After Vedanta*. Albany: State University of New York Press.

———. 2001. *Hindu God, Christian God: How Reason Helps Break Down the Boundaries Between Religions*. New York: Oxford University Press.

Cook, Scott. 1997. Xun Zi on Ritual and Music. *Monumenta Serica* 45: 1–38.

Corpus Christianorum, Series Latina. 1953–. Turnhout: Brepols.

Corpus Scriptorum Ecclesiasticorum Latinorum. 1865–. Vienna: Tempsky.

Couenhoven, Jesse. 2004. Responsibility Without Freedom? A Critique of the Augustinian Doctrine of Original Sin. Ph.D. diss., Yale University.

Courcelle, Pierre. 1950. *Recherches sur les Confessions de Saint Augustin*, rev. ed. [Reprinted Paris: E. de Boccard, 1968.]

Cutrone, Emmanuel J. 1999. Sacraments. In *Augustine through the Ages*, ed. Allan D. Fitzgerald. Grand Rapids, Mich.: William B. Eerdmans.

Csikszentmihalyi, Mihaly. 1990. *Flow: The Psychology of Optimal Experience*. New York: Harper & Row.

Davidson, Arnold. 1994. Ethics as Ascetics: Foucault, the History of Ethics, and Ancient Thought. In *The Cambridge Companion to Foucault*, ed. Gary Gutting. Cambridge: Cambridge University Press.

Davidson, Donald. 1984. On the Very Idea of a Conceptual Scheme. In *Inquiries into Truth and Interpretation*. Oxford: Clarendon Press.

Dawson, David. 1997. Taking Metaphysical Commitments Seriously. *Journal for Peace and Justice Studies* 8, no. 2: 37–44.

de Bary, William, Theodore Bloom, and Irene Bloom, eds. 1999. *Sources of Chinese Tradition*, 2nd ed., vol. 1. New York: Columbia University Press.

de Waal, Frans. 1996. *Good Natured: The Origins of Right and Wrong in Humans and Other Animals*. Cambridge, Mass.: Harvard University Press.

Dihle, Albrecht. 1982. *The Theory of Will in Classical Antiquity*. Berkeley: University of California Press.

Djuth, Marianne. 1999. Will. In *Augustine through the Ages*, ed. Allan D. Fitzgerald. Grand Rapids, Mich.: William B. Eerdmans.

Dodaro, Robert. 2004. *Christ and the Just Society in the Thought of Augustine*. Cambridge: Cambridge University Press.

Dubs, Homer H. 1956. Mencius and Sün-dz on Human Nature. *Philosophy East and West* 6: 213–22.

Eck, Diana. 2001. *A New Religious America: How a Christian Country Has Become the World's Most Religiously Diverse Nation*. New York: HarperCollins.

Eno, Robert. 1990. *The Confucian Creation of Heaven*. Albany: State University of New York Press.

Epstein, Shari. N.d. Social Malaise / Ritual Remedy: A Comparative Study of Durkheim and Xunzi. Unpublished manuscript.

Evans-Pritchard, E. E. 1937. *Witchcraft, Oracles and Magic Among the Azande*. Oxford: Oxford University Press.

Fingarette, Herbert. 1972. *Confucius: The Secular as Sacred*. New York: Harper Torchbooks.

Fitzgerald, Allan D., ed. 1999. *Augustine through the Ages*. Grand Rapids, Mich.: William B. Eerdmans.

Flanagan, Owen. 1990. Identity and Strong and Weak Evaluation. In *Identity, Character, and Morality: Essays in Moral Psychology*, ed. Owen Flanagan and Amélie Oksenberg Rorty. Cambridge: MIT Press.

Fleishacker, Samuel. 1994. *The Ethics of Culture*. Ithaca, N.Y.: Cornell University Press.

Foucault, Michel. 1971. *On the Order of Things: An Archaeology of the Human Sciences*. New York: Pantheon Books.

———. 1977. *Discipline and Punish: The Birth of the Prison*, trans. Alan Sheridan. New York: Pantheon Books.

———. 1978. *The History of Sexuality, Volume 1: An Introduction*, trans. Robert Hurley. New York: Pantheon Books.

———. 1985. *The Use of Pleasure*, trans. Robert Hurley. New York: Pantheon Books.

———. 1986. *The Care of the Self*, trans. Robert Hurley. New York: Pantheon Books.

———. 1997. *Ethics: Subjectivity and Truth*, ed. Paul Rabinow and trans. Robert Hurley and others. New York: New Press.

Frankfurt, Harry. 1988. Freedom of the Will and the Concept of a Person. In *The Importance of What We Care About: Philosophical Essays*. Cambridge: Cambridge University Press.

———. 1999. *Necessity, Volition, and Love*. Cambridge: Cambridge University Press.

Fredriksen, Paula. 1988. Beyond the Body/Soul Dichotomy: Augustine on Paul against the Manichees and Pelagians. *Recherches Augustiniennes* 23: 87–114.

Gadamer, Hans-Georg. 1989. *Truth and Method*, 2nd rev. ed., trans. Joel Weinsheimer and Donald G. Marshall. New York: Continuum.

Geaney, Jane. 2002. *On the Epistemology of the Senses in Early Chinese Thought*. Honolulu: University of Hawaii Press.

Girard, René. 1977. *Violence and the Sacred*, trans. Patrick Gregory. Baltimore: Johns Hopkins University Press.

Godlove, Terry. 1989. *Religion, Interpretation and Diversity of Belief: The Framework Model from Kant to Durkheim to Davidson*. New York: Cambridge University Press.

———. 2002. Saving Belief: On the New Materialism in Religious Studies. In *Radical Interpretation in Religion*, ed. Nancy Frankenberry. Cambridge: Cambridge University Press.

Goldin, Paul. 1999. *Rituals of the Way: The Philosophy of Xunzi*. Chicago: Open Court.

———. 2000. Xunzi in the Light of the Guodian Manuscripts. *Early China* 25: 113–46.

Graham, A. C. 1989. *Disputers of the Tao: Philosophical Argument in Ancient China*. La Salle, Ill.: Open Court.

———. 1990a. The Background of the Mencian Theory of Human Nature. In *Studies in Chinese Philosophy and Philosophical Literature*. Albany: State University of New York Press.

———. 1990b. "Being" in Western Philosophy Compared with *Shih/Fei* and *You/Wu* in Chinese Philosophy. In *Studies in Chinese Philosophy and Philosophical Literature*. Albany: State University of New York Press.

———. 1990c. Relating Categories to Question Forms in Pre-Han Chinese Thought. In *Studies in Chinese Philosophy and Philosophical Literature*. Albany: State University of New York Press.

———. 1991. Conceptual Schemes and Linguistic Relativism in Relation to Chinese. In *Culture and Modernity: East–West Philosophic Perspectives*, ed. Eliot Deutsch. Honolulu: University of Hawaii Press.

Green, R. P. H., trans. 1995. *Augustine: De Doctrina Christiana*. Oxford: Clarendon Press.

Green, Ronald. 1978. *Religious Reason: The Rational and Moral Basis of Religious Belief*. New York: Oxford University Press.

———. 1988. *Religion and Moral Reason: A New Method for Comparative Study*. New York: Oxford University Press.

Gregory, Eric. N.d. Politics and the Order of Love: Modern Variations on Augustinian Themes. Unpublished manuscript.

Grelle, Bruce, and Sumner Twiss, eds. 1998. *Explorations in Global Ethics: Comparative Religious Ethics and Interreligious Dialogue*. Boulder, Colo.: Westview Press.

Guodian Chumu Zhujian. 1998. Beijing: Wenwu Chubanshe.

Hacker, P. M. S. 1996. On Davidson's Idea of a Conceptual Scheme. *Philosophical Quarterly* 46, no. 184 (July): 289–307.

Hadot, Pierre. 1993. *Plotinus, or The Simplicity of Vision*, trans. Michael Chase. Chicago: University of Chicago Press.

———. 1995. *Philosophy as a Way of Life: Spiritual Exercises from Socrates to Foucault*, ed. Arnold I. Davidson and trans. Michael Chase. Oxford: Blackwell.

———. 1998. *The Inner Citadel: The Meditations of Marcus Aurelius*, trans. Michael Chase. Cambridge: Harvard University Press.

———. 2002. *What Is Ancient Philosophy?* trans. Michael Chase. Cambridge, Mass.: Belknap Press of Harvard University Press.

Hall, David L., and Roger T. Ames. 1987. *Thinking Through Confucius*. Albany: State University of New York Press.

Hankey, Wayne. 2003. Philosophy as Way of Life for Christians? Iamblichan and Porphyrian Reflections on Religion, Virtue, and Philosophy in Thomas Aquinas. *Laval Théologique et Philosophique* 59, no. 2: 193–224.

Hansen, Chad. 1995. *Qing* (Emotions) 情 in Pre-Buddhist Chinese Thought. In *Emotions in Asian Thought: A Dialogue in Comparative Philosophy*, ed. Joel Marks and Roger T. Ames. Albany: State University of New York Press.

Harmless, William. 1995. *Augustine and the Catechumenate*. Collegeville, Minn.: Liturgical Press.

Harper, Donald. 1987. The Sexual Arts of Ancient China as Described in a Manuscript of the Second Century B.C. *Harvard Journal of Asiatic Studies* 47: 539–93.

———. 1995. The Bellows Analogy in *Laozi* V and Warring States Macrobiotic Hygiene. *Early China* 20: 381–91.

———. 1997. *Early Chinese Medical Literature: The Mawangdui Medical Manuscripts*. London: Kegan Paul.

Harris, William V. 2001. *Restraining Rage: The Ideology of Anger Control in Classical Antiquity*. Cambridge, Mass.: Harvard University Press.

Harrison, Carol. 2000. *Augustine: Christian Truth and Fractured Humanity*. New York: Oxford University Press.

Hauerwas, Stanley. 1981. *A Community of Character: Toward a Constructive Christian Social Ethic*. Notre Dame, Ind.: University of Notre Dame Press.

Herdt, Jennifer. 2000. Religious Ethics, History, and the Rise of Modern Moral Philosophy: Focus Introduction. *Journal of Religious Ethics* 28, no. 2: 167–88.

Hick, John H. 1977. *Evil and the God of Love*, 2nd ed. New York: HarperCollins.

———. 1985. *Problems of Religious Pluralism*. New York: St. Martin's Press.

———. 1989. *An Interpretation of Religion: Human Responses to the Transcendent*. New Haven, Conn.: Yale University Press.

Hill, Edmund, trans. 1990–97. *Sermons*. The Works of Saint Augustine, Part III, vols. 1–11. Brooklyn: New City Press.

———. 1991. *The Trinity*. The Works of Saint Augustine, Part I, vol. 5. Brooklyn: New City Press.

Hollis, Martin, and Steven Lukes, eds. 1982. *Rationality and Relativism*. Cambridge, Mass.: MIT Press.

Hsu, Cho-yun. 1965. *Ancient China in Transition: An Analysis of Social Mobility, 722–222 B.C.* Stanford, Calif.: Stanford University Press.

Hutton, Eric. 1996. On the Meaning of *Yi* (義) in Xunzi. Master's thesis, Harvard University.

———. 2001. Virtue and Reason in Xunzi. Ph.D. diss., Stanford University.

Ignatius of Loyola. 1991. *Ignatius of Loyola: Spiritual Exercises and Selected Works*, ed. George E. Ganss et al. New York: Paulist Press.

Irwin, Terence. 1988. Disunity in the Aristotelian Virtues. In *Oxford Studies in Ancient Philosophy, Supplementary Volume*. New York: Oxford University Press.

———, trans. 1999a. *Aristotle: Nicomachean Ethics*, 2nd ed. Indianapolis: Hackett.

———. 1999b. Splendid Vices? Augustine For and Against Pagan Virtues. *Medieval Philosophy and Theology* 8: 105–27.

Ivanhoe, Philip J. 1990. Thinking and Learning in Early Confucianism. *Journal of Chinese Philosophy* 17: 473–93.

———. 1991. A Happy Symmetry: Xunzi's Ethical Thought. *Journal of the American Academy of Religion* 59: 309–22.

———. 2000a. *Confucian Moral Self-Cultivation*, 2nd ed. Indianapolis: Hackett.

———. 2000b. Human Nature and Moral Understanding in Xunzi. In *Virtue, Nature, and Moral Agency in the Xunzi,* eds. T. C. Kline III and Philip J. Ivanhoe. Indianapolis: Hackett.

———. 2002. *Ethics in the Confucian Tradition: The Thought of Mencius and Wang Yangming*, 2nd ed. Indianapolis: Hackett.

Jackson, Timothy P. 1997. Prima Caritas, Inde Jus: Why Augustinians Shouldn't Baptize John Rawls. *Journal for Peace and Justice Studies* 8, no. 2: 49–62.

Johnson, Penelope D. 1975. Virtus: Transition from Classical Latin to the "De Civitate Dei." *Augustinian Studies* 6: 117–24.

Kahn, Charles H. 1988. Discovering the Will: From Aristotle to Augustine. In *The Question of Eclecticism: Studies in Later Greek Philosophy*, ed. John M. Dillon and A. A. Long. Berkeley: University of California Press.

Kant, Immanuel. 1960. *Religion Within the Limits of Reason Alone*. Trans. Theodore Greene and Hoyt Hudson. New York: Harper Torchbooks.

Katz, Leonard D., ed. 2000. *Evolutionary Origins of Morality: Cross-Disciplinary Perspectives*. Bowling Green, Ohio: Imprint Academic.

Katz, Sheri. 1999. Person. In *Augustine through the Ages*, ed. Allan D. Fitzgerald. Grand Rapids, Mich.: William B. Eerdmans.

Kearney, Ray, trans. 1999. *Marriage and Virginity: The Excellence of Marriage, Holy Virginity, The Excellence of Widowhood, Adulterous Marriages, Continence.* Works of Saint Augustine, Part I, vol. 9. Hyde Park, N.Y.: New City Press.

Kline, T. C., III. 1998. Ethics and Tradition in the Xunzi. Ph.D. diss., Stanford University.

———. 2000. Moral Agency and Motivation in the *Xunzi*. In *Virtue, Nature, and Moral Agency in the Xunzi,* eds. T. C. Kline III and Philip J. Ivanhoe. Indianapolis: Hackett.

Kline, T. C., III, and Philip J. Ivanhoe, eds. 2000. *Virtue, Nature, and Moral Agency in the Xunzi*. Indianapolis: Hackett.

Knoblock, John. 1982–83. The Chronology of Xunzi's Works. *Early China* 8: 28–52.

———, trans. 1988–94. *Xunzi: A Translation and Study of the Complete Works*, 3 vols. Stanford, Calif.: Stanford University Press.

Knuuttila, Simo. 2004. *Emotions in Ancient and Medieval Philosophy*. Oxford: Clarendon Press.

Krausz, Michael, ed. 1989. *Relativism: Interpretation and Confrontation*. Notre Dame, Ind.: University of Notre Dame Press.

Kraut, Robert. 1986. The Third Dogma. In *Truth and Interpretation: Perspectives on the Philosophy of Donald Davidson*, ed. Ernest LePore. New York: Basil Blackwell.

Kupperman, Joel. 1968. Confucius and the Problem of Naturalness. *Philosophy East and West* 18, no. 3 (July): 175–85.

———. 2002. Naturalness Revisited: Why Western Philosophers Should Study Confucius. In *Confucius and the Analects: New Essays*, ed. Bryan W. Van Norden. New York: Oxford University Press.

Lai, Karyn. 2003. Confucian Moral Cultivation: Some Parallels with Musical Training. In *The Moral Circle and the Self: Chinese and Western Approaches*, ed. Kim-chong Chong, Sor-hoon Tan, and C. L. Tan. Chicago: Open Court.

Lau, D. C., ed. 1992. *A Concordance to the Huainanzi*. Hong Kong: Commercial Press.

———. 1996. *A Concordance to the Xunzi*. Hong Kong: Commercial Press.

Lauritzen, Paul. 1994. The Self and Its Discontents: Recent Work on Morality and the Self. *Journal of Religious Ethics* 22, no. 1 (Spring): 189–210.

Lawless, George. 1987. *Augustine of Hippo and his Monastic Rule*. Oxford: Clarendon Press.

———. 2000. Augustine's Decentering of Asceticism. In *Augustine and His Critics: Essays in Honor of Gerald Bonner*, ed. Robert Dodaro and George Lawless. New York: Routledge.

Lewis, Charlton. 1995. *An Elementary Latin Dictionary, 1891*. London: Oxford University Press.

Lewis, Thomas A. 1998. Vergleichende Ethik in Nordamerika: Methodologische Probleme und Ansätze. *Polylog: Zeitschrift für interkulturelles Philosophieren* 1, no. 2 (December): 87–94. [An English version is also available online: Comparative Ethics in North America: Methodological Problems and Approaches, at http://lit.polylog.org/1/elt-en.htm]

———. 2005. Frames of Comparison: Anthropology and Inheriting Traditional Practices. *Journal of Religious Ethics* 33, no. 2 (Summer): 225–53.

Lewis, Thomas A., Jonathan W. Schofer, Aaron Stalnaker, and Mark A. Berkson. 2005. Anthropos and Ethics: Categories of Inquiry and Procedures of Comparison. *Journal of Religious Ethics* 33, no. 2 (Summer): 177–85.

Leyser, Conrad. 2000. *Authority and Asceticism from Augustine to Gregory the Great*. Oxford: Clarendon Press.

Lieu, S. N. C. 1992. *Manichaeism in the later Roman Empire and Medieval China: A Historical Survey*, 2nd ed. Tübingen: J. C. B. Mohr.

Lindbeck, George A. 1984. *The Nature of Doctrine: Religion and Theology in a Postliberal Age*. Philadelphia: Westminster Press.

Little, David, and Sumner B. Twiss, eds. 1978. *Comparative Religious Ethics: A New Method*. New York: Harper & Row.

Loewe, Michael, ed. 1993. *Early Chinese Texts: A Bibliographical Guide*. Berkeley: Society for the Study of Early China and Institute of East Asian Studies, University of California.

Loewe, Michael, and Edward L. Shaughnessy, eds. 1999. *The Cambridge History of Ancient China: From the Origins of Civilization to 221 B.C.* Cambridge: Cambridge University Press.

Lovin, Robin W., and Frank E. Reynolds, eds. 1985. *Cosmogony and Ethical Order: New Studies in Comparative Ethics*. Chicago: University of Chicago Press.

Machle, Edward. 1993. *Nature and Heaven in the Xunzi: A Study of the Tian Lun*. Albany: State University of New York Press.

MacIntyre, Alasdair. 1970a. The Idea of a Social Science. In *Rationality*, ed. Bryan R. Wilson. Oxford: Oxford University Press.

———. 1970b. Is Understanding Religion Compatible with Believing? In *Rationality*, ed. Bryan R. Wilson. Oxford: Oxford University Press.

———. 1984. *After Virtue: A Study in Moral Theory*, 2nd ed. Notre Dame, Ind.: University of Notre Dame Press.

———. 1988. *Whose Justice? Which Rationality?* Notre Dame, Ind.: University of Notre Dame Press.

———. 1990. *Three Rival Versions of Moral Inquiry: Encyclopedia, Genealogy, and History*. Notre Dame, Ind.: University of Notre Dame Press.

———. 1991. Incommensurability, Truth, and the Conversation Between Confucians and Aristotelians About the Virtues. In *Culture and Modernity: East–West Philosophic Perspectives*, ed. Eliot Deutsch. Honolulu: University of Hawaii Press.

———. 1999. *Dependent Rational Animals: Why Human Beings Need the Virtues*. Chicago: Open Court.

———. 2004a. Once More on Confucian and Aristotelian Conceptions of the Virtues: A Response to Professor Wan. In *Chinese Philosophy in an Era of Globalization*, ed. Robin R. Wang. Albany: State University of New York Press.

———. 2004b. Questions for Confucians: Reflections on the Essays in Comparative Study of Self, Autonomy, and Community. In *Confucian Ethics: A Comparative Study of Self, Autonomy, and Community*, ed. Kwong-loi Shun and David B. Wong. Cambridge: Cambridge University Press.

Markus, Robert A. 1999. Life, Culture, and Controversies of Augustine. In *Augustine through the Ages*, ed. Allan D. Fitzgerald. Grand Rapids, Mich.: William B. Eerdmans.

Martin, Thomas F. 2001. Paul the Patient: *Christus Medicus* and the "*Stimulus Carnis*" (2 Cor. 12:7): A Consideration of Augustine's Medicinal Christology. *Augustinian Studies* 32, no. 2: 219–56.

Mathewes, Charles T. 1999. Augustinian Anthropology: A Proposal and a Partial Map. *Journal of Religious Ethics* 27, no. 2: 195–221.

———. 2001. *Evil and the Augustinian Tradition*. Cambridge: Cambridge University Press.

McKim, Robert. 2001. *Religious Ambiguity and Religious Diversity*. Oxford: Oxford University Press.

Meilaender, Gilbert. 1997. "The Things Relevant to Modern Life": Divorcing Augustine from Rawls. *Journal for Peace and Justice Studies* 8, no. 2: 63–68.

———. 2001. Sweet Necessities: Food, Sex, and Saint Augustine. *Journal of Religious Ethics* 29, no. 1 (Spring): 3–18.

Midgley, Mary. 1995. *Beast and Man: The Roots of Human Nature*, rev. ed. New York: Routledge.

Migne, Jacques-Paul, ed. 1844–64. *Patrologiae Cursus Completus, Series Latina*. Paris.

Miles, Margaret. 1979. *Augustine on the Body*. AAR Dissertation Series, vol. 31. Missoula, Mont.: American Academy of Religion.

Miscellanea Agostiniana. 1930. Vol. 1. Rome: Tipografia Poliglotta Vaticana.

Moody-Adams, Michelle. 1997. *Fieldwork in Familiar Places: Morality, Culture, and Philosophy*. Cambridge, Mass.: Harvard University Press.

Munro, Donald. 1996. A Villain in the *Xunzi*. In *Chinese Language, Thought and Culture: Nivison and His Critics*, ed. P. J. Ivanhoe. Chicago: Open Court.

Nehamas, Alexander. 1998. *The Art of Living: Socratic Reflections from Plato to Foucault*. Berkeley: University of California Press.

Neville, Robert C. 2001a. *The Human Condition*. Albany: State University of New York Press.

———. 2001b. *Religious Truth*. Albany: State University of New York Press.

———. 2001c. *Ultimate Realities*. Albany: State University of New York Press.

Nietzsche, Friedrich. 1967. *On the Genealogy of Morals*, trans. Walter Kaufmann and R. J. Hollingdale. New York: Vintage.

Nivison, David. 1991. Hsün Tzu and Chuang Tzu. In *Chinese Texts and Philosophical Contexts: Essays Dedicated to Angus C. Graham*, ed. Henry Rosemont Jr. La Salle, Ill.: Open Court.

———. 1996. Xunzi on "Human Nature." In *The Ways of Confucianism: Investigations in Chinese Philosophy*, ed. Bryan Van Norden. Chicago: Open Court.

Nussbaum, Martha. 1986. *The Fragility of Goodness: Luck and Ethics in Greek Tragedy and Philosophy*. Cambridge: Cambridge University Press.

———. 1993. Non-Relative Virtues. In *The Quality of Life*, ed. Martha Nussbaum and Amartya Sen. Oxford: Clarendon Press.

———. 1994. *The Therapy of Desire: Theory and Practice in Hellenistic Ethics*. Princeton, N.J.: Princeton University Press.

———. 1995. Aristotle on Human Nature and the Foundations of Ethics. In *World, Mind, and Ethics: Essays on the Ethical Philosophy of Bernard Williams*, ed. J. E. J. Altham and Ross Harrison. Cambridge: Cambridge University Press.

———. 1997. *Cultivating Humanity*. Cambridge, Mass.: Harvard University Press.

O'Connell, Robert J. 1968. *St. Augustine's Early Theory of Man, A.D. 386–391*. Cambridge, Mass.: Belknap Press.

———. 1987. *The Origin of the Soul in St. Augustine's Later Works*. New York: Fordham University Press.

O'Daly, Gerald. 1987. *Augustine's Philosophy of Mind*. London: Duckworth.

O'Donnell, James J. 1992. *Augustine: Confessions*. 3 vols. Oxford: Oxford University Press.

———. 2005. *Augustine: A New Biography*. New York: HarperCollins.

O'Donovan, Oliver. 1980. *The Problem of Self-Love in St. Augustine*. New Haven, Conn.: Yale University Press.

Okin, Susan Moller. 1989. *Justice, Gender, and the Family*. New York: Basic Books.

O'Neill, Onora. 1989. *Constructions of Reason: Explorations of Kant's Practical Philosophy*. Cambridge: Cambridge University Press.

Osborne, Thomas, Jr. 2003. The Augustinianism of Thomas Aquinas' Moral Theory. *The Thomist* 67: 279–305.

Pinker, Steven. 2002. *The Blank Slate: The Modern Denial of Human Nature*. New York: Viking Press.

Poo, Mu-chou. 1998. *In Search of Personal Welfare: A View of Early Chinese Religion*. Albany: State University of New York Press.

Porter, Jean. 1990. *The Recovery of Virtue: The Relevance of Aquinas for Christian Ethics*. Louisville: Westminster / John Knox Press.

Prendiville, John G. 1972. The Development of the Idea of Habit in the Thought of Saint Augustine. *Traditio* 28: 29–99.

Puett, Michael. 2002. *To Become a God: Cosmology, Sacrifice, and Self-Divinization in Early China*. Cambridge, Mass.: Harvard University Asia Center for the Harvard-Yenching Institute and Harvard University Press.

———. 2004. The Ethics of Responding Properly: The Notion of *Qing* in Early Chinese Thought. In *Love and Emotions in Traditional Chinese Literature*, ed. Halvor Eifring. Boston: Brill.

Qu Yuan et al. 1985. *The Songs of the South* [translation of *Chuci*], trans. David Hawkes, rev. ed. London: Penguin.

Ramsey, Boniface. 1999. Mendacio, De/Contra Mendacium. In *Augustine through the Ages*, ed. Allan D. Fitzgerald. Grand Rapids, Mich.: William B. Eerdmans.

Rawls, John. 1971. *A Theory of Justice*. Cambridge, Mass.: Belknap Press of Harvard University Press.

———. 1993. Political Liberalism. New York: Columbia University Press.

Reynolds, Frank, and David Tracy, eds. 1990. *Myth and Philosophy*. Albany: State University of New York Press.

———. 1992. *Discourse and Practice*. Albany: State University of New York Press.

———. 1994. *Religion and Practical Reason: New Essays in the Comparative Philosophy of Religions*. Albany: State University of New York Press.

Ricks, Thomas E. 1997. *Making the Corps*. New York: Scribner.

Ricoeur, Paul. 1970. *Freud and Philosophy: An Essay on Interpretation*. New Haven, Conn.: Yale University Press.

Rist, John M. 1969. Augustine on Free Will and Predestination. *Journal of Theological Studies* 20: 420–47.

———. 1994. *Augustine: Ancient Thought Baptized*. Cambridge: Cambridge University Press.

Rorty, Richard. 1979. *Philosophy and the Mirror of Nature*. Princeton, N.J.: Princeton University Press.

———. 1984. The Historiography of Philosophy: Four Genres. In *Philosophy in History: Essays in the Historiography of Philosophy*, ed. R. Rorty, J. B. Schneewind, and Q. Skinner. Cambridge: Cambridge University Press.

———. 1989. *Contingency, Irony, and Solidarity*. Cambridge: Cambridge University Press.

———. 1994. Religion as Conversation-Stopper. *Common Knowledge* 3, no. 1 (Spring): 1–6.

———. 2000. Response to Brandom. In *Rorty and His Critics*, ed. Robert Brandom. Malden, Mass.: Blackwell.

Rosemont, Henry. 1988. Why Take Rights Seriously? A Confucian Critique. In *Human Rights and the World's Religions*, ed. Leroy Rouner. Notre Dame, Ind.: University of Notre Dame Press.

———. 2000. State and Society in the *Hsün Tzu*: A Philosophical Commentary. In *Virtue, Nature, and Moral Agency in the Xunzi,* eds. T. C. Kline III and Philip J. Ivanhoe. Indianapolis: Hackett.

Roth, Harold. 1999. *Original Tao: Inward Training (Nei-yeh) and the Foundations of Taoist Mysticism*. New York: Columbia University Press.

Rouner, Leroy S., ed. 1992. *Selves, People, and Persons: What Does It Mean To Be a Self?* Notre Dame, Ind.: University of Notre Dame Press.

Russell, Robert P., trans. 1948. Divine Providence and the Problem of Evil. In *The Writings of Saint Augustine*, ed. Ludwig Schopp, vol. 1. The Fathers of the Church, vol. 2. New York: Cima Publishing.

Sage, Athanase. 1990. *The Religious Life According to Saint Augustine*, trans. Paul C. Thabault. New York: New City Press.

Santurri, Edmund N. 1997. Rawlsian Liberalism, Moral Truth, and Augustinian Politics. *Journal for Peace and Justice Studies* 8, no. 2: 1–36.

Schaeffer, John, and Frank Schaeffer. 2002. *Keeping Faith: A Father-Son Story About Love and the United States Marine Corps*. New York: Carroll and Graf.

Schlabach, Gerald. 1998. "Love Is the Hand of the Soul": The Grammar of Continence in Augustine's Doctrine of Christian Love. *Journal of Early Christian Studies* 6, no. 1: 59–92.

Schofer, Jonathan. 2000. Virtues in Xunzi's Thought. In *Virtue, Nature, and Moral Agency in the Xunzi,* eds. T. C. Kline III and Philip J. Ivanhoe. Indianapolis: Hackett.

———. 2003. Spiritual Exercises in Rabbinic Culture. *AJS Review* 27, no. 2: 203–26.

———. 2005a. *The Making of a Sage: A Study in Rabbinic Ethics*. Madison: University of Wisconsin Press.

———. 2005b. Self, Subject, and Chosen Subjection: Rabbinic Ethics and Comparative Possibilities. *Journal of Religious Ethics* 33, no. 2 (Summer): 293–331.

Schuld, J. Joyce. 2003. *Foucault and Augustine: Reconsidering Power and Love*. Notre Dame, Ind.: University of Notre Dame Press.

Schwartz, Benjamin. 1985. *The World of Thought in Ancient China*. Cambridge, Mass.: Harvard University Press.

Sharpe, Eric J. 1975. *Comparative Religion: A History*. London: Duckworth.

Shaughnessy, Edward L. 1993. Shu Ching. In *Early Chinese Texts: A Bibliographic Guide,* ed. Michael Loewe. Berkley: Society for the Study of Early China and Institute of East Asian Studies, University of California.

Sherman, Nancy. 2005. Of Manners and Morals. *British Journal of Educational Studies* 53, no. 3 (September): 272–89.

Shils, Edward. 1981. *Tradition*. Chicago: University of Chicago Press.

Simon, Lawrence H. 1990. Rationality and Alien Cultures. In *Midwest Studies in Philosophy Volume XV: The Philosophy of the Human Sciences*, ed. Peter A. French, Theodore E. Uehling Jr., and Howard K. Wettstein. Notre Dame, Ind.: University of Notre Dame Press.

Slingerland, Edward, trans. 2003a. *Confucius: Analects*. Indianapolis: Hackett.

———. 2003b. *Effortless Action: Wu-Wei as Conceptual Metaphor and Spiritual Ideal in Early China*. New York: Oxford University Press,.

Smith, Jonathan Z. 1978. *Map Is Not Territory: Studies in the History of Religions*. Leiden: Brill.

———. 1990. *Drudgery Divine: On the Comparison of Early Christianities and the Religions of Late Antiquity*. Chicago: University of Chicago Press.

———. 1998. Religion, Religions, Religious. In *Critical Terms for Religious Studies*, ed. Mark C. Taylor. Chicago: University of Chicago Press.

Sober, Elliott, and David Sloan Wilson. 1998. *Unto Others: The Evolution and Psychology of Unselfish Behavior*. Cambridge, Mass.: Harvard University Press.

Sorabji, Richard. 2000. *Emotion and Peace of Mind: From Stoic Agitation to Christian Temptation*. New York: Oxford University Press.

Stalnaker, Aaron. 2001. Overcoming Our Evil: Spiritual Exercises and Personhood in Xunzi and Augustine. Ph.D. diss., Brown University.

———. 2003. Aspects of Xunzi's Engagement with Early Daoism. *Philosophy East and West* 53, no. 1 (March): 87–129.

———. 2004. Rational Justification in Xunzi: On His Use of the Term *Li* 理. *International Philosophical Quarterly* 44, no. 1 (March): 53–68.

———. 2005. Comparative Religious Ethics and the Problem of "Human Nature." *Journal of Religious Ethics* 33, no. 2 (June): 187–224.

Stendahl, Krister. 1976. The Apostle Paul and the Introspective Conscience of the West. In *Paul Among Jews and Gentiles, and Other Essays*. Philadelphia: Fortress Press.

Stock, Brian. 1996. *Augustine the Reader: Meditation, Self-Knowledge, and the Ethics of Interpretation*. Cambridge, Mass.: Harvard University Press.

Stothert, Richard, trans. 1979. On the Morals of the Catholic Church and On the Morals of the Manicheans. *St. Augustine: The Writings Against the Manicheans and Against the Donatists*. Select Library of the Nicene and Post-Nicene Fathers, vol. 4. Grand Rapids: William B. Eerdmans. [Orig. pub. 1886.]

Stout, Jeffrey. 1988. *Ethics After Babel: The Languages of Morals and their Discontents*. Boston: Beacon Press.

———. 2002. Radical Interpretation and Pragmatism: Davidson, Rorty, and Brandom on Truth. In *Radical Interpretation in Religion*, ed. Nancy Frankenberry. Cambridge: Cambridge University Press.

———. 2004. *Democracy and Tradition*. Princeton, N.J.: Princeton University Press.

Swidler, Ann. 2001. *Talk of Love: How Culture Matters*. Chicago: University of Chicago Press.

Tanner, Kathryn. 1997. *Theories of Culture: A New Agenda for Theology*. Minneapolis: Fortress Press.

Taylor, Charles. 1985a. The Diversity of Goods. In *Philosophy and the Human Sciences: Philosophical Papers II*. Cambridge, Mass.: Cambridge University Press.

———. 1985b. Understanding and Ethnocentricity. In *Philosophy and the Human Sciences: Philosophical Papers II*. Cambridge, Mass.: Cambridge University Press.

———. 1985c. What Is Human Agency? In *Human Agency and Language: Philosophical Papers I*. Cambridge, Mass.: Cambridge University Press.

———. 1989. *Sources of the Self: The Making of the Modern Identity*. Cambridge, Mass.: Harvard University Press.

———. 1991. *The Ethics of Authenticity*. Cambridge, Mass.: Harvard University Press.

TeSelle, Eugene. 1970. *Augustine the Theologian*. New York: Herder & Herder.

———. 1994. Serpent, Eve, and Adam: Augustine and the Exegetical Tradition. In *Augustine: Presbyter Factus Sum*, ed. Joseph T. Lienhardt, Earl C. Muller, and Roland J. Teske. New York: Peter Lang.

Teske, Roland J., trans. 1997. *Answer to the Pelagians: The Punishment and Forgiveness of Sins and the Baptism of Little Ones, The Spirit and the Letter, Nature and Grace, The Perfection of Human Righteousness, The Deeds of Pelagius, The Grace of Christ and Original Sin, The Nature and Origin of the Soul*. The Works of Saint Augustine, Part I, vol. 23. Hyde Park, N.Y.: New City Press.

———. 1998. *Answer to the Pelagians II: Marriage and Desire, Answer to the Two Letters of the Pelagians, Answer to Julian*. The Works of Saint Augustine, Part I, vol. 24. Hyde Park, N.Y.: New City Press.

———. 1999a. *Answer to the Pelagians IV: To the Monks of Hadrumetum and Provence*. The Works of Saint Augustine, Part I, vol. 26. Hyde Park, N.Y.: New City Press.

———. 1999b. *Answer to the Pelagians III: Unfinished Work in Answer to Julian*. The Works of Saint Augustine, Part I, vol. 25. Hyde Park, N.Y.: New City Press.

———. 2003. *Letters 100–155*. The Works of Saint Augustine, Part II, vol. 2. Hyde Park, N.Y.: New City Press.

Thomas, Laurence. 1989. *Living Morally: A Psychology of Moral Character*. Philadelphia: Temple University Press.

Troeltsch, Ernst. 1992. *The Social Teachings of the Christian Churches*, trans. Olive Wyon. Louisville: Westminster / John Knox Press.

Twiss, Sumner B. 1998a. Four Paradigms in Teaching Comparative Religious Ethics. In *Explorations in Global Ethics: Comparative Religious Ethics and Interreligious Dialogue,* eds. Bruce Grelle and Sumner Twiss. Boulder, Colo: Westview Press.

———. 1998b. Religion and Human Rights: A Comparative Perspective. In *Explorations in Global Ethics: Comparative Religious Ethics and Interreligious Dialogue,* eds. Bruce Grelle and Sumner Twiss. Boulder, Colo: Westview Press. .

Twiss, Sumner B., and Walter H. Conser, eds. 1992. *Experience of the Sacred: Readings in the Phenomenology of Religion*. Hanover, N.H.: University Press of New England.

Van Fleteren, Frederick. 1999. Nature. In *Augustine through the Ages*, ed. Allan D. Fitzgerald. Grand Rapids, Mich.: William B. Eerdmans.

van Lierde, Canisius. 1935. *Doctrina sancti Augustini circa dona Spiritus Sancti ex textu Isaiae XI 2–3*. Würzburg, Germany: Rita Verlag und Druckerei. [Reprinted as The Teaching of St. Augustine on the Gifts of the Holy Spirit from the Text of Isaiah 11:2–3, trans. Joseph C. Schnaubelt and Frederick Van Fleteren. In *Augustine: Mystic and Mystagogue*, *Collectanea Augustiniana* III, ed. Schnaubelt, van Fleteren, and Joseph Reino. New York: Peter Lang, 1994.]

Van Norden, Bryan. 2000. Mengzi and Xunzi: Two Views of Human Agency. In *Virtue, Nature, and Moral Agency in the Xunzi*, eds. T. C. Kline III and Philip J. Ivanhoe. Indianapolis: Hackett. [Orig. pub. *International Philosophical Quarterly* 32, no. 2 (June 1992): 161–84.]

———. 2003a. Mencius and Augustine on Evil: A Test Case for Comparative Philosophy. In *Comparative Approaches to Chinese Philosophy*, ed. Bo Mou. Aldershot, U.K.: Ashgate.

———. 2003b. Virtue Ethics and Confucianism. In *Comparative Approaches to Chinese Philosophy*, ed. Bo Mou. Aldershot, U.K.: Ashgate.

Wallwork, Ernest. 1999. Psychodynamic Contributions to Religious Ethics: Toward Reconfiguring *Askesis*. *Annual of the Society of Christian Ethics* 19: 167–89.

Wang Tch'ang-tche, J. 1938. *Saint Augustin et les vertus de paiens.* Paris: Beauchesne.

Watson, Burton, trans. 1963. *Hsün Tzu: Basic Writings*. New York: Columbia University Press.

Watson, Gary. 1975. Free Agency. *Journal of Philosophy* 72: 205–20. [Reprinted in *Free Will*, ed. Gary Watson. New York: Oxford University Press, 1982.]

Wetzel, James. 1992. *Augustine and the Limits of Virtue.* Cambridge: Cambridge University Press.

White, Michael J. 1997. Peace or Justice? *Journal for Peace and Justice Studies* 8, no. 2: 69–75.

Williams, Rowan. 1990. Sapientia and the Trinity: Reflections on the *De Trinitate*. In *Collectanea Augustiniana: Mélanges T. J. Van Bavel*, ed. B. Bruning, M. Lamberigts, and J. Van Houtem. Leuven: Leuven University Press.

Wills, Gary. 1999. *Saint Augustine*. New York: Penguin.

Wilson, Bryan R., ed. 1970. *Rationality*. Oxford: Oxford University Press.

Wimbush, Vincent L., and Richard Valantasis, eds. 1995. *Asceticism*. New York: Oxford University Press.

Winch, Peter. 1958. *The Idea of a Social Science*. London: Routledge and Kegan Paul.

———. 1970. Understanding a Primitive Society. In Wilson 1970. [Orig. pub. 1964.]

Wong, David. 1984. *Moral Relativity*. Berkeley: University of California Press.

———. 1996. Xunzi on Moral Motivation. In *Chinese Language, Thought and Culture: Nivison and His Critics*, ed. P. J. Ivanhoe. Chicago: Open Court.

Xunzi. 1983. *Xunzi Jianshi*, ed. Liang Qixiong. Beijing: Zhonghua Shuju.

———. 1988a. *Xunzi Jijie*, ed. Wang Xianqian. Beijing: Zhonghua Shuju.

———. 1988b. *Xunzi Jishi*, ed. Li Disheng. Taipei: Taiwan Xuesheng Shuju.

Yearley, Lee. 1980. Hsün Tzu on the Mind. *Journal of Asian Studies* 39, no. 3: 465–80.

———. 1990. *Mencius and Aquinas: Theories of Virtue and Conceptions of Courage*. Albany: State University of New York Press.

———. 1996a. *Facing Our Frailty: Comparative Religious Ethics and the Confucian Death Rituals—The 1995 Gross Memorial Lecture at Valparaiso University*. Valparaiso, Ind.: Valparaiso University Press.

———. 1996b. Zhuangzi's Understanding of Skillfulness and the Ultimate Spiritual State. In *Essays on Skepticism, Relativism, and Ethics in the Zhuangzi*, ed. Paul Kjellberg and Philip J. Ivanhoe. Albany: State University of New York Press.

———. 1998. The Ascetic Grounds of Goodness: William James's Case for the Virtue of Voluntary Poverty. *Journal of Religious Ethics* 26, no. 1 (Spring): 105–35.

———. N.d. Hsün Tzu: Ritualization as Humanization. Essay manuscript.

Yu, Anthony. 1997. *Rereading the Stone: Desire and the Making of Fiction in Dream of the Red Chamber*. Princeton, N.J.: Princeton University Press.

Index